The COMPLETE ILLUSTRATED *Guide to*

Joinery

The COMPLETE ILLUSTRATED *Guide to*

Joinery

GARY ROGOWSKI

The Taunton Press

The Taunton Press, Inc., 63 South Main Street, PO Box 5506, Newtown, CT 06470-5506
e-mail: tp@taunton.com

Distributed by Publishers Group West

DESIGN: Lori Wendin
LAYOUT: Suzie Yannes
ILLUSTRATOR: Mario Ferro
PHOTOGRAPHERS: David L. Minick, Gary Rogowski, Vincent Laurence

LIBRARY OF CONGRESS CATALOGING-IN-PUBLICATION DATA:
Rogowski, Gary.
The complete illustrated guide to joinery / Gary Rogowski.
p. cm.
Includes index.
ISBN 1-56158-401-0
1. Woodwork--Amateurs' manuals. 2. Joinery--Amateurs' manuals. 3. Woodworking tools--Amateurs' manuals. I. Title: Joinery. II. Title.

TT185 .R73 2002
684.1'04--dc21

2001044293

Printed in Italy
10 9 8 7 6 5 4 3

About Your Safety: Working with wood is inherently dangerous. Using hand or power tools improperly or ignoring safety practices can lead to permanent injury or even death. Don't try to perform operations you learn about here (or elsewhere) unless you're certain they are safe for you. If something about an operation doesn't feel right, don't do it. Look for another way. We want you to enjoy the craft, so please keep safety foremost in your mind whenever you're in the shop.

To Dziadz and Busia. It was through them that I came to be here.

Acknowledgments

I would like to thank all of these people for their help and support.

My undying gratitude to David Minick for jumping into the fray mid-flight to help with the photography. My deepest thanks as well to Vincent Laurence for answering the call of duty to help get my motor running.

Many thanks to Deborah Howell for her patience and support. To Buck and Jimmy. I could not have done it without you boys. To Marc, Angie, Elena, Lenny, Rob, Lisl, Ketzel, Splons, Brooks, and Ed. Thank you all for your understanding. To John and Lydia Rogowski.

My thanks to Lonnie Bird and Andy Rae, brothers in arms.

To Helen Albert and Jennifer Renjilian, whew.

My thanks to all those who have passed through the shop and helped out with the book: Ryan Wynne, Laure Dwyer, Aaron Laird, and Evertt Biedler.

To those who provided me with tools and their expertise: Eliot Apatov, Bill Yost, Terry Anderson, John Eric Byers, Dan Stafford, and Jim Tolpin.

To my students: Matt Cooper, David Waring, Karl Schmidt, Paul Weiss, Cameron Gordon. I wrote this book with Wendy Feuer in mind—thanks Wendy.

The great folks at The Film Lab: Katy, Brian, Matt, and Chris.

Finally I would like to acknowledge the contributions that Charles Hayward, Ernest Joyce, Tage Frid, George Ellis, and Ian Kirby have made to the body of woodworking writing on joinery.

Contents

Introduction

We categorize our furniture making like we do so many of our other human endeavors. There are only so many ways to make a box after all. But we have in our imaginative way, made the most of all the possibilities.

The fact is, there are only two basic joinery systems. Either we use box construction, joining wide panels of solid-wood or plywood materials together, to make our carcases, cabinets, or jewelry boxes. Or we use frame construction to build our chairs, tables, beds, and cabinets. These frames use smaller members fastened together with or without a panel captured within them.

From these two categories spring a wealth of joinery options. A project as simple as a box has a dozen ways to solve the joinery question, and many joints can be used interchangeably. So how do you choose which joint to use?

The function of the piece is the starting point for your joinery choices. Are you building a cabinet to hold the crown jewels or a recipe box destined to be stained with the labors of the kitchen?

Dovetail joints are the best way to join large panels, but a window box doesn't need dovetails to be serviceable.

Next, consider economy—the need for efficiency and speed in your building. What's your time frame? If it's a weekend project, your choice of a joint will make a big difference. Hand chopping dozens of mortises is certainly not time-efficient, but it may be the perfect way to enjoy working at a leisurely pace in a harried world.

The skill you bring to a project also determines which joint you choose, but learning a new method of joinery is a wonderful challenge. We tend to find our methods and stick to them; but remember that each time you cut a joint, you get a little better at doing it.

Joinery affects the design in ways both obvious and quite subtle. That simple box can be built in a dozen ways, but a mitered corner doesn't look anything like one that's finger jointed together. Joinery will also help in the building of some pieces, offering shoulders and edges that help hold a piece together for gluing or pre-assembly work.

Make your joinery choices based on all these factors. One method may work better one day and another method the next. Please also remember that this book is only a guide. No one process, jig, machine, or book can confer mastery. The way to mastering joinery is to make joints. It's the time you spend learning, making mistakes, backing up, and starting all over again. The time you spend in the shop is the real pay-off; the furniture you build a wonderful bonus.

How to Use This Book

First of all, this book is meant to be used, not put on a shelf to gather dust. It's meant to be pulled out and opened on your bench when you need to do a new or unfamiliar technique. So the first way to use this book is to make sure it's near where you do woodworking.

In the pages that follow you'll find a wide variety of methods that cover the important processes of this area of woodworking. Just as in many other practical areas, in woodworking there are often many ways to get to the same result. Why you choose one method over another depends on several factors:

Time. Are you in a hurry or do you have the leisure to enjoy the quiet that comes with hand tools?

Your tooling. Do you have the kind of shop that's the envy of every woodworker or a modest collection of the usual hand and power tools?

Your skill level. Do you prefer simpler methods because you're starting out or are you always looking to challenge yourself and expand your skills?

The project. Is the piece you're making utilitarian or an opportunity to show off your best work?

In this book, we've included a wide variety of techniques to fit these needs.

To find your way around the book, you first need to ask yourself two questions: What result am I trying to achieve? What tools do I want to use to accomplish it?

In some cases, there are many ways and many tools that will accomplish the same result. In others, there are only one or two sensible ways to do it. In all cases, however, we've taken a practical approach; so you may not find your favorite exotic method for doing a particular process. We have included every reasonable method and then a few just to flex your woodworking muscles.

To organize the material, we've broken the subject down to two levels. "Parts" are major divisions of this class of techniques. "Sections" contain related techniques. Within sections, techniques and procedures that create a similar result are grouped together, usually organized from the most common way to do it to methods requiring specialized tools or a larger degree of skill. In some cases, the progression starts with the method requiring the most basic technology and then moves on to alternative methods using other common shop tools and finally to specialized tools.

The first thing you'll see in a part is a group of photos keyed to a page number. Think of this as an illustrated table of contents. Here you'll see a photo representing each section in that part, along with the page on which each section starts.

Each section begins with a similar "visual map," with photos that represent major groupings of techniques or individual techniques. Under each grouping is a list of the step-by-step essays that explain how to do the methods, including the pages on which they can be found.

Sections begin with an "overview," or brief introduction, to the methods described therein. Here's where you'll find important general information on this group of techniques, including any safety issues. You'll also read about specific tools needed for the operations that follow and how to build jigs or fixtures needed for them.

The step-by-step essays are the heart of this book. Here a group of photos represents the key steps in the process. The accompanying text describes the process and guides you through it, referring you back to the photos. Depending on how you learn best, either read the text first or look at the photos and drawings; but remember, they are meant to work together. In cases where there is an

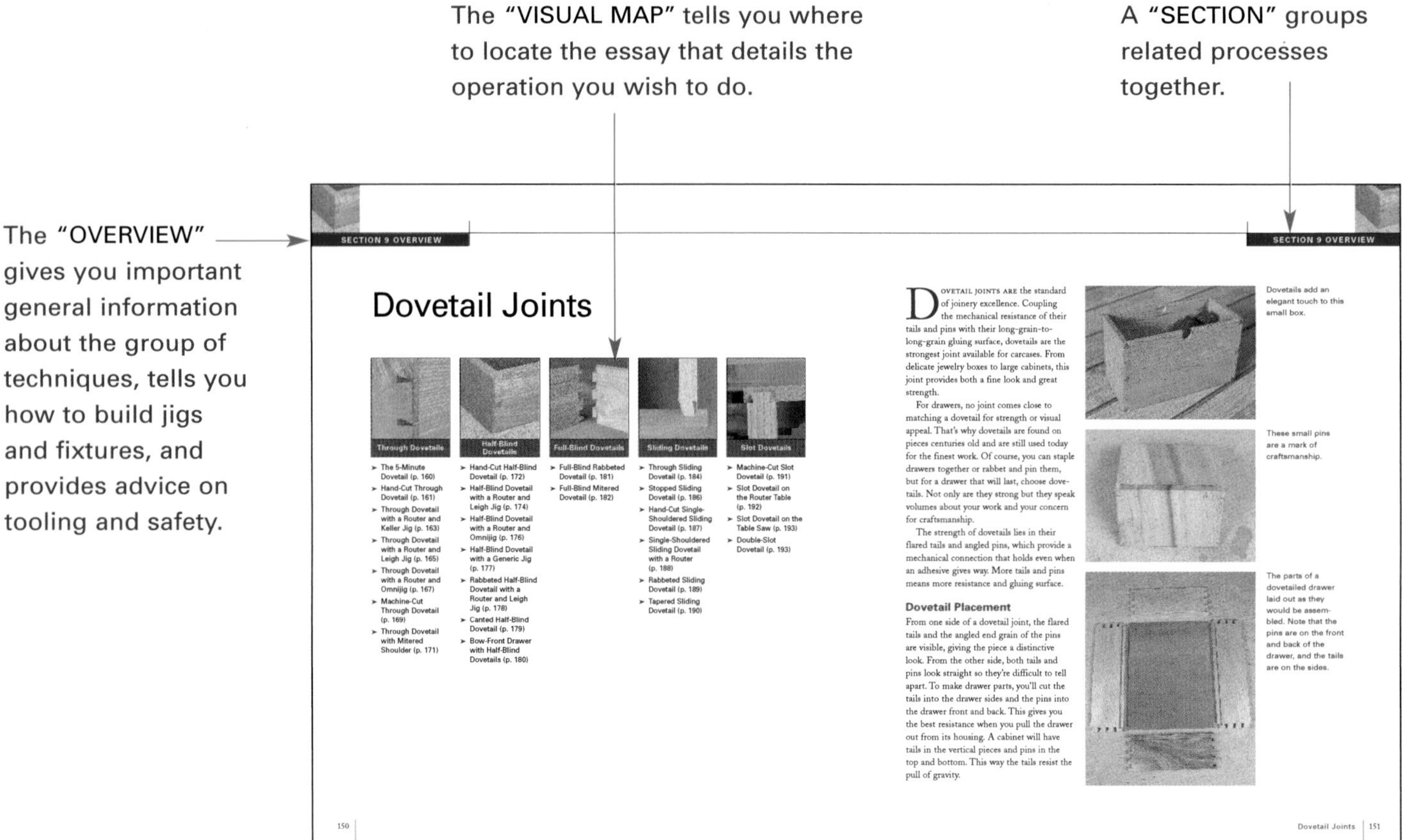

alternative step, it's called out in the text and the visual material as a "variation."

For efficiency, we've cross-referenced redundant processes or steps described in another related process. You'll see yellow "cross-references" called out frequently in the overviews and step-by-step essays.

When you see this symbol ⚠, make sure you read what follows. The importance of these safety warnings cannot be overemphasized. Always work safely and use safety devices, including eye and hearing protection. If you feel uncomfortable with a technique, don't do it, try another way.

At the back of the book is an index to help you find what you're looking for in a pinch. There's also list of further reading to help you brush up on how to use tools and keep them sharp, as well as some general references on design.

Finally, remember to use this book whenever you need to refresh your memory or to learn something new. It's been designed to be an essential reference to help you become a better woodworker. The only way it can do this is if you make it as familiar a workshop tool as your favorite bench chisels.

—The editors

"CROSS-REFERENCES" tell you where to find a related process or the detailed description of a process in another essay.

"STEP-BY-STEP ESSAYS" contain photos, drawings, and instructions on how to do the technique.

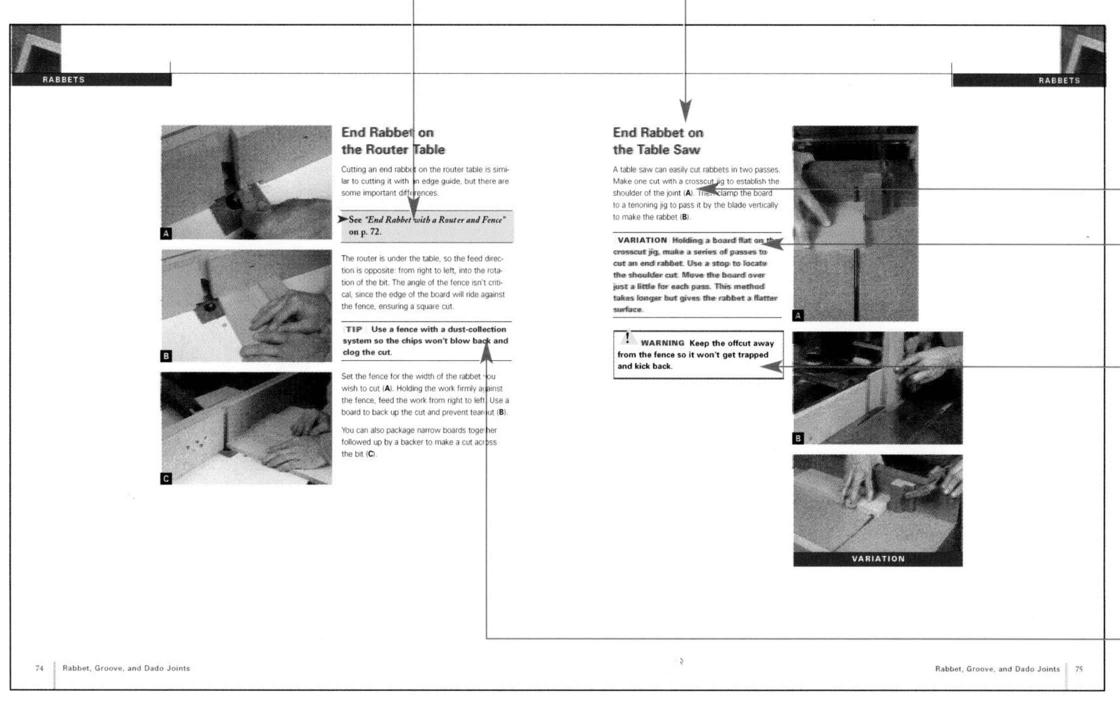

The "TEXT" contains keys to the photos and drawings.

"VARIATIONS" show alternatives for doing a step.

"WARNINGS" tell you specific safety concerns for this process and how to address them.

"TIPS" show shortcuts and smart ways to work.

Hand Tools, page 8

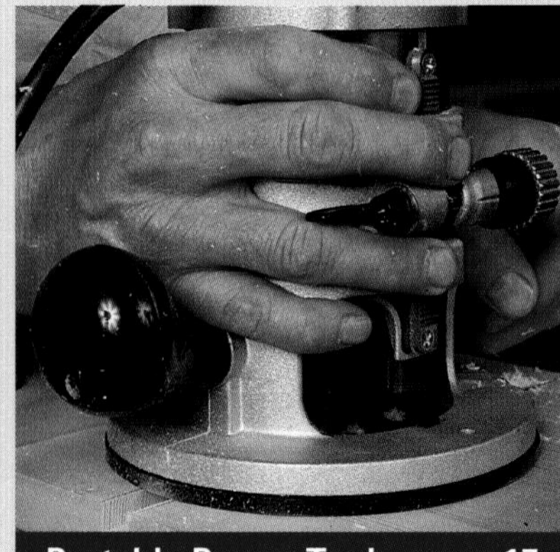
Portable Power Tools, page 17

Machines, page 27

PART ONE

Tools for Joinery

THE FURNITURE MAKER USES a variety of tools for joinery. Hand tools require patience to learn how to use properly, but they offer great precision and satisfaction. Other tools, such as routers, are quick, flexible, and accurate when you know how to guide them effectively. They are also noisy and dusty in their efficiency. Machine tools form the backbone of most woodshops, for they do the bulk of the milling jobs now. But they can also be used quite effectively for certain types of joinery. Machines are fast and designed to do a repeated task endlessly and effortlessly. They are also dangerous when used without safety in mind. Each of these tool systems brings its own set of advantages and problems to the workbench. The experienced furniture maker uses them all, sometimes in combination, sometimes alone. It's simply a question of the desired result.

Hand Tools

THE ACCOMPLISHED JOINER knows when to reach for his dovetail saw, when to grab his router, and when to turn on his table saw. His decision relies as much on the job and the tools available as it does on his experience. After all, there are a dozen ways to cut a mortise. One of the determining factors is how fast you want results. It takes longer to chop all your mortises by hand, but the work is satisfying. And, as with most hand-tool processes, chopping mortises will teach you much about the nature of wood and your tools.

Hand tools for joinery fall into a few broad categories, depending on their use: measuring and marking tools, cutting tools, and boring tools. There are also a variety of incredibly useful accessories—such as benches, jigs, and clamps—that we use in joinery work.

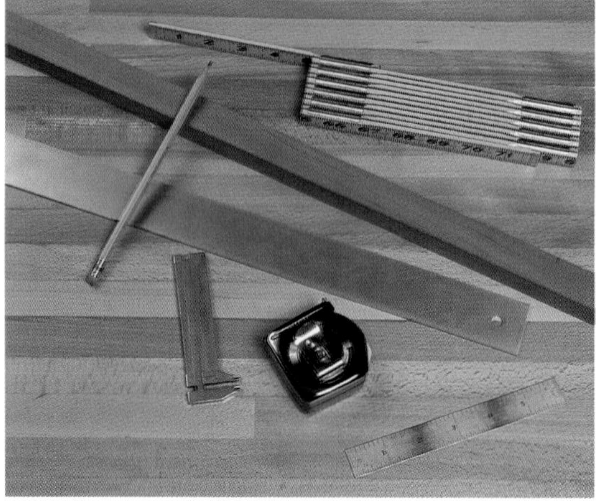

Measure for measure, these tools are as helpful a lot as there are in the shop.

Measuring and Marking Tools

Joinery begins with laying out the cuts. The importance of accurate measuring and marking out can't be overstated. From your layout lines, you make the sawcut, set up the router bit, or lock down the fence.

Measuring tools can be very basic. A straight stick and a pencil are all you really need for measuring. This time-honored method is simple and very effective. However, a variety of tools for measuring have been devised, including tape measures, straightedges, rules, calipers, and squares. Some have scales marked on them and some don't.

When measuring, always remember to keep the *tape measure* or rule parallel to the edge of the board. This ensures more accurate measurements. Also try to use the same tape throughout a job, because tapes can vary in their markings. The true-zero hook on tapes is for measuring both inside and outside a corner. Make sure the movement in the hook doesn't become too sloppy.

Calipers come in different shapes and sizes. Large calipers are very useful for checking dimensions, especially on the lathe. For checking thickness or dado blade widths, I prefer to use a smaller set of calipers. Make sure the caliper jaws close up tight with no gap between them.

Use calipers for checking the thickness of a dado blade.

A steel straightedge can help you lay out joints or check surfaces.

Rules are essential for taking accurate measurements. Use a *depth gauge* for checking depths of cut. Its scale is useful for measuring, but you can check a surface just by seeing if the depth gauge rocks or if any light shows under it.

A *steel straightedge* can be used to lay out lines, check surfaces, and help set up machines. It won't wear out, unless you abuse it, so buy a good true one. They're well worth the investment.

The *6-in. rule* is an ideal tool for laying out joinery. It can be used almost everywhere on a board or machine to help you find the center or help mark out for a mortise or tenon. The better versions have four separate scales as well as two end scales for easily measuring across a gap, such as the bottom of a router base.

Use a *sliding bevel* to lay out any angle. You can capture an angle from an existing board or setup that appeals to you or mark out a pencil line and set the sliding bevel to that. Make sure the sliding bevel can be flipped to either side with no interference from its locking nut.

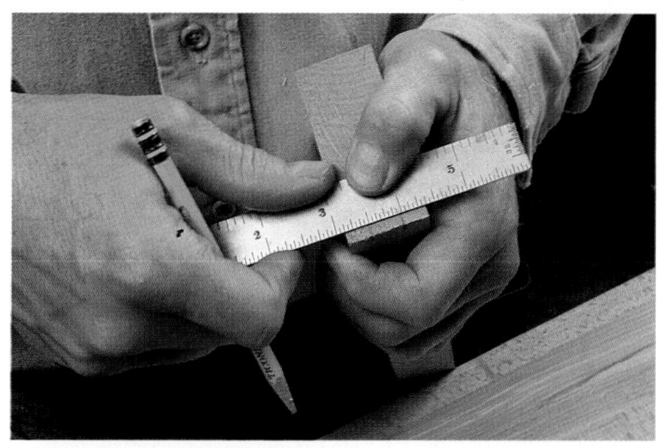

A 6-in. rule, especially one with end scales, is invaluable in the shop.

A sliding bevel helps you lay out angles or set up a sawblade for an angled cut.

A *square* is the one measuring tool most woodworkers find indispensable. There are different types, including the large framing square and its smaller brothers, the try square and engineer's square. For all-around versatility, nothing beats the combination square. You can, of course, measure for square across the end or face of a board using a combination square. But you can also use it as a depth gauge, a pencil gauge, a try square for inside corners, and a 45-degree miter square.

A combination square can be used to check for square both inside and outside a corner and can help when laying out miters.

All squares share several characteristics: None of them likes to be dropped onto the floor or tossed into a toolbox, and they need to be held by the body, not the rule. When using it against the edge of a board, don't press down on it too hard, hoping to see that the board is square. You can end up fooling yourself. Use a soft touch to check any board and always put a light source behind the square. Your eye will be able to see a few thousandths of an inch of error.

Marking tools do only one job: clearly mark out a cut to be made. Keep your *pencil* sharp. Thick pencil lines cause you more trouble than help as you try to split them down the middle with your cut. You need to keep layout lines clean and precise.

A *marking knife* is preferred over a pencil by many woodworkers for laying out joints. In some instances, as when marking out dovetail pins, a pencil just can't get in tight enough. Use a sharp marking knife, dispos-

Use a marking knife when you need to get in tight to an edge to lay out a line.

HOW SQUARE IS YOUR SQUARE?

You can check how square your square is with a simple test. Place it against the edge of a straight board and mark out one pencil line. Flip the square over, line it up on the pencil mark, and check if the measure matches up. If it does, the square is square. If it's within a few thousandths of an inch at the end of 6 in. or 8 in., the square is probably fine for most of the work you'll be doing. But if it's noticeably out of square, hang it on your wall as an ornament. It will do nothing but frustrate your efforts to do precise joinery work.

Check a square by using it to mark out a line. Flip the square over and use the other side to measure the line.

able knife, or even a penknife over a pencil. You need to get in as close as possible to the wood for accurate layout. Use a *scratch awl* for marking center points for drilling or for scribing out joints.

Marking gauges use a knife, pin, or sharpened wheel to mark the workpiece. You move an adjustable head or fence to place the cutter in the proper spot. Hold the fence in tight to the edge of the board as you move along. Most knife- or pin-type gauges need tuning before using. File a bevel into the knife on the side closest to the fence so it pulls the head in closer as the gauge cuts. Wheel-type gauges come with this bevel already ground in place. They do a great job of marking out cross-grain.

Mortising gauges have two pins mounted on one side of the beam. One is adjustable so you can set the width of the pins to the size of the mortise or chisel.

Cutting Tools

Woodworkers use several different types of *handsaws* for joinery. Handsaws do most of the crosscutting to length. Backsaws, which include dovetail and tenon saws, have stiffened backs to hold them rigid during a joinery cut. For the best results, use a saw with teeth filed for the job at hand. Crosscut teeth are filed at a 60-degree angle. Ripsaw teeth are filed straight across and are used for cutting straight down the long grain of a board. Occasionally, you'll call on a saw to cut some curves. Rely on a coping saw, fretsaw, or bowsaw for this job.

Scratch awls are useful for marking center points for drilling.

A wheel-type marking gauge will cut cleanly across the long grain of even a softwood.

This dovetail saw has teeth filed for ripping, which makes it ideal for cutting tenons or dovetails.

Start a cut at one corner of the board. Draw the saw opposite to the way it cuts to get the cut started.

A Japanese-style dovetail saw cuts on the pull stroke and makes a thin kerf.

Paring chisels are best suited for fine trimming work.

Beyond these choices, however, lies another one: Do you want to cut on the push or on the pull stroke? European-style saws all cut on the push stroke. Start each cut by drawing the saw backward at the point where you want the cut to start. Japanese-style saws cut mostly on the pull stroke. This puts the saw under tension as you pull it through the cut, allowing the saw to be thinner with less set to the teeth.

Although you will use entirely different cutting techniques for the pull and push saws, a few things remain constant. Point your index finger when cutting to help guide the cut. Keep the saw to the waste side of the line and, most important, let the saw do the cutting. Concentrate on simply guiding it. Remember, too, that you're always cutting in two directions: For a simple crosscut, you will cut straight across and straight down the edge of the board.

Chisels are owned by just about every woodworker, from the hand-tool zealot to the router fanatic. Keep them sharp, because you can't do good work with dull chisels. It's also far more dangerous to use a dull chisel that's hard to control. Chisels are designed for various purposes: chopping, mortising, shaving, and cleaning out work. Beveled-edge chisels are the standard bench chisel used for almost any chisel work. Their shorter cousin is the butt chisel used for working in tight spaces. Longer paring chisels are used for nothing but taking off the finest shavings.

Mortising chisels can take many shapes. Heavy mortising chisels have thick blades with parallel sides. They use a leather washer set between the handle and the steel to act

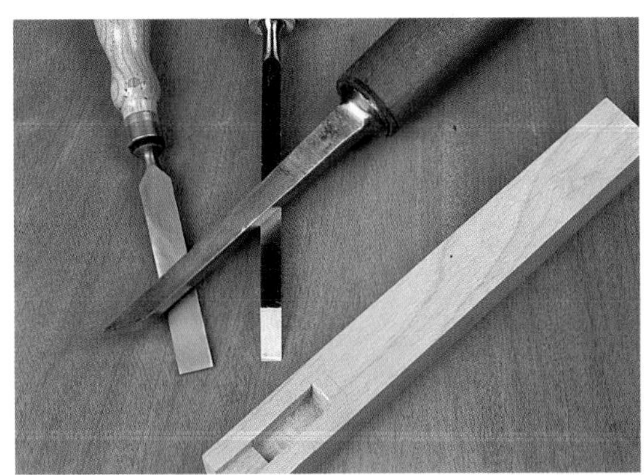

Mortising chisels can take the pounding that mortise work requires.

as a shock absorber. The handle is either very large and rounded or is contained by an iron hoop to prevent mushrooming of the handle's end. The firmer chisel is a smaller type of mortising chisel but has a tapering blade. The blade is small enough that it can be used for chopping or paring.

Handplanes allow you to make fine adjustments to the fit of a joint. Keep several tuned to use just for joinery. Bench planes like a no. 3 or no. 4 smoothing plane are used for fitting joints as well as for truing short edges. Larger jointer planes are used for truing and jointing the edges of boards.

Block planes will handle a multitude of joinery tasks from trimming miter joints and the keys that fit them to trimming wide tenon joints. Planes made specifically for joinery include the bullnose plane and shoulder plane. These tools are designed to take fine shavings off a tenon cheek or shoulder with a plane iron that is as wide as their sole.

Use the mass and length of a no. 7 or no. 8 jointer plane to true up long edges.

A block plane can trim a miter joint before gluing or plane down a miter key after.

Clean up tenon cheeks and shoulders with a shoulder plane.

A rabbet plane uses a mounted fence to guide the cut.

Use router planes for getting inside grooves, dadoes, and even larger joints like a half lap. Rabbet planes are used for cutting rabbets on the edge of boards. They, too, have a blade that extends to their edge. You can clamp on a fence or use a fence mounted to the plane itself. Combination planes can make a variety of cuts when tuned properly and cutting well. Keep the blade supported for the best results.

Drills and Drivers

There are several types of *hand drills* and drivers. The egg beater, Yankee drill, and ratchet-type screwdriver are handy in certain situations for drilling or driving screws. For larger boring jobs, the *brace* is the best tool for the job. Auger bits are common, but for chair work many woodworkers prefer to use a spoon bit for easy adjustment of boring angles.

Although not generally considered joinery tools, good *hammers* and *mallets* are indispensable. A simple leather mallet is perfect for light chopping. For heavier chopping, use a solid-wood carver's mallet. A metal hammer is the best tool for putting in wedges or plugs. When the wooden wedge is in as deep as it'll go, you'll hear the sound of the hammer blow change from a thud to a ping.

The majority of hand boring work is done with a bit and brace.

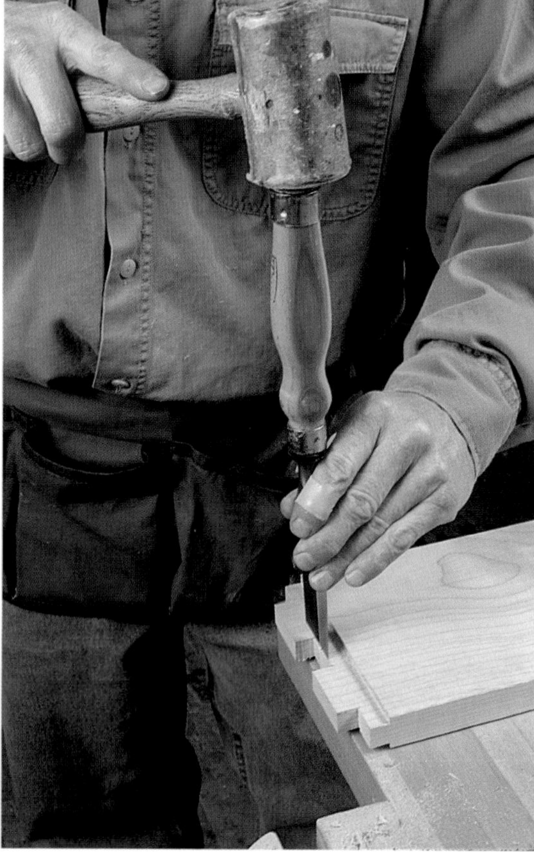

Use a small mallet for precise chopping work.

The dead-blow mallet is also worthy of a spot in the toolbox because of its non-marring yet persuasive nature. It will bang dowels or loose tenons home without mushrooming their ends. You'll also find the dead blow invaluable when checking the fit of joints. This mallet will leave no trace behind when you use it to force a joint apart that is held together too tightly.

Be sure always to use hand pressure to put any joint together. This avoids the risk of shattering the joint by using too much persuasion.

Every shop has an assortment of *screwdrivers.* If you're using slotted screws, grind your screwdriver head to match the screw slot. This will keep the driver engaged more positively and save you from nicked-up screw heads. Use Phillips-head or square-drive screws for more positive control of your screwdriving. Remember to match the driver size to the screw head. Always run a steel screw in a pilot hole to cut the threads of the hole before putting in a brass screw. Brass screws are soft, and you can twist their heads right off.

Holding Jigs

The simplest of *holding jigs* is the bench hook. Make up several lengths for different tasks in the shop, such as plane work, sawing, and sharpening. Another version of the

Use a metal hammer to drive in a wedge. When the wedge can't go any farther, the sound of the hammer blow will change from a thud to a ping.

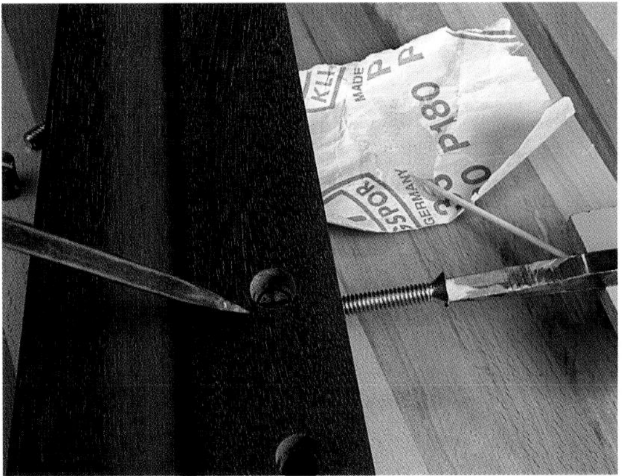

Grind your slotted screwdriver to fit a screw head better.

Match the square drive bit to the screw head for the most secure driving.

Bench hooks hold the workpiece steady when you plane, saw, or sharpen.

Make sure the vise is mounted securely to the bench. A quick-action mechanism and clamping dog are very useful features.

You can never have too many clamps. Collect a variety of them to conquer any clamping situation.

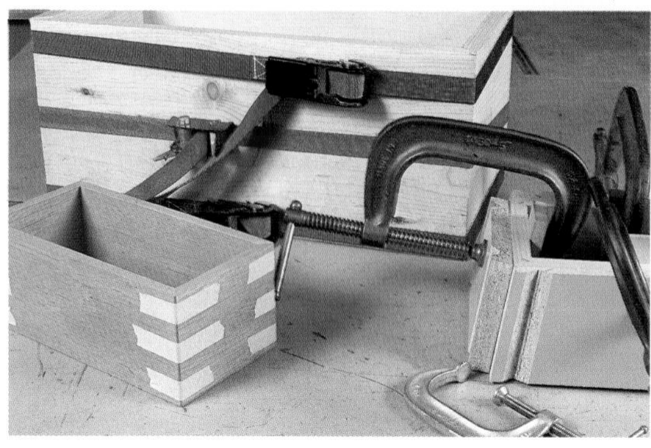
For clamping miter joints, use band clamps or C-clamps with clamping blocks. Masking tape will work for small miter joints that fit together well.

bench hook is the shooting board used for shooting the long edges of boards with a plane. Use a miter shooting board for working miters with a handplane.

Clamping Tools

Bench *vises* are the heavy-duty solution for holding pieces firmly in place while you work on them. Mount one to your bench that has a quick-action mechanism on it. Above all else, however, make sure the vise is sturdy and securely mounted for the best results.

Clamps come in many sizes. Use C-clamps, pipe clamps, or quick-action clamps whenever the situation warrants. Use wooden jaw clamps to hold small pieces for drilling or to clamp down boards without fear of marring the work. When clamping miter joints, use band clamps, C-clamps with clamping blocks, or even masking tape under certain circumstances.

Portable Power Tools

A FRIEND OF MINE ONCE SAID that using the router was the fastest way he knew to screw up a piece of wood. But a router is also one of the most useful portable power tools in the shop for joinery. Learning how to guide and use it precisely may take some time, but once you've developed your skills, you can cut joints with consistency and speed. Portable power tools are fast; but to get the best results, they should be understood before you turn them on. When guided properly, they are unmatched for accuracy and versatility, being limited only by your engineering imagination. Power tools should also demand your respect, because they can turn a moment's lapse into a lifelong memory. Although they are few in type, they are many in number. Portable power tools include saws, routers, biscuit joiners, and drills.

Saws

Few *circular saws* cut with the degree of accuracy required for furniture work. Some tool manufacturers, however, have been designing saws that cut with little or no blade vibration to achieve superior results. The anti-tearout guards available for these saws help protect the workpiece from surface tearout. If you guide a saw with an edge-guide system, your results can improve dramatically.

Circular saw systems now come with dust pickup, anti-tearout guards, and little or no blade vibration for superior cutting results.

A router can cut joinery with precision and speed once you understand how to guide it properly.

Routers and Bits

Routers have become a joinery workhorse because of their versatility. They can be guided by a bearing-mounted bit, an integral fence mounted to the router, or a fence clamped onto the workpiece or a router table. Routers can be used with templates or jigs to align the cuts. They can even be used freehand to aid your joinery work. Learn to guide them successfully, and there is little joinery work they cannot accomplish. The two most common types of routers are the fixed-base and plunge routers.

The *fixed-base router* consists of two separate major parts: the motor and the base. Remove the motor from the base to mount a bit; then adjust the height to set the bit exposure. You make a series of cuts to get down to final depth. Fixed-base routers can be handheld and used topside or be mounted in a router table to work from below.

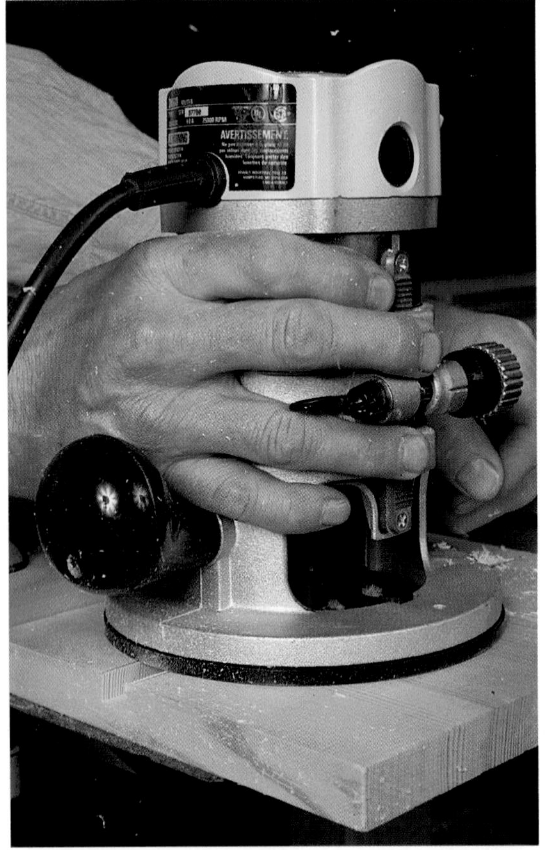

To set the bit depth on a fixed-base router, adjust the motor within its base.

A *plunge router* works best for the job it was designed for: plunging into a cut. The motor stays fixed to the base but moves up and down on spring-loaded columns. You set the bit for the full depth of cut, but get down there in a series of passes. Many plunge routers also have a variable-speed adjustment.

Routers are also designated by the largest bit they can hold. Use a ½-in. router for the most versatility, a better selection of bits, and stronger bit shanks with less flex. When using larger-diameter bits, put the router in the router table and make sure it has a variable speed adjustment so you can decrease the rotation speed.

There are three basic materials used for *router bits:* high-speed steel, carbide tips, and solid carbide. Each has different qualities that make it useful in a particular situation. High-speed steel can take the keenest edge but loses it fast. Use high-speed steel when a cheaper bit is required, when an edge might get damaged, or when you don't mind sharpening after each use. High-speed steel is also found in end-mill cutters, which are very useful for mortising.

Carbide-tipped bits will last 10 times longer than steel bits; but as their edges dull, bits of carbide will flake off. With the smaller diamond honing stones now available, you can sharpen some carbide edges. You will find a great variety of carbide-tipped bits. Solid-carbide bits are great for mortising. They, of course, contain more carbide, which gives them a longer sharpening life.

One way to guide a plunge-router cut is to use a fence.

Bits are also categorized by their shape and use. There are a large variety of straight

bits, single- and double-fluted bits, and straight- and spiral-fluted bits. Single-fluted straight bits are production bits used for quick but rough removal of wood. A double-fluted bit gives a smoother cut. Use spiral flutes for an even smoother shearing cut. These always have one edge in the cut so there's less vibration and chatter. The most common type is the up-spiral flute shaped like a drill bit for removing waste from a hole. Use a down-spiral to avoid tearout at the top of a hole.

Profile cutters have some type of shape cut into them. Look at the router bit to see the negative shape of the cutter so you can imagine the kind of cut you will get.

The bit depth can be set in several ways. Use a rule for precise measuring on the router table. You can also use a piece of wood pencil marked for the proper depth. For repeatable setups, make up a height block you can set the bit directly off of. Be sure to have some bit height blocks for cuts you make often. On the plunge router, the depth of cut is set with the depth stop rod.

ROUTER CUTS

Cutting with the router topside usually calls for moving it left to right across the edge of a board. Note, however, that this can be a counterclockwise direction when, say, making a cut on the perimeter of a mirror frame, but it's a clockwise cut when making the rabbets on the mirror's inside edges. It's best not to think of moving the router in terms of a clock's motions. Think instead of moving into the rotation of the cutter. As the router bit spins, it does spin clockwise. By

All these spiral-flute straight bits are designed for mortising. *Left to right:* solid carbide, carbide tipped with a down-spiral flute, high-speed steel, and carbide tipped.

This dovetail cutter makes a cut that leaves a tail shape behind. It is guided with a template mounted into the bottom of the router.

Use a rule with an end scale to set the bit depth on the router table.

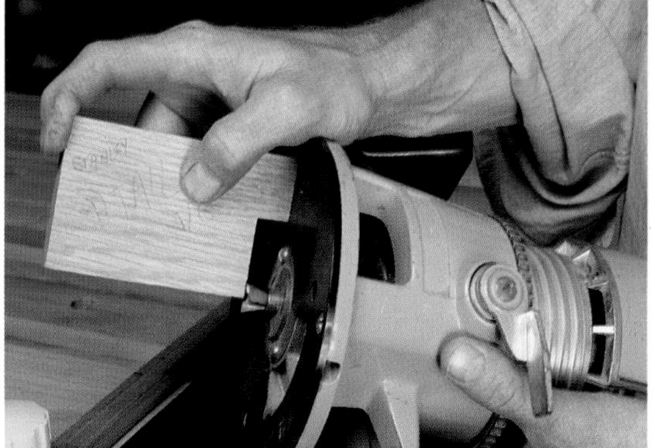

A height block sets up the bit for cuts you make often.

moving the router from left to right along an edge, the cutter pulls itself into the cut as it rotates.

However, if you move a router topside from right to left quite a different result occurs. The router tries to push itself away from the edge of the work, and you scoot along the edge of the board. This "climb cut," as it's called, occurs because the first cutting action of the bit is directly into the edge of the board, which causes the router to push away from the board. If you're not prepared for it, it can be quite surprising. But it's easy to control with a handheld router.

On the router table, everything is reversed. As you look at the bit, it's spinning counterclockwise, and you move the work past the bit from right to left. This direction is into the rotation of the cutter, which causes the work to pull into the bit or fence. The climb cut occurs when you move from left to right on the router table; it may cause

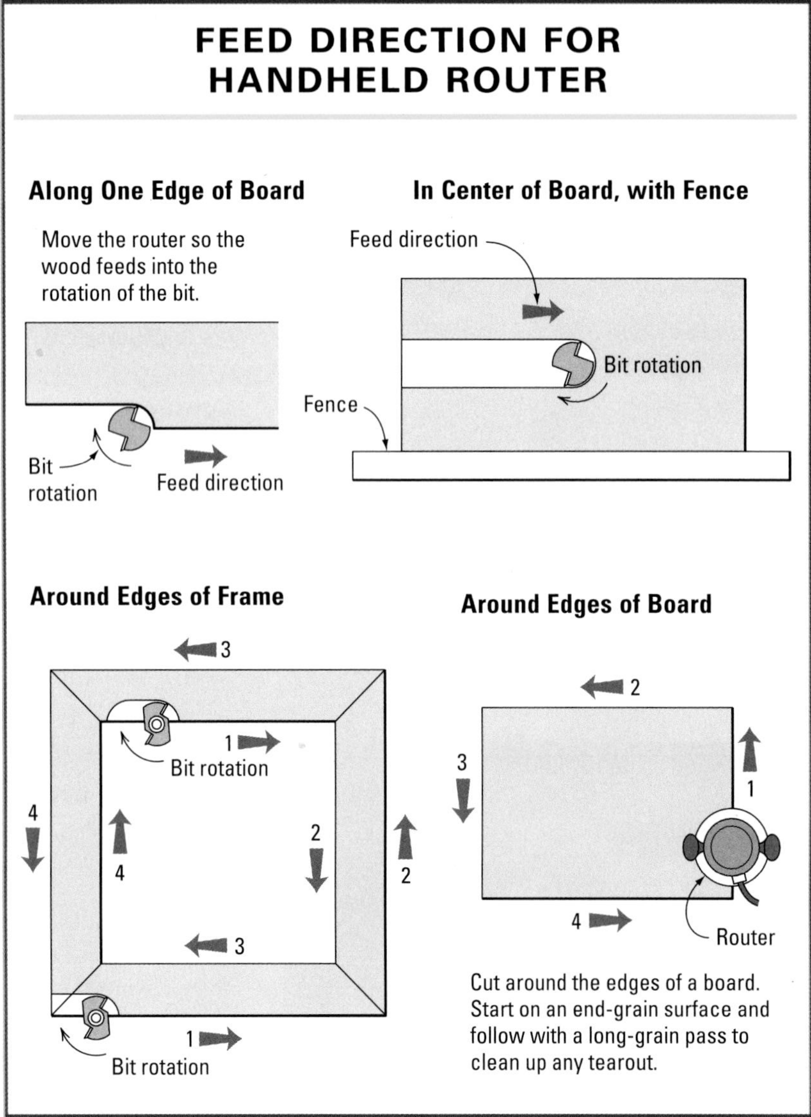

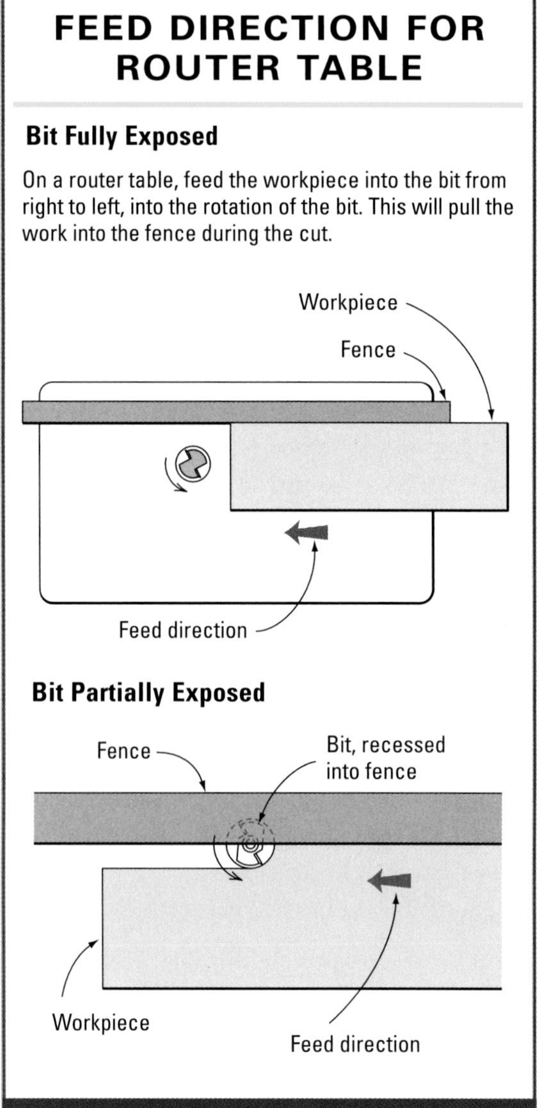

the workpiece to shoot past the bit if you're not extra careful.

There are situations in which a cut causes a lot of tearout. Making a climb cut is a technique for eliminating tearout on long-grain cuts. It cannot be used for short pieces on the router table and is best done topside. Make a scoring pass along the edge of the board to trim the outer fibers of the long grain. Then come back and make the full pass in the proper feed direction. This way any tearout that occurs will be back from the edge and thus removed as the cut is completed.

ROUTER GUIDES

Guiding a router bit is often accomplished by means of a *bearing*, which can be either top or bottom mounted. Use these bits in both the router table and handheld router. The bit can cut in only as far as the bearing will allow. Make sure that the bearing spins freely, with no crunching or roughness to it. One very useful bearing-mounted bit for joinery is the flush-trimming bit. The bit is just as wide as the bearing, so it cuts out exactly the same shape as a template. Use

This spline cutter, in the router table, has a bottom-mounted bearing by which it limits the depth of cut.

CLIMB CUTTING

Normal Cut

The normal feed direction can sometimes produce tearout on the unsupported fibers at the edge, especially when cutting against the grain. Tearout can also occur below the final depth of cut. (Bit rotation is clockwise on a topside cut.)

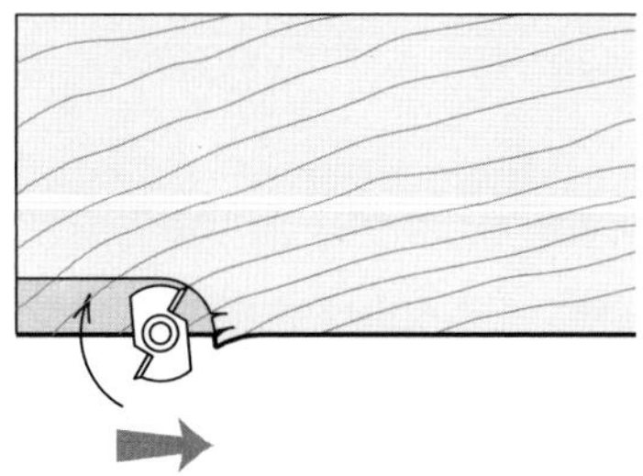

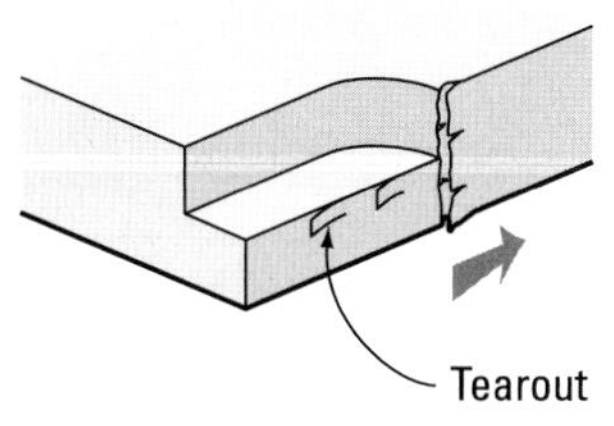

Climb Cut

The climb cut scores the edge as the bit tries to climb out of the cut and push itself away from the edge.

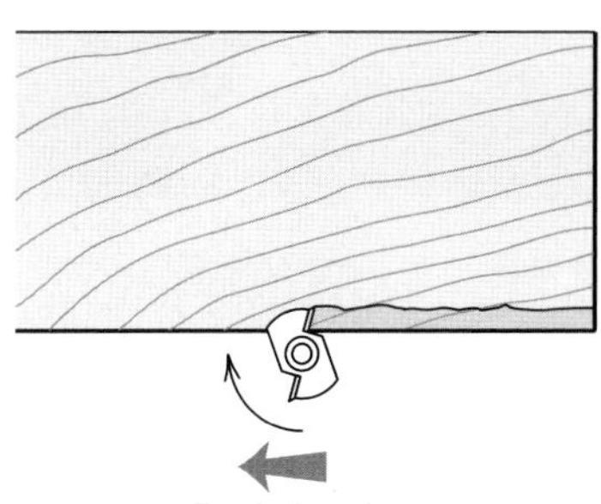

Cleanup Cut

The cleanup pass to full depth will take care of any further tearout. Any tearout that occurs will be set back from the edge.

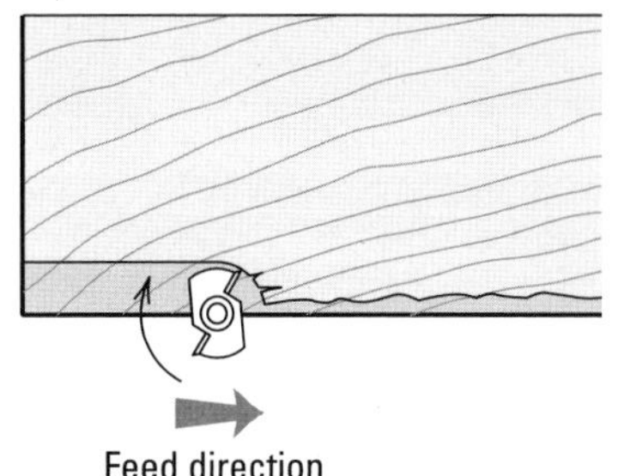

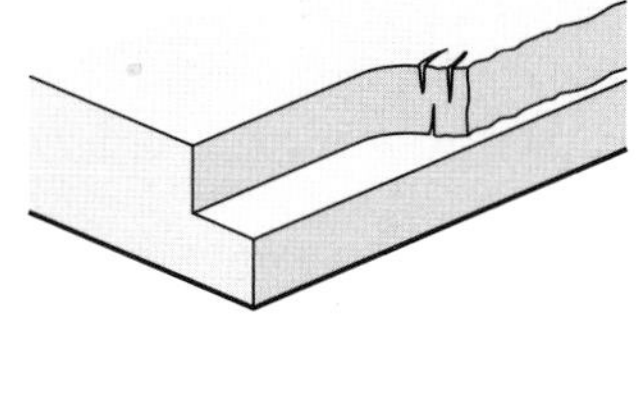

A flush-trimming bit has a bearing that's just as wide as its cutter. The bearing rides against the template, allowing you to cut out a shape that matches the template exactly.

Mount a fence onto the plunge router to make cuts parallel to an edge. An auxiliary fence lets you make a more precise cut.

Guide a topside cut with a straight-edged board clamped to the workpiece. A sub-base with a straightedge on it rides against the fence to direct the cut.

Clamp a fence onto the router table to locate a cut. A vacuum attachment helps collect the dust.

this bit with both shopmade and commercial templates.

Mount a *fence* to the router when making topside cuts parallel to an edge. Most fences have some degree of slop in them, so be sure to tighten them securely into the router and keep all the locknuts tight. Fences benefit from an auxiliary fence to lengthen the bearing surface, making for a surer cut. Move the router from left to right around the edge of the work.

A fence simply clamped onto a board can also guide the router. Make sure the fence is straight and the clamp heads are out of the way. Move the router topside from left to right across the board so the router gets pulled in tight to the fence as it cuts. Make certain you don't rotate the router as you make the cut, because some bases are not concentric with the bit. Some routers now come with a straightedge built into the base to make using a straight fence easier. Sub-bases with a straightedge can be added to the router to help guide straight cuts.

Fences are often used on router tables to guide a cut. Make up a fence that you can attach a vacuum hose to. Be sure any fence you use is square to the table, flat, and without any twist. When using the router table, you move the work from right to left across the bit for most cutting situations.

Template routing is another effective method for guiding a router cut. Template guides, rub collars, or template bushings, as they're called, mount in the bottom of the router base. They are available in a variety of

shapes, sized by the outside diameter (O.D.) and inside diameter (I.D.). Measure the offset of the bit to the template guide and figure in this distance to the template.

The advantage of templates is that, once made up, they're usable again and again. If you don't want to create your own, try some of the commercially available templates. Most of them are dovetail templates, but others can also cut sliding dovetails and mortise-and-tenon joints, with some setup.

Measure the distance from the bit's cutting edge to the template guide's edge to figure out the amount of offset.

Templates let you make repeatable cuts with the plunge router. The template guide is mounted to the router base, which fits in the template's slots.

This jig holds a box steady as you move the workpiece past the bit for a key cut on the router table.

This scarfing jig lets you move the router over the work as you cut the joint.

RIGHT-ANGLE JIG

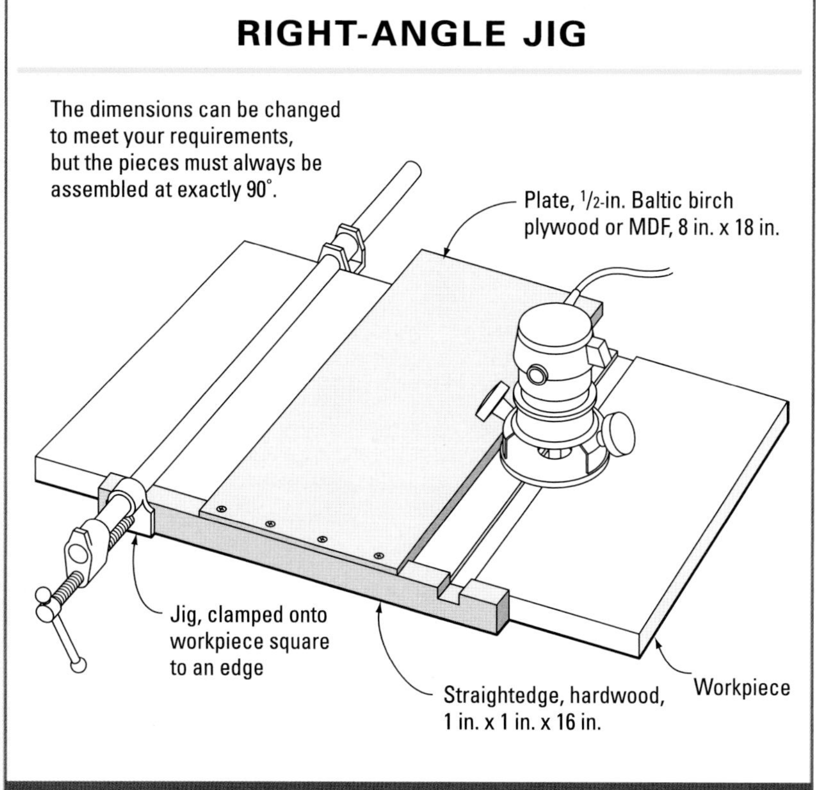

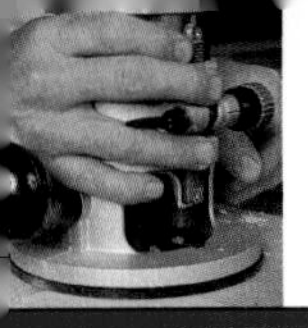

A well-designed router jig will make some repeatable jobs, like mortising, simpler and quicker.

Jigs can guide a router to make many cuts. Simple right-angle jigs are easily constructed in the shop for cutting topside grooves or dadoes. More complex jigs can be created for use on the router table or in the handheld router. Jigs can move the workpiece past the router or help guide the router as it moves past the board. Learn how to design and use jigs to increase your routing capabilities.

Biscuit joiners use a slotting blade to cut biscuit slots. You then insert a pressed beech biscuit, which swells when it comes in contact with the glue.

Biscuit Joiners

Biscuit joinery has replaced doweling and screws in many shops as a fast way of aligning pieces. These joints use a pressed beech biscuit as a loose tenon between two slots

Sheet-good materials, like plywood and medium-density fiberboard (MDF), are perfect for biscuit joinery, because there is always a good gluing surface to cut a slot into.

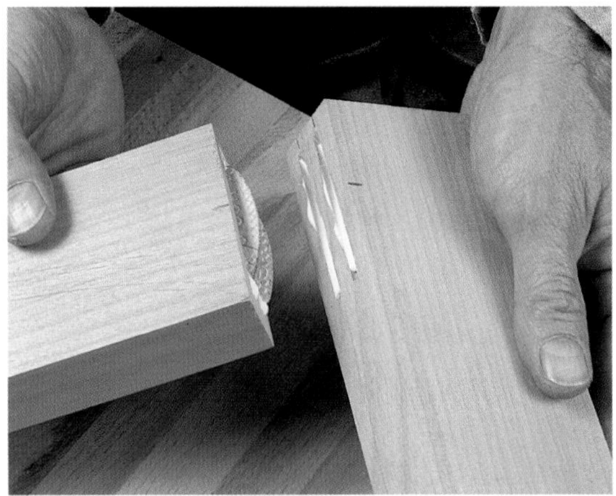

Biscuit joinery works well in frame construction, as each slot is cut into long grain.

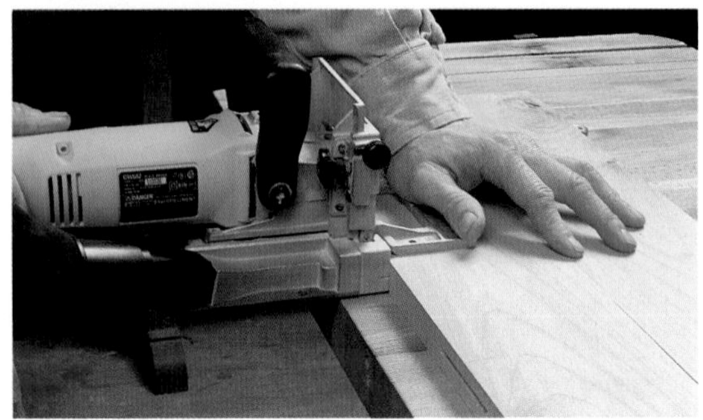

Biscuit joints help you line up boards for edge gluing.

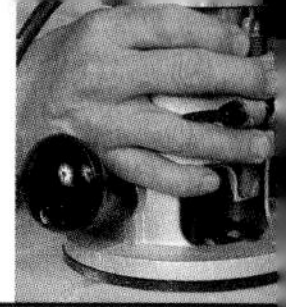

cut in the boards. Biscuits are used for sheet-good joinery, as you can place a slot anywhere in the sheet and still get a good gluing surface.

In solid wood, biscuit joinery is limited to situations in which you can cut slots into two long-grain surfaces. Frame construction fits this scenario. Biscuit joinery is also used in edge gluing, when you need help lining up surfaces.

Drills

Today's drills handle two jobs. They, of course, do our boring work quickly, but they now drive screws for us as well. Corded power drills used to be the standard in most shops. They have now been replaced by cordless units, which range in battery size from 9-volt units for moderate-duty short jobs to 24-volt batteries for tougher, longer jobs.

Choosing a drill is also determined by chuck size. The size designation refers to the largest diameter bit shank that can fit into the chuck. For furniture work, most ⅜-in. drills are adequate. Only on rare occasion do you bore with a ½-in.-shank bit for hand drilling. For small work, some chucks do not spin down small enough to hold on to a bit. If you're working with small-diameter bits, make sure your drill can too.

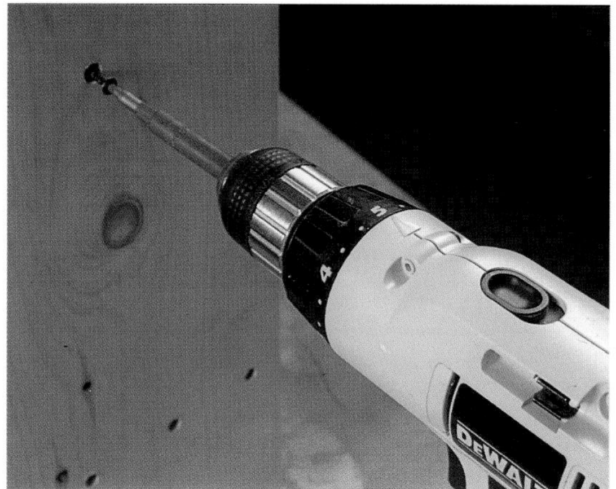

Cordless drills not only bore but also drive screws.

A ½-in. chuck on a cordless drill can handle larger shank bits.

Drilling out for escutcheon pins or brads requires small-diameter drill bits. Make sure your drill's chuck can hold on tight to a small bit.

TUNING YOUR PORTABLE POWER TOOLS

Portable power tools are not built like your hand-crafted furniture. You can improve their accuracy with just a little bit of tuning, which will improve their usefulness for joinery work.

- Check the router base for flatness with a straightedge. Subbases can get warped and should be replaced or sanded flat on a piece of sandpaper or carefully on a belt sander.
- Lubricate plunge-router columns with a spray-type lubricant to keep them moving freely. Clean them frequently to keep off accumulated dust.
- Keep your router bits clean for better cutting. Use an old toothbrush and some oven cleaner to do this job. Soak the bits in the cleaner and then brush off the burned-on gunk. You can also do a little sharpening of the flat side of a router bit with a small diamond honing stone.
- Make sure the router table stays flat. Use a straightedge to see that the weight of the router hasn't caused it to bow or droop in the middle.
- Make sure the router table fence is straight and has a good right angle to the table.
- Test the biscuit joiner fence to see that it's parallel to the cutter. You can add a piece of tape to a fence to fix one that's a little skewed.

Lube the screws by putting some wax on the threads for easier driving.

Driving screws with a drill is now the standard in most shops. Use a variable-speed reversible drill for the job. You will be able to adjust the drill speed for the material and screw you're using. It's easier on your wrists, arms, and hands and, in general, is a much faster and better method. Most cordless drills also have clutch settings that power the chuck. When the resistance setting is reached, the drill stops driving. Always lubricate the screws with wax for easier entry.

Machines

MACHINES ARE DESIGNED to do specific tasks, for example, saws cut wood and jointers flatten a board. But often these machines can also be used to do a joinery task. Other machines are designed specifically for joinery, including boring and mortising machines.

Check each machine's reference surface for flatness. A bow or twist in a table will cause you continuing problems when you try to cut joints. Use a good straightedge to check a table or fence. Make sure all machine surfaces stay clean and free of debris when you use them. Install dust collectors to remove sawdust. *Always* read the manufacturer's safety guidelines and follow them carefully.

Boring and Mortising

Boring and mortising machines bore or rout out holes for mortises. Most produce only round holes because of the rotary action of the bit, but one actually makes a mortise with square corners.

The *drill press* is thought of mostly as a tool for boring out holes for dowels. The holes can go in straight or at an angle. This joinery job relies on the drill press's ability to cut a true hole. No matter the precision of the drill press bearings or chuck, if you use cheap bits the holes will be out of round.

Rely on a drill press to bore out accurate holes, but only if your drill bits are of good quality.

Use good-quality bits and check them for runout or wobble when chucked in the drill press.

The drill press can also bore out mortises when used with a fence. Because a fence locates a cut or hole at a specific distance from an edge, a series of holes can be made to drill out a mortise for a joint. Remember that the fence does not have to be parallel or square to any edge of the drill press table to do this job. It simply has to be located at the proper distance from the bit's center. The drill press can also be fitted with other types of bits for doing mortise work. End-mill and hollow-chisel mortising bits can be mounted in the drill press for mortising operations.

Use a fence to locate your drilling for a series of holes that will create a mortise.

An auxiliary table mounted to the drill press table makes attaching other jigs much simpler.

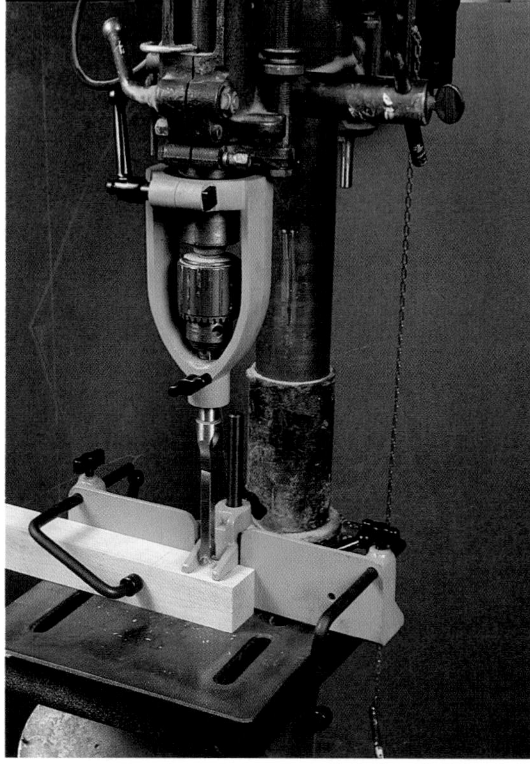

A hollow-chisel mortising attachment can be mounted to the drill press for cutting square holes.

You can use several different jigs on the drill press to help your mortising. An auxiliary table is useful, because most drill press tables are cast iron with ribbing underneath. With an auxiliary table clamped or bolted in place, fastening on other jigs is much easier. Make one from a flat piece of ¾-in. medium-density fiberboard (MDF) with a board glued onto its bottom. Clamp the auxiliary table to the side of the drill press table.

Use a fence for drilling out mortises. The fence should be flat and straight, but it can be clamped at any angle to the table. It needs, however, to be placed at the proper distance from the bit. Each hole is drilled out at that distance, forming a straight line. Some drill presses have tables that adjust for angled holes. Angle jigs will also angle your workpiece to the bit. A vertical drilling jig is useful when you want to help hold a piece for an end-grain hole.

A vertical drilling jig bolts onto the drill press table, which is rotated to vertical. With the jig's adjustable fence, you can locate the work for drilling into the end of a board.

Drill bits for the drill press include twist bits for metal and woodwork, spade bits for rough drilling in wood only, brad-point bits for more accurate centering, multispur bits for larger-diameter holes, and Forstner bits for angled drilling. Always use a piece of scrap to protect the drill press table or auxiliary table when drilling through any board.

Horizontal mortising machines are industrial tools used specifically for boring out mortises. The table moves side to side and

DRILL PRESS JIGS

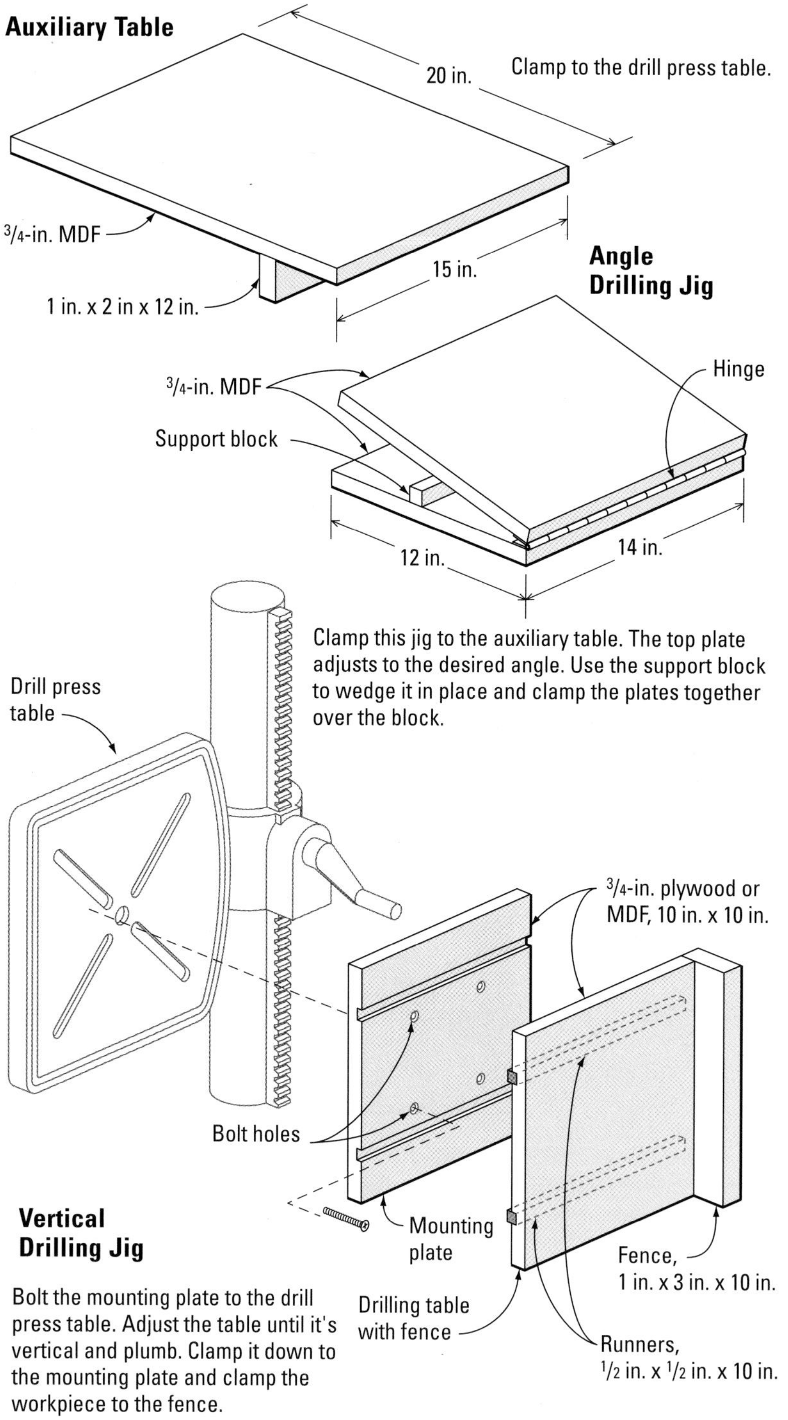

Auxiliary Table

20 in.

Clamp to the drill press table.

3/4-in. MDF

15 in.

1 in. x 2 in x 12 in.

Angle Drilling Jig

3/4-in. MDF

Hinge

Support block

12 in.

14 in.

Clamp this jig to the auxiliary table. The top plate adjusts to the desired angle. Use the support block to wedge it in place and clamp the plates together over the block.

Drill press table

3/4-in. plywood or MDF, 10 in. x 10 in.

Bolt holes

Vertical Drilling Jig

Mounting plate

Fence, 1 in. x 3 in. x 10 in.

Bolt the mounting plate to the drill press table. Adjust the table until it's vertical and plumb. Clamp it down to the mounting plate and clamp the workpiece to the fence.

Drilling table with fence

Runners, 1/2 in. x 1/2 in. x 10 in.

up and down while the motor and bit move into the work. Routing machines like the Multirouter can also bore out mortises, and they have a great deal of versatility. They can do angled work and can cut tenons. Their ability to move in three directions makes them suitable for a variety of mortising operations. The horizontal table holds the work and moves side to side and in and out. The router is mounted in the vertical table and moves up and down. Any horizontal machine needs to move smoothly in its major axes and have no wobble or slop in its tables. Also check to see there's no flex in the table when you put on a long or heavy board.

The *hollow-chisel mortiser* is designed specifically for mortising. Only with significant modification can it do any other drilling job. It requires finely tuned and sharpened bits, but the superior leverage in its gearing gets the square mortising done. The heavier the hollow-chisel mortiser, the better.

Edge Tools

Edge tools are all designed primarily for other tasks. But on occasion they can do some joinery work.

The *jointer* flattens an edge or a face of a board. It will not do this parallel to any other edge or face, as its cutterhead is in line with its reference surface. Make sure the cutterhead knives line up perfectly with the outfeed table of the jointer at top dead center. If the knives are set too high to that table, you will experience snipe at the end of the board when the board comes off the infeed table and drops into the knives. If you're getting a taper cut, your knives are set too low to the outfeed table. They stop cutting as the board moves along its pass, gradually lifting itself off the knives. You can use the jointer for rabbet cuts along the long-grain edge of a board or to joint edges for gluing.

The *planer* cuts the face of a board flat and parallel to another face. Its cutterhead is set parallel to the reference surface, its table. For the best results, you must first flatten

Because of the x-y-z movement of their tables, horizontal routing machines have the flexibility to cut not only mortises but tenons and other joints.

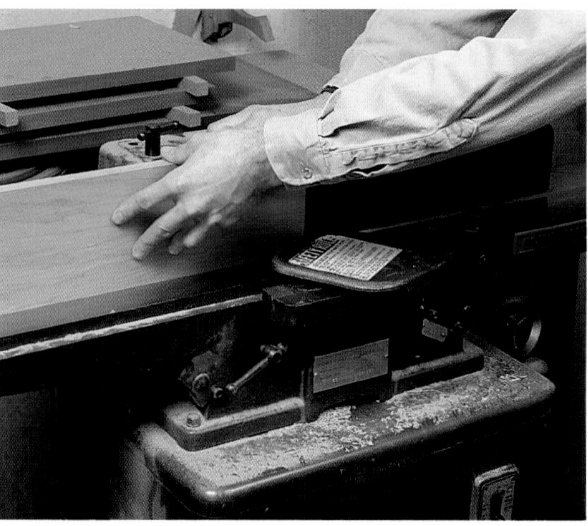

The jointer is used for straightening the edges of boards before gluing.

Use the planer to make stock with perfectly parallel faces for loose tenons or splines.

Lathes can turn round tenons on the ends of square or round stock.

one face on the jointer and then pass the board through the planer. You can also use the planer for making up loose tenon or spline stock.

The *lathe* is used to make round tenons in joinery. A variety of cutting tools will make the tenons.

The *disk sander* can be used for trimming miter cuts. Always work on the left side of a disk sander that spins counterclockwise. This will push the workpiece down into the table.

Saws

The usefulness of saws for joinery depends on their accuracy. The heavier the saw, generally the better. Bearings that run true and good straight fences that lock well are important for any saw. Also use sharp sawblades and never force work through a saw. You can either cut fast or cut accurately. Do not expect to do both with a saw. Use the

Use a disk sander to trim miter cuts. Make sure the table is set square to the sanding disk.

The bandsaw is surprisingly capable of cutting many joints. Make sure the blade tracks true and keep the feed rate slow for the best results.

blade guards supplied by the saw's manufacturer and always use hearing and eye protection.

The *bandsaw* is capable of many joinery cuts when equipped with a sharp blade and true-running wheels and tires. Use a wider blade with fewer teeth per inch (tpi) for joinery rip cuts. A ½-in. 3-tpi or 4-tpi blade is excellent for cutting out tenons or finger joints. For smoother surfaces, use a 6-tpi blade, but slow down the feed rate. For ease, use a fence on the saw that's adjustable. Pencil out the cuts and check to see the blade cuts parallel to the fence. If it doesn't, you'll have to use a clamped-on fence set parallel to the degree of blade drift.

The *miter saw* (chopsaw) was developed as a carpenter's tool. Portable and lightweight, it could be taken to any job site. Now in heavy use in furniture shops, it can produce excellent results when crosscutting boards to length. Clamp stops onto its fence so you can reproduce cuts. The miter saw

Cut finger joints on the bandsaw equipped with a fence and stop block.

The miter saw does an excellent job of crosscutting multiple pieces exactly to length.

Use the miter saw for miter cuts on frame pieces or box parts.

The table saw does the lion's share of the work in most shops. By using different jigs, you can also cut joinery very effectively.

can cut miters on picture frame stock or wide boxes. Use a sliding compound miter saw for cutting half laps or tenons by adjusting the blade depth.

The *table saw* performs most of the routine cutting chores in the shop: cutting sheet goods, ripping stock to width, and crosscutting to length. With the addition of several jigs, however, you can use the table saw for precise joinery work.

BLADES

Carbide-tipped blades are now the industry standard for most cutting jobs. There are four standard blade grinds: alternate-top bevel (atb), alternate-top bevel with a raker or a combination grind (atb/r), flat grind (fg), and triple-chip grind (tcg). The combination blades are the best all-around blades for joinery.

Dado blades are also used for joinery. Better designs give a more flat-bottomed cut, which will save you time in cleanup. Chippers can now be four toothed rather

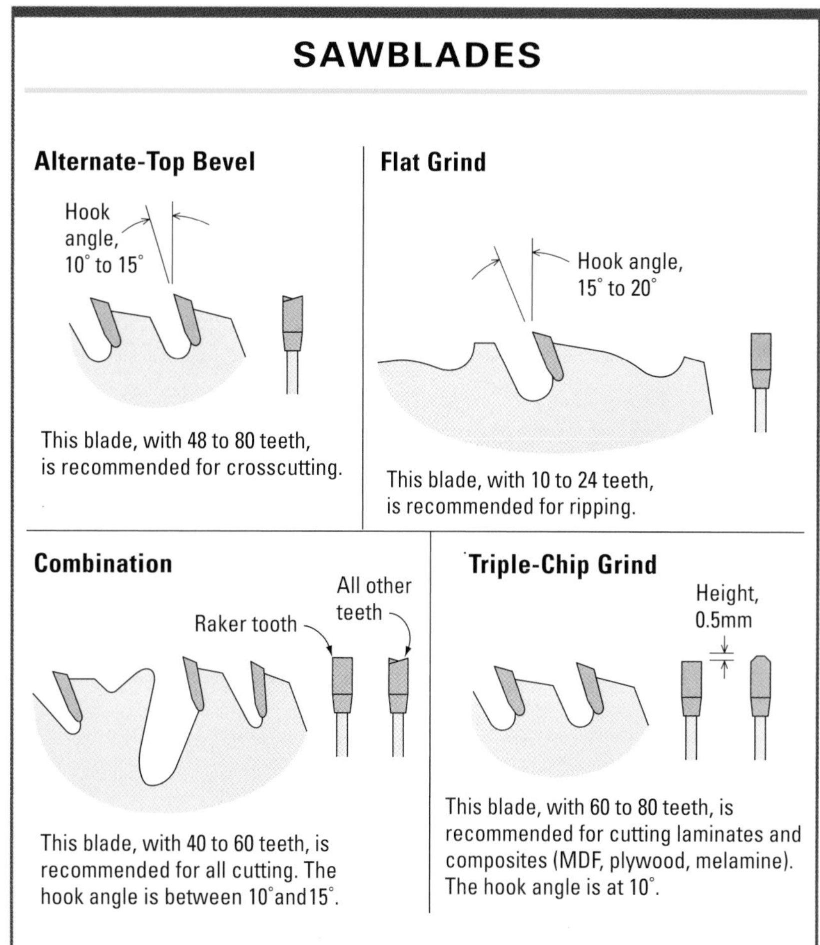

TABLE SAW SAFETY

- Always use the blade guard and splitter.
- Wear eye and hearing protection.
- Raise the blade only one tooth above the surface of the stock being cut.
- Know where your fingers are at all times. Place them consciously on a jig before pushing it through the cut.
- Use push sticks when the fence is closer than a fist's width from the blade. Keep the push sticks near enough to grab at any time.
- Stand to the left side of the fence, pushing the work into it. Keep your head and body just to the left of the blade, out of the path of kickback.
- Keep the blade sharp. Don't force the work past a dull blade.
- Move the work at a moderate feed rate past the blade. If the work starts to ride up on the blade, hold it firmly in place while you dial the blade down and out of the cut. Don't try to force the wood down onto the blade.
- Remember that everything that happens at the fence next happens at the blade and not vice versa. Always keep the workpiece held tight to the fence.
- Keep the board from touching the back half of the blade. Use a splitter to prevent it from drifting into the blade.
- Push the board through the blade and well past it before reaching around to grab it.
- Use a runoff table or roller support to help with long boards or panels. Do not pull the work to feed it past the blade.
- Never feed a board with a hand on the outfeed side of the cut. If the board kicks back, your hand will go along for the ride.
- When using a dado blade, use a slower feed rate and greater caution. The dado blade cuts a wide swath and is more susceptible to kickback.
- When using any metal jig, check to make sure it will clear the blade *before* you turn on the saw.
- Be careful of trapping a small offcut between the blade and fence (or a stop) as the piece may kick back at you.

than two toothed, which makes for a smoother, more balanced, and safer cut.

JIGS

Table saw jigs greatly extend the versatility of the saw as a joinery tool. Use an auxiliary fence on a regular table-saw fence when cutting wide boards that need support. You can also make zero-clearance cuts with an auxiliary fence and save cutting the saw's fence.

The miter gauge that comes with the table saw generally needs some tuning before use. Most have a sloppy fit in their tracks. Drill out the bars and insert commercially

Use a combination blade with an alternate-top bevel grind and a raker tooth to cut a variety of joints.

Use an auxiliary fence to support wider boards on edge. You can also cut into an auxiliary fence when making a zero-clearance cut.

Dado blades are dangerous when misused. Always use a controlled feed rate and push sticks when needed. If possible, keep the fence closer to, rather than farther from, the dado blade.

Aftermarket miter gauges feature positive stops at common angles, adjustable telescoping fences for long stock, and locking adjustable stops.

available expandable gauge blocks. These will give you a tighter and truer fit. Some miter gauges feature locking stops, positive stops at set angles, and adjustable fences. These gauges also benefit from inserting gauge blocks. Cut miters on the miter gauge or make up a picture frame jig. This jig, when built properly, ensures that matching cuts will always yield a square corner.

A crosscut jig is indispensable for tablesaw crosscutting. Bolt on the fence so it locks down more securely. It will also be easier to adjust this way. Use wooden gauge bars of quartersawn stock to minimize the

A picture frame jig has a fence with a square corner set at 45 degrees to the blade. It glides on runners that fit into the miter-gauge tracks.

Be sure your tenoning jig adjusts accurately and moves precisely in its gauge slot.

A crosscut jig rides in the miter-gauge slots. Bolt on a fence so you can adjust it easily for a square cut.

CROSSCUT JIG

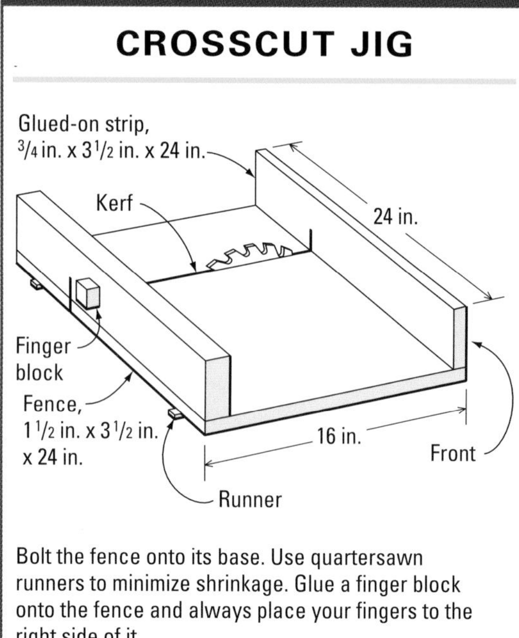

Bolt the fence onto its base. Use quartersawn runners to minimize shrinkage. Glue a finger block onto the fence and always place your fingers to the right side of it.

effect of wood movement throughout the seasons. Clamp stops to the fence to locate cuts.

Tenoning jigs can be bought or be shopmade. Take some time to fine-tune a purchased tenoning jig. A shopmade jig can be very simply made. Keep the screws that hold on the support block higher than your highest possible saw position. Also, make the jig taller than your fence so you can use a clamp on the work. Be careful to never tip the tenoning jig into the blade as you move the work past it.

When you need to move the work past the blade at an angle, make up a jig. Put the fence on a new board at the required angle to hold the work.

Make a tall tenoning jig so you can attach a support block high up on it. Then you can also use a clamp on the work.

Build simple jigs to hold the work at the needed angle to make a cut. This spline miter jig uses only a piece of MDF with a support block screwed to it at 45 degrees.

Use a push stick in situations when your fingers might get too close to the exit spot of a blade.

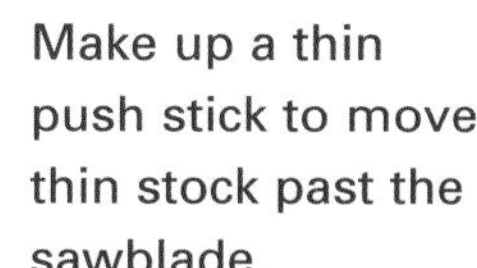

Make up a thin push stick to move thin stock past the sawblade.

Use push sticks whenever the fence gets too close to the blade. A fist's width is my rule of thumb: Smaller than a fist, I use a push stick. Use push sticks for any cut that might put your fingers close to the exit point of the blade. For extra-thin stock use an extra-thin push stick. A featherboard and push stick used together will allow you to cut safely.

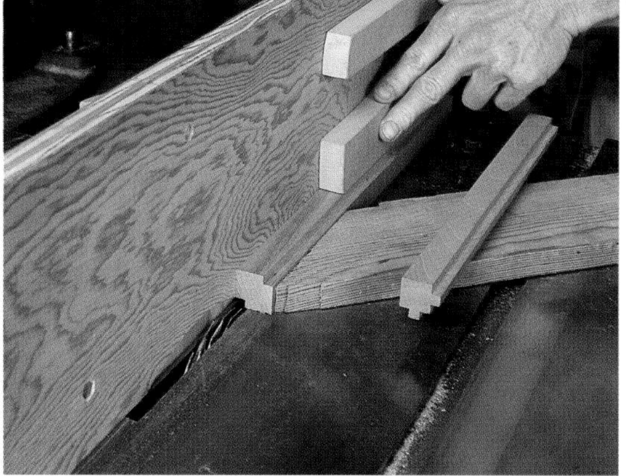

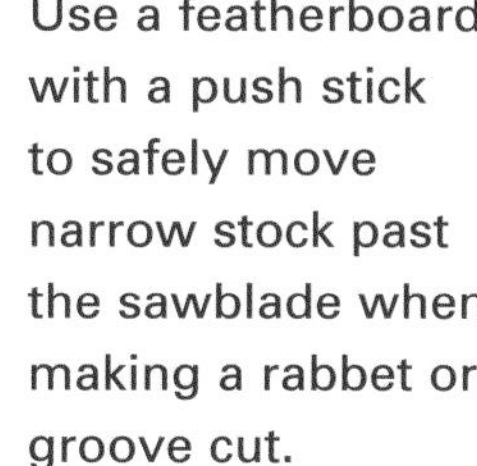

Use a featherboard with a push stick to safely move narrow stock past the sawblade when making a rabbet or groove cut.

Butt Joints, page 40

Rabbet, Groove, and Dado Joints, page 65

Miter Joints, page 105

Finger Joints, page 123

Mortise-and-Tenon Joints, page 138

Dovetail Joints, page 150

PART TWO

Carcase Joinery

CARCASE CONSTRUCTION is quite simply box construction. Boxes are the basic form of cabinets, drawers, bookcases, and chests, including chests of drawers. So the ability to make a stable and sturdy box is essential to woodworking.

Carcases can be made of solid wood, plywood, or other composite materials, such as medium-density fiberboard (MDF). When made of plywood or composites, there are no concerns about grain direction, strength, or movement. But if the carcase is constructed of solid wood, grain direction becomes important.

The long-grain sides of the box provide a good gluing surface, but where the end grain meets the long grain, a mechanical connection must be created. Ideally, an additional gluing surface is formed as well. The many methods for accomplishing this are collectively called carcase joinery.

Butt Joints

Joints with Fasteners

Knockdown Joints

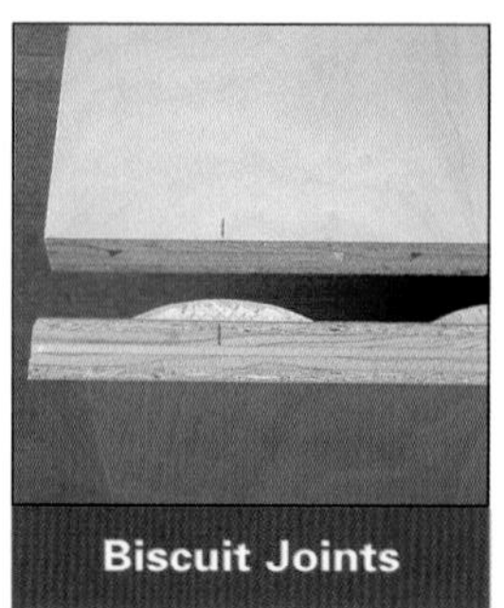
Biscuit Joints

Dowel Joints

BUTT JOINTS ARE THE SIMPLEST WAY of joining boards together to make a carcase. They're easy to cut if you pay attention to keeping them flat and square to both the face and the edge of a board. Angled butt joints, of course, need angles other than 90 degrees cut into the face or edge. With either flat or angled butt joint cuts, always keep the joint flat across its length and width. This will maximize the gluing area and give you a better bearing surface.

For anything other than the most cavalier construction, butt joints require something more than glue. Nearly all butt joints connect long grain (running with the grain) and end grain (cut across the grain). End grain will not bond well, no matter what type of glue you use. The glue will hold for a time; but without fasteners to help, the joint eventually will give way. Fasteners help hold this weak glue bond together.

Choosing Fasteners

One of the first things you need to decide is what kind of fastener to use for strengthening the joints. There are a variety of methods available for fortifying butt joints.

Biscuits are an efficient way to build large carcases; they reinforce the joint and enable accurate alignment.

For a simple butt joint with no fasteners, the edges are just glued and clamped.

This failed butt joint shows its weakness when no fasteners are used.

Driving a nail into a piece of hardwood will often cause splitting.

A butt joint built with knockdown fasteners can be assembled or disassembled on site.

Pocket hole screws, which require a jig for drilling the angled pilot holes, are an excellent reinforcement for carcases.

Nails are the most common way to fasten two boards. Drive a nail through one board into the other. Nothing could be simpler. But often in hardwoods or thin or narrow stock, you risk splitting out the board as you drive the nail. Predrilling a hole with a slightly smaller diameter drill bit than the nail will prevent splitting.

Screws are another fastener used for holding butt joints together, especially in cabinetry. When properly installed, they do a nice job of holding panels tightly together.

Knockdown fasteners can be surprisingly strong if you use them correctly. They allow you to build in the shop and assemble the piece on site, and they make for easy moving or storage. However, these fasteners must be designed into a piece so that they resist movement or tearing out when put under repetitive strain. It is important to use enough fasteners to distribute the pressure along a wide surface to give better holding power. Spread the fasteners out to help with triangulating the support and to ensure the butt joints are flat.

Pocket screws are another method for strengthening butt joints, particularly in cabinetry, where they're often used to fasten face frames to a carcase. They're made for speed, so use them accordingly. You can find commercial jigs to help rout the pockets with great alacrity or use a simple clamp-on jig with a drill and drill bit. Specialized auger-style bits are available for use with commercial jigs and often come with a depth stop. Such bits usually have a smaller diameter at the end for drilling a pilot hole.

Installing Screws

For quick installation jobs, use a taper bit mounted with a countersink head and stop collar. These tapered bits drill a pilot hole for the screw and a countersink for the screw head. If you keep drilling deeper, you can also bore out for a wood plug. A stop collar allows you to index each cut to the same depth. Another method for installing screws is to use a spade bit to drill the countersink holes. Drilled by hand, these holes are prone to tearout, but a sharp bit can make a decent hole.

Finer cabinetwork requires more accurate drilling. Use the drill press, drilling for the screw heads first with a 3/8-in. or 1/2-in. bit. Plug cutters are easy to find for these common sizes. Then use the drill press to drill pilot holes for the screws.

There are situations, however, when a drill press isn't large enough to allow a cabinet side to fit under it. This is when

A tapered bit fitted with a countersink is a quick way to drill pilot holes for screws.

A spade bit can be used to drill countersinks.

For jobs that require accuracy, use a drill press for the pilot holes.

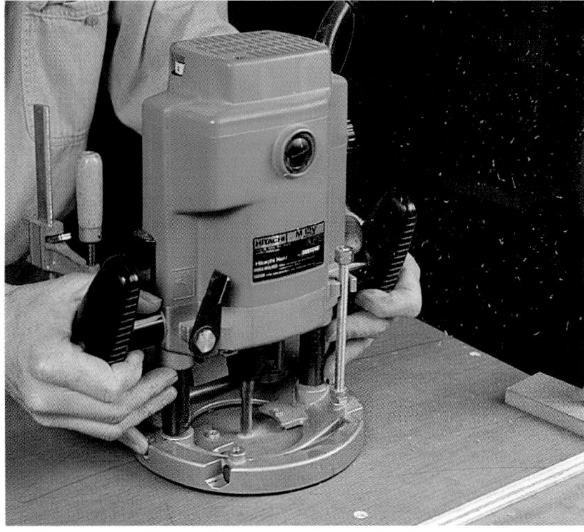

When a piece is too large for the drill press, use a plunge router fitted with a center-cutting bit for accuracy.

the router comes in handy. Use a plunge router to rout holes into a case with a center-cutting bit. This type of bit can act as a drill bit because it has a cutting edge across its bottom. Clamp the router in place so it won't slip and then rout to depth.

When drilling screw pilot holes, use a bit that's the same size as, or maybe even a size larger than, the root of the screws (the part the threads wrap around). The screws will enter with ease but still have good holding power. In some woods, a too-small pilot hole means you'll have trouble driving the screws at all. Heads can snap off or get bunged up by the driver. Be careful to size the bit not just to the screw but also to the wood. A soft wood like cedar can take an undersize hole far easier than can maple or cherry. Pilot holes should be drilled to depth and, in some cases, not even a tad farther. A piece of masking tape wrapped around the bit works as a depth gauge.

When drilling pilot holes for screws, choose a bit that is the same diameter as the root of the screw.

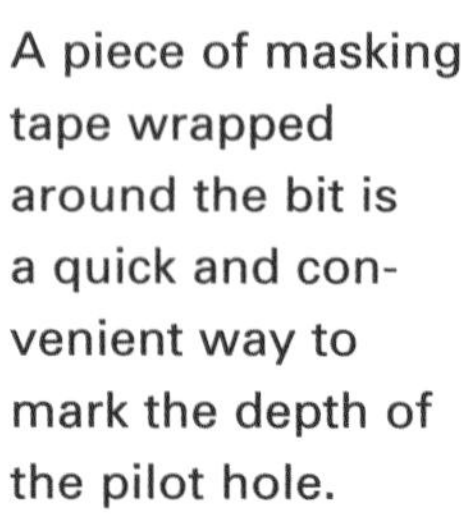

A piece of masking tape wrapped around the bit is a quick and convenient way to mark the depth of the pilot hole.

Hiding Fasteners

In some cases, a fastener gives a decorative look to a piece, such as handmade nails in a country piece or escutcheon pins in a dressy piece. More often, you'll want to disguise the fact that a fastener is holding the joint together. Face it, nail heads are just plain ugly. Fortunately, they can be easily hidden by countersinking the nails and filling the holes with a bit of putty, which is available to match a wide variety of wood species.

Hiding screws takes a little more work. There are several types of wood plugs you can use for covering up screw heads. You can buy different species of mushroom-shaped and round-head plugs. Drill some holes in a piece of scrap with the bit you're using on the project to check the fit of the plugs.

You can also use dowel rod as plugs. Check the fit of the dowel before you buy it. Remember that round dowel rod becomes oval as it dries out over time. It may not fit a round hole very tightly. Also be aware that a dowel rod plug will show end grain on the surface. The dowels can contrast greatly with the surrounding wood, even if they're the

Plugs for hiding screw holes come in a variety of shapes, sizes, and species. Or you can make your own for a perfect match.

same species, because end grain will soak up more finish, making it darker.

You can make your own plugs with a plug cutter and guarantee that the plugs will fit nicely and disappear into the woodwork, so to speak. Be sure to line up the grain of the plug with the grain of the case side.

Tapered plug cutters cut snug-fitting plugs that taper from top to bottom. The plugs enter the holes easily and fill them up entirely, thus eliminating any unsightly gluelines around half of the plug. Drill the plugs out on the drill press but set the depth so they stay in the stock. Then remove the plugs with a screwdriver or cut them off on the bandsaw. Tenon cutters are designed to cut long tenons or long dowels but can be used to cut plugs. They eject the cut plugs, so they're handy when you need a lot.

After cutting the plugs with a tapered plug bit, remove them from the stock with a screwdriver.

A round tenon cutter can be used to make plugs; it has the advantage of ejecting the cut plugs.

Biscuits and Dowels

Biscuits and dowels are used to strengthen butt joints. Biscuit joinery, which has been around only since the 1970s, is relatively new compared to the centuries-old method of nailing; but it's proving to be pretty effec-

BISCUIT JOINT

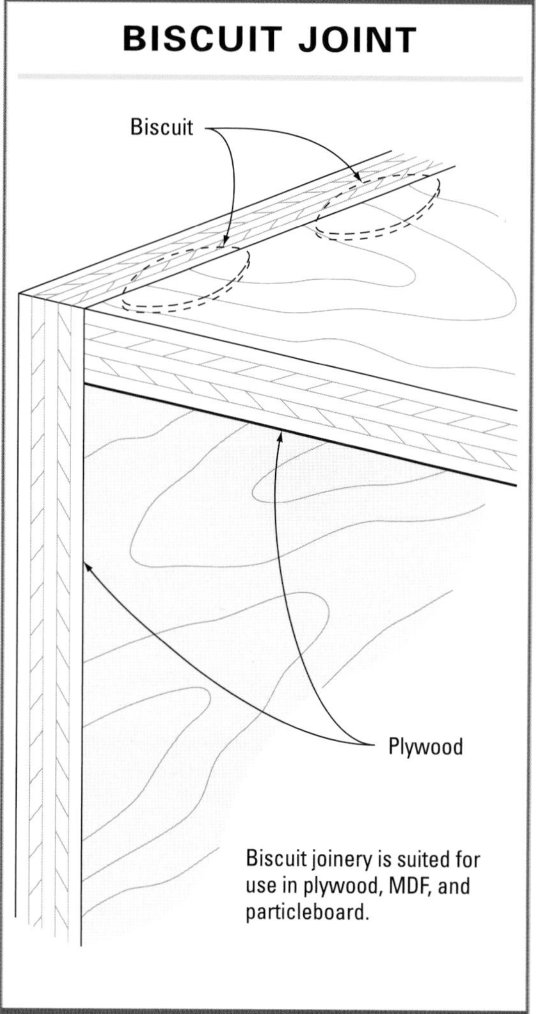

Biscuit joinery is suited for use in plywood, MDF, and particleboard.

Biscuits come in a variety of sizes for different applications.

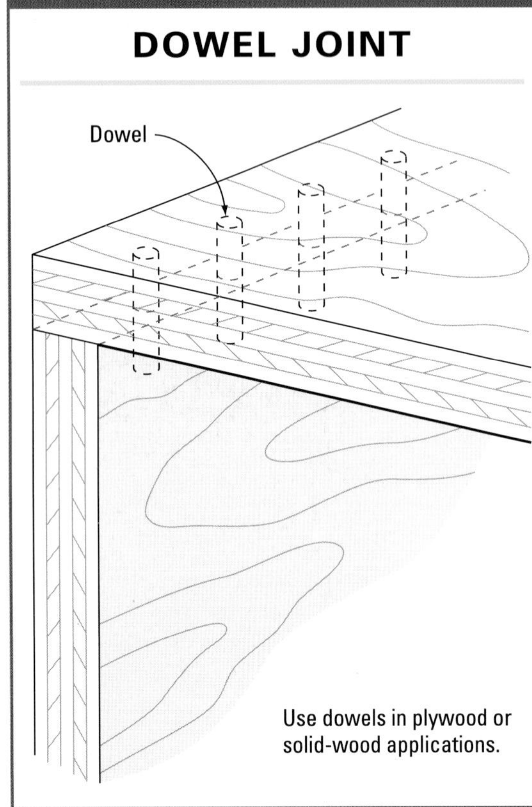

tive for strengthening butt joints, particularly in plywood carcase work.

Biscuits work like a loose tenon or dowel in that you cut a hole in each of your mating pieces and put a glued fastener between them. They differ in that the biscuits are made of compressed beechwood cut on the bias to avoid shrinkage and grain problems. They also swell when they come into contact with a water-based glue. Biscuits come in different sizes for different applications. Be aware that biscuit joinery is perfectly suited for plywood and particleboard construction; but for solid-wood construction—especially solid-wood cabinetry—you may run into situations in which the biscuits cannot be located in optimal long-grain-to-long-grain gluing spots.

Dowels are, of course, an industry standard and are used to put millions of couches, tables, and chairs together. They are the standard because they are quick and have a life expectancy just long enough to keep people coming back for more. Unlike biscuits, which can fail completely and without warning, dowels will rock back and forth, creaking their warning for years before finally giving up the ghost.

Unfortunately, dowels have their downside, too. Their long grain does not always match up with the long-grain surface of the piece; this is especially true when they're used in the face of a board. A dowel hole drilled into long grain exposes end grain, which is not the best gluing surface. Furthermore, as the dowels dry out, they can shrink into an oval, causing an imperfect fit in their round holes. And as the dowels cycle through seasonal changes in moisture content, they can eventually break loose. Then there's the difficulty of aligning parts and checking the fit of pieces drilled for multiple dowels. Finally, even if the dowels are perfectly fitted, too much glue in the holes can create a hydraulic action that won't allow the joint to close up, except with great groans and hammer blows.

All this being said, dowels—if planned for carefully—are very strong in some applications and can be used so there is no evidence of their presence. Blind dowels, however, have led many a woodworker to despair. And no wonder, blind dowels can be extraordinarily finicky if you've been just the tiniest bit sloppy. But they're useful for a variety of applications, including installing box lid handles. If your foresight did not extend to putting a dowel hole into a small or irregularly shaped part before shaping it, use a clamp to hold the part carefully level at the drill press when you drill the dowel hole.

To make a dowel hole in a small or irregularly shaped part, secure it in a clamp before drilling it on the drill press.

The Importance of Square Crosscuts

Everyone's first sawcut is a crosscut. But there's a bit more to this cut than you might think. Straight and square cuts are essential to all joinery and particularly for butt joints. Remember that you're always cutting in two directions when you saw. On a square crosscut, you're sawing straight across a board as well as straight down.

For a butt joint to be accurate, the crosscut must be absolutely square.

Whether crosscutting with a handsaw or a power saw, always give yourself a good straight and visible pencil line. Don't make it too wide and don't try to saw down its middle. Keep the line neat and consistently thin; then place your saw just to the waste side of the line. If the pencil line is between you and the saw, it's easy to see.

When sawing a crosscut by hand, cut just to the waste side of the pencil line.

CROSSCUTTING WITH A HANDSAW

To crosscut with a handsaw, start by drawing the saw in the opposite direction from which it cuts. This helps you establish the kerf in the right spot. If you're using a Western-style saw, which cuts on the push stroke, draw the saw back. Once the kerf is established, begin sawing through the board. A Japanese-style saw cuts on the pull stroke, so it must be started by pushing it.

While you draw the saw backward and forward, use your knuckle as a guide to the first few strokes. Point your finger when you saw, since this helps guide the cut; and try to practice sawing without cutting. Too much

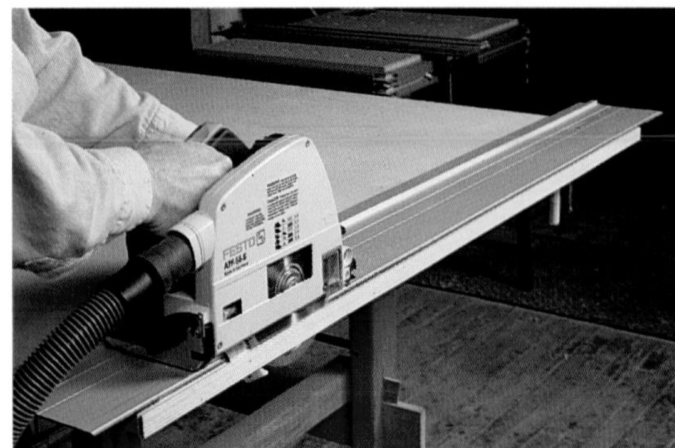
A guide system helps ensure square crosscuts when cutting with a circular saw.

Once used primarily in the building trades, the miter saw is now a popular crosscutting tool in many small shops.

Build a simple crosscutting sled or carriage to make accurate 90-degree cuts on the table saw.

downward pressure when starting the cut makes it harder to saw straight. Let the saw do the work; your job is to keep the blade straight. Keep the workpiece down low so your shoulder is over the cut, and you'll get plenty of cutting power if your saw is sharp.

CROSSCUTTING WITH A CIRCULAR SAW

Circular saws, of course, saw much faster than handsaws, but the key to a good cut is still accuracy. The best way to make a straight cut is to use a straightedge as a guide. A simple board placed in the proper spot will do. Make a practice cut to determine the distance from the cut to the edge of the saw body that rides against the fence. Then put the fence at that distance from the marked line. Commercial guide systems are available for use with the better crosscut saws. The Festo system shown in the top left photo clamps onto the workpiece with a rubber antisplinter guard directly against your marked line. The saw rides on the aluminum channel, helping you make a superb cut. Always support the offcut piece to prevent tearout.

CROSSCUTTING ON THE MITER SAW

In most shops, the miter saw has become the preferred tool for crosscutting. It is portable, accurate (when not abused by too much transporting and knocking about), and convenient. You can set one up right near your bench for use on all those little crosscuts that always need doing. As a general rule, let the saw come to a stop before removing the board. This helps prevent zinging flying offcuts.

CROSSCUTTING ON THE TABLE SAW

The table saw remains my favorite tool for precise sawing. With a good crosscut jig, it is possible to reproduce accurate cuts endlessly. The table saw's only limitation is the thickness of the board it can cut. Longer boards are easy to cut if you use a spacer board as thick as the surface of your crosscut jig. The long board rides on that without tipping as you cut.

Butt Joint with Nails

Your first woodworking project was probably this simple: Butt two boards together and bang a nail in to keep them together. First, mill the stock to size and make an accurate crosscut.

➤ See *"The Importance of Square Crosscuts"* on p. 47.

Clamping and gluing the box together first helps hold the joint while you nail (**A, B**).

When nailing by hand it's up to you to keep the nail going in straight. Sight from the side of the board you're nailing into to see how the nail is progressing and make your corrections early rather than after the nail pokes through the side piece (**C**). Use a nail set to punch the nail heads below the surface of the project so they won't mar anything (**D**).

A

B

C

D

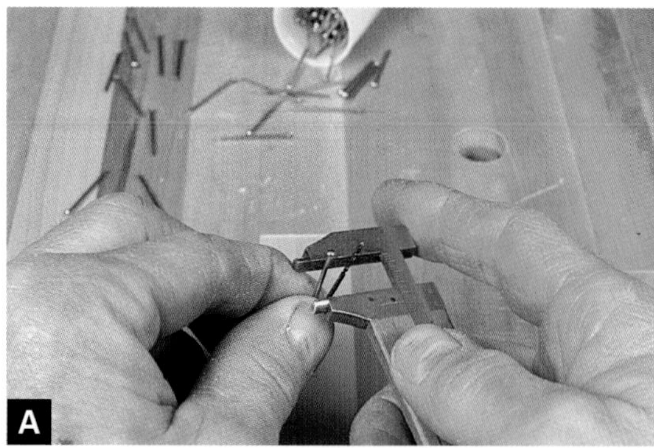

Butt Joint with Escutcheon Pins

Escutcheon pins are a decorative fastener that can be used for strengthening butt joints. First, mill your stock to size and make an accurate crosscut.

➤ See *"The Importance of Square Crosscuts"* on p. 47.

For most woods, predrill pilot holes for the pins to protect against splitting your boards. This will also ensure that the pins will go in exactly how you want them to.

Check the size of the escutcheon pins against the bit size. I use a set of calipers to hold both the pin and a likely bit. If the pin falls out when I take my hand off it, I know it's smaller than the bit (**A**).

Make sure the box is sitting flat or clamp it in the vise to drill for the pins (**B**). As a final step, use a nail set to drive each pin so its head sits just at the surface of the wood (**C**).

Butt Joint with Nail Gun

An air-actuated brad or nail gun works about 10 times faster than doing the job by hand but also adds that much more danger. First, mill the stock to size and make an accurate crosscut.

➤ See *"The Importance of Square Crosscuts"* on p. 47.

Preclamping and gluing the parts to be joined make it easier to keep them straight (**A**). Either you can drive the nails straight into the work or you can slightly angle the gun. Nails driven at a slight angle have better holding power (**B**).

A brad gun, if run with enough air pressure, will automatically bury the nails or brads below the surface of the board. It's then just a matter of filling the nail holes with putty. Water-based putties are a bit nicer to use than solvent-based materials, because they make it easier to clean up your tools. Apply just enough putty to fill the hole plus a bit more. Later, use sandpaper to smooth the putty level with the surface of the wood (**C**).

WARNING A nail gun is aptly named: It fires a nail at a speed and pressure that can seriously injure you or someone else. Keep your fingers away from the surface you're nailing into and make sure no one is in the line of fire.

A

B

C

A

B

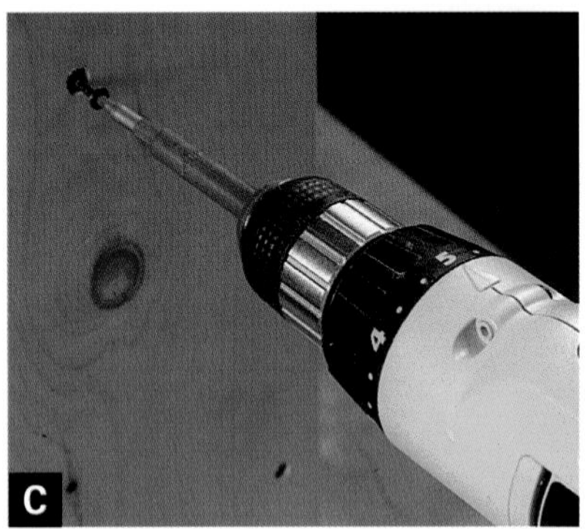
C

TIP

Butt Joint with Screws

Screwed butt joints are similar to nailed butt joints: Only the fastener is different. Screws, of course, provide better purchase in the wood because of their threads. First, mill your stock to size and make an accurate crosscut.

➤ See *"The Importance of Square Crosscuts"* on p. 47.

As for many joints, gluing and clamping the work holds the joint in position until you can add the fastener (**A**). Although driving a screw may not split the wood as easily as a nail might, you still need to predrill and countersink for most applications. Otherwise, the screw head will stand proud of the surface or, as with hardwoods, may not go into the wood at all.

➤ See *"Installing Screws"* on p. 43 for more information.

The quickest way to predill is to use a portable power drill with a taper bit mounted with a countersink head and stop collar on it. If you want to hide the screw head and countersink it, continue drilling and bore out for a wood plug (**B**). Drive the screw in straight and square to the edge being joined.

[TIP] Grease your screw with a little bit of wax to make for easier entry.

If the driver slips out of the screw head, check that you're using the right size driver (**C**).

Butt Joint with Pocket Screws

Clamp the pocket screw jig tightly in place. Place some masking tape on the bit to mark the depth of the holes or set a depth stop. Make sure the depth is shallow enough to keep the screws from breaking through on the other side. Drill out the pocket (**A**).

The screws made for this application have a round Phillips head and self-tapping threads that cut into the wood for fast entry (**B**). It's still advisable to glue butt joints, like the ones on the drawer shown here (**C**), but the pocket screws eliminate the need for lots of clamps.

A

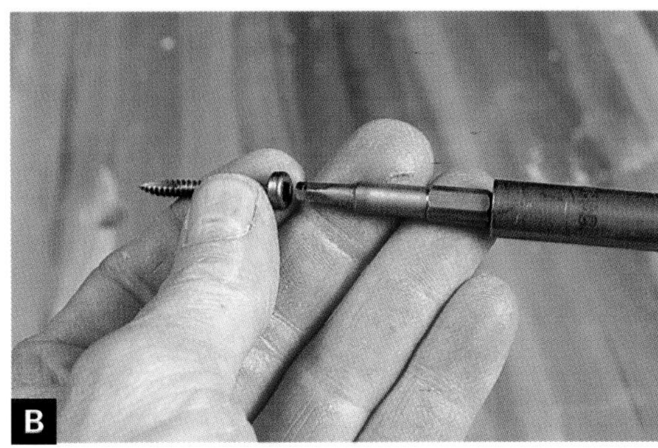
B

C

A

B

C

Plugging Screw Holes

Have all the screws in place and give them one more twist with a screwdriver before plugging their holes. Use a toothpick to apply some glue around the mouth of the hole and align the grain of the plug with the grain of the surrounding wood (**A**). Then hammer the plugs in place, making sure they go in straight.

Once the glue has dried, there are several methods for cleaning the plugs up flush to the surface. A flexible pull saw has very little set on its teeth. This means it's handy for trimming plugs quickly. But remember to be careful of the surrounding wood (**B**).

You can use a good sharp handplane to level the plug. Take a few practice shavings to determine which way the grain runs. Then take the plug down to the surface, slowing the pace as you get closer. You don't want to mar the surrounding wood with an errant handplane pass (**C**).

Leveling Plugs with a Router

A plunge router does a great job of cleaning up plugs very quickly. The trick is to set the bit depth to just shy of the surface (**A**). Use a piece of cardboard and zero the bit to that. This way it will cut just that much shy of the case side (**B**). Place the router over each plug and rout off the extending wood. What's remaining is easy to clean up with a scraper or sandpaper (**C**).

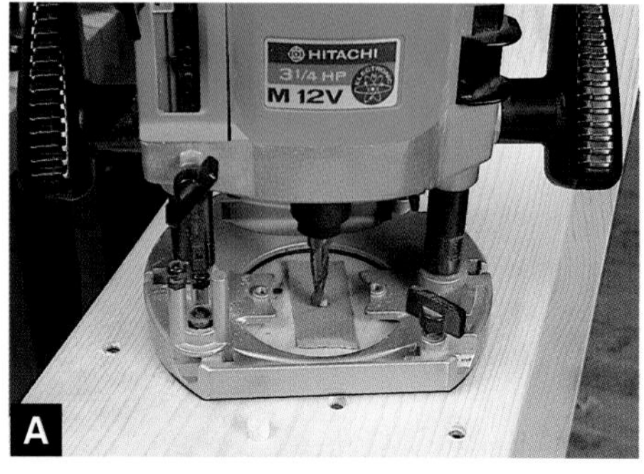

A

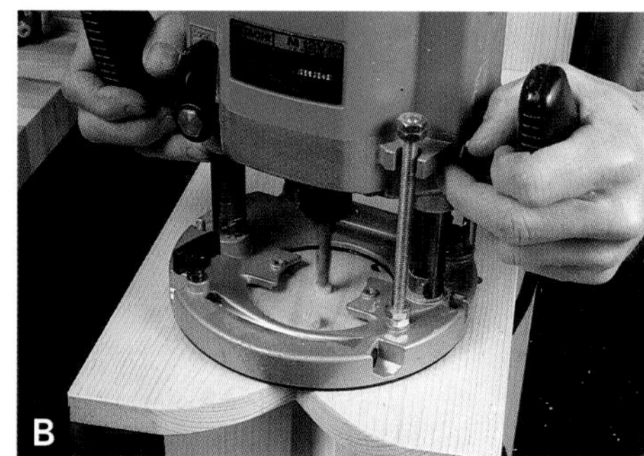
B

C

Making Decorative Plugs

Commercial round plugs may not be quite dressy enough for a project. You can make a number of different types of decorative plugs that really spice up a piece (**A**). Square plugs made of a contrasting wood can be smoothed flush to a surface, left slightly domed, carved, or carved to a peak.

Start by drilling the countersink hole for the screw just as normal. Then square the hole with a chisel. Don't make any squaring lines. Trust your hand and eye and be careful but not overly so (**B**). Then mill the square stock just larger than the holes you've made. To work the stock for the 1/4-in.-square holes shown here (easily and safely), first cut it roughly to width on the bandsaw using a fence (**C**).Then mill it to 1/32 in. larger than the plug hole on the table saw using a thin push stick (**D**). For these plugs, I milled the stock to 9/32 in. square.

A handplane pass removes any saw marks. Then chamfer the end of the square stock with a chisel, file, or sander (**E**).The plug will enter the smaller hole easily, but the oversize stock will fill up any little indiscretions in your chiseling. Then start to clean up the plug with a chisel.

You can, of course, plane or rout the plug flush to the surface, but I prefer to show my handiwork and leave the plugs raised a bit. Take them down with a handplane to about 1/16 in. above the surface and then sand them off with some 120-grit sandpaper to dome them.

To carve a peak into the plugs, you need to carve from the edges up toward the center. Place a piece of scrap laminate on the surface of the wood to protect it. Then lever your sharpest chisel up toward the center of the plug (**F**). Do a few dozen of these and you'll get the hang of it (**G**).

A

B

C

D

E

F

G

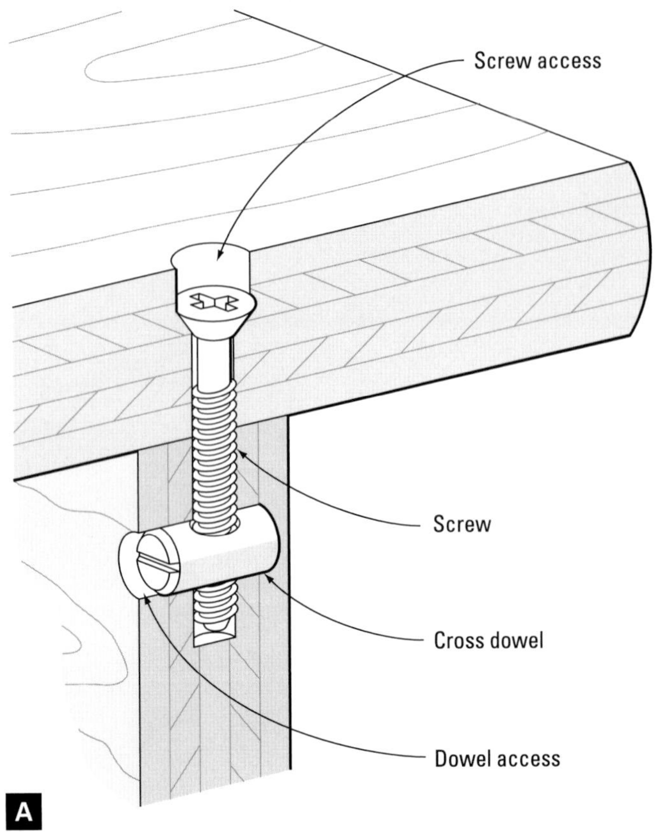

Butt Joint with Cross Dowels

Cross dowels (**A**) are round metal rods made with a threaded hole right in the center of their length. A machine screw then threads into that hole, pulling an assembly tight (**B**).

If you want to hide the dowel, first drill a ½-in. countersink hole. Then drill a hole slightly larger than the ⅜-in. cross dowel, so the dowel enters it easily (**C**). Also drill an access hole for the machine screw to contact the threaded part of the cross dowel. Drill deeply enough for the screw to run all the way through the dowel. Use epoxy to cement a cross dowel that will be hidden under a wood plug (**D**), but align the dowel's screw hole before the glue sets. The dowel has a slotted end so you can turn the dowel with a screwdriver to align it (**E**).

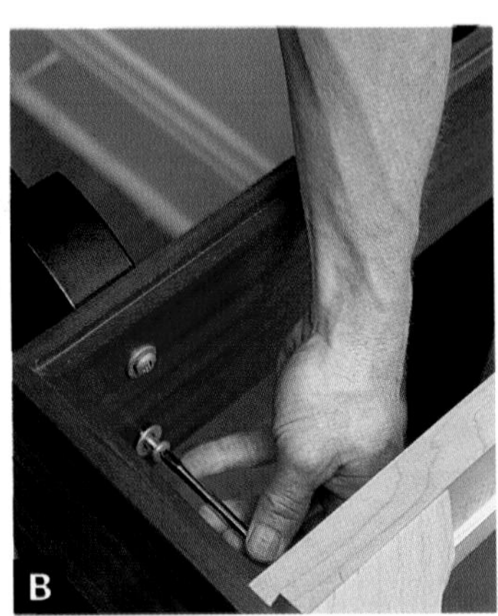
B

C

D

E

Butt Joint with Tite-Joint Fasteners

A Tite-Joint fastener is commonly used in office furniture made of large veneered panels. Such furniture is often designed so it can be assembled on site.

First drill two ⅞-in. countersink holes for the fastener's large barrel assembly and ring. Be sure the centering spur of the bit does not poke through the surface of the veneer (**A**). The multispur bit shown here wouldn't drill deeply enough without poking through, so I had to use the router to reach full depth. Use a top-mounted flush-trimming bit to deepen the hole. The bearing rides against the already drilled-out portion of the hole, and the bit makes the hole just deep enough to allow the connector barrel to sit below the surface of the veneer (**B**).

Next, drill through the edge of the panel with a 7⁄16-in. bit. This access hole is for the connector bolt. Drill deeply enough for the end of the bolt head to poke through the ring (**C**). Rotate the barrel with a ⅛-in. drill bit to tighten the joint. This pulls the bolt head tight against the ring in the mating piece (**D**).

A

B

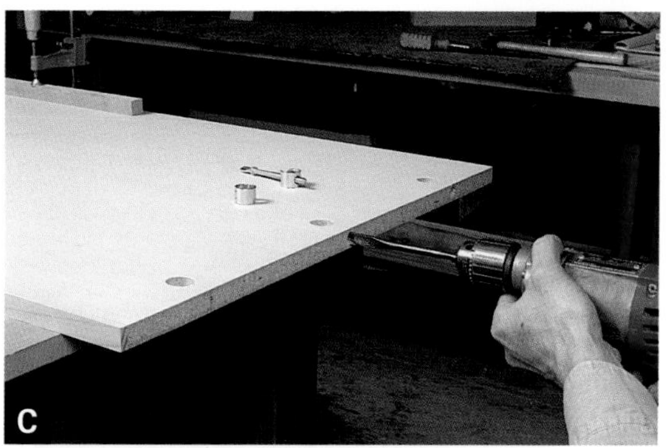
C

D

Butt Joint with Threaded Inserts

Threaded inserts, also called rosans, are made with a wood screw thread on their outside so they can be inserted into the edge of a panel (**A**). Their interior is threaded so a machine screw can fit into them and pull two panels together. They're a bit trickier to use than other knockdown fasteners because they like to go in at any other angle but straight. So take your time with them and get or make a good insertion tool.

Drill into the case end for the threaded insert. Use a centering doweling jig that puts a hole dead center in the panel (**B**). Then remove the jig and redrill with a slightly larger bit than the doweling jig allows. This prevents any bulging that may occur when installing the insert. Or clamp right around the hole during insertion.

Drive the insert with a T-driver, or drive a double-nutted bolt with a socket wrench (**C**). Keep checking the insert to see that it's going in straight from both directions. These inserts are very easy to cant as you drive them in. Once in place, make sure they line up well with the holes on their matching panels (**D**).

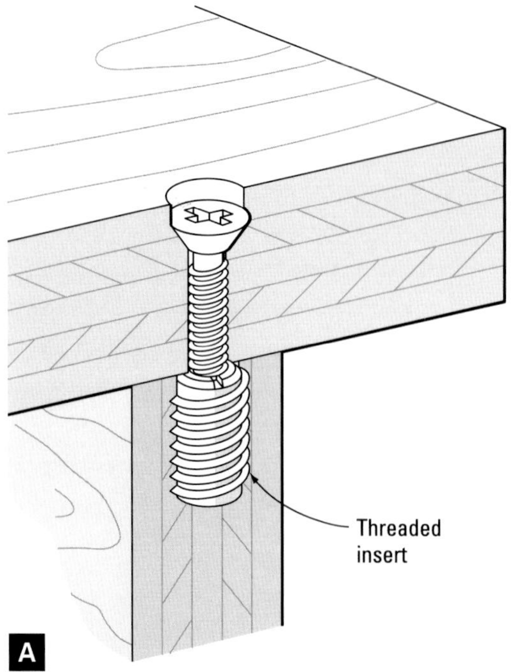

B

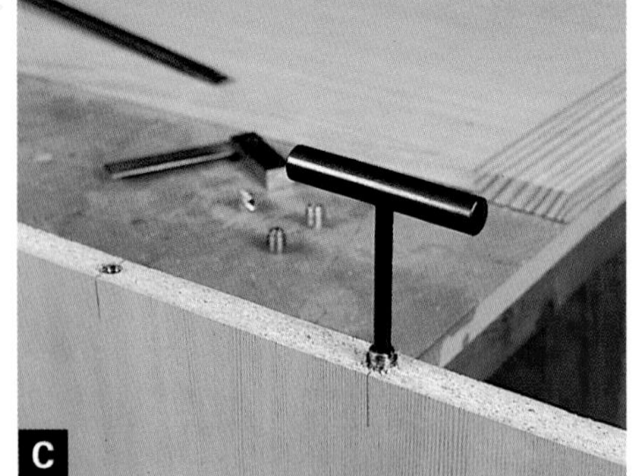

Flush-Corner Biscuit Joint

Mark the cabinet panels for the biscuit slots (**A**). Use as many as will fit into the width of the piece, but be careful near the edges of the panel because you don't want a biscuit slot to show there. Also be sure to set the height adjustment on the biscuit joiner to center the cut in the panel. Check that the height adjustment is locked securely and have the fence locked down in the 90-degree position. Shim the joiner fence if it isn't perfectly parallel to the cutterhead. There is a centering mark for the height on the side of the biscuit joiner shown here. Line it up with the center of the panel or use the scale mounted on the joiner (**B**).

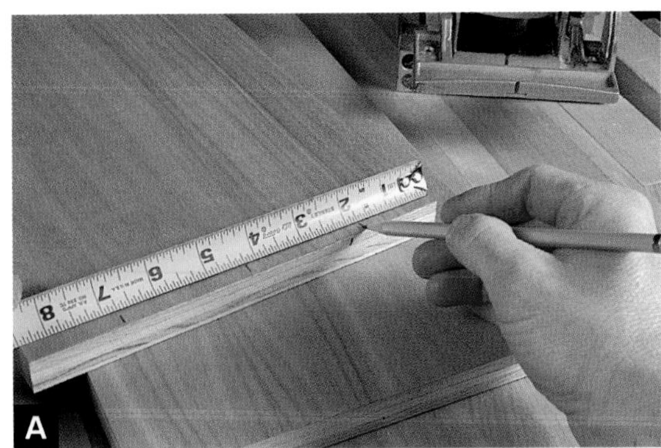
A

B

Use a pencil to mark the position of the biscuits on the boards. You will index the cuts off the outer face of one board and the outer edge of the other (**C**). Your biscuit joiner has a centering mark for the center of the rotation of its cutterhead. Line it up with the pencil marks to make the cuts. Clamp the workpiece down or push it tightly against a stop to hold it firmly in place.

C

When making the biscuit cut, push down firmly on the handle of the machine to keep the joiner flat to the workpiece (**D**). As with any joinery cut, first make a practice cut to check the settings.

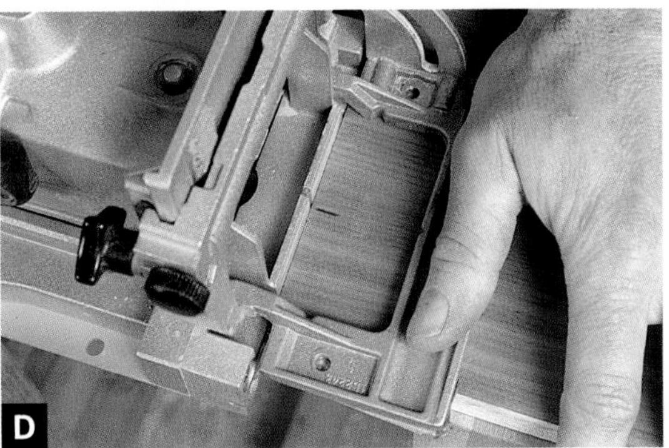
D

(Text continues on p. 60.)

E

F

G

It's easy to make the cuts in the end of a panel; however, it's a bit trickier to make the cuts in the flat of the other panel. Use another carcase panel to support the biscuit joiner when you're making an end cut (**E**). Clamp it in place flush with the top edge of the piece getting cut and keep the biscuit joiner flat on this surface when making the cuts (**F**).

Make the cuts at a moderate feed rate. Too fast a rate only forces the tool to work unnecessarily hard, can cause the motor to stall, and can dull the blade. On the other hand, don't burn the wood by moving too slowly. Use a dust bag on the joiner or, better yet, hook up a vacuum to capture the dust.

Apply glue with a flux brush to the biscuit slot. Don't skimp here, as it's important there's enough glue to swell the biscuit. Expect some squeeze-out when you hammer the biscuit down into place. Make sure it's centered before moving onto the next biscuit (**G**).

> **WARNING Do not hold a small piece with your hand when making a cut with the biscuit joiner; always use clamps.**

Offset-Corner Biscuit Joint

Offset panels, shelves, or dividers that stick into a carcase side anywhere but right at the corner need a different technique for biscuiting. Obviously, you can't use the fence in its locked-down position to locate the cut in the middle of a side. What you use instead is the shelf going into the side. Mark out the position of the biscuits on the shelf. Use a square as a depth guide to place the shelf on the carcase side.

Mark the top or bottom face of the shelf on the carcase side, and mark out the biscuit centers (**A**). Then clamp the shelf down flat onto the carcase side right up against the pencil mark. This will act as a fence for the biscuit cuts. Then cut the biscuit slots on the carcase piece with the fence in place (**B**). Use the biscuit joiner to cut into the ends of the panel as you would for a flush-corner joint.

➤ See *"Flush-Corner Biscuit Joint"* on p. 59.

Remember when gluing that the squeeze-out on an assembly like this can be difficult to clean, so be judicious with the amount of glue you use (**C**).

A

B

C

A

B

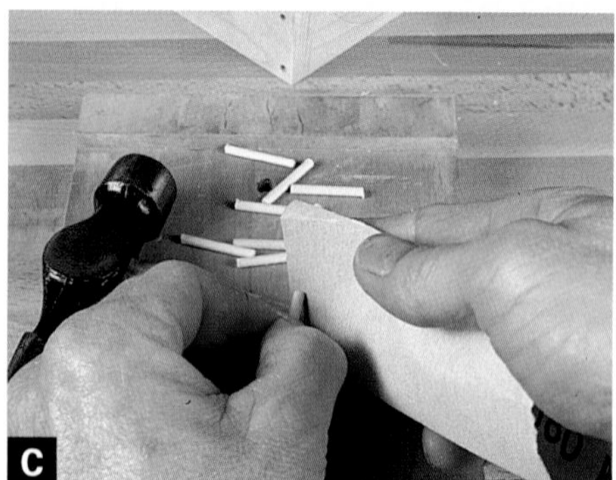
C

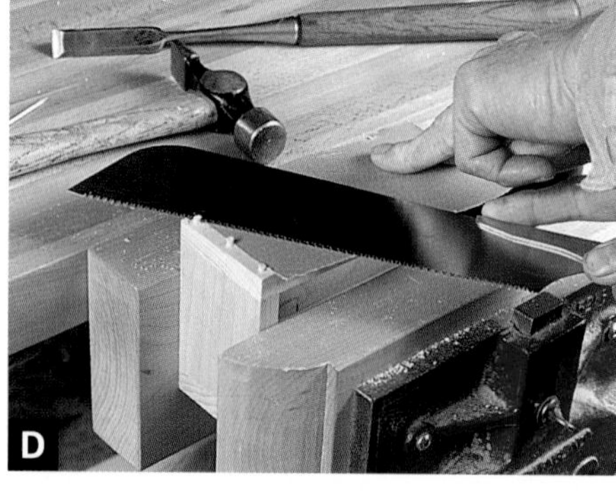
D

E

F

Through Dowel

Strengthen a butt-jointed box with through-dowel pins. They're very simple to drill for and to apply because you do all the work after the box has been put together.

Sight the drill from the side to line up the holes in the box side (**A**). The dowels I used here, although very small in diameter, dried oval and fit too snugly in the holes. Since the holes were drilled so close to the end of the side, I drilled them again 1/64 in. oversize just to avoid any short-grain breakout when I hammered the dowels in. Always check the dowels against the drill bit size before pounding them in.

You can also size the dowels using a dowel pop. Use good, straight twist bits to drill a metal plate with some convenient dowel sizes. Then bang the dowels you want to use through the dowel pop to size them correctly. The metal hole will shear off any distortion that may have occurred as the dowel dried and shrunk (**B**).

Before applying the glue, chamfer the ends of the dowel pins with a bit of sandpaper. This makes entry that much easier (**C**). Once the glue has dried on the dowel pins, use a saw to cut them off close to the surface of the box. Place a piece of cardboard on the surface of the box to protect it and rest the saw on that. This raises the sawteeth off the wood just enough so they won't cut into the box (**D**). Make sure your hand is on the opposite side of the sawteeth as well when it comes through that dowel.

Finally, pare the pins flush to the box surface with a sharp chisel (**E**). The end grain of the pared dowel shows a bit darker than the surrounding wood, creating a decorative effect (**F**).

Blind Dowel with a Doweling Jig

Use a centering doweling jig for drilling dowel holes in a carcase or box parts. Carefully lay out the dowel centers on the workpiece (**A**). Place a few more dowels out near the edges of a board where it's more likely to cup. Use a good brad point bit for drilling the holes. The centering point on these bits helps locate the cut in end grain, which can be difficult to drill accurately.

Measure the depth of the cut and mark the bit with tape while it's in the doweling jig (**B**). Remember to figure in the length of the brad point. When the jig is too close to the end of a board, use another piece of the same thickness to support the jig. Then tighten the jig down onto both boards. This way the jig won't twist (**C**).

After drilling the ends of the box sides, mark out the dowel positions on the mating boards. Use dowel centers in the drilled holes to locate the mating holes; you can use a glued-up spacer to help locate offset parts in their proper positions. Line up the boards and give them a little pop with a hammer to transfer the center points (**D**). To drill the matching holes, use a drill press for the best accuracy. Place a fence and set the bit depth so it goes just far enough without going through the face side of the board (**E**).

Score the dowels several times along their length with saw kerfs. This will allow glue to escape. Then insert the dowels in the ends of each board. Use a height block to tell you when you have driven the dowels in enough (**F**). Once the dowels are in place, put the entire box together. Make sure a dead-blow hammer and some clamps are nearby and ready to go (**G**).

A

B

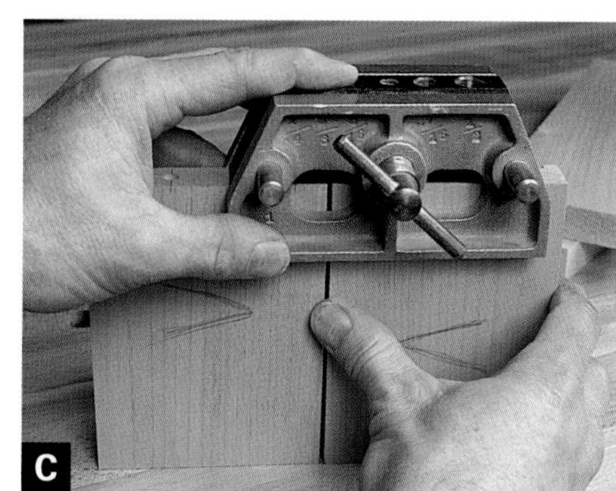
C

D

E

F

G

A

C

B

D

E

F

Blind Dowel with a Template

Cut the template to width to match the board perfectly. Line up the bit on the center marks to drill each of the template holes. Mark one hole and hold the template tight against the drill press fence (**A**).

Unless you have a horizontal boring machine, you'll have to use a drill press with a tilting table to drill vertical holes. A vertical drilling jig holds the piece firmly in place and in the right position (**B**). Hold the template tight to the workpiece with your hands or use nails. Line up the template on both the stop and the edge. Drill all the holes, making sure to clear the bit often to get rid of chips and to keep it cool. Drill the horizontal holes as well (**C**).

➤ See *"Drill Press Jigs"* drawing on p. 29.

Chamfer the dowel ends for easier entry (**D**). You can also chamfer around the dowel holes themselves with a chamfering bit. This gives debris a place to hide if a dowel goes in a bit crooked and some wood fibers tear off.

The dowels shown here were pre-scored to let the glue escape. If yours aren't, score them along their length with some saw kerfs.

As one final aid to assembly, put the dowels in a dowel oven. It's a box with a light bulb suspended from its top (**E**). Put the dowels in a can and place the light bulb right over it. Cook the dowels until they lose some of their moisture. This makes them easier to insert. When the glue hits the dowels, they'll expand back for a tight fit and a joint that will stay put (**F**).

Rabbet, Groove, and Dado Joints

Rabbets

Grooves

Dadoes

Dado Rabbets

Tongue and Groove

Shouldered Dadoes

Drawer Lock Joints

Loose Tongue Joint

RABBETS, GROOVES, AND DADOES are the standard joints of cabinet construction. These simple methods of joinery provide strength and gluing surfaces. They are especially useful when building with plywood and particleboard, because there is no grain direction to be concerned with. In solid-wood cabinets, these joints provide only end-grain-to-long-grain gluing surfaces, which are not optimal; so reserve rabbets, grooves, and dadoes for quickly built cabinets or boxes that will not be used to support heavy loads. Strengthened with nails, screws, or dowels, these joints become much sturdier.

If you take a basic face-to-edge butt joint and add a simple shoulder across the face of one board, you've created a rabbet. The shoulder makes assembly much easier and introduces more bearing surface for the joint.

This mahogany shelf unit was built with rabbets for the corners and dadoes to hold the shelf in place.

Useful in a wide variety of situations, rabbet, groove, and dado joints can hold together large plywood panels as well as the smallest of drawer bottoms. With these joinery methods, you can build simple drawers, small boxes, and freestanding room dividers. They also provide options for fitting panels, drawer bottoms, and cabinet dividers.

What's in a Name?

What's the difference between an edge rabbet and an end rabbet joint? Or a groove and a dado or a housed dado? The distinctions are mostly linguistic.

Rabbets can be either stopped joints, terminating before reaching the end of a board, or through joints, running off the end of a board. You cut end rabbets into the end of boards and use them as cabinet or box joints. This joint yields only a long-grain-to-end-grain gluing surface in solid stock, which is not optimal. In plywood or particleboard construction, fasteners aren't required but are a good idea to help resist racking. Use edge rabbets for letting in cabinet backs or bottom panels for jewelry boxes or drawers, but

The back of this mahogany cabinet reveals both through and stopped rabbets.

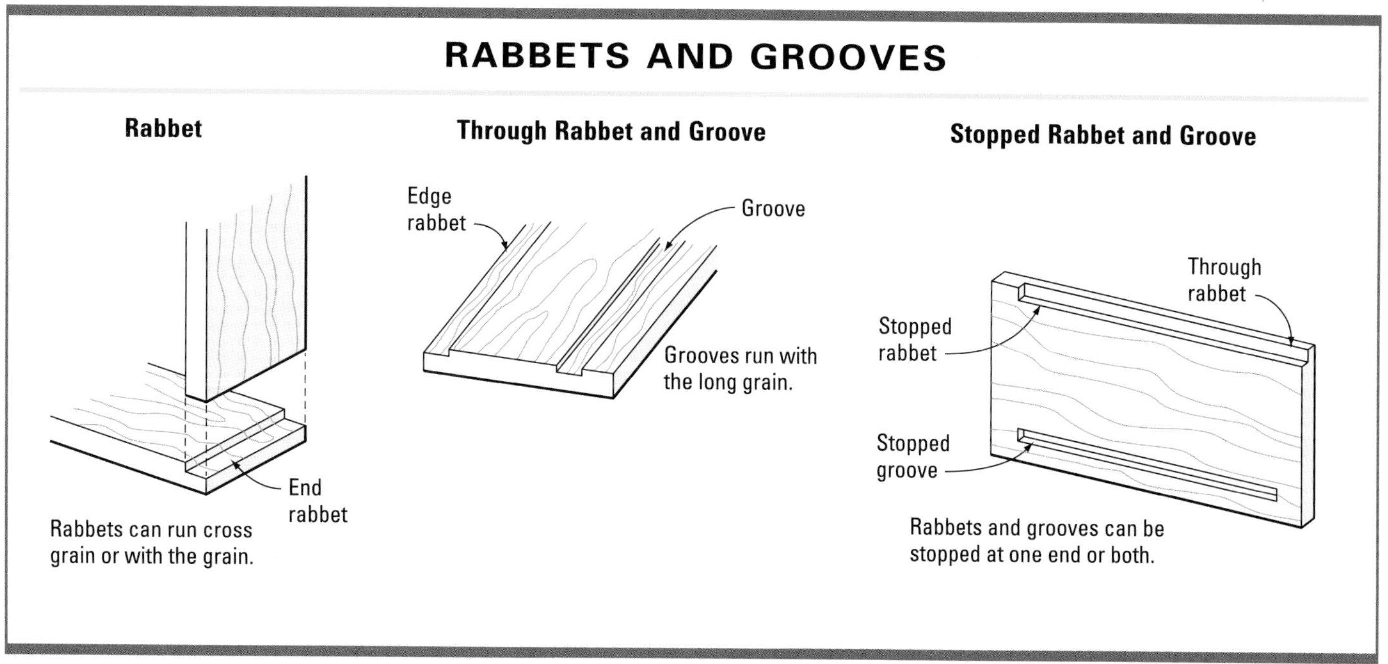

remember that in solid wood you'll need to strengthen the joint for best results. They're also used for lining up long edges for gluing or for shiplap construction. Grooves are long-grain cuts placed parallel to an edge. You can place drawer bottoms or lids in grooves. Grooves can run through or stop short of the end of a board on one or both ends. Keep the groove cuts no deeper than half the thickness of the stock to prevent weakening the board. But for greater strength and a neater look, try to run them at just one-third the thickness of the stock.

Plow a trench down the length of a board and you've made a groove. Run that groove cross-grain and now it's called a dado. Place a board in two dadoes to create a shelf or cabinet divider. Like grooves and rabbets, dadoes can be run stopped or through.

A *housed joint* is one in which the full thickness of a shelf or drawer runner is housed within the dado cut. Through and stopped dadoes, as well as sliding dovetails, can be

This board shows a long-grain stopped groove and a cross-grain through dado.

A housed dado joint, like this cabinet shelf, is one in which the entire thickness of the mating piece is enclosed in the dado.

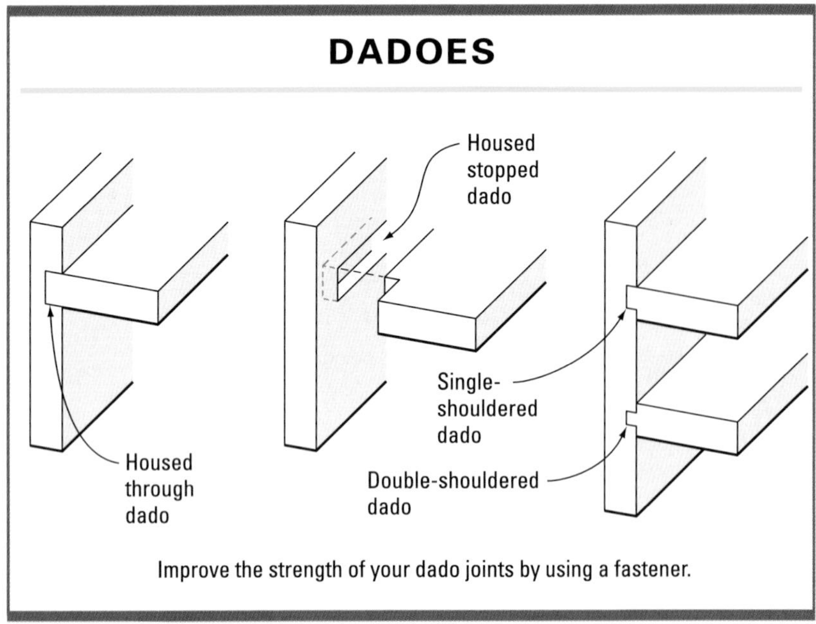

Improve the strength of your dado joints by using a fastener.

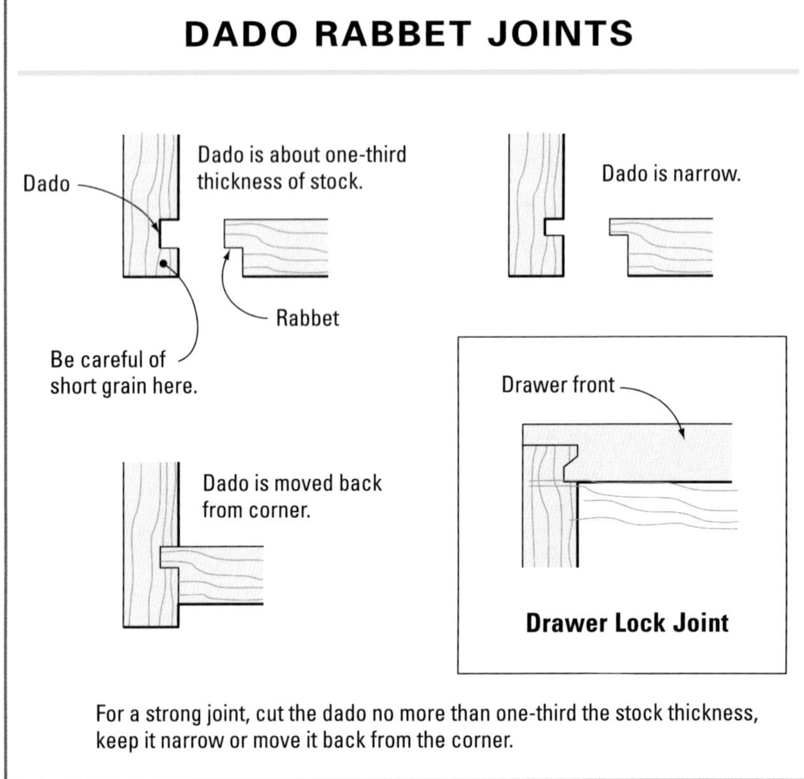

For a strong joint, cut the dado no more than one-third the stock thickness, keep it narrow or move it back from the corner.

housed. In solid-wood construction, housed dadoes need to be carefully fitted for the best strength, since all the gluing surfaces are long grain to end grain. Reinforce these joints with screws or nails.

Instead of fully housing a shelf, you can cut shoulders into the matching piece of the dado joint. This provides a bit more strength, better resistance to racking, and a neater appearance. Dado rabbet joints combine a dado cut with a rabbet to create gluing surfaces. Be careful in solid stock and sheet-good materials of the short grain left by the dado cut. One way to help prevent tearout of this grain is to keep the dado cut narrow and as far from the end of a board as possible. You can also keep the dado and rabbet fairly shallow, no more than one-third the thickness of the stock.

Use the dado rabbet joint for smaller panels or boxes. Larger cases are harder to fit and it's too easy to lever out that short grain when you're maneuvering a large board in and out of the joint. In drawer work, arrange the joint so the dado cut goes onto the side piece. This way the rabbet and dado work to resist the pull of the drawer each time it's opened.

A drawer lock joint is made with a special router bit chucked into a table-mounted router that has a speed-control motor. Run the speed down to about 10,000 revolutions per minute (rpms), as the large bit diameter causes a very fast outer rim speed. Plan on spending a few minutes getting the bit height and fence distance set properly.

A tongue-and-groove joint combines rabbets and grooves to make yet another useful way to connect two pieces of wood. The joint places a tongue, which is a double or single rabbet cut, into a groove. Be sure to

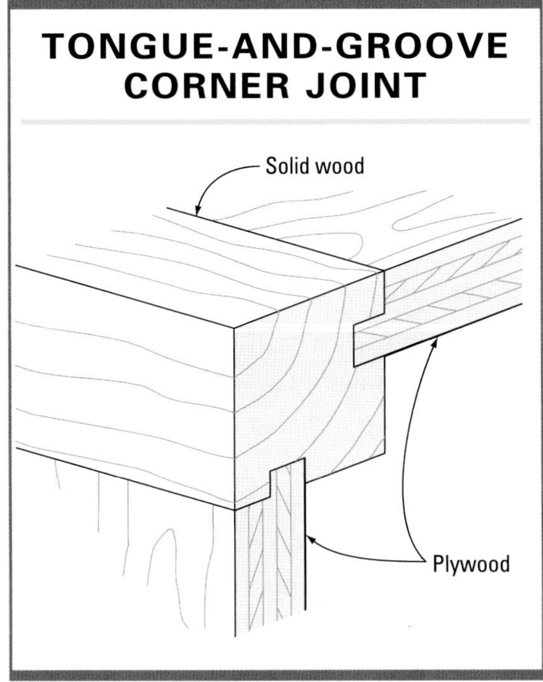

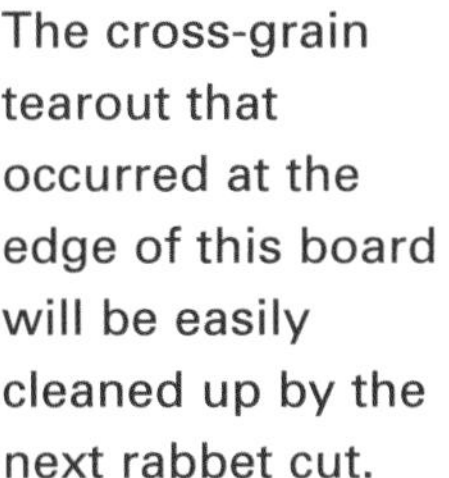

The cross-grain tearout that occurred at the edge of this board will be easily cleaned up by the next rabbet cut.

If the rabbet or groove is cut first, there's a greater risk of tearout when making the cross-grain dado cut.

make the shoulder cuts of the tongue consistent with one another and to keep the depth of the tongue just less than the full depth of the groove. This allows a little room for expansion or for glue. Check the cut first on a piece of scrap. With plywood panels there are no concerns about grain direction, so feed from left to right around the edge.

Grain Direction

When cutting rabbets, grooves, and dadoes, be careful not to tear out the grain. Special attention must be given when cutting cross-grain to avoid tearout at the edge of a board where a blade or cutter emerge. There are several methods for eliminating tearout. The first and easiest is always to make your cross-grain cuts first and then finish up with any long-grain rabbet cuts. The final cuts will remove any evidence of tearout.

You can also place masking tape over the edge where the cutter or blade will emerge. Or you can score the cut with a good marking knife to define the exit point of the blade. These methods work well when a precious veneer or edging must be maintained and cannot be followed by any cleaning rabbet cut. But in other situations, you can simply make all your stock 1/8 in. wider than needed. Make all your cross-grain cuts with no regard for tearout; then trim off the extra 1/8 in., which will also remove any tearout.

Cutting Methods

There are several methods for cutting this group of joints from the laborious but effective hand chopping with a chisel to the more satisfying cuts that can be made with a well-tuned rabbet plane. Routers and table saws do the lion's share of grooving and dado work and are well suited for it. But be particularly aware that machine-made stopped cuts present a special problem. Any machine-made cut that is stopped short of an edge or end will leave a rounded corner. This is due to the rotational action of the blade or bit. But note the difference between a router and a sawblade stopped cut, shown in the top photo below. The contrast is impressive because it's so great; the router-cut joint is much cleaner.

My preferred method for cutting stopped joints of this type is to use the router. But my reasons are not just because there's less cleanup. There is also less risk of an accident. Anytime the back half of a sawblade comes in contact with wood there is a risk that the powerful force of the blade will lift the work up and off the table and throw it into your lap. If you're hanging onto the back part of the board as you're trying to lift it off the stopped cut on the table saw, bad things can happen. Even if you place stops on the saw fence, using the table saw for these cuts is risky. In contrast, a bit chucked into a table-mounted router pushes the work into a fence. Kickback can't occur. And top-side routing presents little kickback danger if you use the right size bit and take small depths of cut.

Stopped table saw and router cuts. The pencil marks show how much wood still needs to be removed.

To adjust the fit of rabbet, groove, and dado joints, use a handplane to take down the male part.

Fitting Joints

Rabbets are fairly simple to fit, as they require only letting in by the thickness of a piece or perhaps just a bit less. Grooves and dadoes, however, are notorious for not fitting and not fitting pass after pass. Then, all of a sudden, the fit is like putting a kid's foot in his dad's shoe.

Sneak up on a fit for these joints by cutting the female portion of the joint just undersize. Then work on the male part with a handplane, sharp chisel, scraper, or sawblade to make it fit. Sanding will only round off parts and make for a sloppy fit and a sloppy look.

Solid-wood pieces can be handplaned to fit. It's a good idea to have one face already planed and then do the fitting on the second face.

Sheet-good material can be scraped to fit. Make pencil marks across the board to indicate the face that needs to have material removed. When the pencil line disappears you know you've made it across the entire face of the board. Check its fit to the dado, and if it needs more, remark it and scrape or plane it again consistently across the face.

Hand-Cut End Rabbet

Hand-cut rabbets require careful marking out and straight cutting. Mark the rabbet joints on the end and face of one board with a marking gauge (**A, B**). In solid stock, set the gauge line for just less than the thickness of the stock to be joined; this is easier to clamp and glue up. Make the sawcut on the board's end with a ripsaw or a dovetail saw. On wide boards, clamp the board in at an angle so you can see both gauge lines better. Cut at an angle down to the shoulder gauge line; then flip the board around and cut the other side (**C**). A sawcut between the two cuts completes the cheek cut. Then make the shoulder cut. You can also clamp on a fence to guide the shoulder cut.

Clean up a rabbet shoulder with a shoulder plane (**D**). Be sure to cut in from both edges toward the middle to avoid tearout. Or place a board just in line with the shoulder line to back up the cut. A rabbet plane is designed to cut this joint. Make sure the cutter is properly sharpened and the plane properly tuned. You can clamp a fence to guide the cut or use the plane's fence. Use the depth gauge on the plane to index each of the rabbets accurately (**E**).

A

B

C

D

E

A

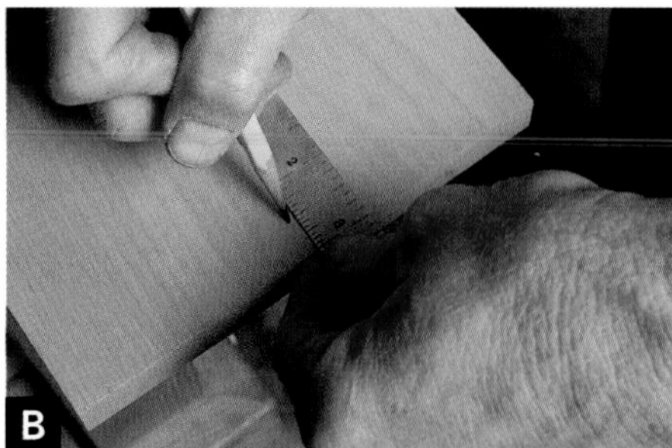
B

C

D

E

F

G

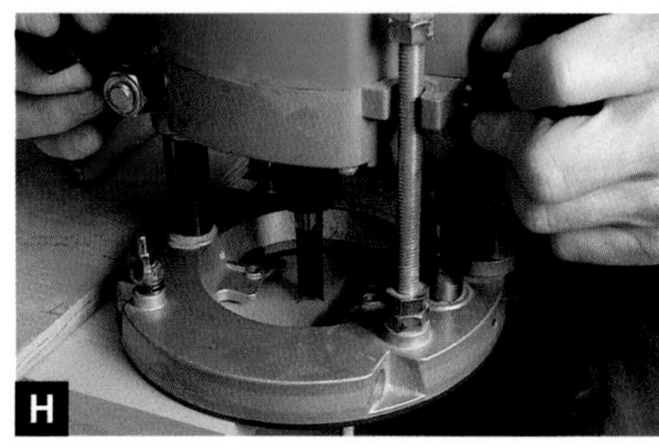
H

I

End Rabbet with a Router and Fence

Use a straight bit and fence to make end rabbet cuts topside with a router. Select a bit as large as the rabbet you wish to cut. If it's slightly undersize, first just take a trim pass on the outside edge. An auxiliary fence attached to the router fence helps guide the cut better because it gives you more bearing surface (**A**).

Mark the depth of the rabbet on the workpiece. On a plunge router, set up the depth stop for the final depth (**B, C**). Make a deep rabbet in a series of passes (**D**). At the end of the cut be careful of tearout. You can stop just short of the end and run back into the cut for the last 2 in. to avoid this. This method can also be used to cut edge rabbets.

Topside cuts can also be guided with a right-angle fence clamped on. The fence is just a straight piece of stock with a jointed straightedge. Measure the distance from the end of the router base to the outer edge of the bit (**E, F**). This is the offset, which determines the placement of the fence. Make sure the fence is square to the edge (on a right-angle jig, this should automatically be square) (**G**).

➤ See *"Right-Angle Jig"* drawing on p. 23.

Clamp the fence securely to the work and the bench. Double-check your bit position against the pencil mark (**H**). To produce matching rabbets, cut a spacer to the width of the distance from the edge of the board to where the fence should be set. Glue a board to the end of that spacer to make lining up even simpler (**I**).

End Rabbet with a Router and Rabbeting Bit

Special bearing-mounted rabbeting bits cut end rabbets very efficiently. These bits now come with changeable bearing sets to change the width of the cut. Choose the bearing for the size rabbet you wish to cut (**A**).

Set the full depth of the rabbet (**B**). Move the bit into the work until the bearing contacts the edge of the board. Feed the board at a moderate pace and work from left to right along an edge (into the rotation of the bit) (**C**). Make the cut almost all the way across the board, but stop just short of the end to avoid tearout. Feed back into the board for that short distance to clean up the rabbet. For deep rabbets, take several progressive cuts until the bearing contacts the edge of the board.

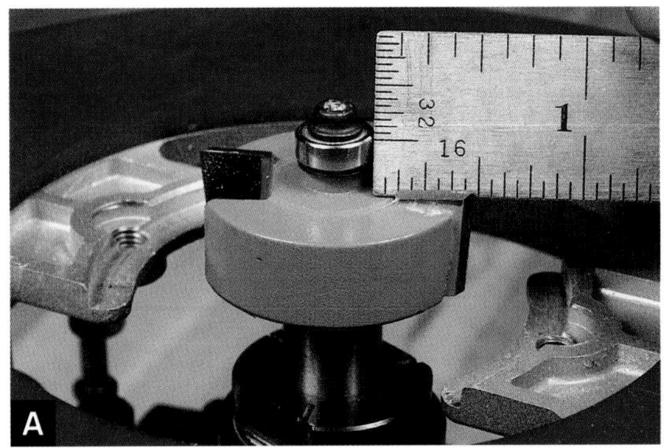
A

B

C

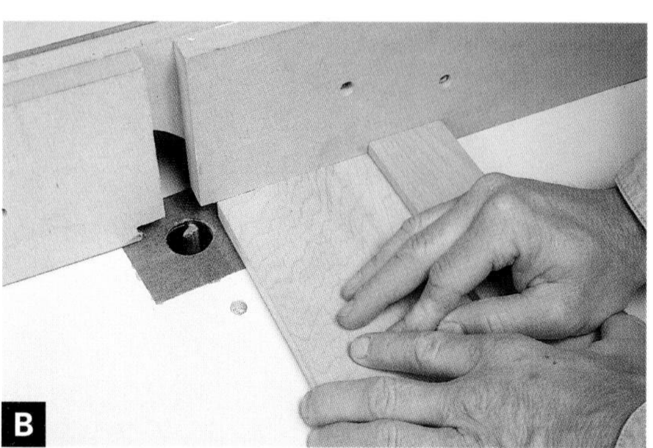

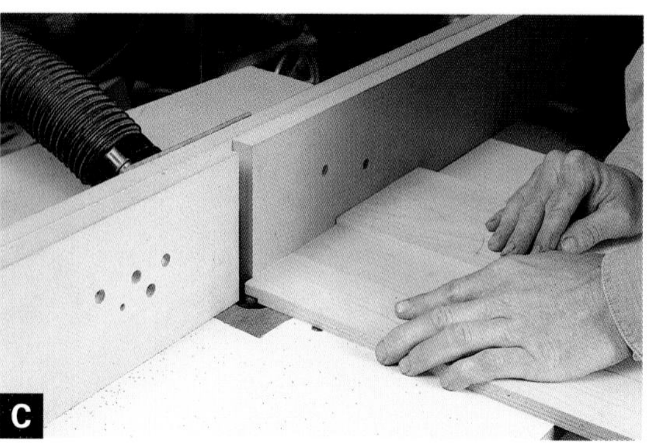

End Rabbet on the Router Table

Cutting an end rabbet on the router table is similar to cutting it with an edge guide, but there are some important differences.

➤ See *"End Rabbet with a Router and Fence"* on p. 72.

The router is under the table, so the feed direction is opposite: from right to left, into the rotation of the bit. The angle of the fence isn't critical, since the edge of the board will ride against the fence, ensuring a square cut.

[TIP] Use a fence with a dust-collection system so the chips won't blow back and clog the cut.

Set the fence for the width of the rabbet you wish to cut (**A**). Holding the work firmly against the fence, feed the work from right to left. Use a board to back up the cut and prevent tearout (**B**).

You can also package narrow boards together followed up by a backer to make a cut across the bit (**C**).

End Rabbet on the Table Saw

A table saw can easily cut rabbets in two passes. Make one cut with a crosscut jig to establish the shoulder of the joint (**A**). Then clamp the board to a tenoning jig to pass it by the blade vertically to make the rabbet (**B**).

[VARIATION] Holding a board flat on the crosscut jig, make a series of passes to cut an end rabbet. Use a stop to locate the shoulder cut. Move the board over just a little for each pass. This method takes longer but gives the rabbet a flatter surface.

! WARNING Keep the offcut away from the fence so it won't get trapped and kick back.

A

B

VARIATION

A

B

End Rabbet with a Dado Blade

A dado blade makes excellent end rabbet cuts. Assemble the dado head to the correct width (**A**). Use shims, if necessary, to get that width. Make sure the grind on the chippers and the blade are lined up so they yield a nice flat-bottomed cut. Use a miter gauge to move the work past the blade (**B**). When making multiples, use a stop on the gauge fence to index the cut.

Strengthened End Rabbet

Solid-stock end rabbets don't have any optimal long-grain-to-long-grain gluing surface to be very strong. Put in fasteners to strengthen the joint on solid-wood carcases. Plywood and particleboard carcases glue up with better results but also need fastening to counteract the effects of racking on the case (**A**).

Drive screws into a rabbeted plywood carcase. Make them long enough to have some holding power but be sure to drill straight into the sides.

➤ See *"Installing Screws"* on p. 43.

Dowel pins also work well to hold a plywood end rabbet together. Angle the drilling just a bit to get more holding power (**B**). Pin a double-rabbet joint in solid stock with small dowels (**C**). Be careful with the drilling and keep the pin diameter small in relation to the size of the rabbet to avoid problems with short grain at the end of the joint.

A

B

C

Hand-Cut Edge Rabbet

Before hand cutting edge rabbets, mark the rabbet lines. This locates the cut and improves your accuracy (**A**). Don't let the marking gauge follow the grain of the board as you mark. Keep the gauge tight to the edge.

Clamp a fence onto the board to guide a through cut. Keep the plane square in the cut; it's easy to tip it and make an angled rabbet (**B**). The no. 78 rabbeting plane shown here has a fence to guide the rabbet cut. Use one hand to keep it in tight to the edge of your board (**C**). Run the fence to either side of the plane, depending on the grain direction of the cut.

A

B

C

A

B

C

D

E

F

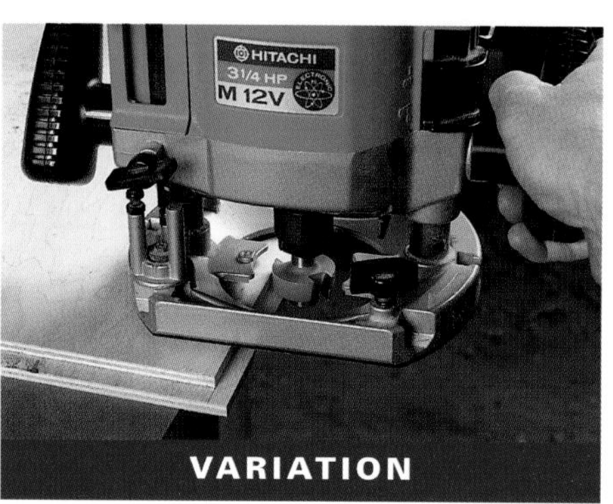

VARIATION

Edge Rabbet on the Router Table

Use a straight bit in the router table to make edge rabbets. Straight bits work well because their small diameter leave very little wood to clean up. Place the router table fence just at the proper distance from the cutting edge of the bit to the fence (**A**). Rotate the bit so one cutting edge is farthest from the fence. The fence itself does not have to be parallel to any edge of the table for your cut to be parallel to the edge of the board. Photo **B** shows how a bit that's larger than the required rabbet is captured in the fence. Holding the edge of the stock firmly against the fence, feed the work from right to left (**C**).

To make a stopped rabbet, clamp a stop onto the fence or router table to stop the cut (**D**). Move into the stop slowly at the end of the cut to avoid jarring the weak short grain of the board.

Routing a rabbet in solid wood can often cause tearout at the edges of the cut. This is especially true when the cut goes against the grain of the wood. Slow down your feed rate, take small depths of cut, and consider a climb cut to pre-score the grain (**E**).

➤ See *"Climb Cutting"* drawing on p. 21.

Stopped rabbets on a cabinet back will leave you with some cleanup work, but this is preferable and far safer than making a table saw stopped cut (**F**).

[VARIATION] Make your rabbeting cuts topside with the proper size rabbeting bit. Move left to right along the edge.

Edge Rabbet on the Table Saw

Use the table saw to make through edge rabbet cuts with ease and accuracy. An effective, if slow, method is to hold the workpiece flat to the table and make a series of passes with the single blade. Another technique uses just two through cuts. Place the board flat to the table to make the first cut. Always know where the exit point of the blade is so you can keep your hands well clear (**A**).

Use an auxiliary fence attached to the saw fence to help support the board.

Then make a second pass holding the work vertically (**B**).

> **WARNING Don't trap the offcut piece between the blade and the fence or you'll get kickback.**

A

B

Edge Rabbet with a Dado Blade

Dado blades make easy work of through rabbets and can cut in one pass. Assemble the dado head to the size of the rabbet to be cut (**A**). An auxiliary fence can capture the dado blade edge within it so the cut can be made right up to the edge of the board (**B**). Set the fence so the cut is made on the edge nearer the fence (**C**). This helps prevent kickback, particularly if the work rides up on the dado blade. Keep the feed rate slow and use a push stick.

A

C

B

A

B

C

Edge Rabbet on the Jointer

You can use the jointer to cut edge rabbets. Shiplap joints for a cabinet back are cut with this method. Use it only for cuts with the long grain of a board.

Remove the cutterhead guard and set the fence to expose only as much cutterhead as is needed for the width of the rabbet (**A**). Set the infeed table for a light pass of 1⁄32 in. to 1⁄16 in., depending on the wood you're cutting and the sharpness of your knives (**B**). Make a pass and use a push stick (**C**). Then reset the infeed table for another 1⁄32-in. to 1⁄16-in. pass. Continue until you're down to full depth. The board rests on the rabbet on the outfeed table as you make the cut, so be sure you have a good grip on the wood and that it's flat before you begin cutting.

Hand-Cut Groove

Groove cuts made by hand need careful alignment to keep them parallel. Mark out the groove lines with a mortising gauge set to match the required width. Set the gauge off a convenient chisel size (**A**). Keep the gauge tight to the edge as you mark out both sides of the groove. Press down enough so you can see your lines easily. Then make a V-cut with a chisel along the length of both groove lines (**B**). Flip the chisel bevel side down so it won't dive into the wood as you cut. Remove just enough wood to form a small trench.

Use a backsaw to cut to depth. Keep it firmly placed in the groove line, especially at the start of each cut. A piece of tape on the sawblade placed at the depth of cut indicates when you've cut deep enough (**C**).

A stopped groove needs a slightly different approach than a through cut. Make the stopped cut first with a chisel, thus establishing a stop for the sawcut (**D**). Then make the sawcuts up to the chiseled-out stop.

Chop out the waste between the two sawcuts with a chisel (**E**). Work with the grain to prevent tearout ahead of the cut.

A router plane is very handy for cleaning the groove exactly to depth (**F**).

VARIATION A no. 45 or no. 55 combination plane also works great for cutting or cleaning up through grooves. A straight cutter ground to match your groove width does the work. Just take small depths of cut to keep the plane properly aligned and cutting well. Be sure your fence clears any bench stops or dogs.

A

B

C

D

E

F

VARIATION

Groove on the Router Table

The router table is the best tool for making stopped groove cuts. You can use stops clamped onto the fence or table, and there is less cleanup and little or no danger of kickback.

Always match the bit width to the stock that goes in the groove (**A**). Most sheet-good material these days is undersize rather than oversize, so check the thickness of the stock carefully before routing a groove. Take a practice pass in scrap wood, and remember that it's always better to cut a little less than the thickness of the stock. Adjust the bit cutting height to ⅛ in. for most materials. Set the fence distance to the bit with the bit rotated so one cutting edge is closest to the fence (**B**). Holding the work firmly against the fence, feed from right to left across the bit (**C**).

When making a stopped groove, carefully mark the fence to show you where to begin and end the cut. Hold a piece of scrap up to the bit. Then rotate the bit until it pushes the scrap away from it. Where the scrap stops moving is the position of the outer edge of the bit. Mark this on the fence and square this line up so you can easily see it. Do the same on the other side of the bit, and you'll have two lines on the fence that indicate the width of the bit (**D**).

Mark the stopped cuts on the workpiece. Line the first stopped cut line with the left edge of the bit as marked on the fence. Then clamp stops on the fence or table at the rear end of the board (**E**). Move the board along to line up the second cut against the right edge of the bit and clamp another stop for it.

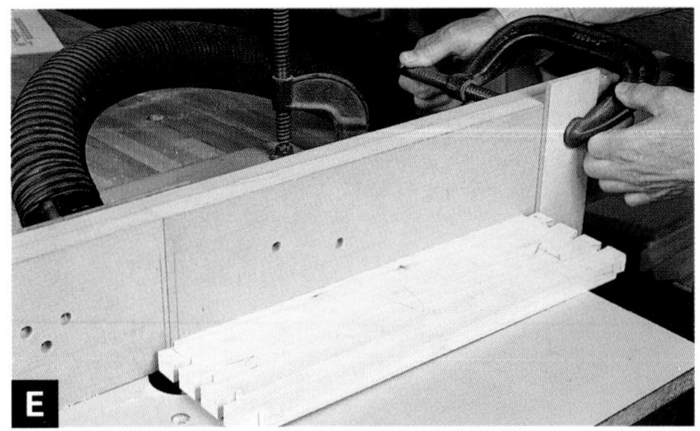
E

TIP Chips are likely to bunch up against the far stop on the outfeed side of the router table fence as you make a cut. Put a fat shim, such as a piece of ¼-in. plywood, underneath the stop before clamping. Then remove the shim so the debris can be blown away as you cut.

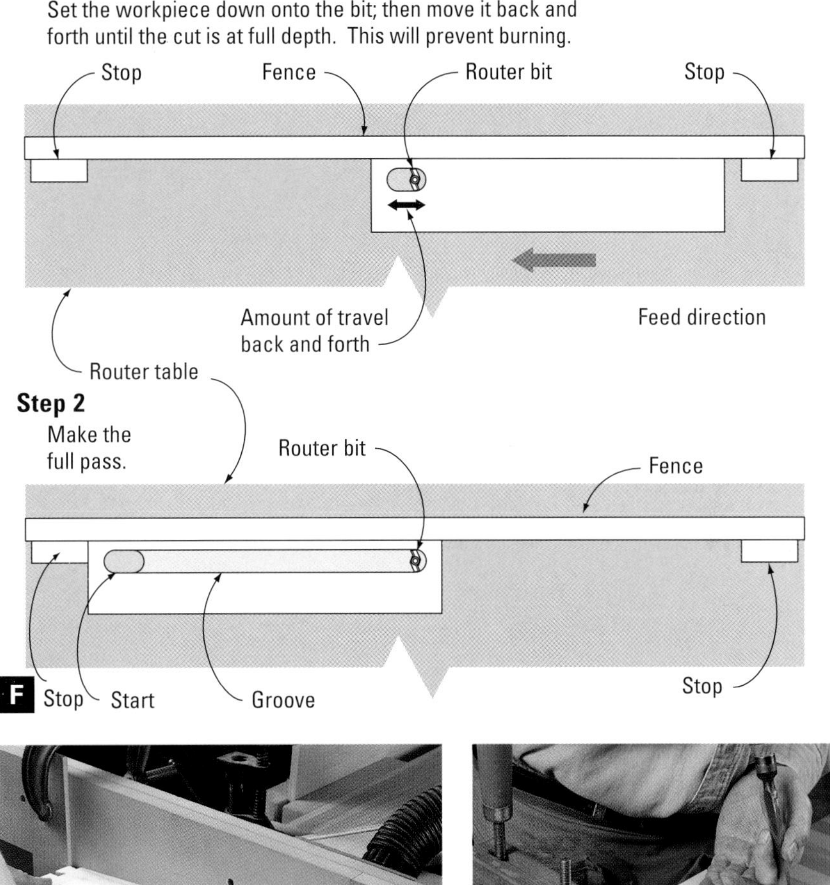

F

With the workpiece above the bit, carefully lower the right end against the stop block to the right. Now lower the left end into the bit. To prevent burning as the bit cuts to depth, slide the workpiece back and forth for just a short distance as you drop down onto the bit until you reach full depth (**F**). When you're at depth, move all the way back to the first stop to make sure it's cleaned and then proceed with the cut. Lift the board off the bit at the far end of the cut by pushing into the fence firmly but gently (**G**). This keeps the board in line with the cut. You can also push into the end stop to help lift the wood off the bit.

After cutting the stopped groove, clean the round corners with a chisel. Line up a wide chisel flat against the side walls of the groove and walk it over to the stop mark to establish your lines (**H**). Then chop down to depth.

G

H

A

B

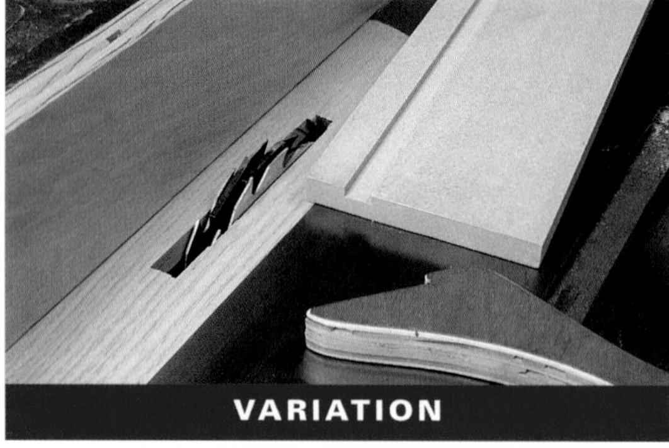
VARIATION

Through Groove on the Table Saw

The table saw is well suited for making through groove cuts. Make certain the workpiece edge is flat and that there is no debris along the saw fence. Use a push stick on small boards. A combination or rip blade makes groove cuts easily in solid-wood or sheet-good stock (**A**). A wider groove can be made with a single blade by making a series of cuts. Just move the fence over after each pass to establish the extra width (**B**).

[TIP] If the groove cut is centered in the workpiece you can make a cut, flip the board edge for edge, and make a second cut with the same fence setting.

Remove the remainder of the waste material with a chisel or router plane, or just move the fence over in very small amounts each time to remove every bit of waste.

[VARIATION] Dado blades were designed for jobs like cutting through grooves. They remove large amounts of wood in a hurry, but take care to feed the work through at a moderate rate. Also use a push stick or hold-down device to keep the workpiece flat to the table. Make a deep groove in a series of passes rather than in one large deep cut.

Hand-Cut Through Dado

Square a board to the workpiece to help guide the sawcut (**A**). Make sure the guide board edge is straight and square and mark the depth of cut either onto the sawblade or at the edges of the workpiece. Keep the sawblade held tightly to the guide edge as you cut down to the depth (**B**). Finish cleaning out the dado by carving out most of the waste with a chisel. Then use a router plane to clean to depth (**C**).

A

B

C

A

C

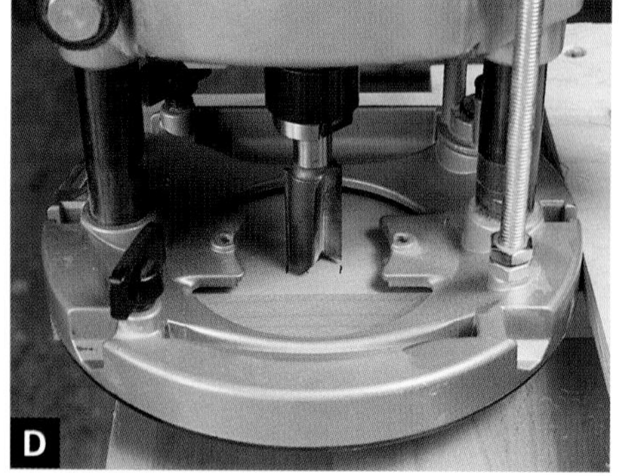
D

B

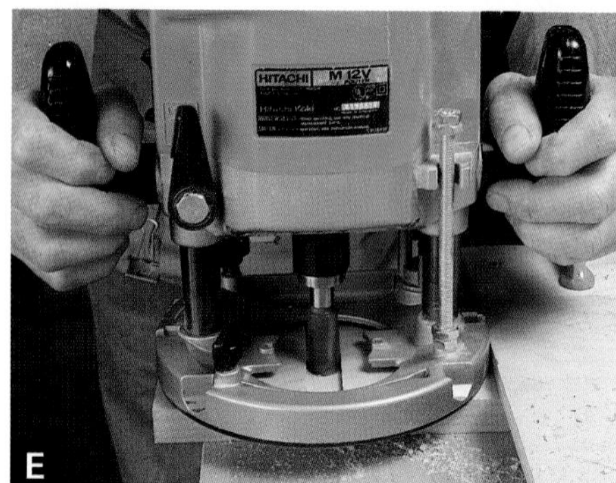

E

VARIATION

Through Dado with a Router

A topside dado pass with the router on a wide panel needs careful alignment. A right-angle jig guides the cut for a through dado. Select a bit for cutting the dado. When making a housed dado, don't assume that the bit will perfectly match your material. Leave the dado slightly undersize and trim the part that slides into it until it fits (**A**). Measure the distance from the edge of the router baseplate to the edge of the bit (**B**). Place the jig on the work, making sure it is square (**C, D**). Run the base tight to the jig or put in a template guide and run it tight to the edge of the jig (**E**).

See *"Right-Angle Jig"* drawing on p. 23.

[VARIATION] Commercial clamps or fence systems can be used to guide the work, especially for sheet-good material. The fence system shown here (by Festo) uses a straightedge fence that is placed in position onto the plywood; the router rides along the guide rail. Use a spacer board to set the fence in exactly the correct position. It lines up flush with the edge of the panel. Make the cut and then use the spacer to line up the matching cut on the opposite panel.

Through Dado on the Router Table

Set the fence for the distance from the edge of the board to the dado (**A**). Cut the dado on the router table using a straight bit.

To make a dado that's wider than your widest bit, use a spacer block during the first pass. Put the spacer in place between the workpiece and fence. This pushes the work just a bit farther away from the fence. Then remove the spacer to make the second pass. This ensures that you will always be cutting into the rotation of the bit when moving from right to left on the router table (**B**). Use a backer board to support the pass and to protect the exit hole from tearout. As you make the pass, be sure all the boards are lined up tight to the fence and don't let them angle or shift (**C**).

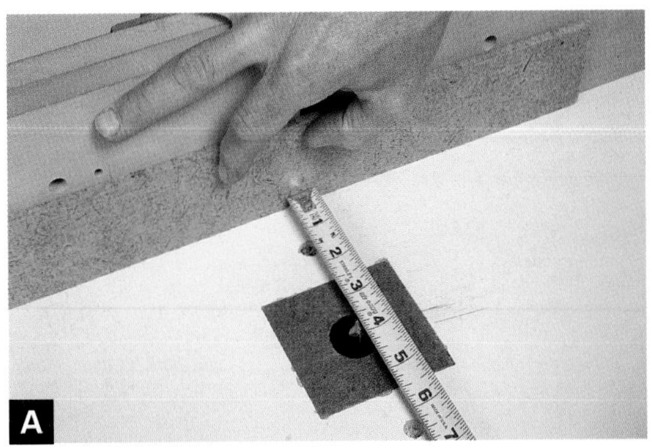
A

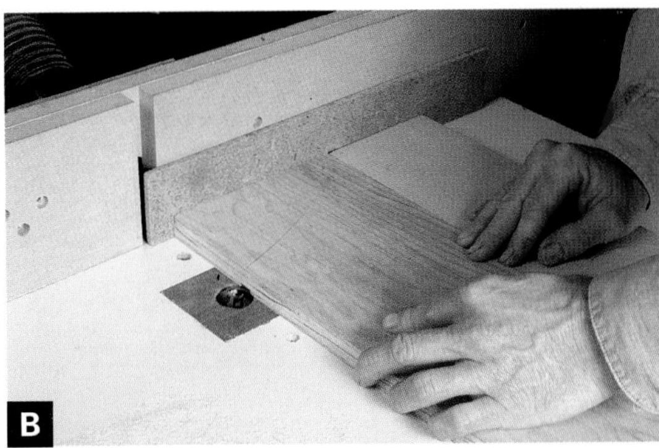
B

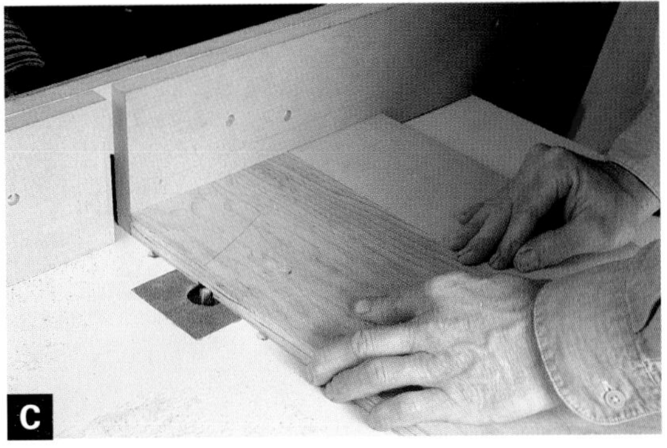
C

A

B

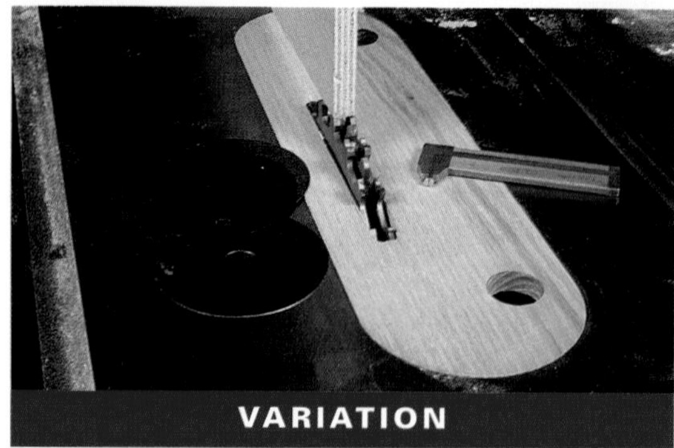
VARIATION

Through Dado on the Table Saw

To cut a through dado on the table saw, use a crosscut jig to make a series of passes. Set up stops for each side of the dado cut. If all your work is cut perfectly to length, then all the dadoes will be the same size (**A**). Be sure no debris gets between the end of the board and the stops, as this will cause an inaccurate cut. Make a pass and then move over just a little for each subsequent pass.

On a narrow board, it's simple to make the two end cuts, cut away all the remaining wood in the middle, and then clean the dado with the saw-blade (**B**). After making all the rough cuts, move the jig so the board is sitting right over the top of the blade. Then move the board back and forth over the blade between the stops to clean up the cut. Do this in a series of passes.

[VARIATION] A familiar method for cutting through dadoes on the table saw is to use a dado set. Match your dado package to the stock thickness. If you don't have a designated crosscut jig for dadoing, use a miter gauge to move the work past the dado blade.

Stopped Dado with a Router

Stopped dadoes do not show through at the end of the board. They are best made with the router, and you can do this topside with an auxiliary fence attached to the router fence. Begin by marking out the joint clearly (**A**); then trust your eye and steady hand with the router to stop the dado pass in the right spot (**B**). If you can't see through the router base to the joint mark on the workpiece, mark the position of the router base instead. Place the router just over the end of the joint with the bit properly rotated. Use a pencil to mark the position of the base and bring the router to that point with each pass (**C**). You could also use a right-angle fence to guide the router (**D**).

➤ See *"Through Dado with a Router"* on p. 86.

A

B

C

D

A

B

C

D

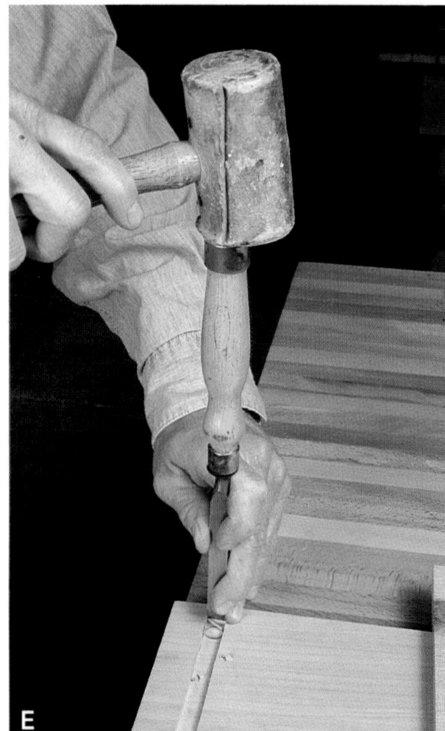
E

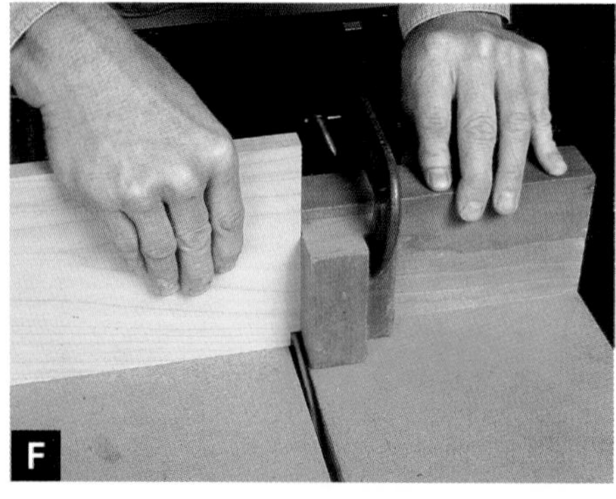
F

G

Stopped Dado on the Router Table

You can make stopped cuts on the router table. Begin by using a pencil to mark out the location of the bit (**A**). The most accurate method of reproducing stopped cuts is to place stops directly on the router table or its fence (**B**). Use the pencil marks to help locate the stops. Check your setup before cutting into good wood. As for other stopped joints on the router table, you'll need to lower the work onto the bit at the front of the cut and lift it off at the back (**C**).

➤ See *"Groove on the Router Table"* on pp. 82–83.

After cutting the stopped dado, clean up any fuzz raised by the cross-grain cut by slicing it off with a sharp chisel (**D**). Then chop the end of the dado square (**E**).

Next, the housed section of the joint needs to be notched to fit the dado. Use a handsaw or the table saw to notch this piece (**F, G**).

Make sure that you cut only as deeply as you need to. Dry-assemble your cabinet or case and check the inside-to-inside measurement; use this as a guide when cutting back your piece.

Shouldered Dado

The more common form of the shouldered dado is shown here; it looks balanced and provides a bit more strength than a simple housed dado. Make your through dado cut first, using the method of your choice (as shown on pp. 85 to 88). The dado should be smaller than the thickness of your stock by twice the amount you want for the shoulder.

Make each shoulder significant enough to provide some resistance to racking; ⅛ in. or so should do. Since you're cutting cross-grain move somewhat quickly across the bit chucked in the router table to avoid burning the end grain of solid stock (**A**).

TIP Let your backer board take the brunt of any tearout. This keeps the workpiece edges clean.

Keep the full depth of cut to no more than half the thickness of the stock. Any deeper and you run the risk of weakening the board. My own preference is to run only one-third as deep as the stock thickness. This is deep enough to be strong and looks better.

Cut both shoulders on the mating board with a straight bit chucked in the plunge router and use a fence (**B**). This method works well if you don't tip the router and you keep your shoulders lined up. Put good pressure down on the router base right over the wood. Make the first pass and then just nip off the end of the second pass and check the fit before finishing the entire cut. You can also make this rabbeting cut on the router table or table saw. Clean the joint with a shoulder plane, rabbet plane, or bullnose plane if it's just short of fitting (**C**).

A

B

C

A

C

Single-Shouldered Dado

A single-shouldered dado is simple to cut and simple to fit. Make the dado pass for a single-shouldered dado in the same way as you would for any other dado joint, through or stopped (**A**).

Cut the rabbet into the piece to be set into the dado with a handheld router or on the router table. On the router table, you can use a zero-clearance fence and the same bit height setting to cut both parts of the joint. Cut the dado first; then, holding the board vertically, rout the end rabbet cut into its end (**B**).

➤ **See *"End Rabbet on the Router Table"* on p. 74.**

Fit the joint by planing or scraping the uncut face until it enters the dado. Put pencil marks across the board, take cleaning passes across the entire width of the board until the pencil marks disappear, and then check the fit (**C**).

Dado Rabbet on the Router Table

For a flush-corner dado rabbet joint, you want to place the dado cut in the board so it's just as far from the edge as the mating piece is thick. Use the thickness of the stock as a gauge to check the cut, but first make a cut in a piece of scrap to double-check the setup (**A**). Then make the dado cut using a straight bit in a table-mounted router.

TIP **Gang two boards together for better support going along the fence.**

Make sure you do not rock the pieces, especially near the clearance hole of the router table fence (**B**).

On the router table, you can keep the bit height setting the same for the rabbet cut as for the dado cut. You just have to move the fence over to establish the proper size for the rabbet. A zero-clearance fence that completely captures the bit will help minimize any tearout. Or run a gauge line on the inside face of the rabbeted board (**C**). Another option is to first take a light pass across the face of the boards and then reset the fence for the full and final cut. You can also make the rabbet cut holding the board flat on the table, but you'll have to reset both the bit depth and fence setting to make the cut.

A

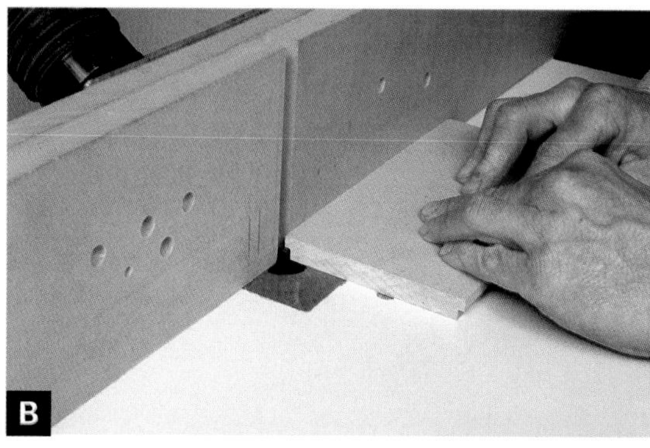

B

C

Dado Rabbet on the Table Saw

Set up a small dado package and cut the dado part of the dado rabbet joint on the table saw with a single pass of the blade. Use the stock to set the table saw fence the proper distance away from the dado blade (**A**). You can pass a wide board right past the blade to make the dado, holding it tight to the fence, but use a push stick or a miter gauge to help out. Make the rabbet cut the same way or use a crosscut jig. Clamp on a stop to limit the depth of the rabbet. Use a dado setup or a single blade to make the rabbet cuts (**B**).

Dado Rabbet by ¼-¼-¼ Table Saw Method

An efficient method for building drawers, the ¼-¼-¼ technique is used in busy cabinet shops where time is money. All the settings are made and double-checked and then every part of a drawer, including the groove for the bottom, is cut using the same setup.

Set the dado package at a ¼-in. width. Set the blade height at ¼ in. and put the fence ¼ in. away from the blade. Use an auxiliary fence for support later on in the cut. Make cuts first in scrap wood, checking all three important measurements (**A**).

First make the cross-grain cuts past the dado blade. Gang two boards together for better support or use a miter gauge to move the board safely past the blade (**B**).

The rabbet cut is done vertically. Here's where that taller auxiliary fence comes in handy. Pass the drawer side past the blade, holding it tightly to the fence. The board should not tip or rock as you make the cut (**C**). Next, make the through grooves on all the boards. Be sure to run all the cuts with the bottom edge of each piece running against the fence (**D**). A drawer face is added on after the drawer box is assembled.

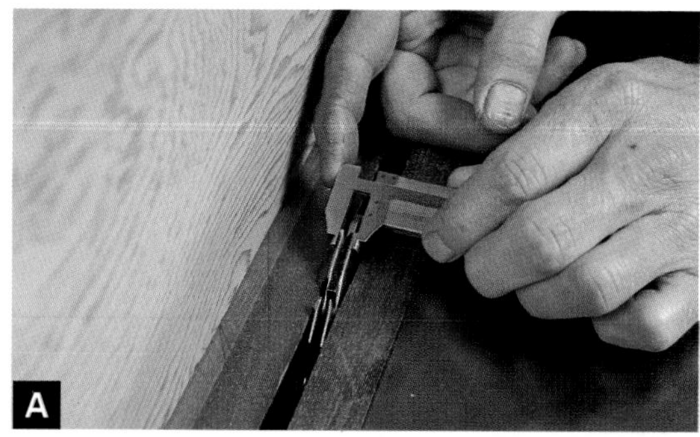
A

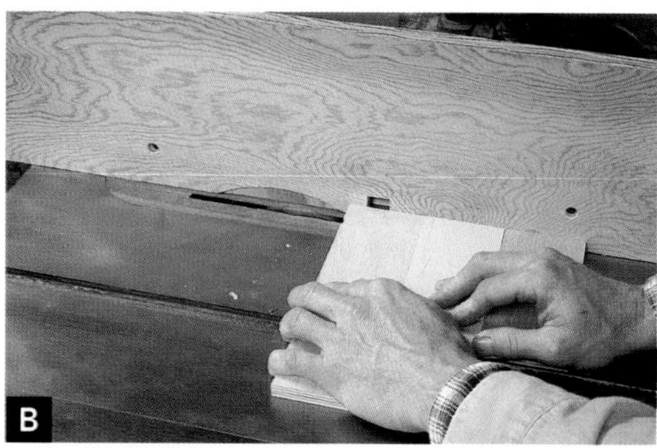
B

C

D

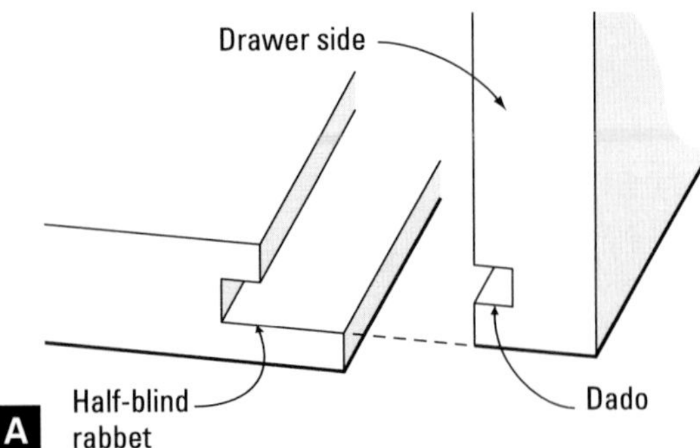

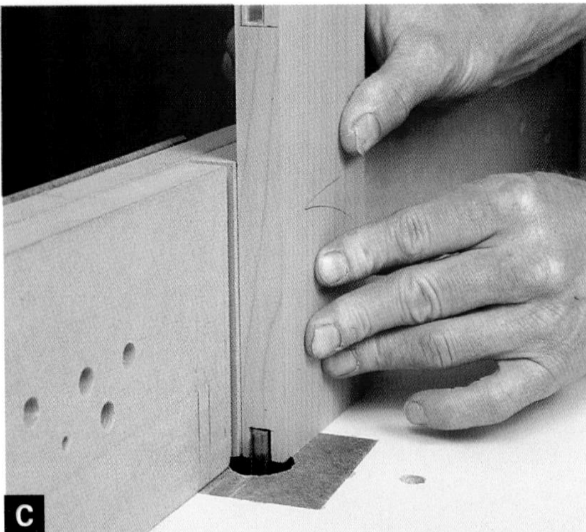

Half-Blind Dado Rabbet on the Table Saw

The half-blind dado rabbet joint has limited strength but it's a useful method when you want a simple reproducible joint that won't show from one face (**A**). For this example, I'm building a drawer.

Set the fence for a dado cut on the drawer side about two-thirds of the thickness of the drawer face back from the edge. Use just the width of a sawblade to make this cut (**B**). You can use a crosscut jig with a stop clamped to it for these cuts.

Pass the drawer face vertically past the dado blade to establish the tongue and dado in the end of the drawer face. Or use a router bit in the router table, but first be sure to make a few waste passes on the table saw to remove most of the wood (**C**).

Trim the end of the tongue off on the table saw so it fits the depth of the dado slot (**D**). Trim off the end of this waste first so the offcut isn't trapped between the stop and the blade. The final fitting of the joint can be done by trimming the end grain of the side piece or the inside face of the drawer, depending on which part of the joint needs fitting.

[TIP] Use the cutoffs to check the bit or dado width to see that it matches the set-in of the first dado cut.

Drawer Lock Joint

On the router table, make the horizontal cut for a drawer lock joint in a piece of scrap plywood (**A**). Next, make the vertical cut with the bit just emerging from the fence.

TIP Use a zero-clearance fence with dust collection and run your router at its lowest speed.

Play around with the bit height to get that perfect fit and check the setup in some scrap (**B**). Adjust the bit lower if the joint is too tight, because the dado cut in the joint is always the same width. The tongue gets smaller with less bit showing at a lower height. I find that just about 15⁄32 in. is optimal for a good fit, but remember that you can also adjust the fit by the placement of the fence. Set the fence too far from the bit, and the joint may fit but the corner won't be flush. Set it too close, and the joint won't fit properly. Keep moving the fence while adjusting the bit height until you get the joint to fit.

A

B

Rabbeted Drawer Lock Joint

It is possible to make a rabbeted version of the drawer lock joint by exposing more of the bit. Waste some of the wood first on the table saw set up with a dado blade (**A**). Then place the fence at the proper distance and feed the board slowly past the bit (**B**). The rabbeted drawer face will allow you to use a full or partial overlay drawer (**C**).

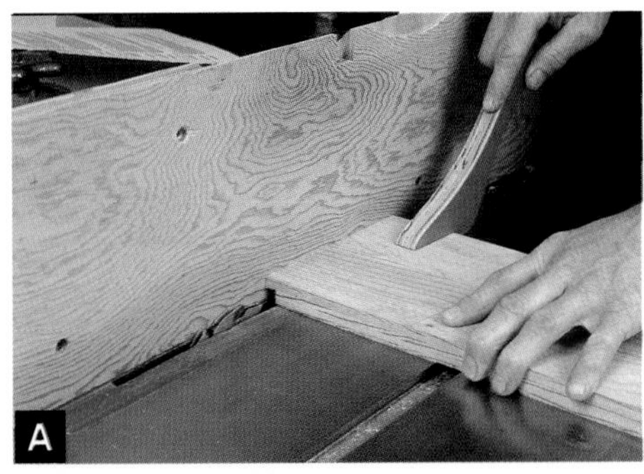
A

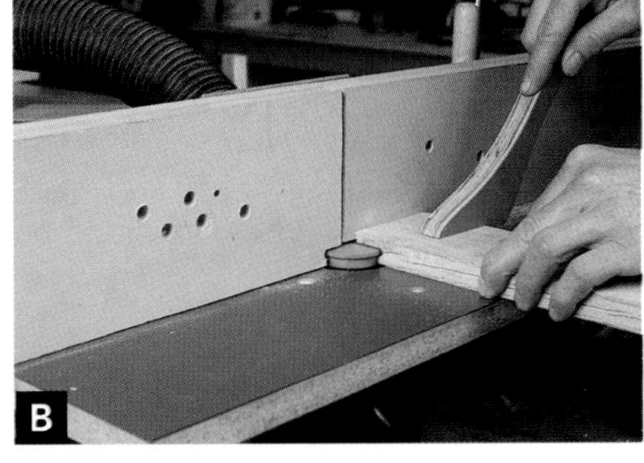
B

C

Hand-Cut Tongue-and-Groove Joint

Combination planes work well for plowing a through groove cut. The no. 45 plane shown here, like all combination planes, needs careful alignment so the iron is well supported during the cut (**A**). Don't let too much blade be exposed or you'll experience chatter.

Tongue cuts can be made with a rabbeting plane (**B**). Keep the plane square to the edge of the board so the shoulder remains square to the tongue. Set the plane fence so the tongue is almost as deep as the groove.

Tongue-and-Groove Joint with a Router

The groove is cut using a straight bit chucked in a plunge router. Using a plunge router allows you to easily control the depth of cut. The cut is guided by the router's edge guide fitted with an auxiliary fence (**A**). Since edge cuts like this are precarious, mount another board next to the workpiece to support the cut (**B**).

You could also use a slotting cutter in a router table to make the groove cut. Or you could clamp on a second fence to the router base and trap the workpiece between the fences (**C**).

Use a rabbeting bit topside to cut a tongue on a plywood panel (**D**). Make sure that the cut is deep enough to hold but not so deep that it weakens the tongue.

Tongue-and-Groove Joint on the Router Table

Place a bearing-mounted slotting cutter in the router table for cutting the groove. Make sure that the depth of cut—the distance from the bit edge to the bearing—is right for your job. You can change out bearings to adjust the depth of cut as required (**A**). Or you can hide the cutter inside an adjustable fence so only as much bit as needed pokes out (**B, C**). Slotting cutters will also cut the tongue. Adjust the bit height so you're cutting a rabbet first on one face and then the other (**D**).

The stock has to be flat with parallel faces for this method to work. Make sure you press the work down flat to the table as you pass it by the bit.

A

B

C

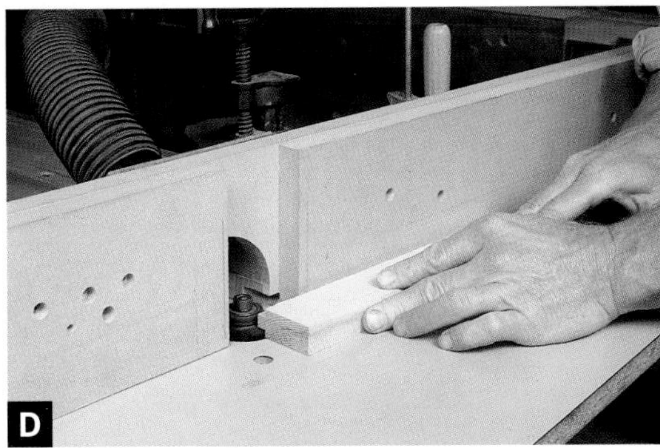
D

A

B

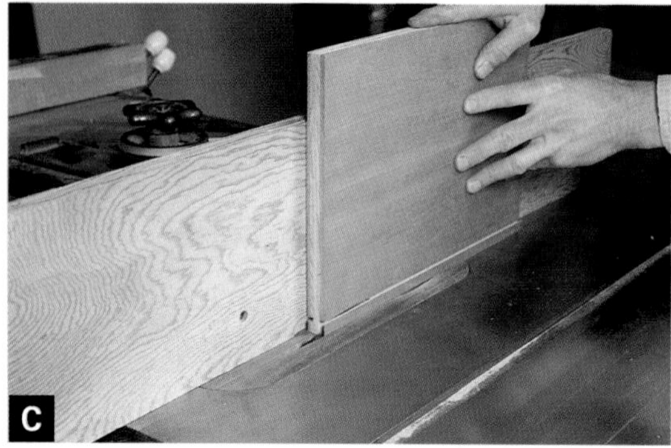
C

D

Tongue-and-Groove Joint on the Table Saw

The table saw makes through groove cuts like any other rip cut. Keep the workpiece held flat to the table and fence and use a moderate feed rate. If necessary, support the workpiece with an auxiliary fence (**A**). A single pass over the blade will cut a ⅛-in.-wide groove. A dado set will, of course, make a large groove much more quickly. Flip the board face for face to center a larger groove cut.

A single blade will cut the tongue. Make the first two cuts horizontally to establish the shoulders of the tongue (**B**). These cuts are made like two rabbet cuts with their shoulders lining up. Make the second pass holding the workpiece vertically to cut the sides of the tongue (**C**), but keep the waste piece away from the fence so it's not trapped by the blade, causing kickback. Set the blade height for just under the shoulder cut. Clean up any leftover waste with a chisel. Use an auxiliary fence for better support of the workpiece. Check the fit of the tongue before committing all your cuts.

You can also use a dado blade with an auxiliary fence to cut the tongue. The auxiliary fence allows you to zero the dado blade right next to the fence (**D**). By doing this, you minimize the danger of kickback, but remember to use a push stick. Make sure the workpiece edge is square so the tongue shoulders are square and in line with one another. Do this cut in scrap, checking the fits of the shoulder and the tongue separately. Adjust the fence setting and blade height accordingly.

Tongue-and-Groove Corner Joint

The tongue-and-groove corner joint offers some design options as well as good strength for plywood cases, but remember that the joint described here is usable only for plywood or other sheet-good material.

To set up for flush outer faces on this corner joint, place a straight bit in the router table and use a fence to index the cut. Set the fence to make the groove cut in the corner piece using the plywood stock thickness as a gauge. Index the cut from the outer, or face, side of the plywood and corner piece. When setting up the cut, be sure to use a piece of scrap cut from the same material (**A**).

Given the available choices, I think it's best to keep the solid corner just a hair taller than the plywood. Make a practice cut first to check this setting. To keep things simple, make this tongue-and-groove joint a through joint.

Cut the first groove; then flip the board to cut the next. Have the solid-wood corners clearly marked to indicate the face sides that run to the table and fence (**B**). For deep grooves, take several passes to get down to full depth or waste some of the material on the table saw first and then set your bit for a final height. Make the tongue cut in the plywood. You want a snug fit with a bit of room for glue at the bottom of the joint (**C**).

➤ See *"Tongue-and-Groove Joint with a Router"* or *"Tongue-and-Groove Joint on the Router Table"* on pp. 98–99.

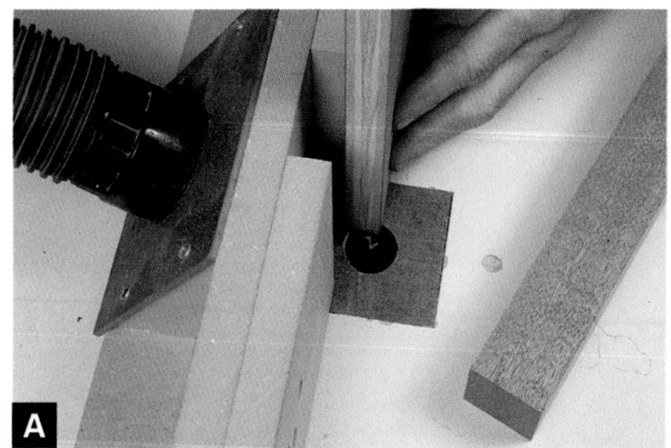

A

B

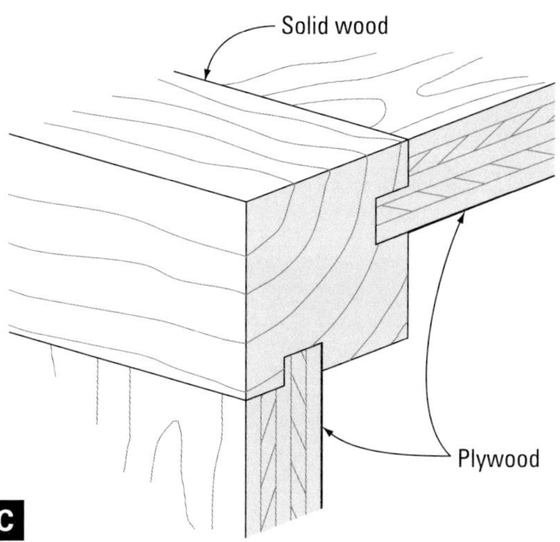

C

Flush-Corner Tongue-and-Groove Joint

For a flush-corner tongue-and-groove joint, groove the plywood instead of the solid-wood corner (**A**). Center the groove cut in the plywood by making a pass with first one face and then the other against the fence. Or you can use a dado blade to make one full pass.

To cut the tongues, make the outside cuts first. Have the corner block clearly marked for face sides. The finished corner piece sits near the blade. In photo **B**, the second pass has just been made.

After the two outer passes, make the two inner cuts. Drop the blade height just a hair so the last cut leaves the waste piece just in place and doesn't trap this potential projectile. As always, check the setups in scrap, including blade height and fence distance (**C**). Clean up the tongues that need work with a chisel or shoulder plane.

A

B

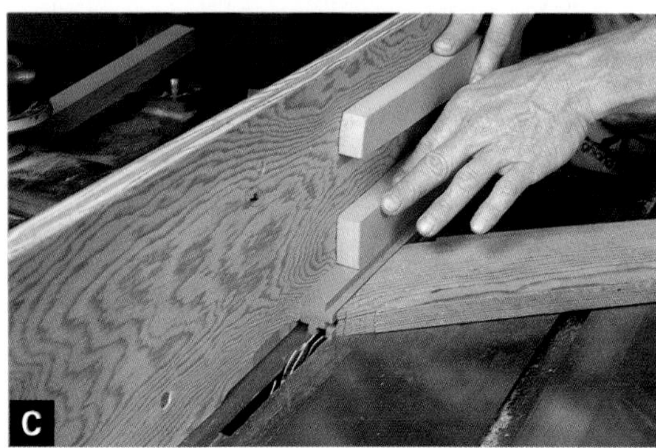

C

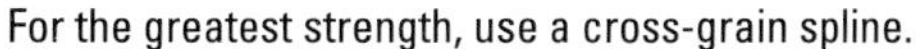

Making a Loose Tongue

Another method of tongue and grooving is to use a loose tongue that fits into grooved boards (**A**). A loose tongue is simply a spline glued in between two groove cuts. Make it fit snugly, with just a little room for glue. The tongue shouldn't fall out of the joint when testing its fit; nor should you have to hammer it in place, except when you apply the glue. When using any sheet-good material, you can use a plywood tongue, as there is no concern with shrinkage. Solid-wood tongues can be used for joining solid-wood sides. Run the spline with short cross-grain for the greatest strength.

Make through groove cuts on the table saw or with a straight bit and plunge router.

➤ See *"Through Groove on the Table Saw"* on p. 84.

Or make stopped groove cuts on the router table with a straight bit (**B**). Clamp stops onto the fence and drop down onto the bit. Have the bit set at full height and use ⅛-in. to ¼-in. table inserts to raise the board up. After each pass, pull out an insert. Or reset the bit height after each pass. Be sure to index off the face side of each board for the groove cuts.

Fit splines that are too thick by scraping or planing them. Not only will sanding round their edges but also it is too difficult to control with any hand-held sander (**C**). Check the fit of the tongue along the entire length of the grooves.

(Text continues on p. 104.)

For the greatest strength, use a cross-grain spline.

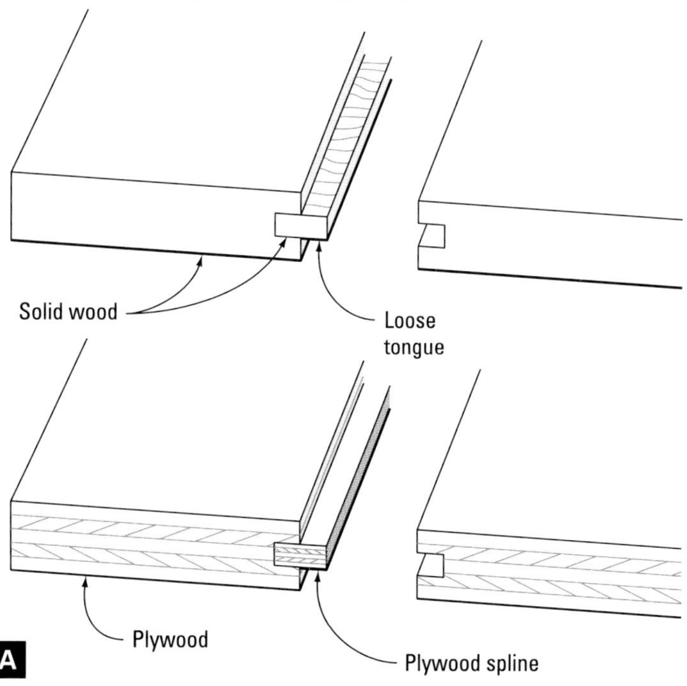

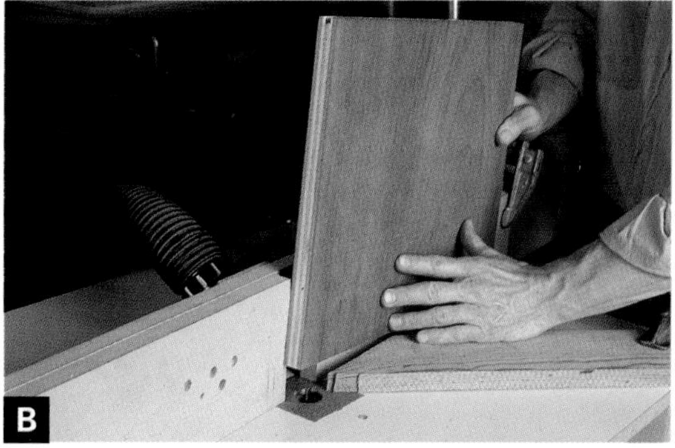

D

E

A solid corner joint can also use loose tongues, but this is only possible with plywood or sheet-good case sides. The shrinkage of solid sides to a solid corner running cross-grain would cause the joint to fail or the case to rack horribly out of square.

Use a slotting cutter on the router table, but match its groove cut to the thickness of the spline, if you can (**D**). Grind a cutter down to match undersize plywood if you need to make a number of these joints for a project. Remember to make the corner stock a bit larger than the plywood stock as well, to give strength to the corner after grooving. You don't want those groove cuts meeting up inside your corner block.

Through groove cuts can be dressed up with a false tongue fitted at the outside of the joint. Make a false tongue out of a nice contrasting material, such as mahogany (shown here) or walnut (**E**).

Miter Joints

Compound Miter

Biscuited Miter

Splined Miters

Keyed Miters

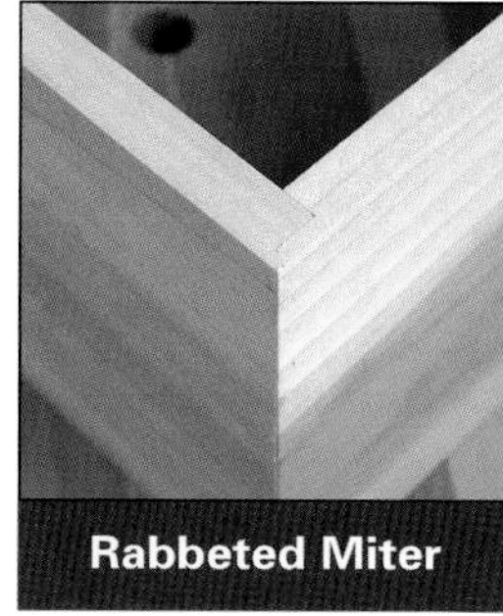
Rabbeted Miter

Lock Miter

Carcase miter joints offer the woodworker a unique kind of joinery because they yield a consistent long-grain pattern running around the perimeter of the case unobstructed by any end grain. Boxes are never disturbed by the appearance of darker end grain showing in the finger or tail of a joint. Carcases never show plywood veneers or substrates.

This, of course, looks very clean and neat; but, regrettably, a miter joint that's held together only by glue is weak. Because the wood in a miter joint is neither long grain nor end grain but somewhere in between, you create a less-than-optimal gluing surface. It's not a bad gluing surface; it's just not a good one. By using glued-in blocks, keys, splines, or biscuits, you can improve the strength of a miter joint considerably.

This miter joint shows the half-long-grain/half-end-grain of the miter joint. The miter box in the background uses keys to strengthen the joint.

The miter cuts on this small box made of wide stock show how the smallest error can be compounded.

To make accurate miter cuts with a circular saw, be sure to use a fence to guide the cut.

Cutting Miter Joints

Cutting miters creates another level of concern. Your cuts must be absolutely true and square to an edge for a simple miter. Compound miters complicate your setup. Consistency, then, is crucial for any carcase miter. All your cuts must be exactly at the required angle. An error of half of a degree adds up to a lot in both the look and fit of a miter joint; and the thicker the stock, the wider the joint and the larger the gaps. Cutting accurately will minimize your fuss factor.

Cutting miters is best suited for power tools when constructing carcases from wide panels and even boxes from smaller parts. Accuracy is crucial in making this joint well, and power saws can make miter cuts accurately and repeatedly with ease.

CIRCULAR SAW

The circular saw I grew up with couldn't crosscut straight much less miter accurately. Saws today will make angled cuts precisely when you lock in the blade angle and speed. By using a guide rail system, you can also locate the cut along its entire length.

COMPOUND MITER SAW

Compound miter saws are limited by how wide a board they can cut, but for most small cases and boxes this saw will do just fine. Sliding compound miter saws can handle wider cuts. Make sure the piece you're cutting is always well supported. Set up a stop to duplicate cuts that are the same length.

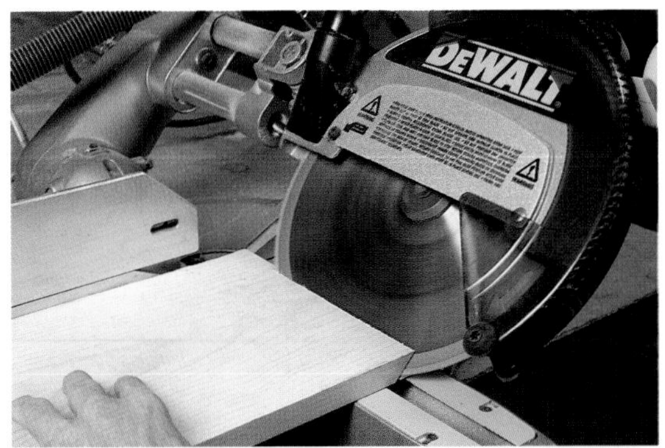

The sliding compound miter saw is a champion at making multiple miter cuts. A standard miter saw can also be used, but it is limited by the width of the stock it can cut.

TABLE SAW

The tilting arbor table saw makes miter cuts with relative ease. Your stock does have to be flat and your blade angle right on the money. The miter gauge acts as a guide for the cut, but use an auxiliary fence to help support the board. You can also clamp stops to the fence.

Set the miter gauge to 90 degrees and double-check the squareness of its cut with the sawblade set at 90 degrees. Then tilt the blade over to 45 degrees. I prefer to make my cut so the waste piece falls to the outside edge of the blade. Use a combination square or a miter square to check that the blade is set exactly at 45 degrees. Set the stop inside the saw cabinet to index the cut each time.

A tilting arbor table saw can make very accurate miter cuts when the blade is set at the correct angle.

Make test cuts and check for 45 degrees with a miter square before making the cuts in the workpiece.

ROUTER TABLE OR SHAPER

A miter can also be cut on the router table using a miter bit or shaper cutter of the correct angle. If the stock is true and flat, this is a highly accurate way of cutting miters, especially miters of specific angles. The lock miter, a strengthened form of this joint, can easily be cut in this way using a specialized bit. To create this joint on the router, you need to make some practice cuts until you have the bit height set properly.

Shaper cutters and router bits come in a variety of angles for cutting miters.

A miter cut can be adjusted and trued with a block plane.

A disk sander is a quick way to clean up a miter cut. Use a jig that ensures the miter stays true.

DONKEY'S EAR SHOOTING BOARD

Clamp in a vise.
Handplane
Base
Cleat
Fence
Angled base
Workpiece goes here.

Truing Miter Cuts

Not every saw makes a perfect cut and not every blade leaves a smooth enough surface for gluing. If you have a tuned-up block plane or low-angle bench plane, you can judiciously clean up a miter cut with a few light passes. Clamp the workpiece in your vise and work from both ends in toward the middle. Don't try to adjust the angle too much if it's not correct, because you'll then start to remove wood from the length of a board.

A donkey's ear shooting board is a jig used for holding wide boards to true up miter cuts. Clamp it in a vise and set the workpiece against the stop on the jig. Push into the stop with the bench plane to trim a miter. The flat, square sides of the bench plane will locate on the jig base to line up the cut.

A disk sander can true up miters quickly. The sander table has to be set exactly at 90 degrees for this trimming. Use the left side of the disk sander so the disk pushes the work down into the table. The jig rides in the miter gauge track in the table. A board or fence cut with a perfect 90-degree angle is screwed to the runner. As long as you use each side of this fence to true up each side of the miters, they will always be complementary angles. Wider boards will require a taller fence to support them.

Gluing Miter Joints

With nothing to prevent these joints from slipping around, clamping miter joints can be a four-handed job in a two-handed shop. And if you'll be adding glue blocks or keys to the joint, then using bar clamps along the sides of the box tends to put too much pres-

Compound Miter Angles

These angles (in degrees) are for a four-sided miter joint.

Side Tilt	Blade Tilt	Miter Gauge Angle
5	44¾	85
10	44¼	80⅛
15	43	75½
20	41½	71¼
25	39¾	67
30	37¾	63½

sure on first one side and then the other. It makes it almost impossible to use normal clamps to clamp up a miter joint. Only if your box is a square can you use clamps across the diagonals. So careful and directed clamping of a different kind is required for assembling miter joints. The options for clamping miter joints include simple masking tape, band clamps, and clamped or glued-on clamping blocks.

Always do a dry run of your gluing assembly. This will help you determine the method of clamping. Then get everything in place for the assembly, including the glue. Yellow aliphatic resin glues set up much quicker and require faster clamping times than plastic resin glues or epoxies. But they'll also show less of a glueline in most woods.

Masking tape works best on small boxes. Band clamps are cumbersome and require a sailor's dexterity with ropes to ensure quick and even clamping pressure. They're quick, but they don't always provide enough specific pressure on the joint. Clamping blocks

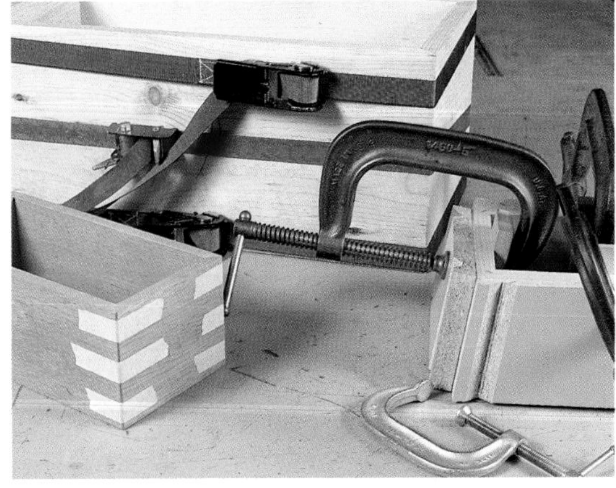

Clamping miters requires some ingenuity. Here are three useful methods: masking tape for small boxes; and band clamps and clamped-on clamping blocks for larger carcase work.

Clamping blocks can be glued on to ease assembly of a carcase. You can remove them after assembly with a chisel and handplane or belt sander.

provide the best pressure across a miter joint, but they're time-consuming to make and place securely.

Before assembly, sizing a miter joint is always a good idea. Sizing fills the pores of the joint with glue before the final glue-up, preventing a starved glue joint, which occurs when too little glue stays on the surface of the joint. Wipe the joint down with glue, scrap off the excess, wait half a bit and then reapply the glue for the final assembly.

Strengthening Miter Joints

Miters require some kind of strengthening for the best and longest-lasting results. The joint is a mix of long grain and end grain, so it's not optimal as a gluing surface. The

STRONGER MITERS

Glue Blocks

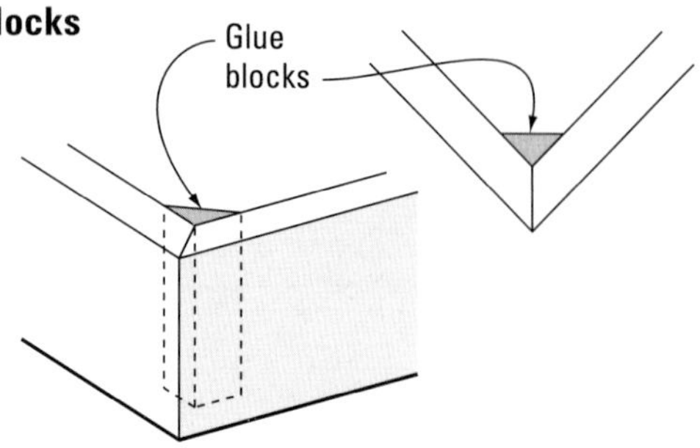

Glue blocks

Keys

Set keys about two-thirds into the miter.

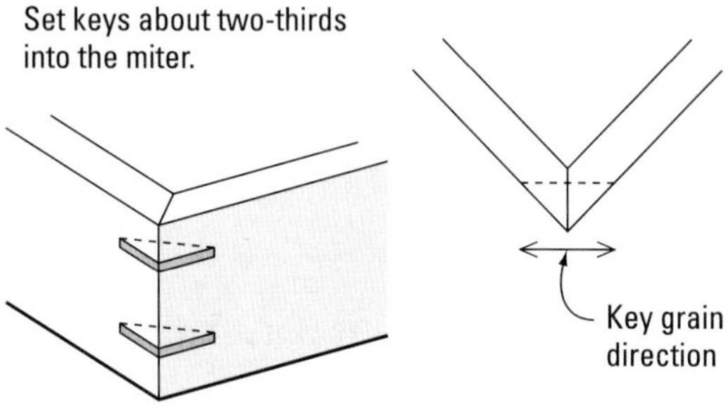

Key grain direction

Dovetail Keys

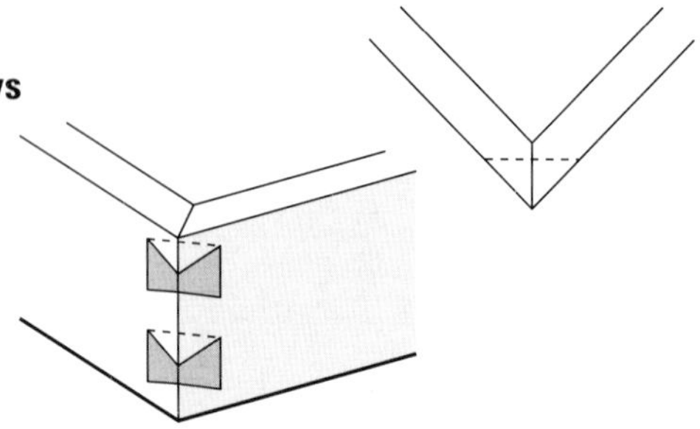

Splines

Make the spline cut about two-thirds of the way in from the corner, which allows you to make it longer and, therefore, stronger.

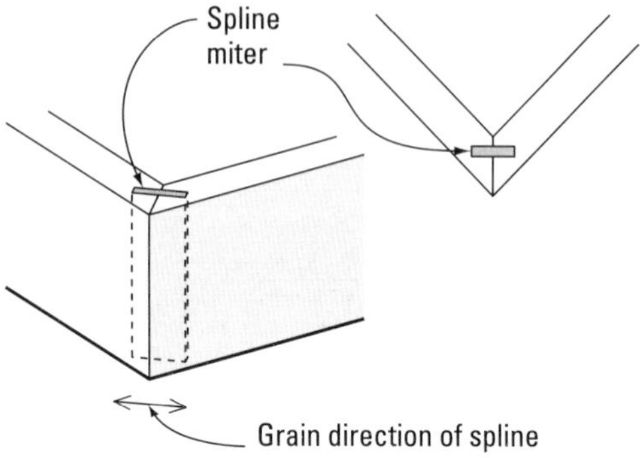

Spline miter

Grain direction of spline

methods for beefing up the joint are usually hidden from view.

Glue blocks applied to the inside of a small carcase provide added strength to a simple miter joint. Make sure that all surfaces are clean and flat before applying the glue. Hold the block in place for a minute or so until the yellow glue dries enough to prevent the block from moving. Or tape the glue block in place until it dries.

Splines act like loose tongues. Both sides of the miter joint are grooved, and a loose spline is placed between the mating boards. Keep these cuts toward the inside corner of the joint, because you can get a greater depth of cut there. The grain direction of the spline in a solid-wood case follows the grain direction of the wood. Use plywood splines for plywood carcase construction.

Keyed miters can give a decorative look to a box or carcase. Glue up the piece first, trusting your true-fitting miters to hold. After the glue has set, clean up the box or case with a sander, scraper, or handplane. An especially decorative look can be achieved with *dovetails keys,* sometimes called "mock dovetails."

A glue block added to the inside of a case is a traditional way of reinforcing carcase miter joints.

Compound Miter on the Table Saw

Set the table-saw blade and miter gauge to the proper settings for the number of sides and required angles (**A**). Set each independently of the other. Make a practice cut for the angle of the miter gauge and check that with an angle gauge or sliding bevel and protractor. Then make a practice cut for the tilt of the blade and check that. Continue to make several practice cuts to check the setups for accuracy and consistency.

➤ See *"Compound Miter Angles"* chart on p. 109.

TIP Try using a fitting system, such as the Tru-Fit, with your miter gauge. These blocks help take the slop out of the miter gauge bar, thus helping you make more accurate cuts.

Make one set of crosscuts for each end of all the boards (**B**). Flip the miter gauge around backward with the exact same angle setting, but cut on the other side of the blade and use a stop to index the length of each cut. Make the matching set of cuts (**C**).

These joints will probably need splines or keys for the best strength. Next, trim the edges of the case at the angle you want the sides to be tilted. For the 10-degree tilt shown here, I tipped the sawblade to 10 degrees and cut the top and bottom edges (**D**).

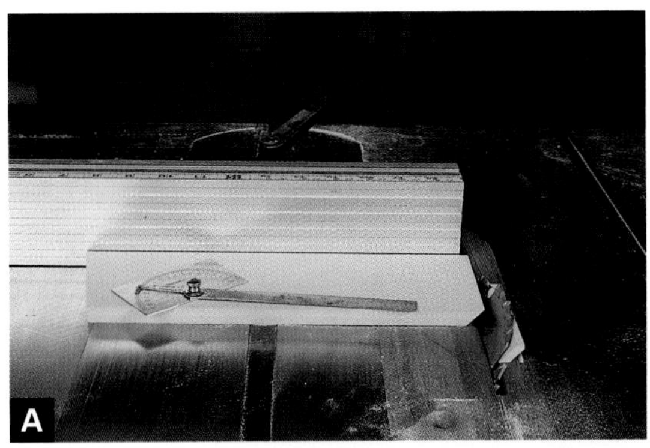
A

B

C

D

A

B

Biscuit-Reinforced Miter

For biscuit-reinforced miters, first make the miter cuts using your preferred cutting method.

➤ See *"Cutting Miter Joints"* on p. 106.

Biscuits placed across a miter joint do a good job of adding strength and are not visible (**A**). Check your cut first on a piece of scrap stock to make sure the biscuit joiner is set for the right depth of cut. You don't want the biscuit slot to go through the board. Clamp the workpiece securely before making the biscuit cut.

Next, size the miter joint with a light application of glue. Then put glue in the slots and across the faces of the joint and finally bring the boards together (**B**).

Splined Miter

The first step to making a splined miter is to cut the miters on the table saw (**A**). The blade angle for cutting the spline is already set after making the miter cuts. Place a fence close to the blade and, using the miter gauge, run the workpiece past the blade. Double-check the blade height and fence settings in scrap material (**B**). For saws that tilt toward the fence, place the fence on the opposite side of the blade.

Splined compound angle miters require that the cut be made vertically past the blade with the blade set at its determined cutting angle (**C**).

VARIATION Make up an angle jig to support a mitered board as it moves across the router table. The one shown here is made of medium-density fiberboard (MDF) and has enough room so the workpiece can be securely clamped to it. Place a straight bit in the router table and pass the jig past the bit. For deeper splines, make several passes to get to a full depth of cut. Pass the jig from right to left into the rotation of the bit, which will push the jig in tight to the fence.

A

B

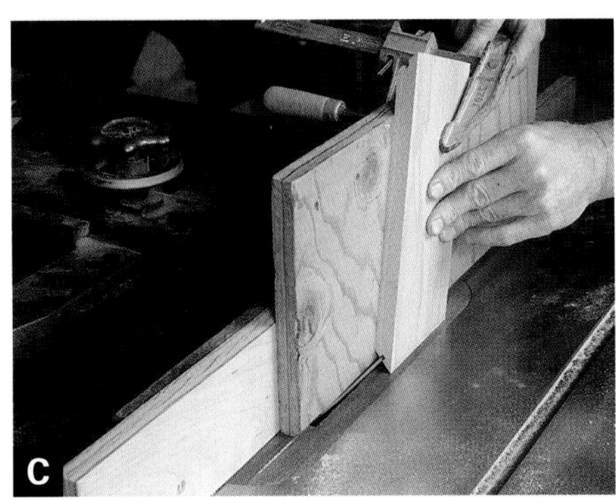
C

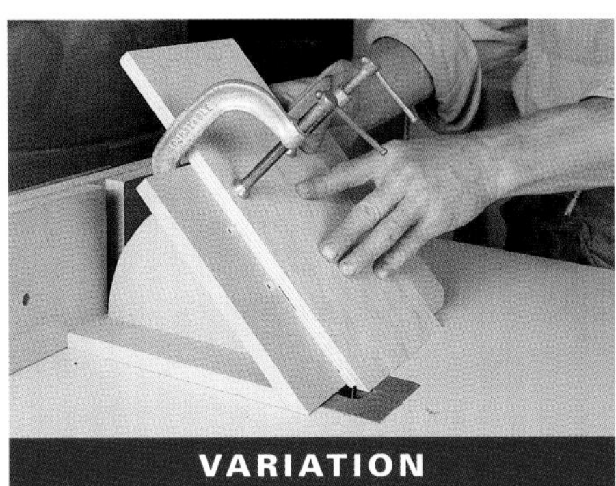
VARIATION

Plywood Splines

A

B

Use plywood splines for miters cut in sheet-good materials, such as plywood and medium-density fiberboard (MDF). It's much better if the plywood is already pretty close to the proper thickness. Then all that's required is to scrape it to fit the spline cut (**A**). Dress up a plywood spline miter joint by placing a bit of hardwood just at the end of a cut (**B**). Run the grain direction of the wood spline the short way across the joint.

A

B

C

D

Solid-Wood Splines

Use solid-wood splines in boxes or cases made of solid wood. Mill them out of a straight-grained piece of stock. The grain direction must run the same way as the sides of the box so their shrinkage directions are the same. This means you'll be working with wide short-grain pieces that are hard to mill with a jointer or planer and that tend to break along their width. However, in their length where they need to be strong to hold the joint together, they are impossible to break.

First mill up a board as wide as your box or even a bit wider. Then crosscut a section to length on the table saw. Take this wide piece to the bandsaw and trim it close to the required thickness of the spline, using a fence to run against (**A**). Use a pencil as a push stick. A practice cut will show you if you're close enough in thickness.

Set the spline onto a bench hook and use a block plane to finish off the fitting (**B**). Be careful not to break the short grain; but if you do break a spline, the pieces will still work in the joint. The break won't be seen and the joint itself won't be compromised.

Double-check the length of the spline and trim it if needed in place on the joint (**C**). If the spline is close in length, a few passes with a block plane should be all that's necessary to clean it up. Leave the splines a bit wide and, after gluing, you can clean the ends off with a file, chisel, or plane. Spline miters make gluing a miter joint a bit easier, because the joint can't slip around during assembly (**D**).

Hand-Cut Keyed Miter

Veneer keys can be made to look almost invisible if you match the veneer to the box material. Make sawcuts into the box right at the corner using a backsaw or dovetail saw (**A**). Try to keep the cuts consistent in depth so the kerfs look the same. You can also cut them in at an angle for a little better holding power.

If the veneer is too thick for the saw kerf, take a hammer and pound the veneer flat until it just fits into the kerf (**B**). When you apply glue, the moisture in it will swell the veneer, locking it tightly in place. Use a chisel to pare back the veneer so that it is flush (**C**). Veneer keys, well matched to their surrounding wood, can almost disappear.

A

B

C

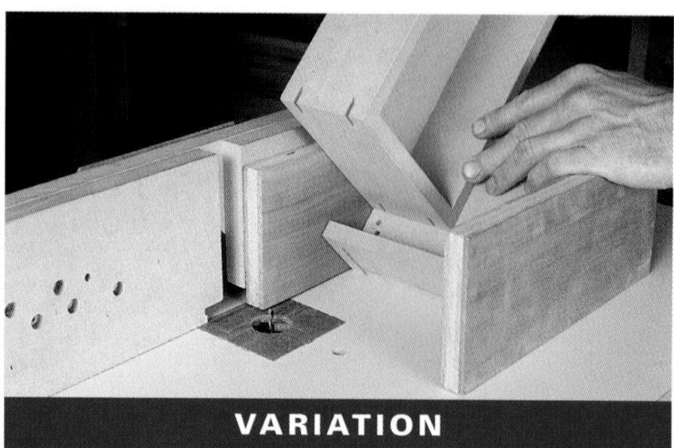
VARIATION

Keyed Miter on the Router Table

You can make key cuts on the router table using a straight bit and a key miter jig. The jig supports the box during the cut. It's made of one flat board with a fence mounted to it at a 45-degree angle.

[TIP] Keep any fasteners you use to mount the fence higher than the highest possible height of the router bit.

Mark out the locations of the keys on the box. Then set the fence in position next to the jig, and measure from the jig (**A**). If the cuts are placed symmetrically, you can make one pass, flip the box around edge for edge, and make a second pass. You will have to support the box in tight to the jig as you pass it over the bit.

[VARIATION] For better support, make a miter jig with a 90-degree cradle in it to hold your box or case. Hold this in tight to the fence and pass the whole jig by the bit. You'll have to measure off the fence with the jig in place.

Keyed Miter with a Router Template

It's difficult to cut keys into large mitered carcases. Instead of trying to come up with a method for holding a large piece steady on the router table, use a plunge router, straight bit, and a template guide to make the key cuts (**A**).

On a squared-up piece of plywood or MDF exactly the same width as the carcase, mark out the center and end lines for the key cuts (**B**). Mount a straight bit the same width as the template guide in the router table. Set up a fence and take some practice cuts to check the fence distance.

Start the cut in the center of a slot, pushing down gradually until you break through the plywood. Or you can drill out a starting hole for the bit. If you place the key slots symmetrically, then you need to set the router table fence for only one cut; just flip the template to make the matching cut (**C**). The template guide should slide easily in the routed slot. Wax it if necessary.

Cut straight across the joint. Note that the length of the template cut is not critical. The length of the key slot depends on the depth of the router bit (**D**).

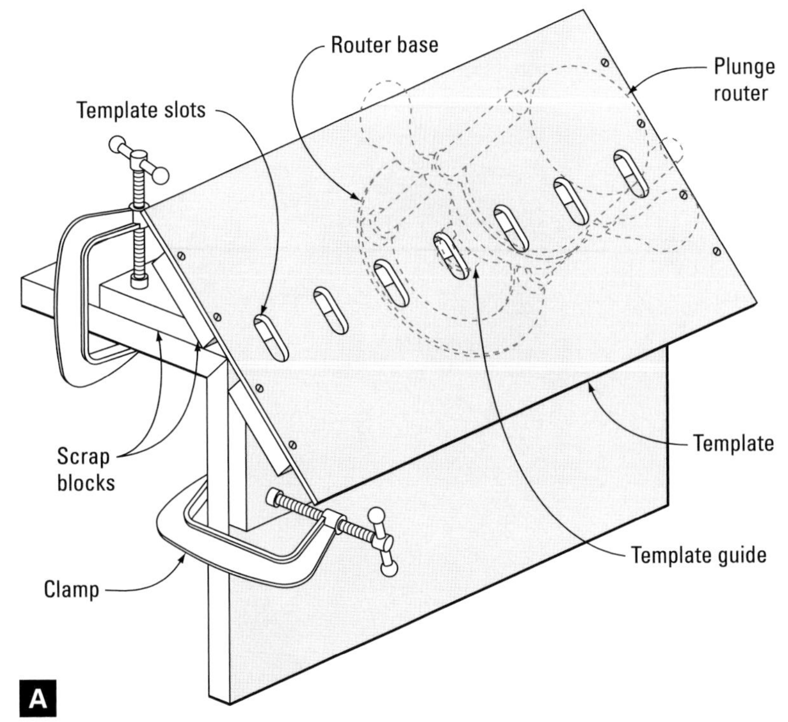

A

B

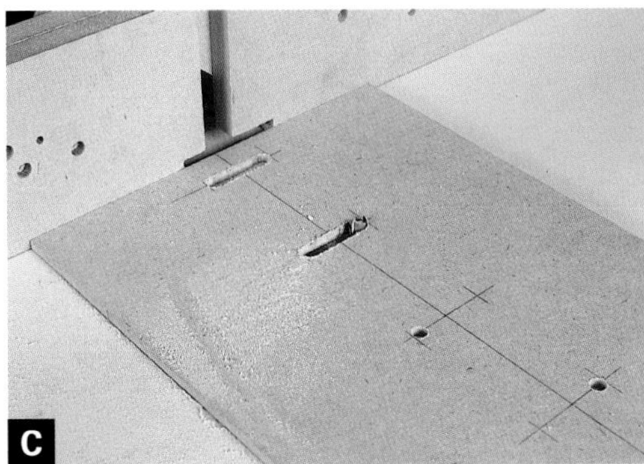
C

D

A

B

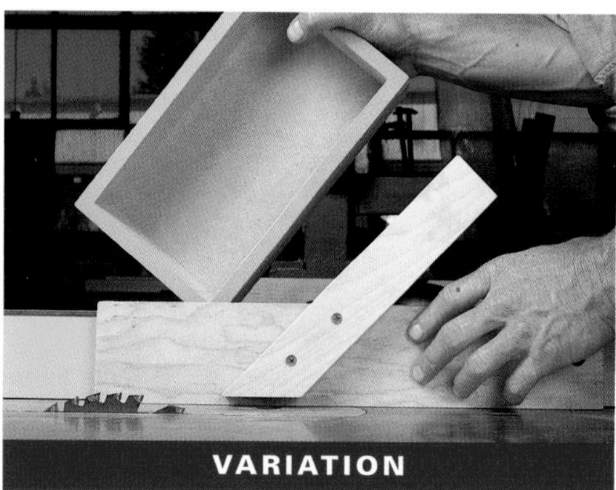

VARIATION

Keyed Miter on the Table Saw

To cut keyed miters in large cases on the table saw, make a larger cradle to hold the carcase. Clamp the key miter jig right to the crosscut jig. The support pieces that hold the jig arms together also act as stops for locating the case in the jig (**A**). A backer board prevents tearout on the face side of the carcase. Use double-sided tape to hold the backer board in place and clamp the workpiece securely to the jig (**B**).

[VARIATION] Use the small key miter jig against the table saw fence to make key cuts in small boxes.

Making and Applying Straight Keys

The first step in making straight keys is to cut the key stock roughly to width and thickness on the bandsaw. Cut it to size on the table saw, being sure to use a push stick on this thin material.

Key stock has its grain running along with the long grain of the box (**A**). Fit the keys snugly into the slots. Use a block plane to trim the keys to fit. A bench hook with a thin stop on it can hold the keys while you plane. Use a hammer to put the keys in place and make sure they seat down all the way across the key cut (**B**).

Trim off the excess key material carefully on the bandsaw. Keep your eye on the blade as it comes past the top of the box to make sure you don't cut into the box itself (**C**). Do a final cleanup on the keys with a block plane, working down away from the corners with each stroke. Notice that all key stock looks darker once it's cleaned up flush with the sides of a box. This is because you're exposing a 45-degree-angle surface, which is partly end grain. This will always show up a little darker than long grain, especially after you apply a finish.

A

B

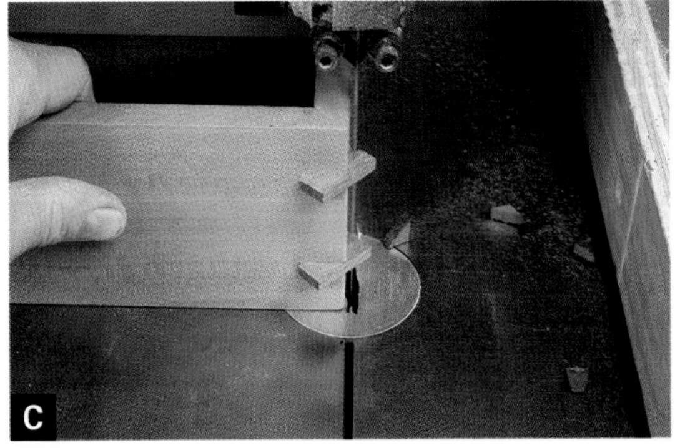

C

Dovetailed Keyed Miter

Dovetailed keyed miters add a decorative touch to any case. Use the same key miter jig as you would to make a straight key cut (**A**).

➤ See *"Keyed Miter on the Router Table"* on p. 116.

For this joint, use a dovetail bit to make the cut. To save wear on your dovetail bit, waste some of the cut first with a straight bit. Then you can cut the slot with a single pass with the dovetail bit.

Mill the key stock just oversize of the bit diameter. Cut the key stock with the same dovetail bit using a fence that captures the bit within it (**B**). Set the bit a little higher than the key cut to make fitting easier. If the key doesn't fit, make the trim pass on the router table. Move the fence away from the bit so more cutting edge is exposed. Take one pass, check the fit, and then flip the stock to cut a second pass, if needed (**C**). Keep moving the fence over until you get a snug fit. You can also trim the bottom of the key stock. This long-grain surface is easy to plane and it effectively decreases the width of the key by a shaving.

After gluing, trim the keys with a bandsaw and clean the sides of the box with a handplane or sander. Use a chisel to remove any excess glue, which will ding up a plane blade (**D**). Always work in from the corner of the box or you risk tearing out the corner of the key.

Rabbeted Miter

To make a rabbeted miter, cut the rabbet part of the joint first with a dado blade. Match the set-in of the rabbet to the thickness of the matching stock (**A**). Use a miter gauge mounted with an auxiliary fence and run the stock against the fence. Make the miter cut on the table saw with the blade tipped to a 45-degree angle. Use the miter gauge again to support the piece (**B**).

Mark the matching piece for the spot where the miter should end (**C**). Now cut the matching miter on the *left* side of the blade so the blade tips into the cut. You'll have to adjust the blade height carefully for this cut (**D**). Then cut the shoulder off square using a crosscut jig (**E**).

A

B

C

D

E

Lock Miter

Use a lock miter bit only in a speed-controlled table-mounted router (**A**). Set the speed for about 10,000 rpm to slow down the rim speed of this large-diameter bit.

First, make a cut horizontally (**B**). Use a zero-clearance fence with the dust-collection system running. The matching cut is done vertically (**C**). There is only one correct bit height setting that makes this joint fit well. You'll need to make several practice cuts in scrap wood to get the results you want (**D**).

Finger Joints

Finger Joints

Halved Joints

Finger joints have a distinctive look and are very strong. They offer lots of good gluing area from all the long-grain surface on each of the fingers. But since they're always a through joint, the end grain shows, which may be fine for those old card catalog trays in the library but may not be appropriate in other situations. You'll have to decide whether this look works for the boxes or carcases you're designing.

Part of your decision of whether to use finger joints depends on how you cut them. If you prefer hand-cut joints you're better off using through dovetails. With dovetails, you can space the fingers of the joint as you like and gain the added benefit of the mechanical resistance of those tails and pins. Finger joints are ideal for situations in which you need to make lots of boxes.

Wide finger joints are useful for large carcases, like this blanket chest. For strength in this application, the joint is pinned.

Finger joints are through joints, showing their darker end grain after finish has been applied. They can provide a decorative look to small boxes.

Cutting Finger Joints

The simplest method of cutting finger joints is with a table saw jig. A good dado blade and a jig that tracks well in a miter gauge slot can cut dozens of these joints repeatedly. They offer excellent amounts of optimal gluing surfaces and can be very attractive.

There are also router dovetail jigs that you can use to cut finger joints, with some small modifications or different cutters. When the router or table saw jig is working properly, you can create hundreds of finger joints that all fit together perfectly. These methods leave regularly spaced fingers, but there are also ways to create some variety in your finger joints by making your own templates.

A table saw jig is the easiest way to cut finger joints. A key the same size as the finger is used to index the spaces.

Commercial jigs for routing finger joints are available, but you can also make your own templates for variably spaced joints.

Counting Fingers

Laying out finger joints requires some planning. Decide first on the width of the fingers. Then cut the stock to a width that is a multiple of the finger width. This will yield the most regular-looking finger joint. But keep in mind that the joint should also always end up with an odd number of fingers so that the joint looks symmetrical; that is, there should be a finger or a socket at the top and bottom of each corner. An even

NUMBER OF FINGERS

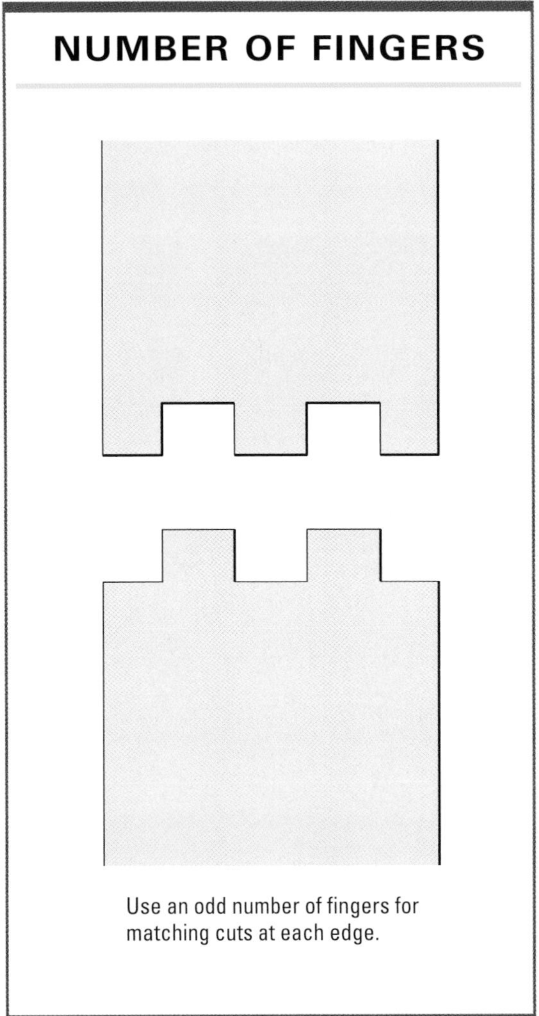

Use an odd number of fingers for matching cuts at each edge.

An odd number of fingers (counting the fingers from the end) will give you fingers at both ends. An even number of fingers gives you a finger at one end and a socket at the other.

If the fingers protrude from the joint, you'll need to make clamping cauls to fit around them.

If you cut the fingers slightly less than the width of the stock, you can clamp a caul right over the joint for easy assembly. Cleanup is also pretty simple; the long-grain surface needs to be taken down only a scant 1/32 in.

number of fingers will give you a finger at one end of the joint and a socket at the other.

Laying Out Thickness

Finger joints, like all through joints, need careful setting out. If you want the finger joints to sit proud, lay them out for the thickness of the stock plus the amount you want them to sit proud. Proud finger joints will protrude from the corners of a carcase, as they do in the blanket chest shown on p. 124.

Flush corners can be made in one of two ways. The first is to cut them to the thickness of the stock plus about 1/16 in. so the finger joints stick through. After assembly, the excess thickness is removed. The disadvantage of this method is that you'll need to make clamping cauls to fit around the protruding fingers to get the best clamping pressure.

The second way to make flush corners is to use a pencil or strike a gauge line to lay out fingers that are slightly less than the thickness of the stock. I find this method much simpler to use, because I can clamp right over the joint with any type of covered or waxed caul (don't glue the caul to your work). Plus it's easier to knock off the proud long grain than it is to plane or sand off protruding fingers. With only a bare 1/32 in. to remove, a handplane or sander can do the work quickly, while also removing any nicks or dings that may have found their way into your pieces during assembly.

Halved Joints

The halved joint, which is a very simple and decorative joint, is really an oversize finger joint. Consider what the joint yields for a gluing surface when deciding if it's the best joint for a piece you're building. Most of the joint is end grain resting against long grain. Without much long-grain-to-long-grain gluing surface, the halved joint must be strengthened to provide the best staying power. Nails, pins, screws, and dowels are all options for locking this joint in place.

The beauty of the halved joint, of course, is how easily it can be shaped. And shaping the joint doesn't greatly affect its strength. This joint can be fastened to call attention to the contrast of the end grain against the long grain.

Cut halved joints by hand or on the table saw. Make the layout lines clear and all the cuts straight and square. Work from one side of the joint, cleaning and adjusting it as necessary; then mark to its mating partner.

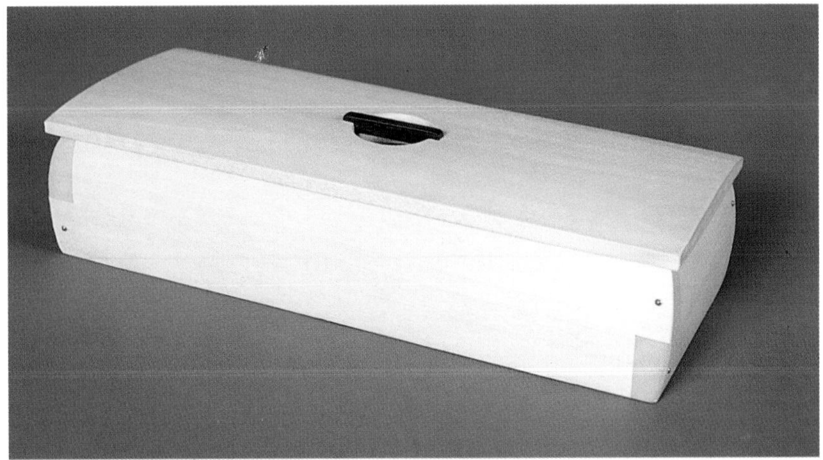

A halved joint gives an elegant simplicity to this small box built by the author.

Small boxes built with half joints can be easily shaped using hand or power tools, without sacrificing the strength of the joint.

Finger Joint on the Table Saw

Set up a dado blade as wide as the fingers you want. Be sure to make the carcase or box as wide as some multiple of the finger cut so you end up with full fingers at both edges of the piece. Use a miter gauge with miter gauge blocks fit to it to take up any slack (such as a Tru-Fit system), or put an auxiliary fence between two miter gauges. Then take a single pass through the fence with the dado blade (**A**).

Next, mill a piece of scrap that is exactly as wide as your dado package. This will be your indexing pin. Make it out of a hardwood, like maple, and long enough that you can cut it in two. Put one indexing pin in the slot cut into the fence by the dado blade (**B**).

Move the auxiliary fence over to the left of the blade by the thickness of one finger cut. Use the second indexing pin as a spacer between the blade and first pin to measure that distance precisely (**C**). Be careful here, because if you move the pin too far from the blade your fingers will be too tight. Have the second spacer pin pressed in right between the blade and indexing pin. Clamp or screw the auxiliary fence right in place here.

[**TIP**] **You can also take one or two passes with a handplane on the spacer to shrink the fingers slightly, making them a bit looser.**

Put the first board snug up against the indexing pin and take a pass (**D**). Then set the finger slot you just cut over the indexing pin and make the second pass (**E**). Continue with this process until all the finger cuts are made. Always keep the boards vertical and square to the saw table (**F**).

To make the matching cuts on the second piece use the spacer pin again. Set it between the indexing pin and the blade. Then place the board up next to it. This will set the board the proper distance away from the pin for its first pass (**G**). After making the first pass, just butt the finger slot right up to the indexing pin for the second cut. Continue as before, lifting the board up and onto the indexing pin after each pass has been made. The fit should be snug enough to hold together on its own, but not so snug you have to hammer it together (**H**).

E

F

G

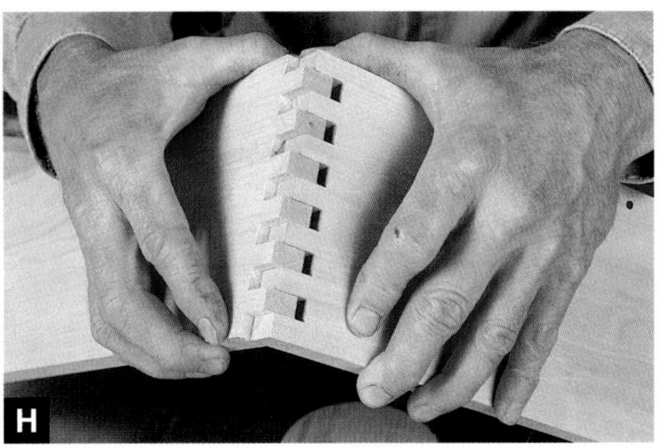

H

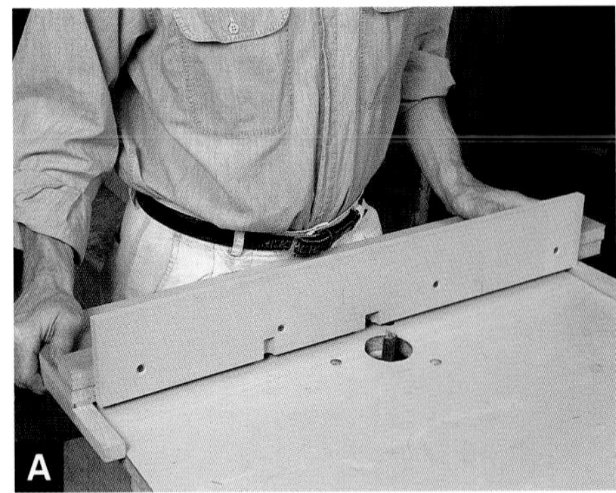
A

B

C

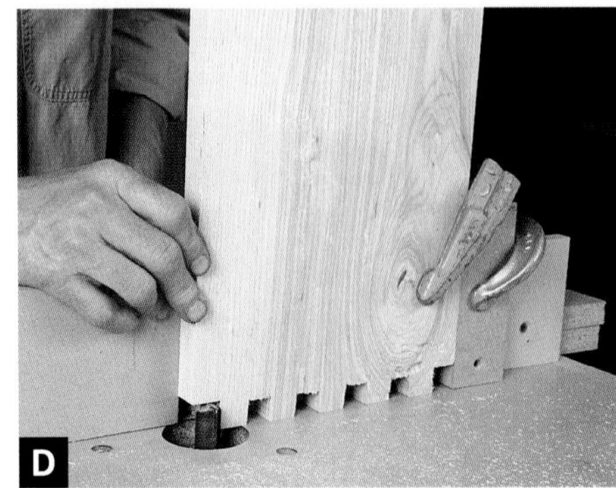
D

E

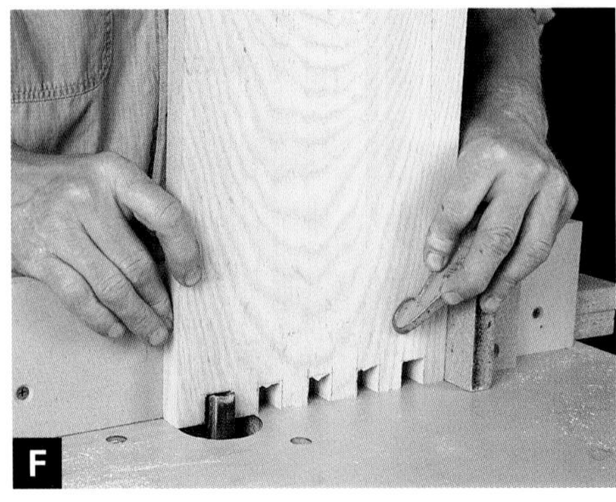
F

Finger Joint on the Router Table

To make larger or variably spaced finger joints or when working with wide boards, make the joints on the router table. Use a sliding table that fits around the edge of the router table or use a miter gauge, if you have a slot for one in your table (**A**). Mark out the finger joints on one board (**B**), and trim away most of the waste in the finger sockets on the bandsaw (**C**). Mount a wide straight bit in the router and set it for the full depth of cut.

Position the stock in the jig so it sets the first finger cut in exactly the right spot and clamp a stop block onto the jig. Then take a pass for the first finger. For symmetrical fingers, flip the board edge for edge to make the second cut (**D**). A spacer block will move the stock away from the stop for the second cut. Use a series of spacer blocks as wide as the finger cuts to move the board over for successive cuts (**E**). Use a spacer block exactly as wide as your router bit to index the matching cuts off the existing stop. Use paper shims between the stop and spacer to adjust the fit of the fingers (**F**).

Finger Joint with a Shopmade Template

To create finger joints of any size or pattern, make a template on the router table using the standard method.

➤ See *"Finger Joint on the Router Table"* **at left.**

You'll use a flush-trimming bit to cut the fingers, so make the template exactly the size of the fingers you want (**A**). When making the template for the wide finger slots shown here, you'll have to slide the board back and forth over the bit to establish the area between each finger.

Mark out the finger joints using the template. Rough out finger sockets first with the jigsaw (**B**). Then clamp the template onto your stock or stick it down with double-sided tape. Make sure the ends and edges line up perfectly. A top-mounted flush-trimming bit will cut the finger sockets out. Make one pass and lower the bit. The bearing will then ride on the part of the wood you just cut. Do the work in a series of passes to get to full depth (**C**). You'll need to clean up the round corners with a sharp chisel (**D**). Work from both faces in toward the middle.

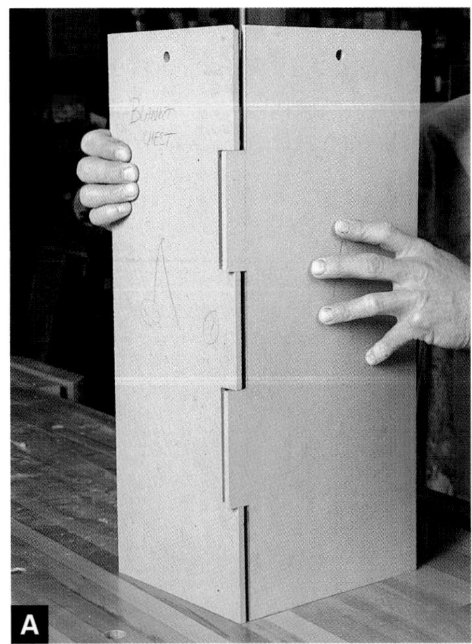
A

B

C

D

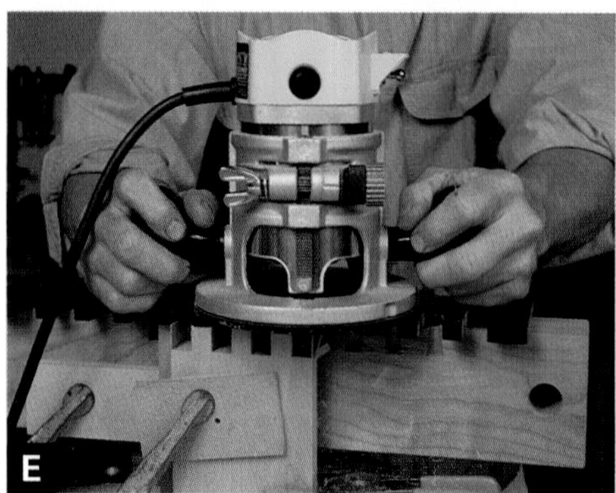

Finger Joint with a Keller Dovetail Jig

The Keller dovetail jig uses an offset trimming bit for cutting finger joints. For the joint shown here, use the straight finger side of the dovetail template. A top-mounted bearing on the 9/16-in.-diameter bit fits snugly between the fingers of the dovetail template. Put two boards together with their ends perfectly aligned but offset on their edges by 9/16 in. Use a 9/16-in. spacer to make this job simple (**A**).

Mark out the center of one board and place this center mark in the jig in the middle of a finger slot (**B**). Clamp the boards in the jig and clamp a stop onto the jig to index the rest of your finger joint cuts (**C**).

Mount the finger jointing bit in the router and set the bit depth to the thickness of the template plus the thickness of the stock less just a hair. Mark a piece of scrap with the proper distance to use as a ruler (**D**). Locate the base of the router on the template after switching it on. Then move straight into the wood with no tipping or lifting of the router (**E**).

Finger Joint on the Bandsaw

Don't rule out the bandsaw for making finger joints. It can do surprisingly good work if the blade is sharp and you have a good adjustable fence on it.

Lay out the finger spacing and mark out the joints. Also lay in a gauge line (**A**). You must be able to accurately and easily adjust the fence on your bandsaw to make these finger joint cuts. Clamp a stop on the fence to limit the depth of cut (**B**). Make the first finger cut. Flip the board and make the matching cut on the other side of the board. Now do all the cuts on the two sides or end pieces (**C**).

For the matching board, use a spacer between the fence and the board that's as wide as the bandsaw blade (**D**). Then make the matching board cuts. For more fingers re-adjust the fence and cut the rest of the fingers along with their matching cuts until all the cuts have been made.

Next, rough out the waste on the bandsaw. Use a narrow blade to make the tight curve cuts (**E**). Trim as close to the gauge line as you can freehand. Then set the fence to cut right to the line. It will be easier to do this on the board with a finger socket at its edges (**F**). Don't cut into the fingers. For sockets between fingers, put the blade as close as you can to the gauge line and let the blade start to cut. With a slow feed rate, it will eventually move over to the line (**G**).

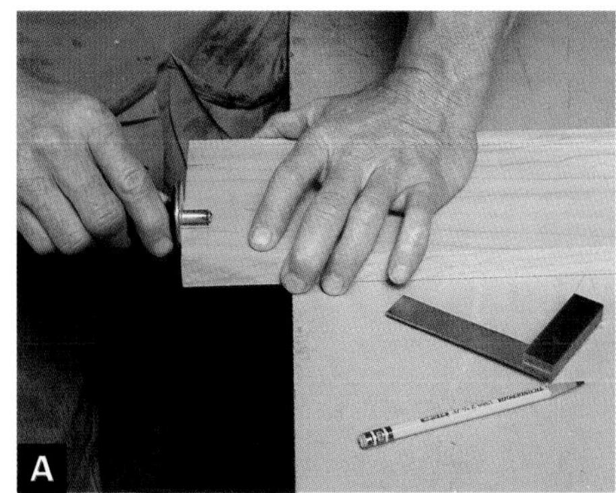
A

B

C

D

E

F

G

A

B

C

Angled Finger Joint on the Table Saw

The first step in making an angled finger joint is to crosscut the ends of the boards at their predetermined angle (**A**). Next, make a fence that will be set onto the miter gauge at that same angle. Mill some boards that will act as spacers; one long edge of the boards should be cut to the appropriate angle.

➤ See *"Finger Joint on the Table Saw"* on p. 128.

Screw the square edge of one board to the auxiliary fence of the miter gauge and the angled edge to a new auxiliary fence (**B**). Then set in another spacer board at a higher location until it just fits tight between the two fences. Screw this board in place. Then cut the fingers with a dado blade, indexing and using a spacer pin (**C**).

Hand-Cut Halved Joint

To begin a hand-cut halved joint, use a marking gauge to lay out all the shoulder cuts. These will run along the cross-grain of the boards. Mark both faces of each board and don't forget to mark across the edge that connects these faces. The cheek cut, which runs with the grain, can be just penciled onto the face. Do this for just half of each joint (**A**). Place the board in the vise vertically and low enough so there's no movement or vibration as you saw. Saw to the waste side of the line straight down to the gauge line (**B**).

After sawing, chop on the gauge marks with a chisel. Drag the chisel along until you feel it just drop into the gauge line. Make a light chopping cut; then turn the chisel over and clean up the cut. Make several more light passes and then move to the other face. Keep the cuts perfectly vertical. Then put the board in the vise and chop on the gauge line that's on the edge of the board. This will connect all three chopping lines together and form the plane that you want the shoulder to lie in (**C**).

Then use the saw again to saw close to the marks to remove the waste. Now use a wide chisel to clean the shoulder cut down to the gauge lines. You can undercut the shoulder a little, but do so away from any edge or face (**D**). Check the fit of the shoulder and cheek to see that they're square and flat (**E**). Then you can mark to the other mating piece with a marking knife. Push one board into a bench dog or stop, and butt the other piece right up to it, lining up its shoulder cut on the inside face of the other board. Be sure to indicate which corners go together so you can find this easily during assembly (**F**).

A

B

C

D

E

F

A

B

Halved Joint on the Table Saw

Before cutting a halved joint on the table saw, use a marking gauge to lay out all the shoulder cuts on one board. These will run cross-grain along the boards. The cheek cut, which runs with the grain, can be just penciled onto one face.

➤ See *"Hand-Cut Halved Joint"* on p. 135.

Set up the sawcuts off one board and the rest will be identical to it. Clamp a stop on the crosscut jig to index the shoulder cuts. I set these cuts for slightly less than the thickness of the stock. This makes it easier to glue up (**A**). Keep the stop close to the cut and not at the far end of the board. This way if any debris gets between the board and the stop it won't cause an errant cut.

For the vertical cut, do just the opposite so you don't trap the offcut between the stop and the blade (**B**). Otherwise, this will cause kickback. When making the cut, hold the board square to the stop and flat to the crosscut jig fence and table. Set the blade for a cut just under the shoulder cut.

Strengthened Halved Joint

The halved joint needs to be strengthened with pins, screws, or dowels because its gluing surface is minimal. Lay out and cut the halved joint using your preferred method.

➤ See *"Hand-Cut Halved Joint"* on p. 135.

Mark out hole locations on the joint with a scratch awl (**A**). Measure or eyeball their positions. Set the drilling depth by pulling the drill bit out only as deep as you need (**B**). You can also mark the drill bit depth with a piece of masking tape (**C**). Make sure when you drill that you line up the drill on the edge of the box as an aid so you drill straight into the joint.

Keep dowel diameters small to avoid short-grain problems at the end of the joint when you hammer in the dowel. Also make sure the dowel pin is as close to round as you can find. Dowels have a tendency to dry out oval over time.

Cut the dowels a little long. Then chamfer their ends with some sandpaper.

Use a toothpick to apply glue to the holes; glue put on the dowels will get scraped off as the pins enter the holes. Drive in the dowels using a metal hammer. You'll know to stop pounding when the sound of the blows changes from a dull thud to a pinging sound (**D**).

After the glue has set, trim off the ends of the dowels with a saw or chisel. Don't take too big a bite with the chisel, as this may cause tearout in the dowel below the surface of the surrounding wood. Just pare away at an angle, taking small passes. Do this from several directions until the dowel is flush with the surface of the box (**E**).

A

B

C

D

E

Mortise-and-Tenon Joints

Stopped Joints

Through Joints

A SERIES OF STOPPED mortise-and-tenon joints across the width of the panels creates a carcase with strong but hidden joints. These joints offer greater strength than a simple housed dado, because they have more long-grain-to-long-grain gluing surface. To take advantage of the long grain, however, there must be several tenons across the width of a panel.

If you take the joints through and wedge them, you create not only great strength but also a design detail in your cabinets. Make the tenons long enough for loose wedges to avoid shearing out the short grain left at the end of a tenon.

Grain Direction

Cut the mortises by hand with a mallet and chisel or by machine with a plunge router, hollow-chisel mortiser, or drill press. What you must remain aware of when laying out the joints is the direction of the long grain of each of the pieces, both for the mortise and for the tenon.

The vertical piece, which contains the mortises in the type of carcase construction discussed here, will actually show more end grain than long grain. This end grain is almost useless as a gluing surface for the joint. Racking stresses will knock the cabinet or bookcase apart in short order. So your job is to optimize the long grain by putting in as many mortise and tenons as you can to maximize the gluing surface.

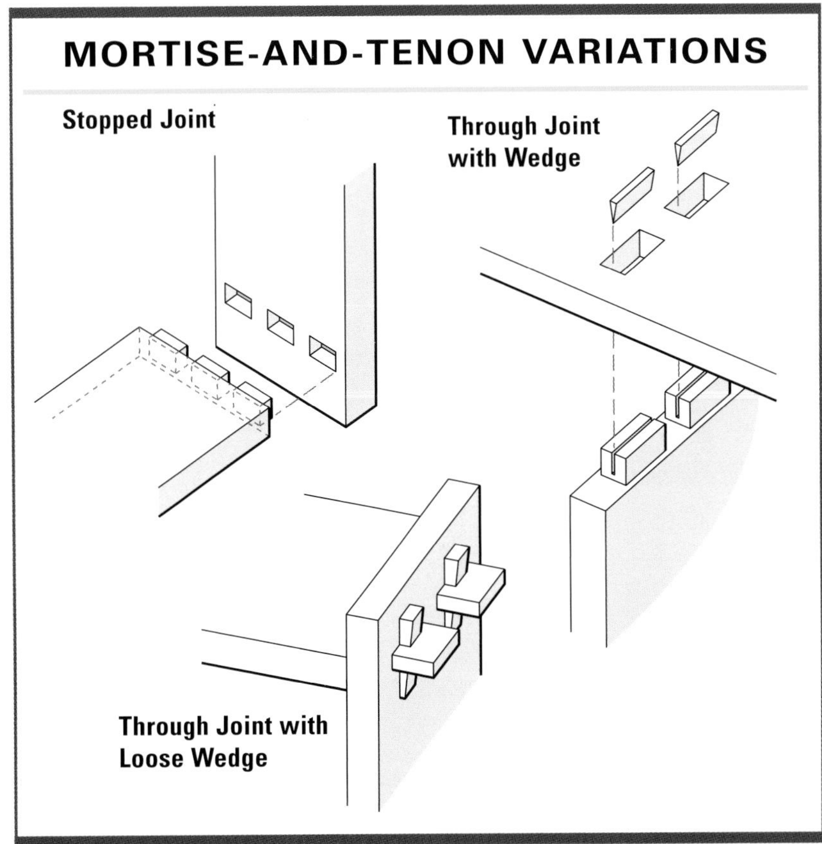

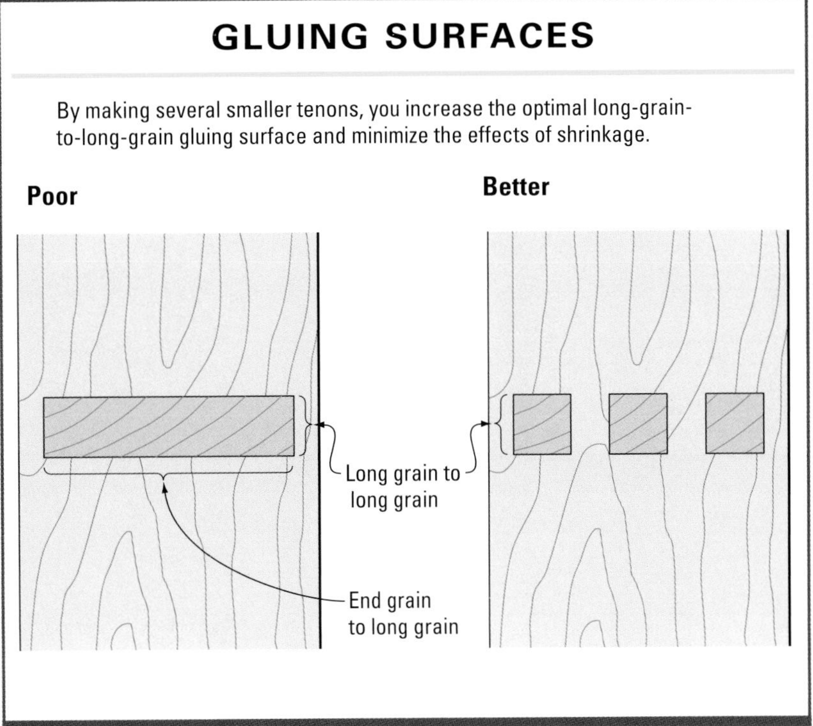

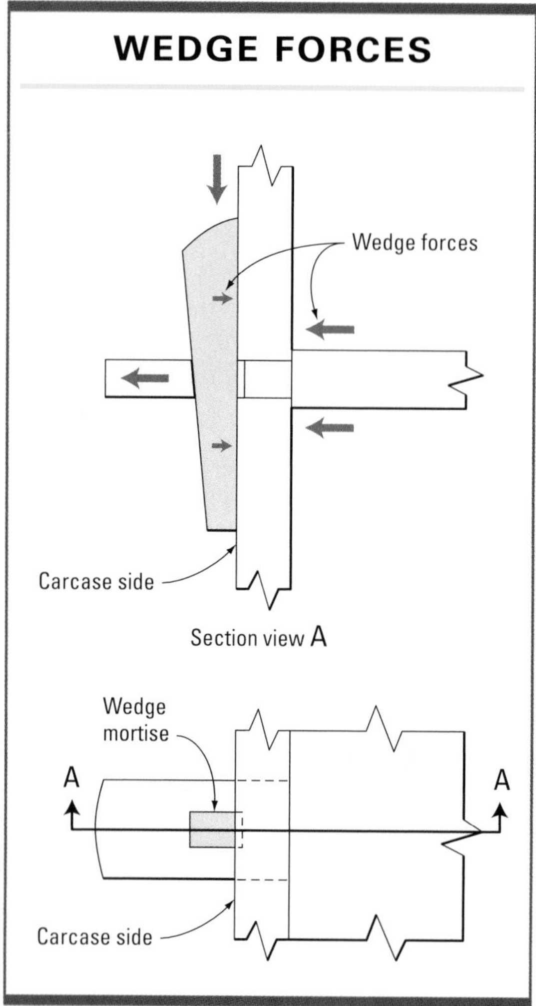

Always make sure there's enough wood at the end of the tenon to prevent the short grain from shearing off.

Strengthening Through Tenons

Through mortise and tenons are greatly strengthened by the addition of a wedge. With this method, the joint can fit loosely, because the insertion of the wedge locks everything in place, like the parking brake on a rusted-out '54 Chevy. The wedged joint provides pressure at three places. The back of the wedge pushes against the outer face of the carcase, which in turn pushes against the end of the wedge mortise. The wedge also pushes down into its mortise. All this force pulls the shoulders of the tenon in tight to the inside face of the carcase. The result is a joint that locks rigidly in place.

The only note of caution is to keep enough wood at the end of the tenon to prevent any shearing of the grain when the wedging force is applied. Although it took about 25 wallops with a hammer to break the tenon shown in the photo at left, it did break. The wedge was eventually forced through the mortise to the point at which the short grain at the end broke out. When the short grain is even shorter, there's a much greater risk of shearing it out when banging home a wedge.

Hand-Cut Stopped Mortise

To begin hand-cut joints, lay out the mortises on the panels. Double-check the matching panels to make sure your layout lines are correct (**A**).

Next, drill out the waste with a bit and brace. Don't forget about the lead screw on the bit; you don't want that coming through the other side. Mark the bit or take only light cuts (**B**).

Finally, square the mortises out with a chisel that's as wide as the mortise (**C**). Lever out the waste when you get deeper into the mortise, but be careful not to round over the edges of the mortise (**D**).

A

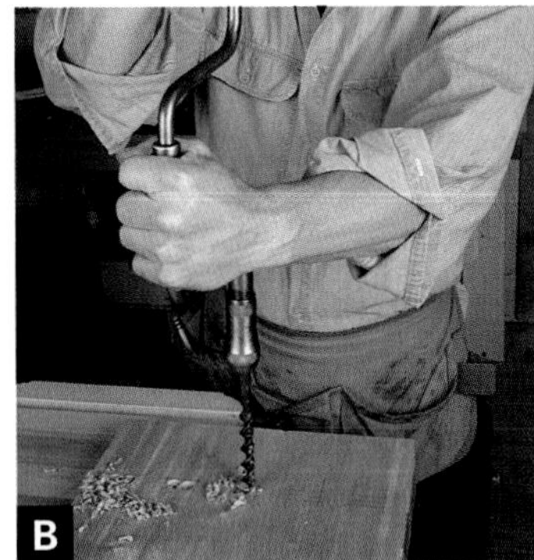
B

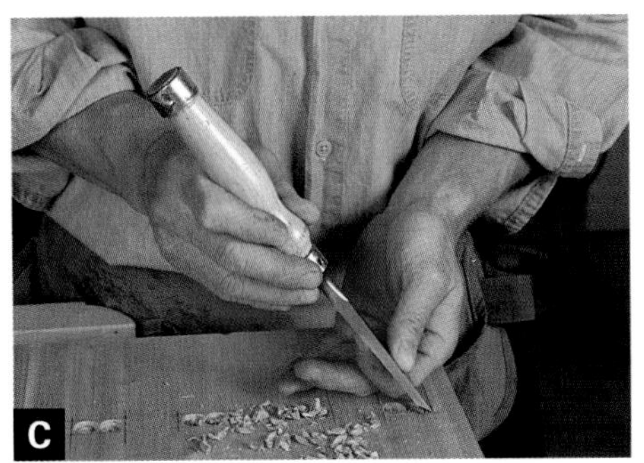
C

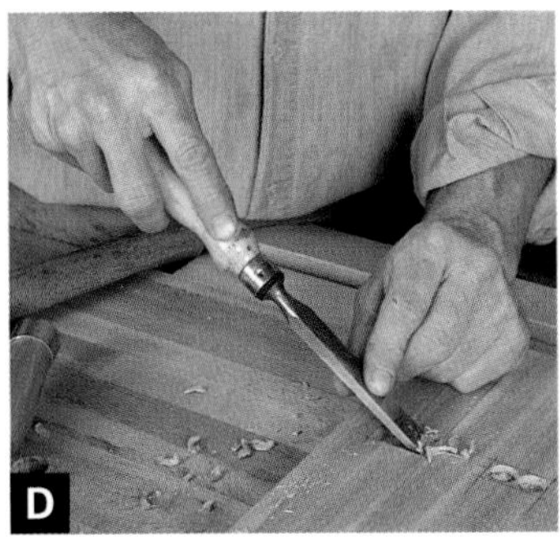
D

Stopped Mortise with a Plunge Router

The first step for cutting stopped mortises with a plunge router is to lay out the mortises on the panel. Clamp a straightedge or right-angle jig to the panel. Remember to figure in the offset of the router base to the cutting edge of the bit (**A**).

Line up the bit over the end of the mortise with the bit properly rotated; then mark out the position of the router base on the panel. Move up to this mark with each pass (**B**). Or stop the cuts by using a piece of scrap clamped to the panel to act as a stop for the router base (**C**). Make the passes moving into the rotation of the bit.

Chop the mortise corners square. Check your work with a "drift," which is a piece of scrap as wide as the mortise. Take off material where the drift fits too tightly or not at all (**D**).

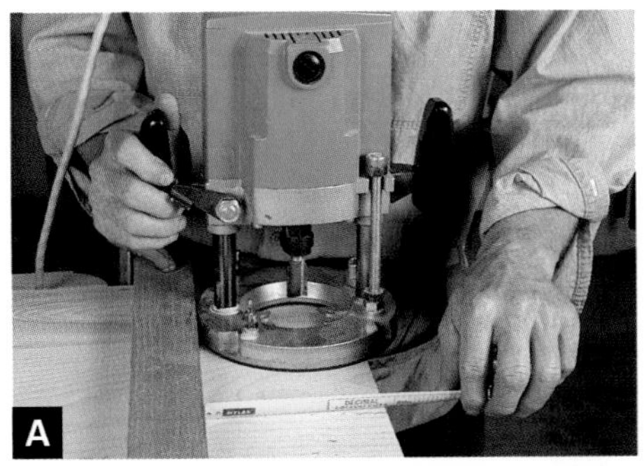
A

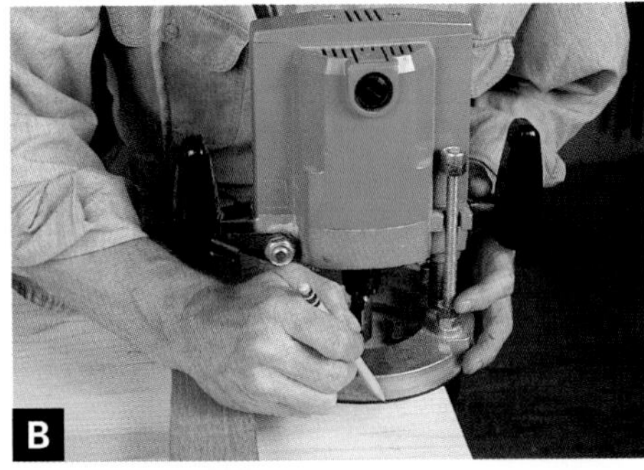
B

C

D

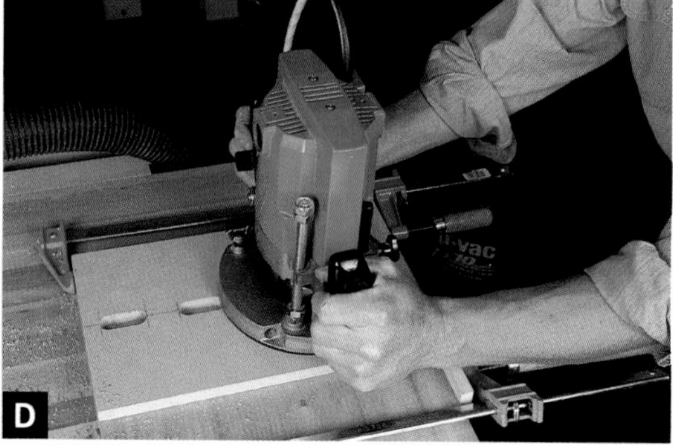

Stopped Mortise with a Router and Template

Template work requires knowing the offset of the bit's cutting edge to the template guide. Do the math or measure the distance and figure this into the template. The width of the mortise will be set by the router bit diameter (**A**).

Mill a piece of ½-in. medium-density fiberboard (MDF) or plywood as wide as the side panel. Lay out a centerline on it and mark out the position and length of the mortises. Set up the router table with a straight bit as wide as the template guide.

Clamp the fence at the proper distance from the bit and put stops in place to limit the cut (**B**). Rout through the template for each mortise. For evenly placed mortises, cut one mortise slot, flip the template, and rout the matching slot. For easier starting, predrill one end of the mortise with an undersize bit. Make certain the template guide slides easily in the template. Wax it if necessary.

Glue and screw a fence to the template. This makes it simpler to locate the cuts on the workpieces. Predrill the template for the screw holes, particularly on the edges of MDF (**C**).

Use the template guide and a plunge router to cut the mortises (**D**). Use an air hose to blow out any debris that collects in the template or have a vacuum handy to suck away the chips.

Stopped Mortise with a Hollow-Chisel Mortiser

Hollow-chisel mortisers are limited by the distance from the hollow chisel to the column. Make sure the mortise can fit under the bit. Set the bit inside the hollow chisel, close enough to cut but not so close the two will burn. It's a very fine line between the two. All bits like this benefit from a good sharpening before cutting (**A**).

Mark out the mortises and set up a fence to index the cuts. Then set the bit depth of cut. Use some spacer blocks to help hold the workpiece down if the clamp doesn't fit right on the surface of the wood. The clamp is useful, particularly when you are trying to get the bit out of the mortise.

First make the two outer cuts in the mortise (**B**). This way the bit will always have some wood to center on. Otherwise, the bit will try to wander as you plunge for the cut. Keep the hollow-chisel exit hole pointed to the side so the hot chips don't fall on your hand (**C**).

A

B

C

A

B

C

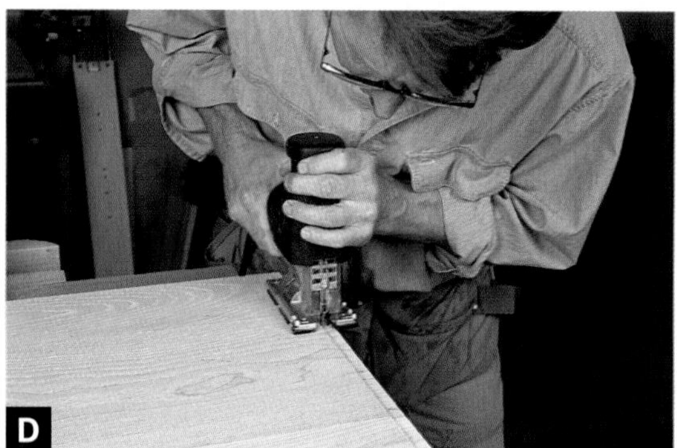
D

Stopped Tenon on the Router Table

Stopped tenons can be cut on the router table. First, set up a wide bit to cut the tenon faces and to establish the shoulder of the joint. Have a backer board at the ready to eliminate tearout at the backside of the pass (**A**). Since the outside corner of the tenon will be cut off, make a nibbling cut on the second face to check the fit to the mortise. You can check it with calipers or place it in the mortise to see if it fits (**B**).

Lay out the tenon position off the mortises and cut the cheeks by hand with a backsaw. Be sure to not saw past the shoulder (**C**). Then clean between the tenon cuts with a jigsaw (**D**). Get as close as you can with the cut, but leave the final cleanup for the chisel. The two router-cut shoulders will give surfaces to index the chopping cuts.

Through Mortise with a Router and Template

To cut a through mortise using a template, set your router bit to stop just short of the outside face of the panel. Place a thin piece of cardboard, or a piece of scrap the same thickness, on the bench next to the workpiece. Don't forget to put the template in place. Set the router on the template and plunge down to the cardboard shim. Lock the depth in place and double-check it once for comfort (**A**).

Rout from the outside face in when using a template to cut through mortises. This way, if by chance you do rout all the way through, any tearout will occur on the inside face of the piece. Rout all the mortises and then clean them carefully. If your depth setting is accurate, you should be able to break through what's left of the wood with a pencil (**B**).

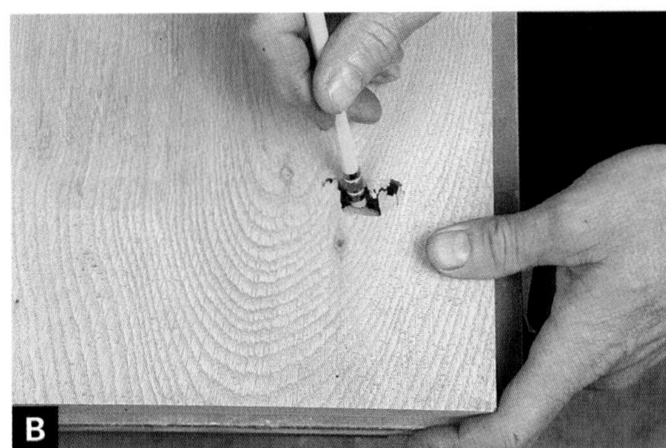

Square the corners of each mortise with a chisel from both faces. Do the inside face first to get your practice strokes in before making the more visible cuts on the outside face (**C**).

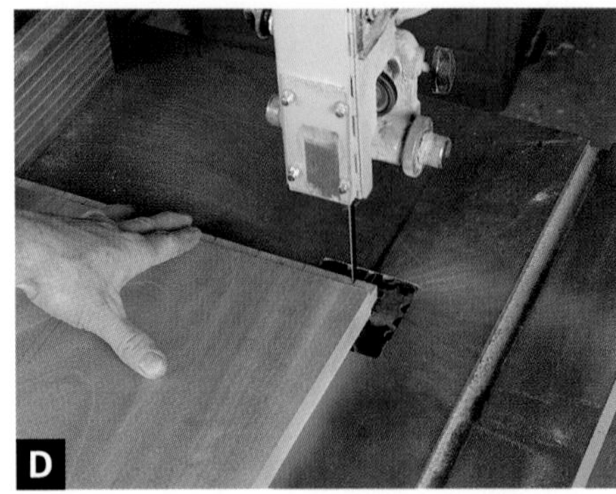

Through Tenon with a Plunge Router

The first step for cutting through tenons with a plunge router is to set up the router with a wide bit and fence. Have an auxiliary fence in place as well to help support the cut. Cut the first tenon face on all the boards of the case. Hold the fence tight into the end of the board, especially at the beginning and end of the pass. Keep good pressure down on the router with your hand over the board (**A**).

Cut the other face of the tenon in the same fashion. Check the fit of the tenon on one end before committing to the entire cut. If you leave the joint a bit oversize, fit it to the mortises with a shoulder or bullnose plane (**B**). When the joint fits tight along its height, you're only halfway there. This part of the joint is long grain to end grain so it's not important as a gluing surface. Make it fit close, but don't sweat too much over this direction.

Now mark out the more important tenon cheeks off the mortises. Hold the boards on edge to register them (**C**). Cut the tenon cheeks on the bandsaw, being sure to not saw past the shoulder line (**D**). Also trim out most of the waste between the tenons, cutting close to the shoulders.

Next, reset the bit depth to rout between the tenons, establishing the full shoulder (**E**). Place the router over a slot between tenons, hold the fence in tight, and plunge down through. Or you can push the bit down to depth and slowly nibble away from the side at the waste. Make sure you don't run into the tenons. You'll find that the wood and bit tell you which method is preferable in a particular situation. Finally, clean the round corners at the tenons with a chisel.

Loose Wedged Through Mortise and Tenon

You can strengthen a mortise-and-tenon joint by using a wedge. After fitting the through tenons in the mortises, mark the face edge of the panel onto one of the tenons. The fit of the tenons can be relatively loose. The strength of this joint comes from the wedge (**A**).

A

Next, lay out the mortise for the wedge so the mortise actually extends inside the case. This way the wedge won't run into the back side of its own mortise.

➤ See *"Strengthening Through Tenons"* on p. 140.

The mortise for the wedge needs to be cut on an angle to match the angle of the wedge.

➤ See *"Making Loose Wedges"* on p. 149.

B

Make a router template out of some ¼-in.-thick plywood or MDF. Glue a thin angled board to the bottom side of the template to angle it the proper amount. Cut this board on the table saw at about 7 degrees. Pencil in a centerline on the template for the mortise (**B**). Then rout out the template slot on the router table, remembering to figure in the offset of the bit to the template guide. Try to use a smaller-diameter bit so the round corners aren't too large.

(Text continues on p. 148.)

C

VARIATION

Use a pencil to mark the center of the tenon; then line up the template centerline to the mark and clamp it in place. Next, rout for the angled mortise. Chop the mortises square after routing, but remember to keep the 7-degree angle (**C**). Since the back side of this mortise extends into the case side don't worry about its being angled, too. It won't help or hurt the joint. Place a sliding bevel set at 7 degrees near the mortise and gauge your chiseling off of it. Put a slight bevel around the entrance and exit of the mortise to prevent any tearout that could occur when you drive the wedge through.

Another means for reinforcing through tenons is to insert a wedge or wedges into a kerf cut into the tenon.

➤ See *"Mortise-and-Tenon Variations"* drawing on p. 139.

VARIATION To avoid making an angled mortise, use double or folding wedges in a straight mortise. Mortise straight down through the tenon using a plunge router with a template and template guide. Remember not to angle the template. Or you can just mark out the tenon and chop the mortise in square from both faces. Then use two wedges with their angles facing each other. Their straight backs will fit against the straight wall of the mortise and the case, but their wedging action against each other will lock the joint fast.

Making Loose Wedges

To work effectively, the wedges and their mortises must be cut at matching angles. Some examples of wedge shapes are shown in drawing **A**.

First mill the wedge stock to the proper width so it fits easily through the wedge mortise. Then make a simple taper jig for the bandsaw to cut the wedge angle. The jig rides against the bandsaw fence (**B**). Cut a notch in a piece of scrap at the wedge angle and as far into the scrap piece as you want the wedge to be thick. Place the wedge stock on edge into this notch and set the fence for the proper distance to cut the wedges.

Clean and trim the wedges with a handplane set up in a vise. Use a push stick to save your fingertips (**C**). Or you can trim the wedges with a chisel or carefully on the belt sander.

You may want to leave this type of mortise and tenon unglued so you can knock the joint apart, but you can also glue it up solid. Bang the wedges in with a metal hammer until the sound changes from a thud to a ping. When that happens, you know you've gone far enough (**D**).

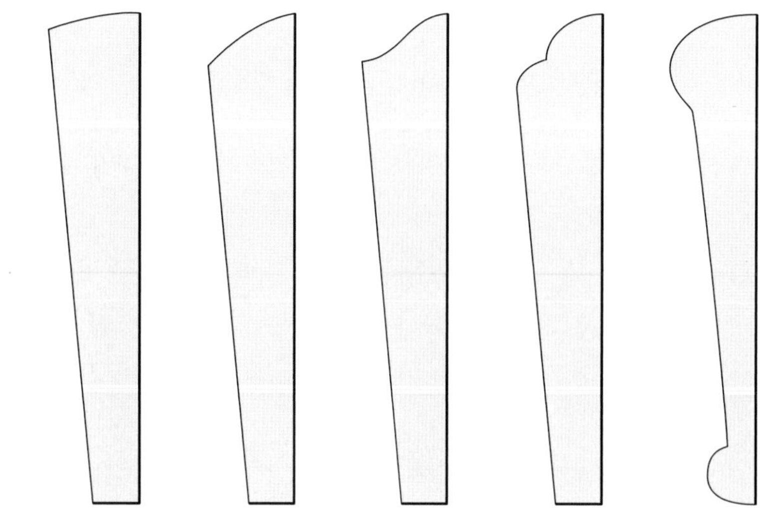

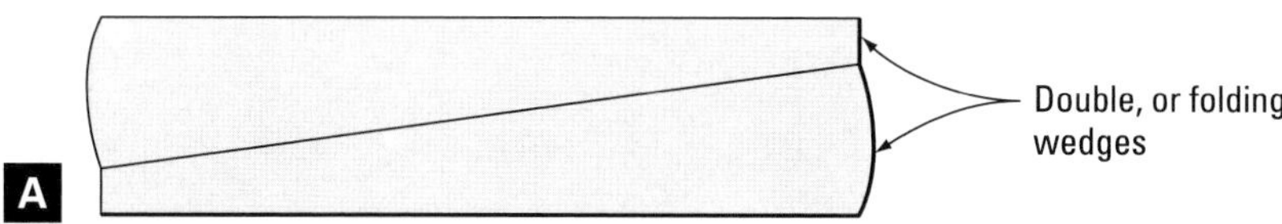

A

B

C

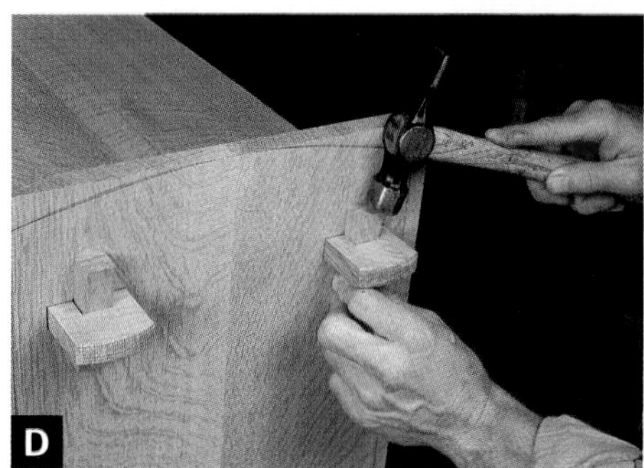

D

Dovetail Joints

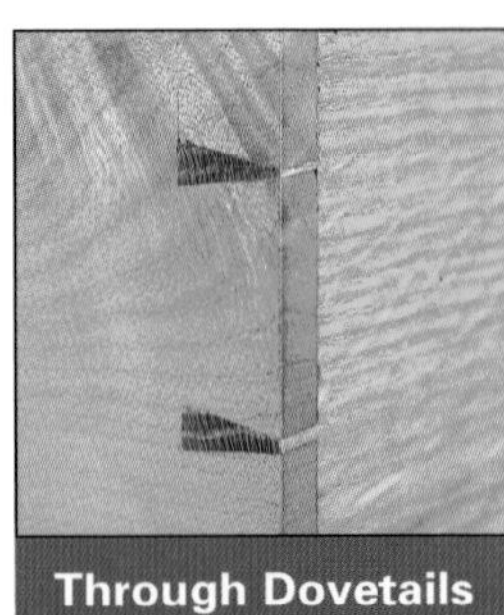

Through Dovetails

Half-Blind Dovetails

Full-Blind Dovetails

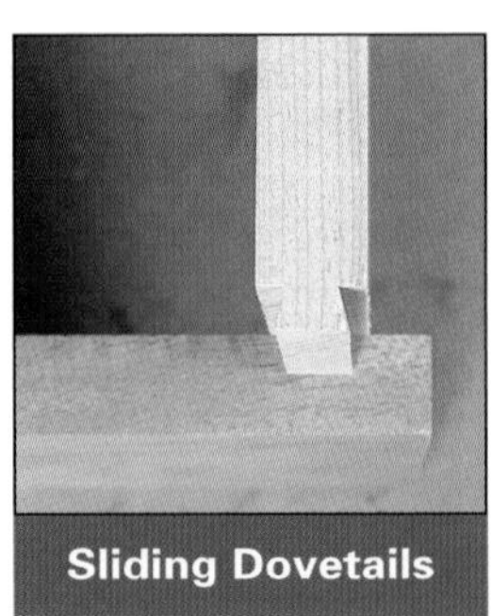

Sliding Dovetails

Slot Dovetails

DOVETAIL JOINTS ARE the standard of joinery excellence. Coupling the mechanical resistance of their tails and pins with their long-grain-to-long-grain gluing surface, dovetails are the strongest joint available for carcases. From delicate jewelry boxes to large cabinets, this joint provides both a fine look and great strength.

For drawers, no joint comes close to matching a dovetail for strength or visual appeal. That's why dovetails are found on pieces centuries old and are still used today for the finest work. Of course, you can staple drawers together or rabbet and pin them, but for a drawer that will last, choose dovetails. Not only are they strong but they speak volumes about your work and your concern for craftsmanship.

The strength of dovetails lies in their flared tails and angled pins, which provide a mechanical connection that holds even when an adhesive gives way. More tails and pins means more resistance and gluing surface.

Dovetail Placement

From one side of a dovetail joint, the flared tails and the angled end grain of the pins are visible, giving the piece a distinctive look. From the other side, both tails and pins look straight so they're difficult to tell apart. To make drawer parts, you'll cut the tails into the drawer sides and the pins into the drawer front and back. This gives you the best resistance when you pull the drawer out from its housing. A cabinet will have tails in the vertical pieces and pins in the top and bottom. This way the tails resist the pull of gravity.

Dovetails add an elegant touch to this small box.

These small pins are a mark of craftsmanship.

The parts of a dovetailed drawer laid out as they would be assembled. Note that the pins are on the front and back of the drawer, and the tails are on the sides.

➤ DOVETAIL DESIGN GUIDELINES

The strongest arrangement is when the tails and pins are exactly the same size. When superior strength is not required and a more refined look is desired, make the tails roughly two to three times the size of the pins.

- When hand cutting, it's more convenient to make the pin size just bigger than the width of a chisel. Then the chisel will fit between the tails to chop out the waste.
- Tail and pin angles should be kept between a range of 1:8 and 1:5 to avoid any short-grain problems at the tips of a tail.
- Lay out half pins at the corners for most dovetail joints. This gives the best strength.

TAIL AND PIN LAYOUT

Regular Spacing

For regularly spaced pins, draw in the centerlines for the half pins. Put a ruler on one centerline and divide up the remaining space by the number of tails you want.

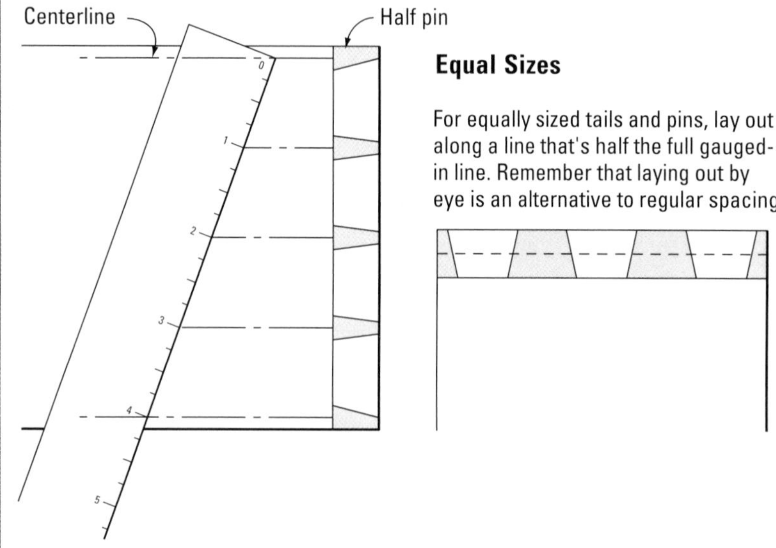

Equal Sizes

For equally sized tails and pins, lay out along a line that's half the full gauged-in line. Remember that laying out by eye is an alternative to regular spacing.

Dovetail Variations

The through dovetail is the signature of fine craftsmanship. But because dovetails are used in a wide variety of applications, they have been modified to fit different purposes.

The through dovetail, though strong, can always be seen on both sides of the carcase. This is an advantage if you want to show off your work and want to use the exposed dovetail as part of the design. Sometimes, however, you want to hide one side of the joint, such as on drawer fronts. That's where the half-blind, or lapped, dovetail proves its merits.

HALF-BLIND DOVETAILS

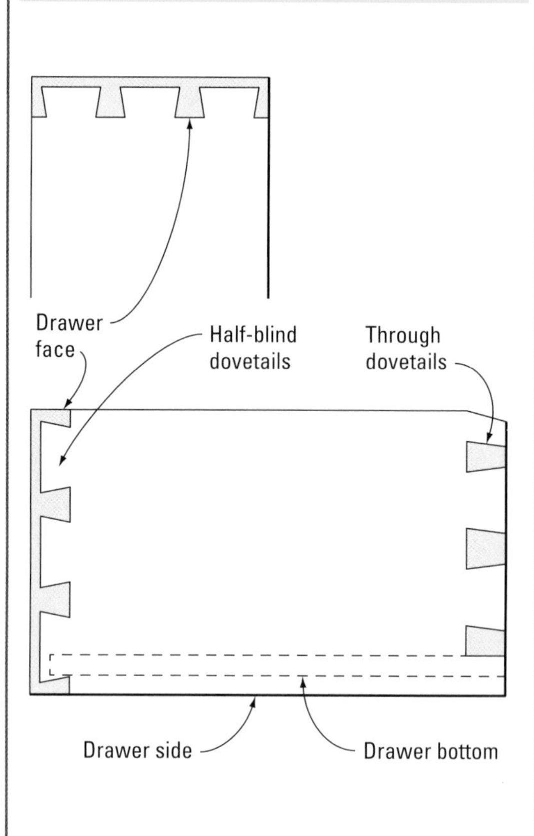

Full-blind, or secret, dovetails are hidden from view and are used in situations where great strength is required without the intrusion of a highly visible joint. Secret double-lapped dovetails were once commonly used on box and tray construction, yielding plenty of strength without revealing the cause. They can also be used on carcases where only the thin end grain line of the lap will show from either the top or side of the case. Their fancier cousin, the mitered blind dovetail, was and still is used for putting together very fine casework, such as desks, boxes, and clocks as well as the details of fine cabinetwork like plinths and cornices.

Sliding dovetails are used in both carcase and drawer construction. In carcases, they help prevent the bowing out of case sides.

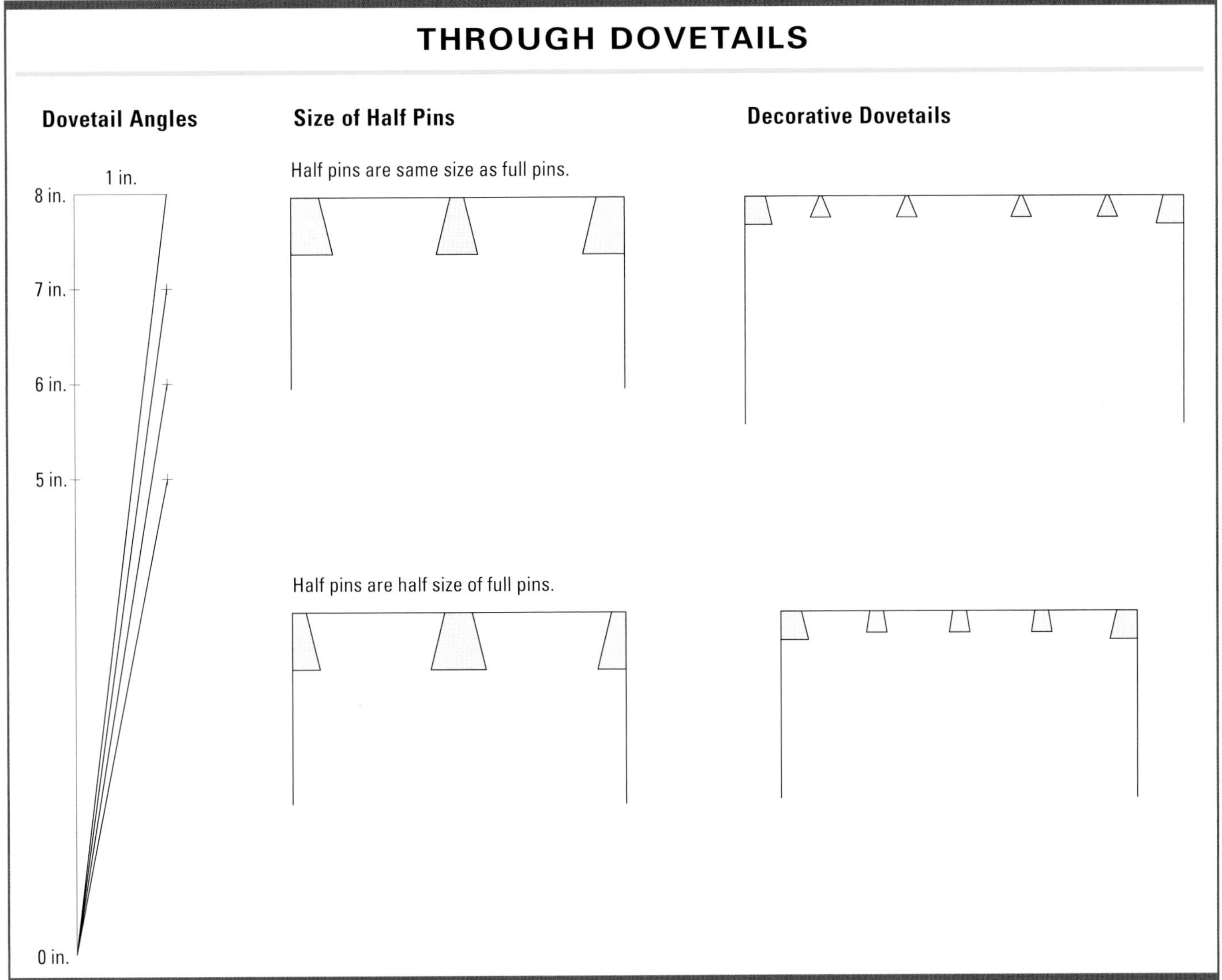

FULL-BLIND DOVETAILS

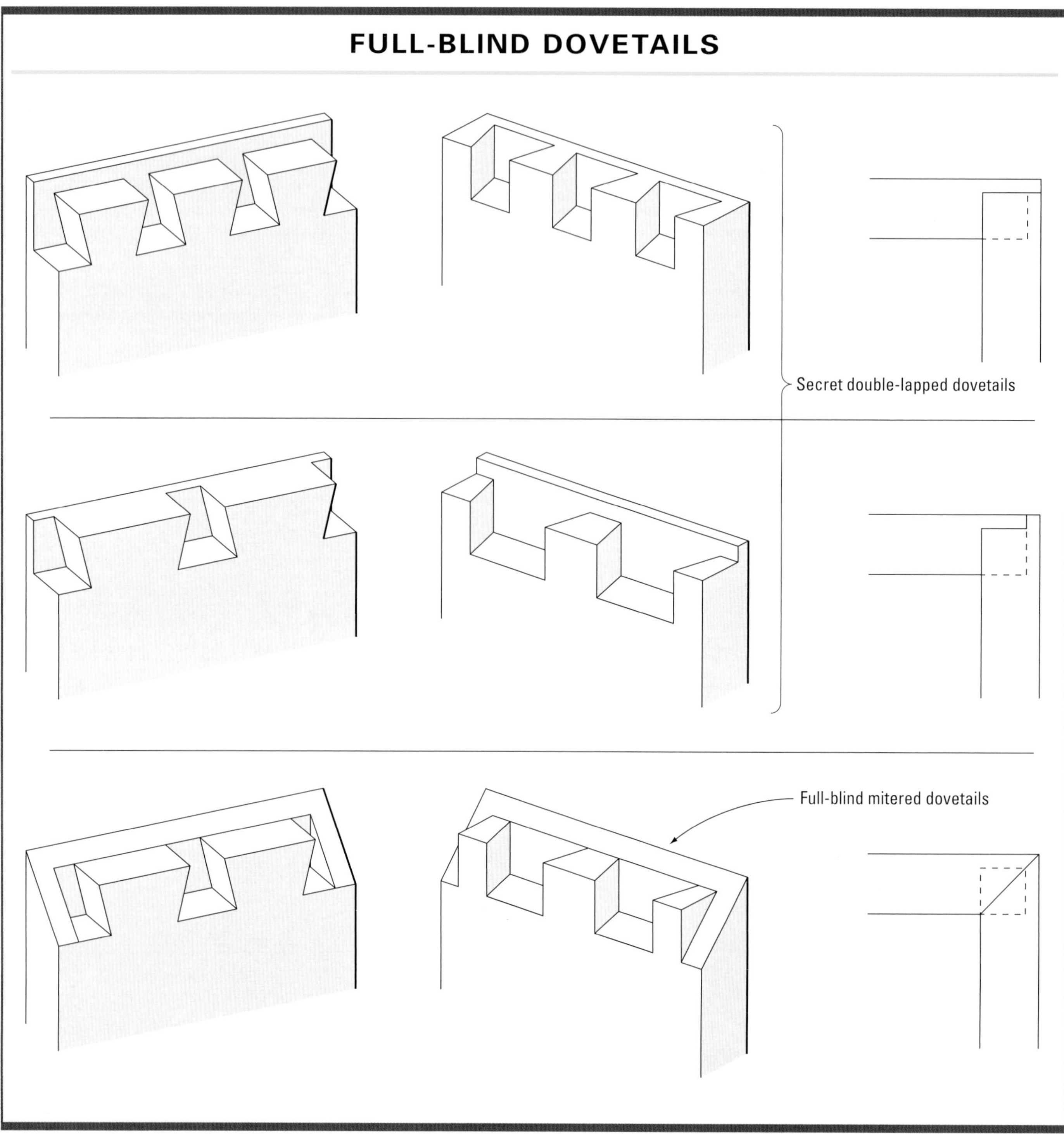

Drawers that require an overhanging front can be built with sliding dovetails for the drawer box. These will allow an overhang that conceals, for example, drawer slides.

Slot dovetails are used for carcase construction in which smaller members help hold the case together. These short dovetails slide into place at the top of a leg or the corners of a solid carcase side to lock a case in place. The top rails then also provide a means of attaching tops to carcases.

SLIDING AND SLOT DOVETAILS

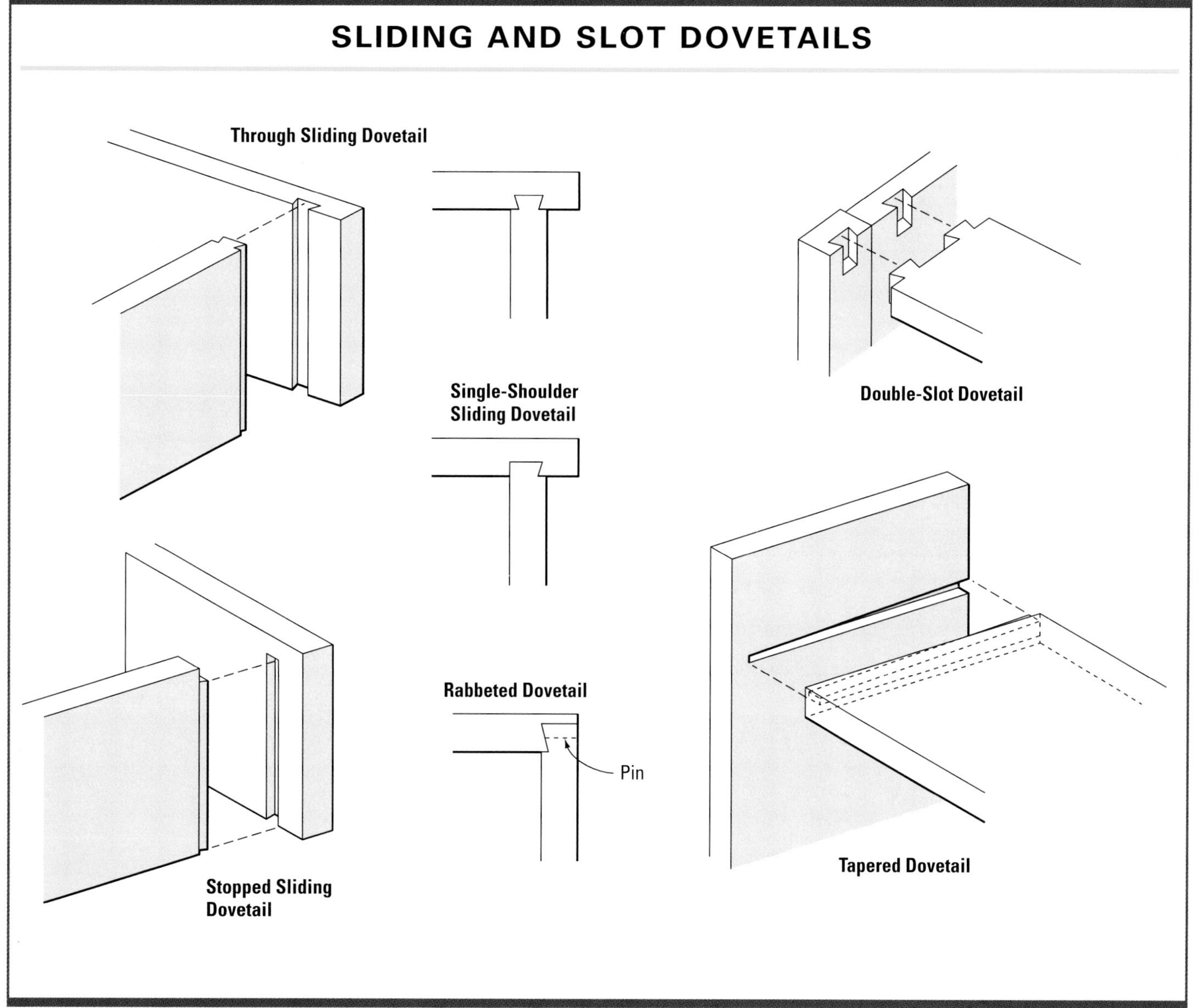

➤ TAILS OR PINS FIRST?

A tempest in a teapot controversy rages over which to cut first: tails or pins. As always, try both methods and find the one that makes the better sense for you. I cut tails first on most of my dovetails. One advantage to this is that it allows me to cut the tails on several stacked pieces that are held together in a vise. But with impossibly small decorative pins and for all blind dovetails, you must cut the pins first. For all other dovetails—through and especially half-blind dovetails—I find that the tails are easier to design, lay out, and cut. But half of the woodworking world doesn't agree! Experiment to see which method you prefer.

Tips for Hand Cutting Dovetails

With practice anyone who can handle a chisel and can saw to a line can learn to hand cut through dovetails. Making them fit just right can be achieved with a couple of refinements during cutting.

Some people like to angle the tail board in the vise, so that the line of cut is perpendicular to the bench or floor. While this practice allows you to cut straight down, I recommend learning to cut at the correct angle while keeping your tail board straight in the bench. It's very important that you keep the saw square to the board during this

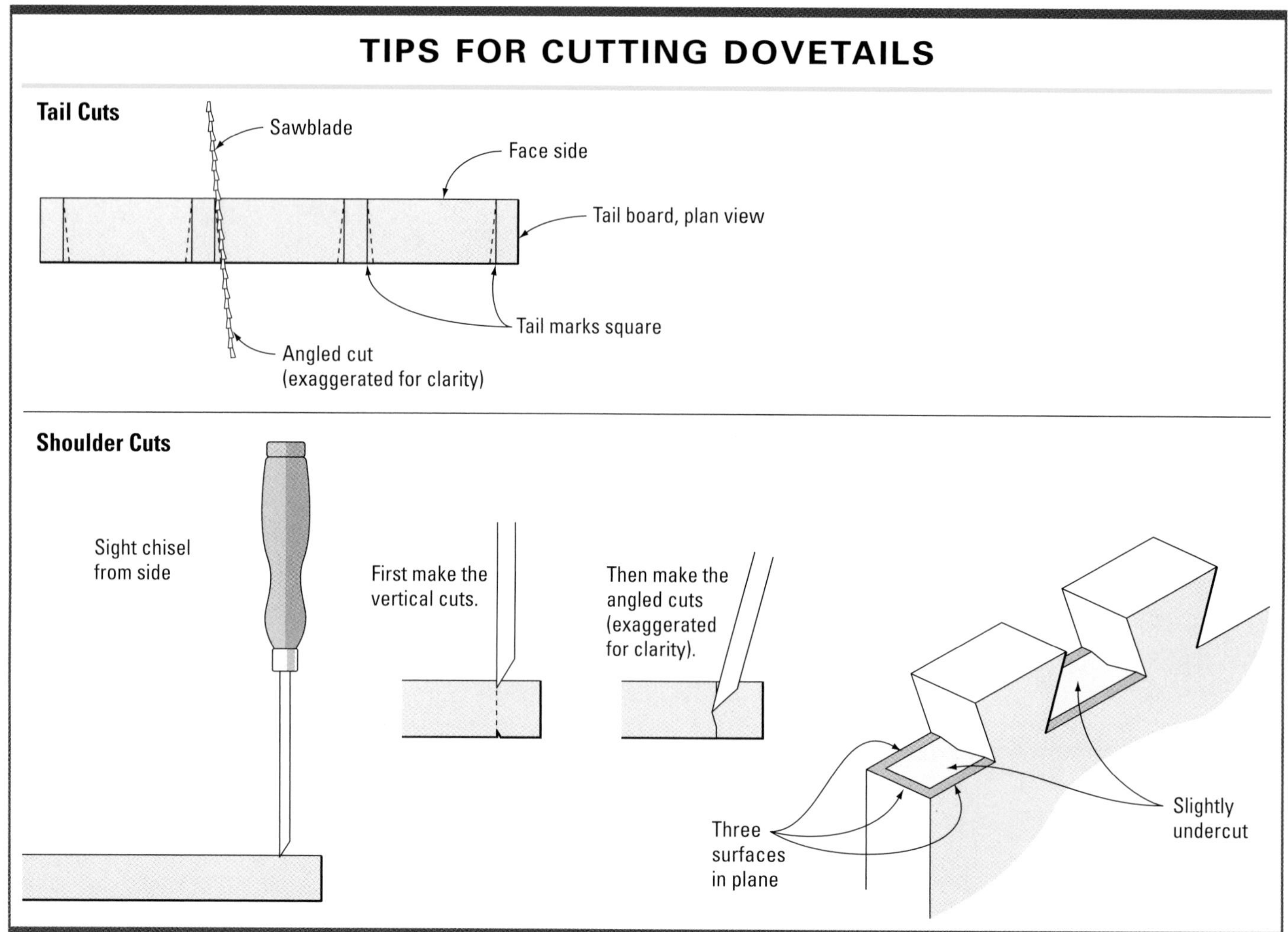

process, or you'll end up with gaps in the final joint.

To make the meeting point of the pin base to the tail board look crisp, it's important that you cut cleanly to the gauge line. One way to ensure this is to first make a light vertical cut with the flat side of the chisel against the gauge line. Next make an angled cut from the waste side toward the line. Keep chopping down this way until you've established a crisp shoulder, then continue chopping out the waste.

Slightly undercutting the waste toward the center helps the joint seat properly. High spots prevent the joint from going together, and since this is end grain, there's no advantage in terms of gluing surface.

Dovetail Fixes

Dovetails can be challenging to cut accurately, especially in a wood like pine or fir. Softwoods are actually harder to work in than a consistently grained hardwood, because they can be crushed easily. One thing to keep in mind for your hand-cut work is that everyone makes little mistakes when sawing. Fixes are often required even for the steadiest of hands. Here are some simple tricks.

Angle the cut of your tails ever so slightly so the tail is angled in two directions. Then when the joint goes together it will compress the fibers for a perfect fit. This is a technique you can, of course, use for hardwoods as well; but some of those woods will not "squish" together at all. So choose your angle of error very carefully. By angling your sawcut just a tad, you'll cut tails that are a hair wider at their outside face. When you clamp them home, they will fill up any small indiscretion.

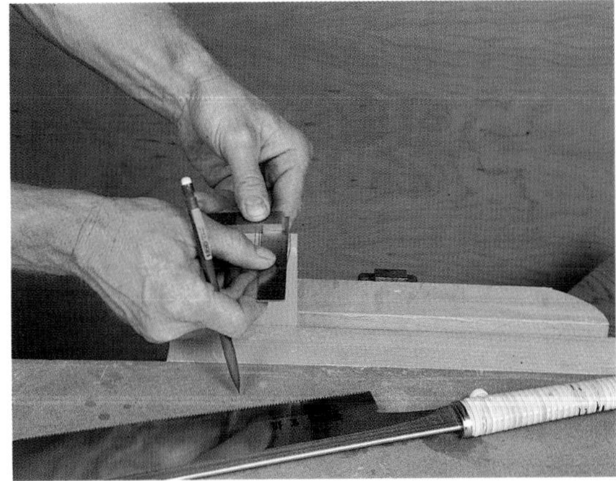

In softwoods, you can angle the cut of your tails very slightly so the tail is angled in two directions. When the joint is assembled, it will squeeze the wood fibers for a tight fit.

To fix an undersize pin, glue on a piece of scrap wood and clamp it with masking tape. When the glue dries, resaw the pin to the correct dimension.

Repairing mistakes is easy *if* you keep your scrap wood. Never ever throw away the scrap from a project until it's complete. Especially keep all the offcut ends from your dovetail parts, as these are perfect matches in grain and color. You can glue slivers of wood onto dovetail pins that were cut too small. Tape works well as a clamp or use a spring clamp. Then recut the joint once the glue has dried.

Router Dovetail Jigs

Hand cutting dovetails is only one option. There are a number of good dovetail router jigs on the market. Some are capable of cutting only through dovetails, whereas others can cut only half-blind dovetails. The most versatile can cut both these dovetails and several other joints as well. But the real difference among the jigs is how they make the cuts.

When using a through dovetail jig, like the Keller jig, you cut one board at a time using first a dovetail bit with a top-mounted bearing and then a bearing-mounted straight bit. These bits follow the jig template fingers so the size and spacing of the joint are set.

The Keller dovetail jig uses a template and bearing-mounted bits. Each board is cut separately.

DEPTH OF CUT IN A HALF-BLIND JIG

Raised Bit

Bit

Pin

Router bit

Pin socket

Raising the dovetail bit makes the pin narrower, but the size of the pin socket doesn't change.

Lowered Bit

Bit

Pin

Pin socket

Lowering the dovetail bit makes the pin wider.

The crucial part here is setting up the jig accurately to its backer board. This determines the width and thus the fit of the pins. The depth of cut is not the crucial factor for accuracy once the jig is set up.

Combination jigs, like the Omnijig, can cut both through and half-blind dovetails. These jigs use template guides that run in finger templates.

The Leigh jig uses a finger template with a variety of different dovetail cutters. The finger assembly is adjustable vertically and horizontally in and out to the jig for different thicknesses of stock. It also adjusts for the size tail and pin you want, and it flips over 180 degrees for each of the tail and pin cuts. In other words, it is infinitely adjustable and complex.

First set these jigs up for the tail cut; then, with a change in the position of the finger template, they automatically cut the pin to match. The advantage of these jigs is that you can adjust for the spacing and number of tails and pins. You can also fine-tune the fit of the pin to the tail. Getting a perfect fit requires some fiddling, which is where the head scratching comes in. But for versatility and results, they're hard to beat—once you've mastered the system.

A half-blind dovetail jig places both boards in the jig with the inside faces of each board showing. You use a router fitted with a specific dovetail bit and a template guide; the guide rides in the template when you make the cuts. The joint size and spacing are set. These jigs require very careful bit depth adjustment because the tails and pins are both cut at once. Set the bit too low and the pins are cut too tightly and the joint won't fit. Set the bit too high and the joint is loose. The best strategy for using one of these jigs is once it's set up and the bit is cutting perfectly, *don't ever move the bit!* If you don't have one router you can dedicate to half-blind dovetails, however, make up a height block that will index your bit depth each and every time you pull out the jig.

Warming Up

It seems that woodworkers are among the few who are silly enough to launch into some critical procedure—such as cutting dovetails in an expensive wood—without the benefit of warming up. But warming up is about as universal a technique as we have for physical endeavors. We stretch before running, we draw large circles on a drawing pad before sketching, we practice throwing and catching before the big game. Everyone warms up, except those of us who cut dovetails.

Before you start cutting into your expensive hardwood, give yourself 5 minutes to practice. I've included a little exercise to help you warm up. Use this exercise for just 5 minutes before launching into your work and you'll thank yourself later.

➤ **See *"The 5-Minute Dovetail"* on p. 160.**

If you haven't cut dovetails for a while, it will help your hands and eyes remember the process. If you're about to cut your first dovetails, the exercise will help you learn the steps for cutting this joint easily and will improve your confidence.

The Omnijig cuts both through and half-blind dovetails.

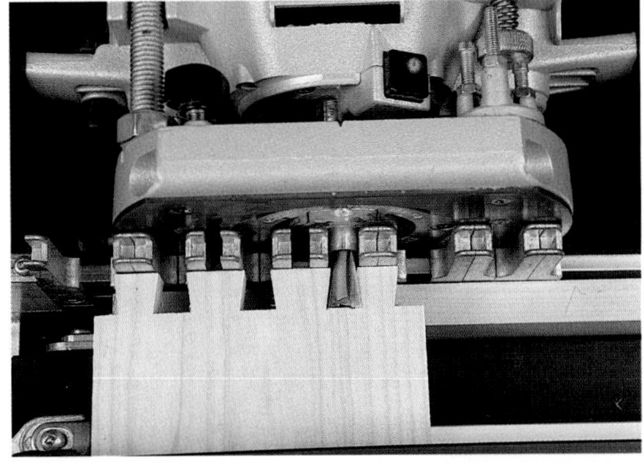

Adjusting the fingers on the Leigh jig lets you created variable spacing, giving a more pleasing look to your through dovetails.

Half-blind-dovetail jigs use a template, template guide, and dovetail bit. The boards are placed inside for the single-pass cut across both of them.

The author's collection of "5-minute dovetails." These were cut by students while they were learning the basics of hand-cutting dovetail joints.

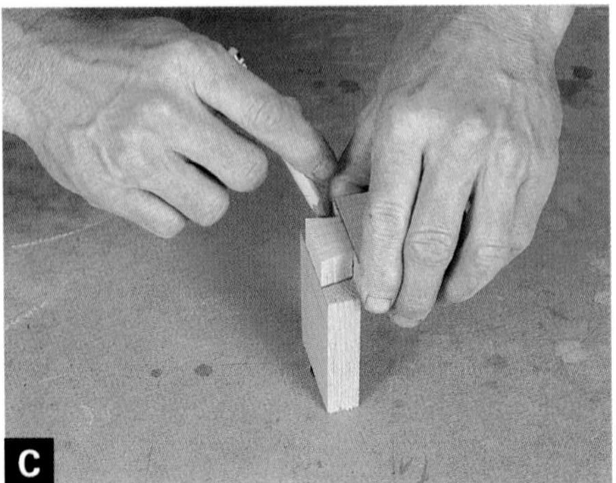

The 5-Minute Dovetail

Use this exercise to warm up before cutting your actual workpieces. You will need a dovetail saw, a pencil, a chisel, and mallet.

First, mill two small pieces of stock: ⅝ in. by 2 in. by 3 in. Use a soft hardwood, such as soft maple or alder. Mark out the thickness of each piece on the other with a pencil (**A**). Then place one piece vertically in a vise.

Begin by sawing the tail. Saw down to the pencil line but at a slight angle. Remember: straight across and at an angle down to the pencil line. Cut first one side and then the other. Don't worry about how the tail angles turn out. You will mark out whatever their shape is onto the pin piece. Then turn the piece in the vise and make the straight shoulder cuts (**B**).

Mark out the tail board onto the pin piece (**C**). Put a pencil mark on what wood needs to come out. Also mark the face of each piece for ease of reassembly. Remember that you're making a right-angle corner here. Then place the pin board in the vise vertically.

Saw to the waste side of the lines down to the pencil line. You'll saw at an angle but straight down. When you've made the cuts for the tail socket, notice that you've also created two half pins (**D**).

With a chisel, chop out on the pencil mark to remove the waste. Chisel from both faces in toward the middle and use a cleaning pass every once in a while to remove the waste (**E**). Fit the tails and pins together.

Hand-Cut Through Dovetail

To begin hand-cut through dovetails, set the marking gauge for slightly less than the thickness of the stock. Put lines around the four sides of the tail boards but only on the faces of the pin boards. The half pins don't require any gauge lines at the outside edges (**A**).

A

Set up a sliding bevel for the tail and pin angle. For best results, keep the angle ratio somewhere between 1:5 and 1:8. Lay these angles out on a square-edged board. Measure up 5 in. and over 1 in. to get a 1:5 slope (**B**). Lay out the tails on the gauge line. Mark out all the tails on the face sides of the boards. Then square the lines across the end grain as well. Mark these angles down the far side of the board with the sliding bevel as a double-check for your sawing.

B

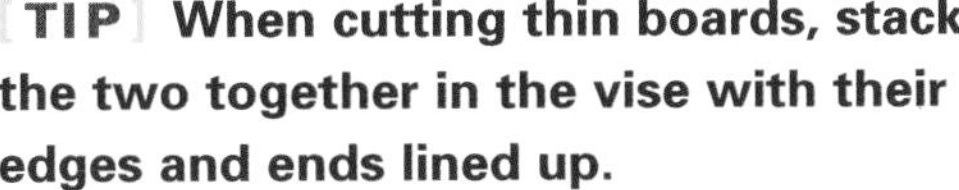
[TIP] When cutting thin boards, stack the two together in the vise with their edges and ends lined up.

Cut the tails with a small-kerf dovetail saw. Keep the board straight in the vise and learn to angle the saw for the tail cut. Start the cut on the far edge, cutting in the reverse direction of the sawteeth to establish the cut. Then gradually lay the saw down across the end of the board, making sure it's square across the board. Next, tilt the saw to cut the tail angle and saw just down to the gauge line (**C**).

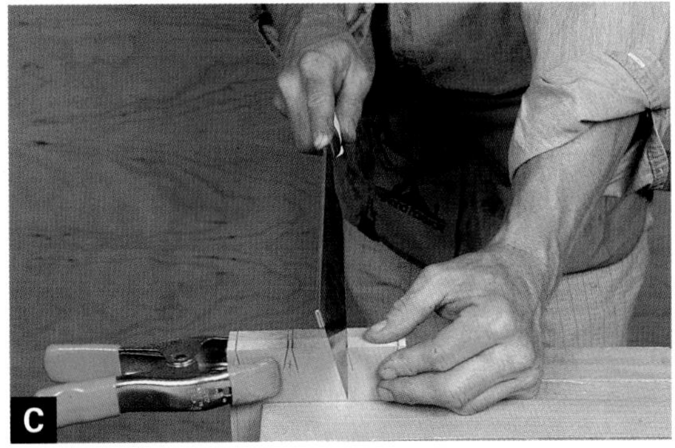
C

Remove the waste by holding the chisel right on the gauge lines. Sight to the side of the chisel when chopping. This way you can see that you're holding the tool truly perpendicular for the start of the cut. Make sure the corners of the tails are

(Text continues on p. 162.)

D

E

F

G

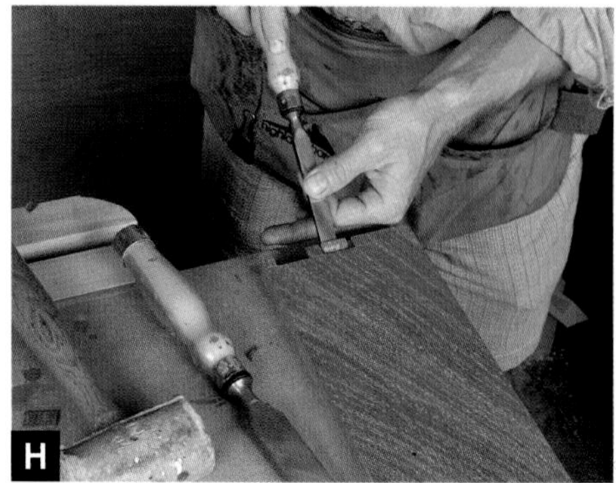
H

I

clean and the shoulders are flat or even a bit undercut. After completing a few chopping passes, angle the chisel just a little to undercut the shoulders (**D**).

Chop the half pin sockets from both faces and the edge to establish three flats all in one plane. Then saw off the waste close to these cuts down to the tail. Finish up by paring the end grain down to those lines. You can undercut the shoulder just past the first chopping marks as well (**E**). Get all the tails right and ready before moving to the pins.

Mark the tails out onto the pin board. Mount the pin board high enough in the vise so you can easily line up its edges with the tail board and another flat board. I put a handplane on its edge and rest the tail board on it. Use a sharp marking knife to transfer the tail shape onto the end grain of the pin board (**F**). Draw square lines from those marks to the gauge lines.

Cut the pins at an angle to the face but straight down the board to the gauge line (**G**). Remember to stay on the waste side of the line with your saw.

Chop away the waste on the pin board with a chisel. Make the first chopping passes very light; flip the chisel bevel side down and clean up the waste. Make sure the board is securely fastened to the benchtop with a clamp or pushed up against a bench dog or stop (**H**).

A well-cut dovetail joint should go together with hand pressure and have just enough room for the glue, which swells the wood a bit. After checking the fit, use a scrap block and hammer or use a dead-blow hammer to carefully take the joint apart (**I**).

Through Dovetail with a Router and Keller Jig

When using a Keller jig, first cut the tails using the provided bit. It rides in the template with the straight fingers. The dovetail bit cuts the sockets for the pins as it creates the tails. Its size and angle matches the size of the angled fingers of the pin template. Thinner tail boards can be stacked together for gang routing. Use a stop against the edge of the board to index subsequent tail cuts (**A**).

The bit depth is important but not crucial for the successful use of this jig. Set the bit depth for just less than the sum of the thickness of the jig (½ in.) plus the thickness of the stock.

Use a wood block marked with the proper depth setting as a ruler to easily span the wide hole in the router base (**B**). Mark the center of the tail board on its end and center it between two of the fingers. Clamp the board in place.

A

B

WARNING Always double-check the bit depth before starting to rout. Make sure the bearing will contact the finger template and that the bit cannot run into the stop or clamps.

(Text continues on p. 164.)

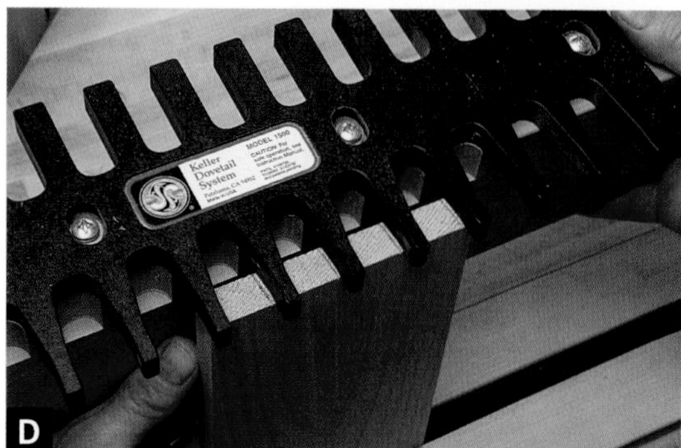

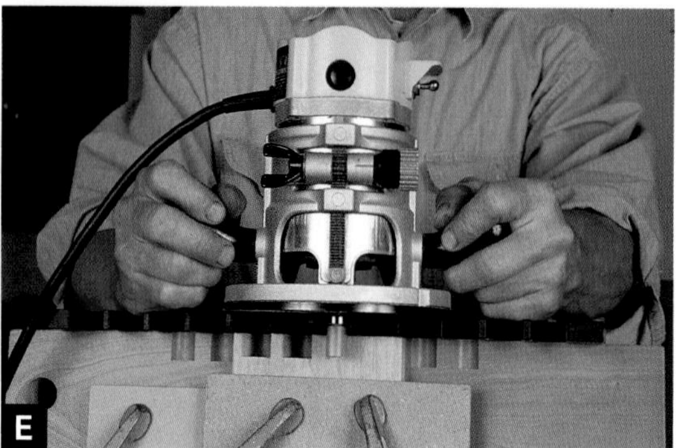

After cutting the tails, place the pin board in a vise and set the tail board onto it. Use a handplane on edge or a piece of scrap to raise the tail board to the height of the pin board. Then lay out the tails onto the pin board with a marking knife (**C**).

The backer board that the Keller jig sits on is the crucial part of the setup. Its placement determines the width of the pins, and this should be done when you first get the jig. See how the tail shapes, which are marked on the end of the pin board, match the finger angles of the pin template (**D**). Moving the angled fingers in or out in relation to the backer board establishes how tightly or loosely the tails will fit.

Mount a straight bit in the router to cut the pins. Clamp the pin board in the jig with its face side facing away from the jig. If you use a stop to index all the pin cuts, you'll need to mark out only one board (**E**).

! WARNING Be careful to set the router down first at the edge of the jig and then move it into the workpiece. Do not come down onto the jig with the bit turning. And make sure the router doesn't tip or rock in the middle of the cut.

Through Dovetail with a Router and Leigh Jig

For the Leigh jig, all the boards are cut vertically for through dovetails. Clamp a spacer board as thick as the stock in the top of the jig (**A**). Set the finger assembly in place to lay out the joint and rotate to the through-pin mode. The pin mode shows tapered fingers on the outside of the template closest to you. It's easier to visualize and lay out the joint this way, even though you'll cut the through tails first. Clamp the tail board in place right under the finger assembly and up against the side stop (**B**).

Adjust the fingers for the number of tails you desire and the spacing that looks good to you. Move a few extra fingers over at the right end of the board just to support the router base during the cut (**C**). Tighten down all the guide fingers.

Next, flip the finger assembly over 180 degrees to the through-tail mode. This mode is color coded and is marked with a through-dovetail icon (**D**). Note that the fingers are straight and will match the spacing laid out with the pins. Move the scale to the ≤1 mark and lock the finger assembly in place. Mount the proper template guide and dovetail bit in the router and set the bit depth to slightly less than the thickness of the

(Text continues on p. 166.)

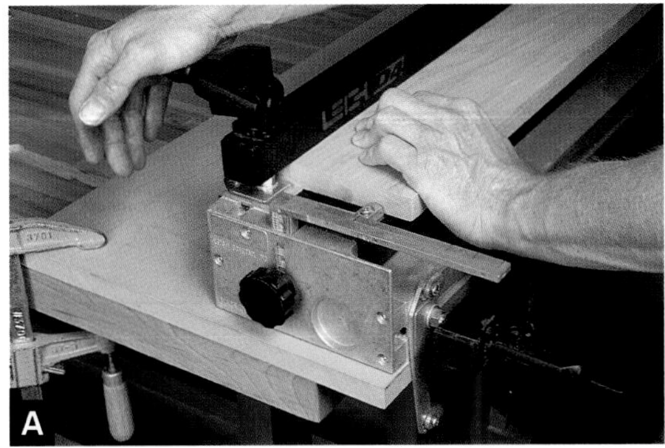
A

B

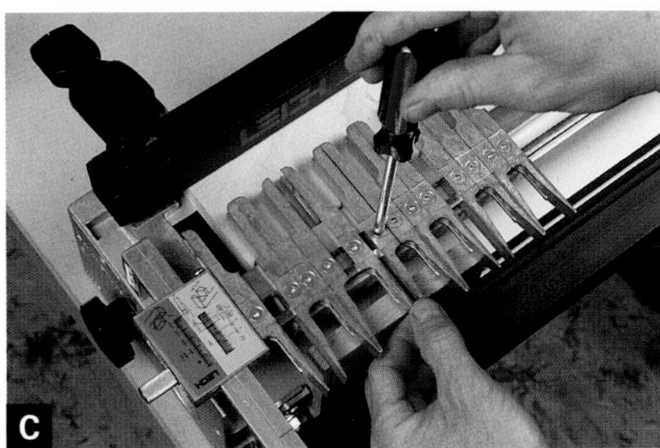
C

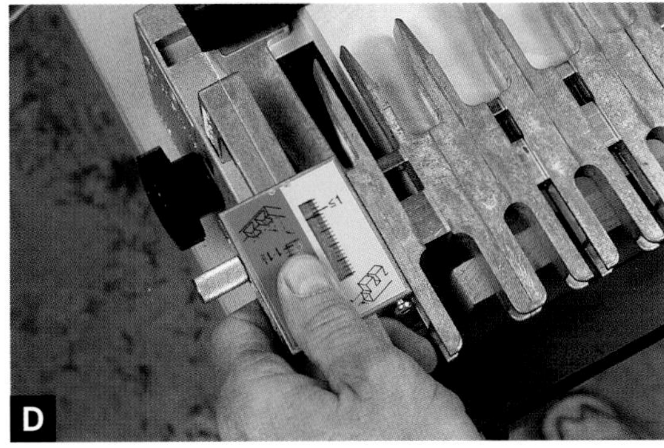
D

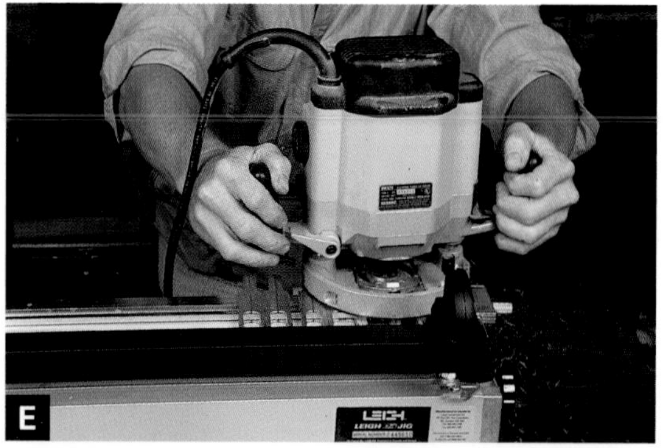

E

F

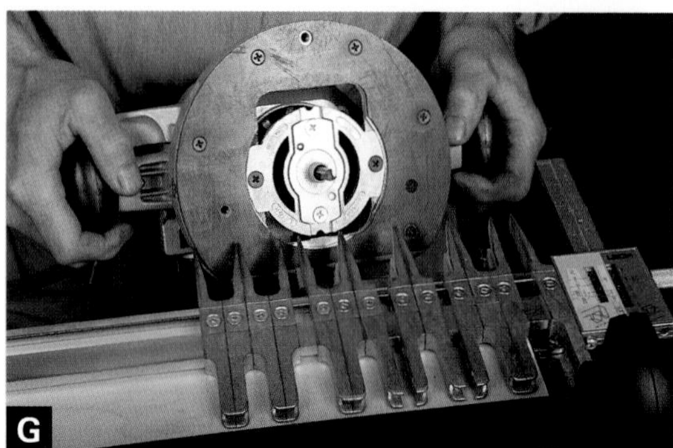

G

H

finger assembly plus the thickness of the stock. Keep the router base flat on the finger assembly throughout the cut (**E**). Rout all the tails now.

Rotate the finger assembly back 180 degrees to the pin mode (**F**). Don't loosen or adjust the guide fingers. The fit of the joint can be adjusted by moving the finger template in or out in relation to the jig. Because the guide fingers are tapered, the farther out from the jig the finger assembly sits, the wider the pins will be. Adjust the finger assembly for a tight fit, based on the pin width as indicated on the scale. Don't forget to take into account variations in bit and template guide size. Mount a straight cutter in the router and use the same template guide as before (**G**). Rout from left to right, moving slowly in between each of the fingers.

Make a practice cut in scrap wood and check the fit. Record the scale setting when the joint fits the way you want it to (**H**).

Through Dovetail with a Router and Omnijig

The Omnijig cuts through dovetails with the boards clamped vertically in the jig. You'll need to adjust the finger template in and out to the jig because both the tail and pin template fingers face outward, in the same direction. Their placement, which is set by bracket spacers, determines whether you're cutting tails or pins. Bracket rod nuts allow for fine-tuning the fit. Dovetails are cut with specific bits and template guides.

Adjust the front clamp bar for the stock. Put in a piece of scrap thicker than the stock on the top of the jig and adjust the top clamp bar to lock this scrap board in place (**A**). Use one long scrap board or two short ones across the top of the jig so the clamp doesn't bend out of shape. Position the thick and thin spacers on the bracket rods close to the jig (**B**).

Next, place the finger assembly to the outside of the spacers and lock it down so it's resting on top of the scrap board. Mount the tail board face side out under the front clamp, against the left stop and right underneath the finger assembly, lining it up with the top of the scrap board (**C**).

TIP **Use a piece of scrap ⅛ in. to ¼ in. thicker than the stock. The finger assembly and tail and pin boards line up on this scrap piece. Since you're making a through cut, the bit will cut through the boards but miss cutting into the jig.**

(Text continues on p. 168.)

A

B

C

D

E

F

G

Adjust the template fingers for the spacing desired. Note that the straight part of the fingers is over the end of the tail board. Set the dovetail bit at a depth equal to or slightly less than the thickness of the stock plus the thickness of the template (**D**). Rout the tails at one end; then rotate the board counterclockwise to cut the tails at the other end (**E**).

To cut the pins, reposition the template between the thin spacer or the bracket rod nut and the first of the three black washers, and adjust the side stops ½ in. Or use a ½-in. spacer at the front left stop. Mount the pin board face side out in the jig and clamp it tightly in place. Note how the angled fingers now sit over the end of the pin board (**F**).

Mount a straight bit and the proper template guide in the router and rout between the fingers. If the fit is too tight, turn the bracket rod nuts clockwise to make the pins smaller. If the fit is too loose, turn them counterclockwise to move the finger assembly out, thus making the pins larger (**G**).

Machine-Cut Through Dovetail

You can use the table saw and bandsaw to cut dovetails. Lay out the pin cuts first on your wood using a sliding bevel to mark out the angle.

➤ See *"Hand-Cut Through Dovetail"* on p. 161.

A

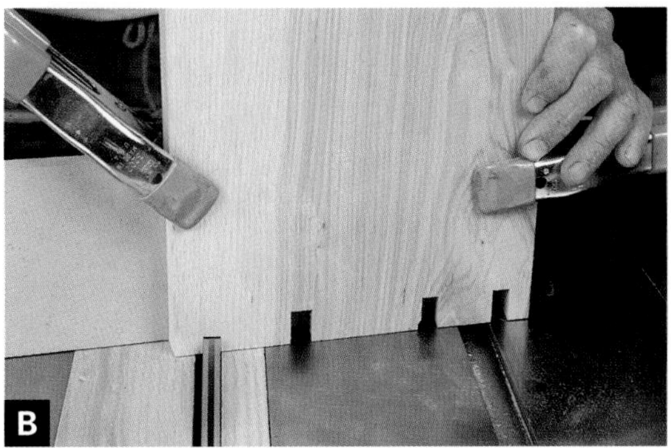

B

Set up a dado blade on the table saw to cut the pins. The size of the dado should be smaller than the tail socket. The blade depth is set for slightly less than the thickness of the stock. Angle the miter gauge to the tail and pin angle required and use an auxiliary fence on the miter gauge to help support the board during the cut (**A**).

Cut one side of each of all the pins for a carcase, lining up the cuts by eye (**B**). Don't worry if the pins aren't all exactly the same size. No matter how the pins come out, you will mark out their shapes onto the tail boards. Just cut as close as you can to the layout lines. Re-angle the miter gauge the opposite way for the second set of cuts to make the other side of the pins.

WARNING Make sure the dado blade doesn't cut into the miter gauge when you angle it for the second set of cuts.

(Text continues on p. 170.)

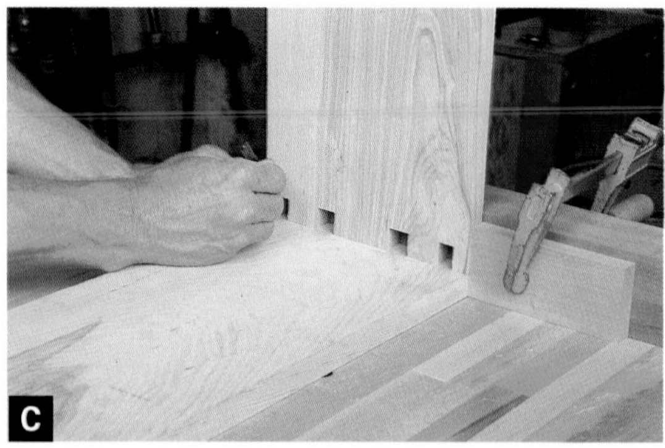
C

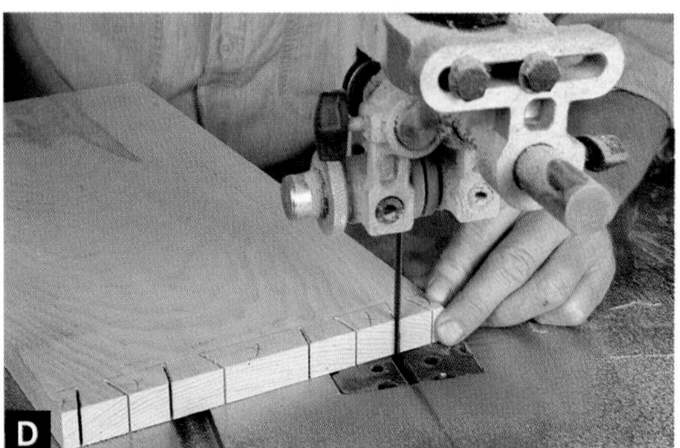
D

E

Set up two stops on the bench. Push the tail board into one stop and line up the edges of the two boards with the other stop. Mark the pins on the tail boards. Be careful to hold the marking knife in tight to the pins. Don't let it follow the long grain (**C**).

Run a pencil down the knife lines to make them clearly visible and mark out the waste. Use the bandsaw to cut right next to the lines (**D**), but be sure that the blade is always on the waste side of the lines. Don't saw past the gauge lines.

Chop the shoulder lines by hand from both faces in toward the middle to finish up. Pare the joints to fit, starting at one end and working your way across the board to the other end. Don't try to fit all the tails and pins at once (**E**). Be sure to number each of the corresponding parts of each joint.

Through Dovetail with Mitered Shoulder

The advantage of a through dovetail with a mitered shoulder is a more refined look than the standard through dovetail. Although the end grain still shows on both sides, the front edge meets in a clean miter rather than a butt joint (**A**).

Lay out the dovetail joint to allow for the miter at one edge. Place gauge lines on both faces and only one edge of the tail board. Lay out the miter cut at the other edge of the board with a pencil and the miter square on a combination square. Then cut the through tails, but don't angle the last cut near the miter. It's a straight-sided cut (**B**). Next, cut the miter with a dovetail saw. Make the pin cuts after marking them out from the tails (**C**).

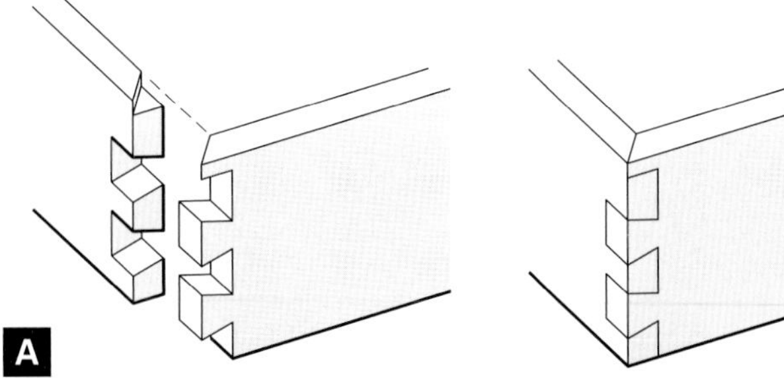

A

B

C

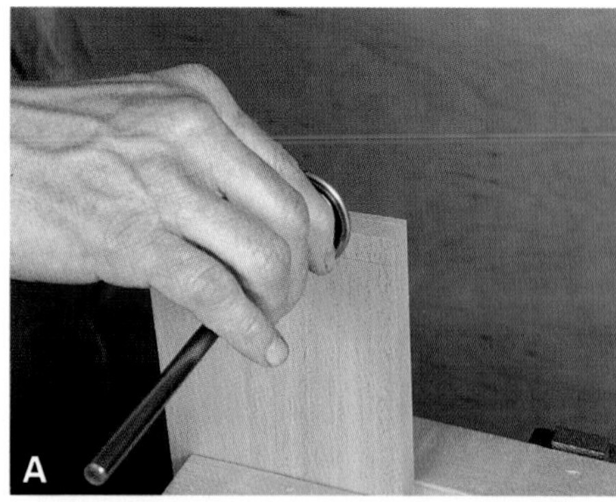

Hand-Cut Half-Blind Dovetail

Half-blind dovetails are commonly used for building drawers. The joint shows from only the drawer side, where it is lapped into the drawer face.

➤ See *"Half-Blind Dovetails"* on p. 152.

The joint requires two different gauge lines on the drawer face because it doesn't come through. One line marks out the thickness of the tail stock as usual. Gauge a line on the inside of the drawer face at just less than the thickness of the drawer side. The other gauge line marks out the depth of the lap. Put it in on the drawer face end at about three-quarters of its full thickness (**A**). Use this last gauge setting to mark out the tail boards across their faces and edges (**B**).

Lay out and mark the tails onto the drawer sides. Set a sliding bevel for the angle, between 1:5 and 1:8 is common. The size of the tails is generally two to three times the size of the pins, but above all be sure to make the pin size convenient for chopping out (**C**).

Cut the tails with the board held perfectly vertical in the vise. Angle the saw to make the tail cuts straight across the board. Practice will improve your ability to make these cuts accurately (**D**).

Use a chisel to chop out on the gauge lines. Make the first passes fairly light, because the chisel acts as a wedge and can move off the line if you're too heavy with the hammer blow. Clean up the waste with some cuts made straight into the board (**E**). Make sure the corners of the tails are clean and that the area across the pin sockets are all flat. You can undercut this area a little to help with the fitting.

Clamp the drawer face in the vise. Set the tail board or drawer side onto it and use a handplane on edge to support the other end of the tail board. By raising both boards up, you can more easily line up their edges with a flat piece of scrap. Line up the end of the drawer side with the gauge line on the end of the drawer face. Use a knife to mark out the tails on the end of the pin board while holding the tail board down tightly (**F**). No matter how the tails came out, their shape is now transferred to the matching board.

Reverse the pin board in the vise. Cut the pins holding the saw at an angle. Cut down to both of the gauge lines and no farther (**G**).

Then clean up the cuts with a chisel. Make the first chopping cut very light; then clean up the waste by holding the chisel bevel side down (**H**). Continue removing the waste from both directions until you're down to the gauge lines. Make these surfaces slightly undercut to create a good-looking joint (**I**).

Fit the joint one tail at a time and don't force the work. Always look for the shiny spots that indicate where a joint is rubbing. Pare these spots first. Work from one end of a board to the other when adjusting the fit (**J**).

F

G

H

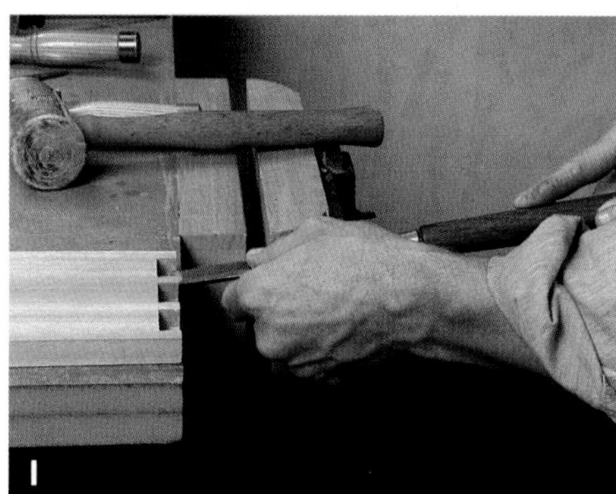
I

J

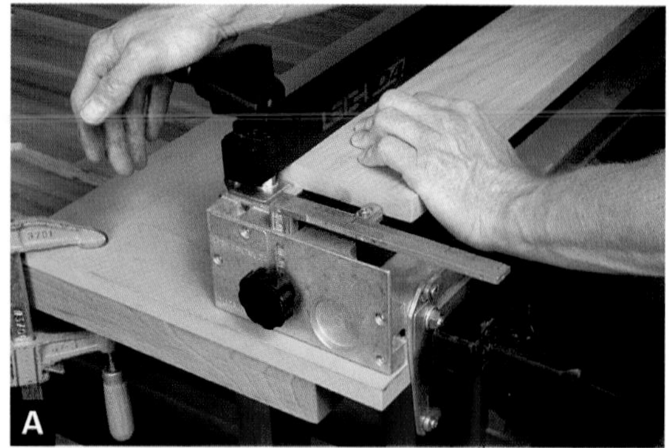

A

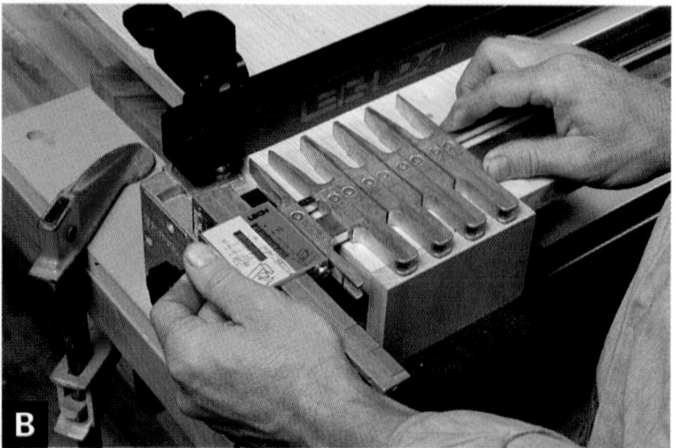

B

C

Half-Blind Dovetail with a Router and Leigh Jig

The Leigh Jig cuts half-blind dovetails one board at a time. It uses one dovetail bit to make the cuts set at a specified depth to give the best results. You can adjust the finger assembly for different thicknesses of stock as well as different tail sizes and spacings. The jig requires specific dovetail bits and template guides.

Mount a spacer board on top of the jig and clamp it in place (**A**). Adjust the height of the finger assembly for the spacer board. Rotate the finger assembly into the half-blind tails mode, which is color coded and displays a half-blind-tail icon; then place it on top of the spacer. Set the scale at the tail board thickness, less a hair (**B**).

Mount the tail board vertically in the jig, butting it right up under the finger assembly and tight against the side stop. Raise up the finger assembly a tad to make it easier to adjust the fingers for the layout desired (**C**). Adjust the fingers for the spacing you want and lock all the guide-finger screws down. Add an extra set of fingers or two at the end of the board to prevent your router base from tipping.

Reset the finger assembly down onto the scrap. Mount the router with a 7⁄16-in. template guide and 1⁄2-in. bit. Set the bit height for the depth indicated in the manual based on the bit angle you've chosen. The depth of cut affects the fit of the joint because it determines the size of the pins. The deeper the cut, the larger the pin. Be sure to practice with some scrap to find the correct depth setting.

➤ See *"Depth of Cut in a Half-Blind Jig"* drawing on p. 158.

Make a climb cut along the edge of the board, moving right to left. This scores the face of the board and eliminates any tearout (**D**). Then rout between all the guide fingers, moving left to right. After routing all the tails, remove the tail board and put a piece of scrap vertically in its place in the jig, projecting above the top face of the jig by ⅛ in. Place it flush against the side stop.

D

Then set the pin board horizontally in the jig with its edge flush up against the face of the scrap board (**E**). You can raise up the finger assembly to make all this work a bit easier. Flip the finger assembly 180 degrees to the half-blind-pins mode and set the scale equal to the tail board thickness (**F**). Drop the finger assembly back down onto the pin board. Rout the pins, moving left to right in a series of small passes.

E

Once the pins are cut, remove the pin board and check the joint's fit (**G**). If the joint is too loose, lower the bit slightly and make test cuts in two new boards. When the bit setting is correct, write it down or make a height-setting block to set your bit for the next time you make this joint.

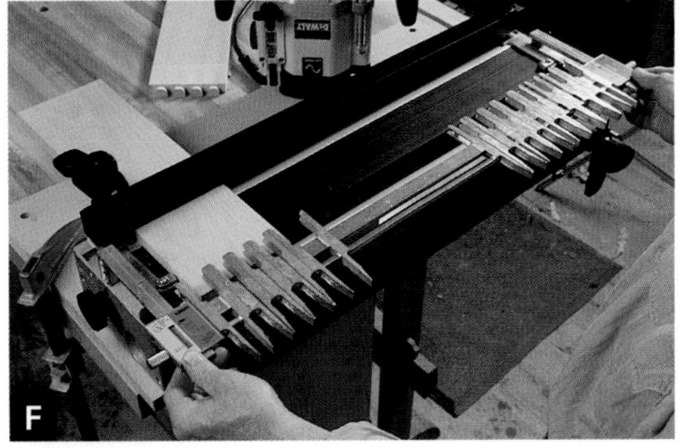
F

WARNING Do not make any climb cuts into the pin board. You will be cutting into end grain, and any cuts made from right to left will cause a severe jerking of the router as it tries to pull itself into the wood.

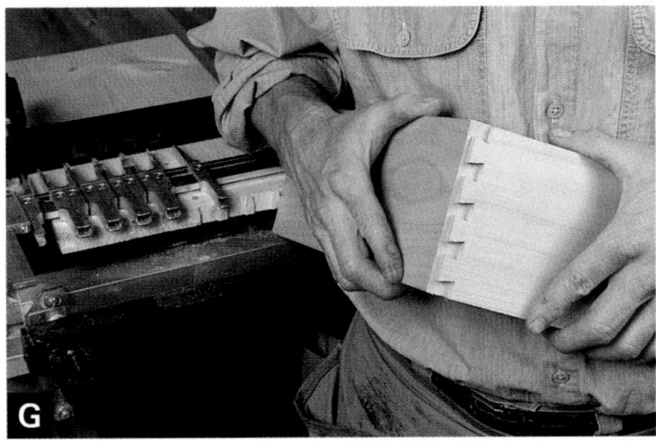
G

A

B

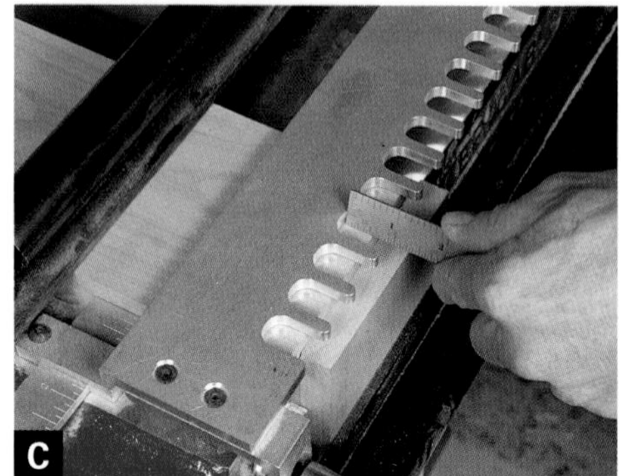
C

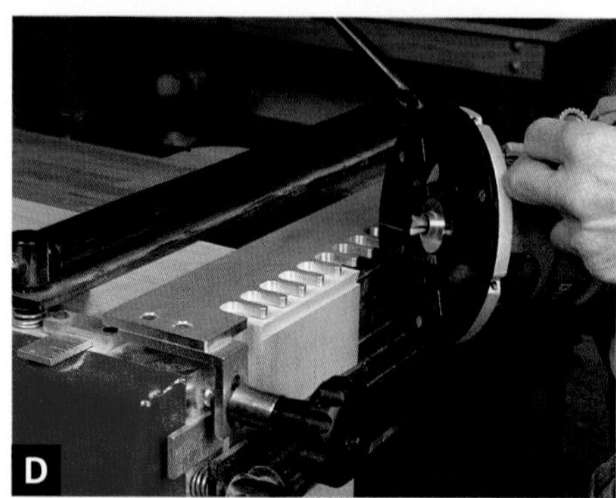
D

E

Half-Blind Dovetail with a Router and Omnijig

The Omnijig cuts half-blind dovetails in both boards at once using a finger template, ½-in. dovetail bit, and ⅝-in. template guide. Mount the template guide first; then insert the dovetail bit into the router. Set the bit depth for approximately 19⁄32 in. Loosen all the sliding stop bars and move them out of the way. Check the manual for final side stop adjustment. Adjust the clamp bars for the thickness of the stock.

For this example, I'm cutting half-blind dovetails for a drawer. Place the drawer side vertically in the jig with its inside facing out. Raise it higher than the surface of the jig and butt it up against the side stop (**A**). Place the drawer face flat in the jig with its inside facing up and its end butted up to the face of the drawer side. Then reset the vertical piece so its end lines up flush with the top of the horizontal piece (**B**).

Set the bracket spacers so the bottom of one of the template finger slots sits approximately 19⁄32 in. from the end of the drawer face. Check this depth and check the side stop placement so the two boards are offset by 7⁄16 in. (**C**). Make a climb cut first across the outer face of the vertical board, moving from right to left to prevent tearout (**D**). Then rout between each of the fingers carefully, from left to right. Make sure to go fully into each of the fingers (**E**).

Half-Blind Dovetail with a Generic Jig

Generic jigs cut both boards at once. You will need a dovetail bit and the proper template guide to ride in the finger assembly. Always make practice cuts in scrap wood before cutting your good stock. The depth of cut is crucial here for a good fit.

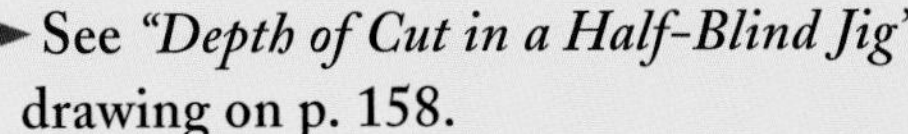

➤ See *"Depth of Cut in a Half-Blind Jig"* drawing on p. 158.

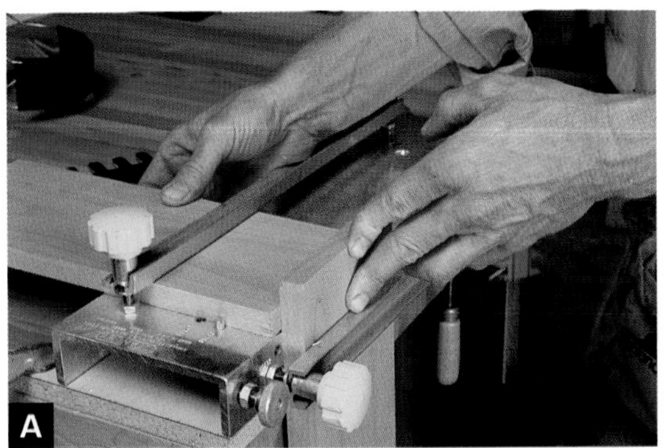

A

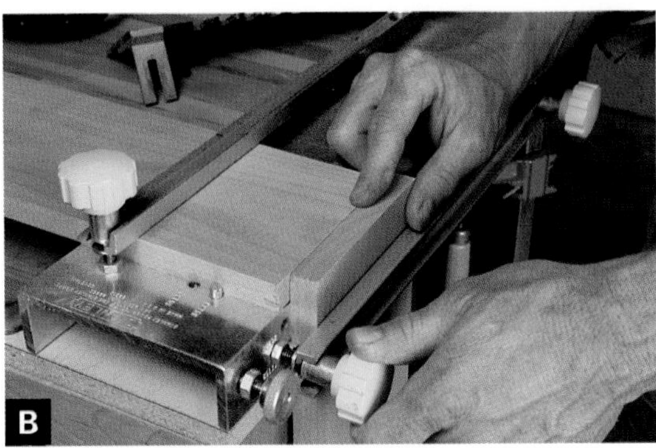

B

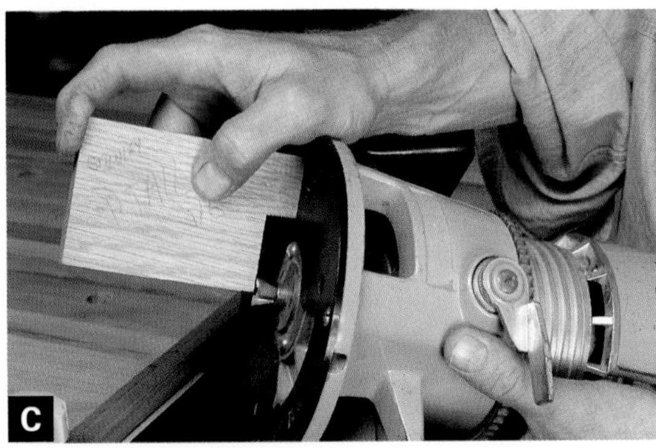

C

D

Place the tail piece, or drawer side, vertically in the jig with its inside facing out. Set it in high and butt the pin board, or drawer face, right up to it with its inside facing up. Make sure both boards register against their side stops (**A**).
Reset the vertical board's end to line up flush with the face of the horizontal board and clamp it firmly in place (**B**).

Place the bit in the router and set its height. This is the critical part for the fit of the joint; so when you find the right height setting, make up a height block to index the bit each time. Or dedicate a router and bit to that jig and never change the bit (**C**).

Turn the router on, set the edge of the base down on the edge of the finger template, and move into the work. Don't come straight down onto the finger assembly and do not tip or lift the router while making the cut (**D**). Make a first pass across the face of the vertical board, moving from right to left. This climb cut will help prevent tearout. Then move into each of the fingers, carefully moving from left to right. The final step is to come back and retrace the cut, making sure you've entered into each of the fingers as deeply as you can go.

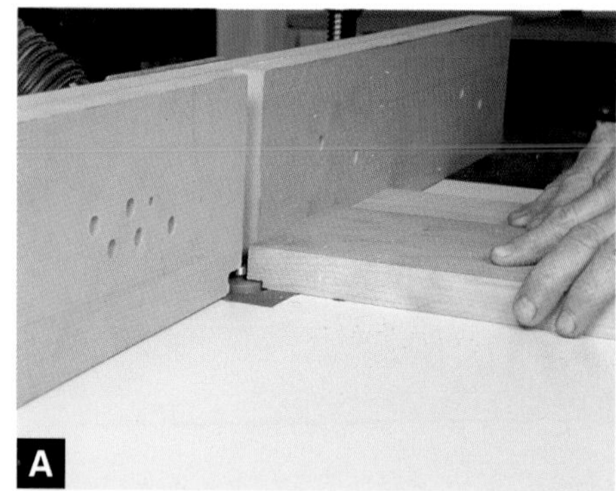
A

B

C

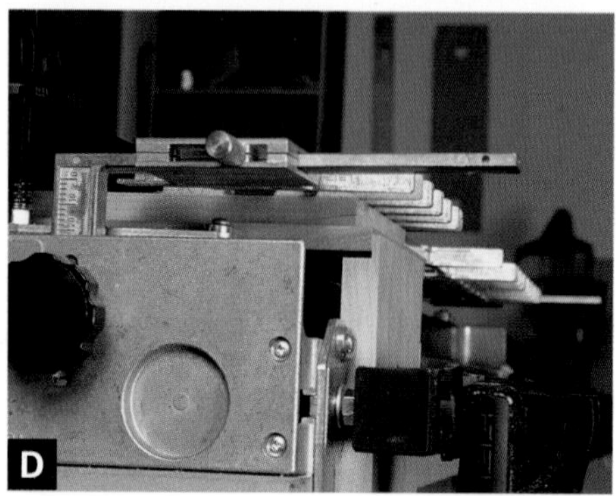
D

E

Rabbeted Half-Blind Dovetail with a Router and Leigh Jig

With the Leigh jig, rabbeted dovetails are cut like half-blind dovetails. You place one board at a time in the jig and cut the first vertically and the second horizontally. But to set in the drawer side for the rabbeted front, first cut a rabbet around the drawer face. Make a matching rabbeting cut in the end of a scrap board. Use a ⅜-in. rabbeting bit on the router table to make the rabbet around the perimeter of the board. Use a backer board to prevent tearout on the back side of the cut (**A**).

Make up a spacer block as deep as the rabbet cut. Use double-sided tape to hold it against the side stop. This will push the drawer side out by the amount of the rabbet. Mount the drawer side right up next to the spacer and right under the straight finger assembly (**B**). Cut the drawer side. Make a climb cut first across the face of the board, moving from right to left. Then move into each of the fingers carefully to full depth, moving from left to right (**C**). Make all the tail cuts with the spacer in place.

Next, remove the spacer and place the rabbeted scrap board vertically in the jig. Mount the rabbeted drawer face out from the jig's front face by this amount by butting it into the rabbeted scrap piece (**D**). As always, make practice cuts in scrap before committing your good wood to this cut (**E**).

Canted Half-Blind Dovetail

Canted, or angled, dovetails for drawer fronts require different layout techniques than regular half-blind dovetails. This is because regular tail angles set at the degree of drawer face tilt yield short grain at the tips of the tails (**A**).

First cut the drawer sides to the required angle. Lay out the gauge line on the tail board, running the gauge tightly against the drawer side end (**B**). Then set the sliding bevel for one angle to mark out one side of the tails. Reset it to a matching angle to mark out the other sides. These angles are set by putting the sliding bevel tight up to the end of the board, but the angle is adjusted to compensate for the board's cant. In other words, lay out the tails along lines parallel to the edges, not to the end, as if the end were square rather than angled (**C**).

Once the marking is complete, cut the joint by hand.

➤ See *"Hand-Cut Half-Blind Dovetail"* on p. 172.

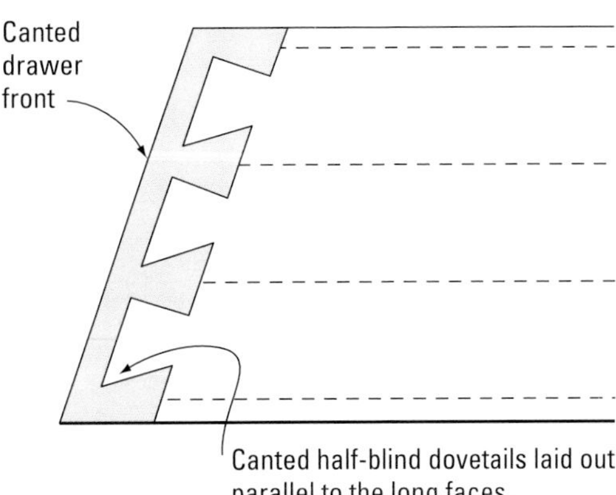

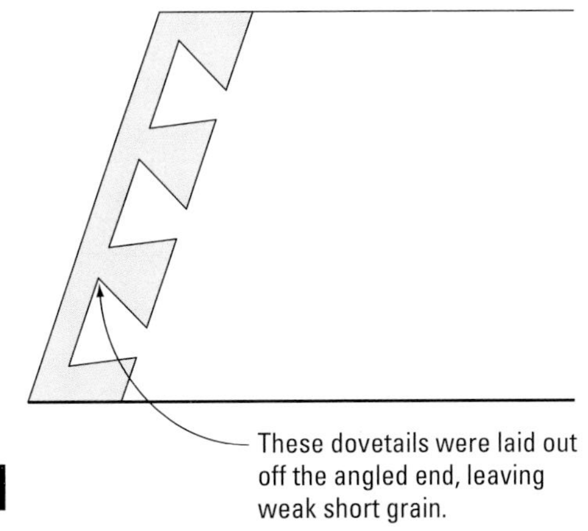

A

B

C

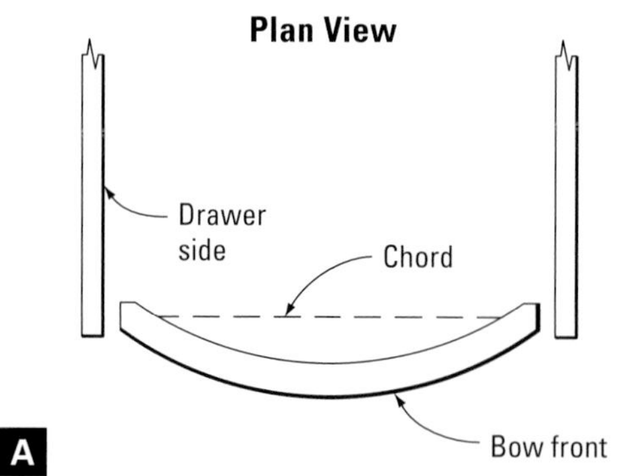

A

B

C

Bow-Front Drawer with Half-Blind Dovetails

Bow-front drawer faces require dovetails that come in perpendicular to the chord of the arc of the drawer face (**A**).

Make up a template for the arc of the drawer face. You can use it to mark out both the inner and the outer curves, but remember that the curves will not be concentric. (Over a distance this short, it's not critical.) Leave two small flats on the inside face of the drawer front when laying out the curves. You can also cut out the drawer face curves and then plane two flats parallel to the chord of the arc. The flats should be almost as wide as the thickness of the drawer sides. The shoulders of the drawer sides will rest on these flats (**B**).

Then cut the drawer side tails as usual.

➤ See *"Hand-Cut Half-Blind Dovetail"* on p. 172.

Once the tails are cut and cleaned, set the drawer face in the vise and place the tail board on it to mark out the pins (**C**). Support the tail board with a piece of scrap. The pins are cut straight into the drawer face like half-blind dovetails.

Full-Blind Rabbeted Dovetail

Full-blind rabbeted dovetails hide the tails and pins of the joint in what looks like a simple rabbet. The end grain of the rabbet can show from either the top or the side of the carcase. Cut the pins on this joint first, because it's easier to mark out for the tails from the pins.

For a joint with rabbeted pins, mark a gauge line that's slightly less than the thickness of the tail stock onto the pin board. Then set in a line for the rabbet cut so it will leave about a square section for the tails and pins to rest in. Lay out gauge lines on the tail board that match the rabbet cut (**A**). Cut the rabbet on the table saw with a dado blade or with a rabbeting bit on the router table.

Make a dovetail gauge out of a piece of cardboard or brass shim stock. Lay out a pleasing tail angle on the shim stock and cut it with a pair of scissors. Use the dovetail gauge to lay out the tail sockets and pins onto the rabbeted pin board (**B**). Saw the pins at an angle with a dovetail saw.

➤ See *"Hand-Cut Half-Blind Dovetail"* on p. 172.

To clean the tail sockets quickly, use a plunge router with a small-diameter straight bit. Use a climb cut rotation—right to left—with the router well supported to get a cut that's easier to control. Set the depth to cut almost to the rabbet depth (**C**). Then use a chisel to chop out on the gauge lines and clean the tail sockets down to the rabbet (**D**).

Mark to tail boards, holding the pin board vertically on each of them (**E**). Cut the tails to fit.

A

B

C

D

E

Full-Blind Mitered Dovetail

Full-blind mitered dovetails reveal only a miter joint to the world; the tails and pins are hidden inside the miter. Both boards must be the same thickness to make the miter work well.

Set a marking gauge exactly to the thickness of the boards (**A**) and mark this on only the inside faces of the boards. Then mark the miter from the outside corner of one board to this gauge line (**B**). Next, set up a rabbeting bit to cut rabbets on all of the boards. The rabbets should be cut at about two-thirds the full thickness of the stock. Cut back just to the miter line, which will leave a triangular section with about equal legs. Use a marking knife to score the miter line on both edges of all the boards.

Lay out the pins using a dovetail gauge.

➤ See *"Full-Blind Rabbeted Dovetail"* on p. 181.

The half pins at the outside edges should be set in from the edge to allow for the miter. Saw the miters down to the shoulder with a dovetail saw as cleanly as you can. You will fit and clean them later on (**C**). Hold the saw at an angle when you cut the pins. Don't worry if the saw nicks into the wood at the top of the cut, but don't cut through what will be the miter.

Clean out the pins, chopping carefully on the gauge line and down to the rabbet. You can use a router and straight bit to speed up waste removal (**D**). Don't remove the square rabbet yet, as it will help support the boards for marking out (**E**). Set the pin board onto the tail piece and butt the two boards into a stop. Line up their edges carefully and mark the tails with a marking knife. Then rough out the miters with a chisel (**F**).

Use any plane with an iron that extends across the width of its sole, such as the skew block plane shown here, to help trim the miters down to a true 45-degree angle (**G**). Make up a wide 45-degree miter block and clamp it to the board to help support the plane cuts.

Full-blind mitered dovetails require careful fitting to ensure that the miter closes up perfectly. Hold the saw at a double angle when cutting the tails (**H**).

Rout to depth to clean up the waste. Then use a chisel to clean out the pin sockets and half-pin sockets carefully just up to the gauge and miter lines (**I**).

F

G

H

I

A

B

C

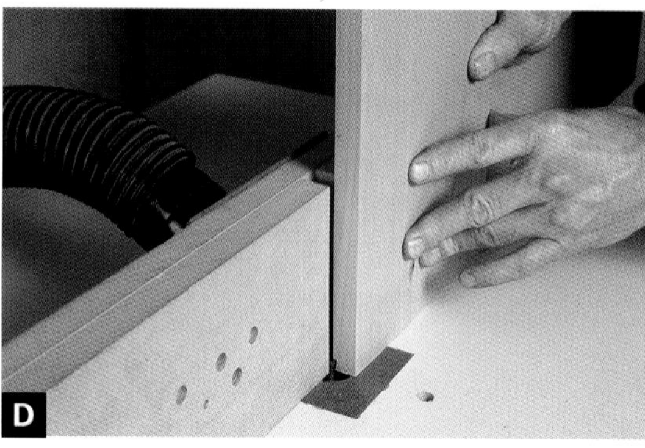
D

Through Sliding Dovetail

Before starting to cut sliding dovetails, make sure the stock is flat and remove all the milling marks. If you handplane, sand, or scrape your work after you cut the joint, you will affect its fit (**A**).

Make the dovetail slot first. For a ½-in. dovetail, use a ¼-in. straight bit on the router table to rough out the slot. Leave this cut just short of full depth. Run the end of the board against a fence set so that the straight bit is centered in the final dovetail slot position (**B**).

Mount the dovetail bit and set it to full depth. You get only one try with this cut at full depth. Make a pass, keeping pressure down on the board to keep the cut consistent in depth. Run the pass twice if you have any doubts about it. Use a backer board to prevent tearout or cut the stock ⅛ in. oversize in width so there will be enough wood to cut away the inevitable tearout. Use a table insert in the router table to cover up as much of the bit as possible (**C**).

Cut the tail section on the router table, holding your workpiece vertically. Don't reset the bit height. It will perfectly match the first cut. Set the fence over the bit so only a portion of it is showing. Cut one face side of all the joints and then cut the other faces. Fine-tune and adjust the fence by cutting into a piece of scrap that's the same thickness. If you need to cut more off the tail, use a pencil to mark the fence position on the table, loosen the fence clamps, and then tap it a little away from the pencil mark to expose more bit. Each movement of the fence will give you two possible cuts, one on each face (**D**).

If you think you're very close with the fit but don't want to risk it, hedge your bet by placing a paper shim between the fence and the workpiece. This will kick the work out a few thousandths of an inch from the fence. A dollar bill gives you a 0.003-in. shim (**E**). If the joint is still too tight, remove the shim and take another pass. On narrower boards, a handplane pass off the board's face will put you that much closer to the bit for a slightly narrower tail cut.

Before starting to fit the joint, take a single handplane pass off the end grain of the tail (**F**). This gives you just a little sliding room and some room for glue. Alternatively, you could set the bit depth for the male cut just a hair lower than the height of the female cut. If the tail still binds up in the slot, double-check the depth of the cut with a depth gauge. Or use a combination square as a gauge. Make sure the depth is consistent (**G**).

WARNING Always be aware of the exit point of the bit on the router table. Place your hands in a safe spot—away from this hole.

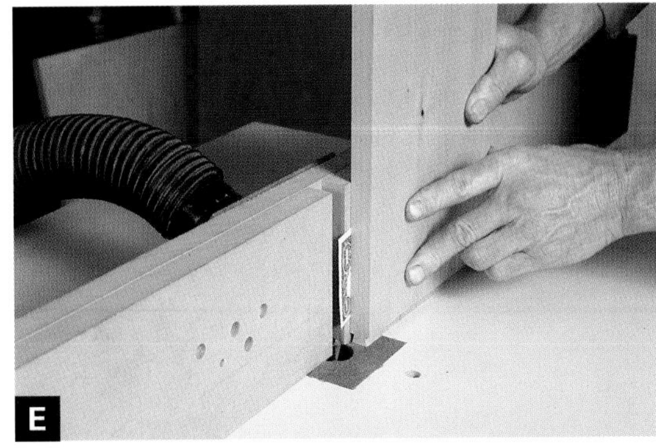

E

F

G

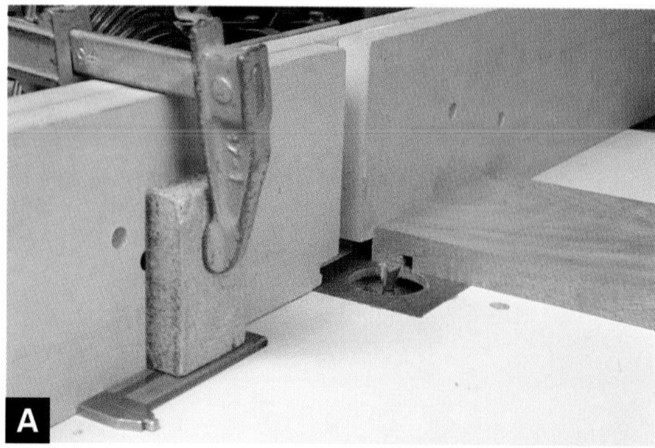
A

B

C

Stopped Sliding Dovetail

Cut a stopped sliding dovetail exactly as you would a through version, but put a stop on the router table fence to limit the cut. Use a spacer under the stop to raise it up so debris doesn't pile up against it, affecting the accuracy of the stop (**A**).

Chop the end of the dovetail slot square or leave it round and cut back the tail enough to miss the round corners. After cutting and fitting the tail, trim off a section of it to allow for the stop. Use a backsaw to cut away the waste. Then walk a chisel around from the router-cut shoulders to establish the flat (**B**). The shoulder can be slightly undercut. Or set up the table saw to trim the shoulder accurately.

A sliding dovetail should slide about halfway together with just hand pressure before it binds up. But the only way you'll get it apart is with a mallet. Clamp a piece of scrap that fits just under the slot and use that as a stop to bang the board against. Make sure the dovetailed piece doesn't cant on you as you're banging it free. On a through sliding dovetail, you can check each end of the male and female parts of the joint, but with a stopped sliding dovetail you can check the joint from only one side so be precise with your cutting (**C**).

Hand-Cut Single-Shouldered Sliding Dovetail

A single-shoulder sliding dovetail is relatively easy to fit because one side remains flat.

➤ See *"Sliding and Slot Dovetails"* drawing on p. 155.

Determine the angle of the tail and set up a sliding bevel (**A**). Mark out a board on both ends with this angle and plane it to match (**B**). Clamp the angled fence or saw guide onto the workpiece and place the saw against it to make the cut (**C**). Be sure to hold the saw tightly in place and don't saw past the depth marks.

Now use the other straight side of the saw guide to line up the straight cut. Make sure it's square to the board's edge (**D**). Then saw the straight side to depth (**E**).

Remove the waste with a chisel and mallet (**F**). Then use a router plane to take the cut down to depth (**G**).

Use the sliding bevel to mark out the tail board with its angle and mark out the position of the tail's shoulder. Set the saw guide in the vise to line up with the tail marks and, using a wide chisel, cut out the tail (**H**). To fit the joint, use a handplane to take wood off the back face of the tail board (**I**).

A

B

C

D

E

F

G

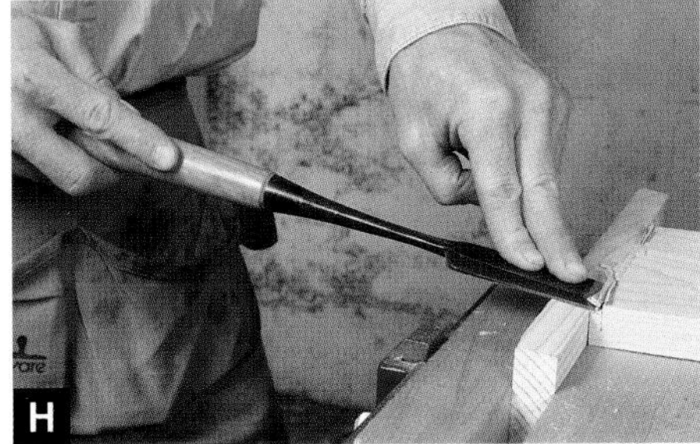
H

I

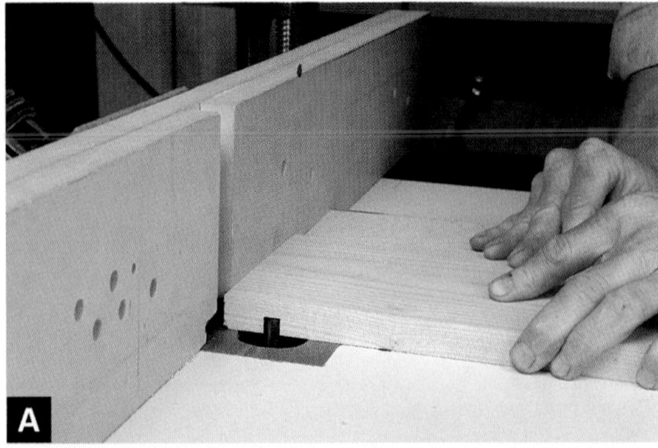
A

B

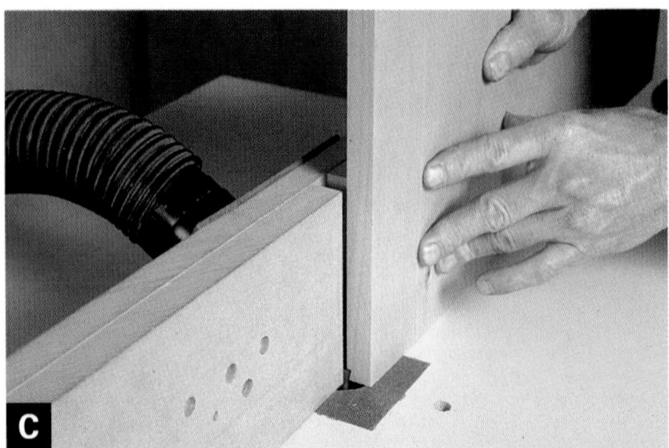
C

D

Single-Shouldered Sliding Dovetail with a Router

When cutting a single-shouldered sliding dovetail with a router, first mill the stock a hair thicker than the width of the dovetail bit so you'll have some fitting room. Use a straight bit first, but don't center the bit in the dovetail slot. Set the fence so that you cut one side of the dovetail slot with the straight bit. Set the bit for the full depth of cut after several cleaning passes and use a backer board to prevent tearout on the back edge of the piece (**A**).

Set the dovetail bit to depth and make one pass, cutting the dovetail side of the slot. Make sure that you're always moving into the rotation of the bit (**B**).

Cut the tail on one face only (**C**). Fit the tail by planing the flat side of that board. Draw pencil marks across the board and remove wood consistently across the face with a tuned handplane or even a scraper. This will make the tail a bit smaller. Recheck its fit until it slides home (**D**).

! WARNING When enlarging a router cut slot, make sure that the feed direction for the second cut is into the rotation of the bit. You are usually contacting only one side of the bit, and a normal feed direction may actually yield a dangerous climb cut. You may have to feed from left to right, instead of the more common right to left, to avoid this.

Rabbeted Sliding Dovetail

Make a rabbeted sliding dovetail in a drawer face just like any rabbet cut on the router table. Hold the board flat to the table, but use a dovetail bit to make the cut. Use a backer board to protect the back edge of the work from tearout.

Set up a fence so that the bit cuts at a depth just less than the thickness of the stock (**A**). Make a series of passes until the board rides along the fence for the final pass, or waste some wood first on the table saw and then make one cleanup pass on the router table.

Don't reset the bit height for the matching tail cut, as it already perfectly matches. Move the fence over so that the bit is captured in the fence. Make the drawer-side dovetail while holding the piece vertically (**B**). Take a light pass and re-adjust the fence away from the bit until the two boards mate perfectly (**C**). Reinforce the joint with dowel pins for the strongest construction.

A

B

C

A

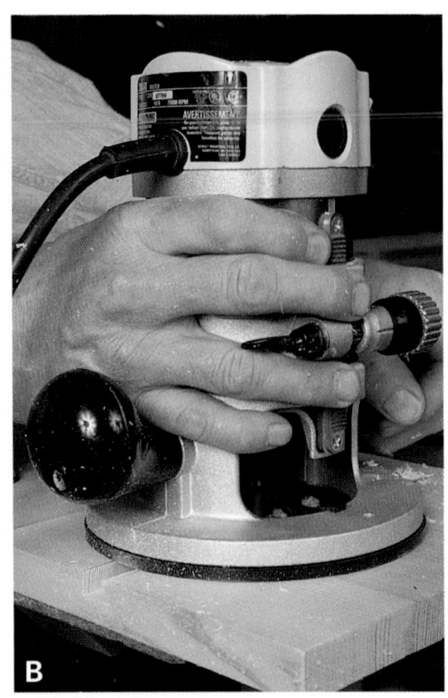
B

Tapered Sliding Dovetail

Tapered sliding dovetails eliminate the binding and fitting problems of sliding dovetails. The joint has an angled slot and tail, which fit loosely right up until the joint is almost together, when it locks into place.

Use a right-angle guide with an auxiliary fence against it and clamp these onto the workpiece. If you mark the position of the dovetail slot in pencil, you'll be able to place the fence more easily using the dovetail bit in the router as an aid. Rough out the slot first with a straight bit (**A**). Cut to full depth with a dovetail bit, making sure to keep the router base tight to the auxiliary fence (**B**).

C

Place a ¹⁄₁₆-in. shim between the auxiliary fence and the right-angle guide exactly at the lead edge of the workpiece. Then rout the tapered side of the slot. Be sure to put the shim at the edge of the board, not at the edge of the fence. If the sliding dovetail is a stopped cut, square up the end of the cut with a chisel. Use a spacer block to index the cut for the matching carcase side. This will place it in the proper position (**C**).

➤ See *"End Rabbet with a Router and Fence"* on p. 72.

D

Rout the tapered tail on the router table using the same router bit, which should now be captured in the router table fence. Tape on the ¹⁄₁₆-in. shim to one face of the board right at its edge. This kicks the workpiece out from the fence to make the tapered cut. Cut the other side of the tail running the board's face flat to the fence (**D**).

Hand-Cut Slot Dovetail

The first step for a machine-cut slot dovetail is to cut the tail of the carcase rail. You mark out from this tail onto the carcase side. Set up a marking gauge and mark the shoulders. Be sure that the shoulder-to-shoulder distance is correct, checking it with the carcase dry-assembled. Lay out the angle of the tail with a sliding bevel or just judge by eye. Clamp the rail in a vise and cut the tail with a dovetail saw (**A**).

Mark out the tail shape onto the carcase side with a marking knife. Support the rail end with a piece of scrap or handplane turned on edge. Use a square to line up the rail to the carcase side (**B**). Then mark out the thickness of the rail onto the carcase side with a marking gauge. Square the lines down from the knife marks of the tail to this gauge line. Saw at an angle to cut the socket for the tail (**C**).

Clean the socket with a chisel. You can undercut these surfaces just a little to help with the fitting (**D**).

Cut the single-shouldered version of the slot dovetail in the same way, just don't put in the second shoulder. Mark out and cut the tail. Lay out the slot in the carcase side. Cut the slot in the carcase side, as shown in photo **C**.

Fitting the joint now only requires using a handplane to plane the rail's flat side until it fits (**E**). As with any mortised joint, always put a small shoulder on the bottom of the joint to hide any dents or damage around the edge of the slot cut (**F**).

A

B

C

D

E

F

A

B

C

Slot Dovetail on the Router Table

You can cut carcase slots using a dovetail bit in the router table. Set up a fence at the proper spot to cut each side of the slot. Cut the closer side of the slot first. Use a stop to limit the depth of cut (**A**). You can waste some wood first with a straight bit or drill out some waste on the drill press. Square up the round corners with a chisel.

Dry-assemble the carcase and cut the carcase rail to fit just snug between the slots in the carcase sides (**B**).

Cut the tail on the carcase rail on the router table using the same dovetail bit. But first rough out the cheek and shoulder of the tail on the table saw and bandsaw. Then hold the rail vertically on the router table to make the pass and use a backer board to support it (**C**).

Slot Dovetail on the Table Saw

Another method of cutting the tail on the carcase rail is to use the table saw. Crosscut the shoulders first using a crosscut jig and a stop to index the cuts. Set the blade height so it comes just up to the marked-out joint (**A**).

Next, adjust the blade to the proper angle and run the rail past the blade using the miter gauge. Put a stop on the miter gauge fence to index the cuts. Make certain the blade height is set just under the shoulder cut (**B**). Clean up the corners of the shoulders with a chisel.

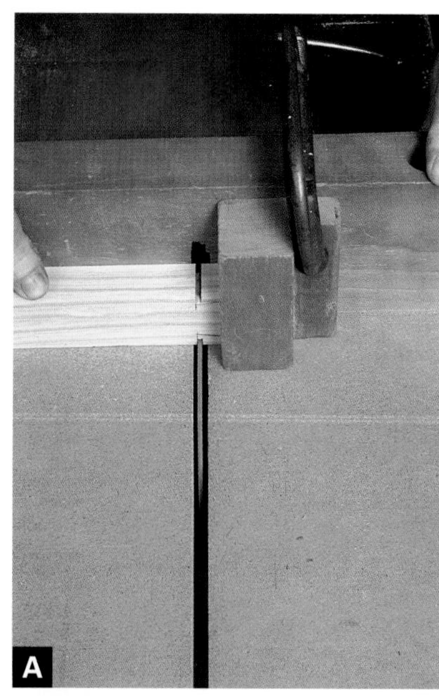

A

B

A

B

Double-Slot Dovetail

Carcase rails often need greater width to keep the carcase sides from twisting. Use double-slot dovetails in these situations. When the slot comes uncomfortably close to the outer face of a carcase piece, cut back the length of one of the tails with a handsaw. Even ⅛ in. can make a difference (**A**). Then mark out the two tails onto the carcase side and fit the rail carefully to the carcase (**B**).

Butt Joints, page 196

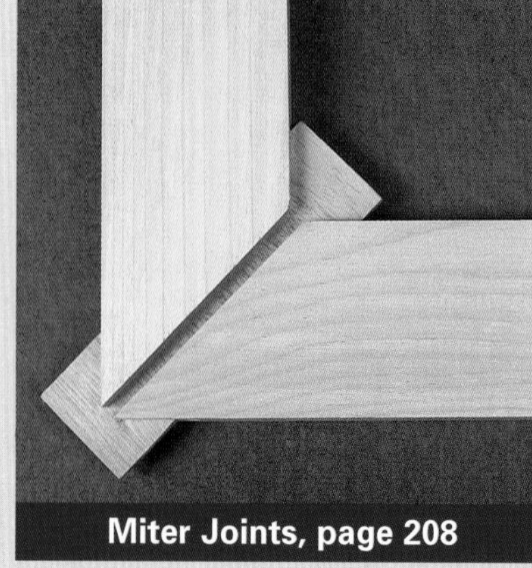

Miter Joints, page 208

Lap and Bridle Joints, page 230

Scarf and Splice Joints, page 258

Edge Joints, page 268

Mortise and Tenons, page 290

PART THREE

Frame Joinery

FRAME JOINERY IS THE SECOND MAJOR structural system we employ in furniture making. Used to construct a range of pieces, frames are made up of smaller, lighter members than the wide panels of carcase work. Frames can be used alone to build mirrors, picture frames, and bed headboards or joined together at their corners to create tables, chairs, and stools. But frames can also capture panels within their edges, allowing us to build larger pieces, such as cabinets and desks.

Because of the smaller size of frame members, a variety of joinery options are available for holding them together. Choices include butts, miters, mortises and tenons, and lap joints. Some of these joints are the same ones that help build carcases; but here they are redesigned for smaller structural members to maximize gluing surface without sacrificing strength.

Butt Joints

Screwed Joint

Pocket-Hole Joint

Doweled Joints

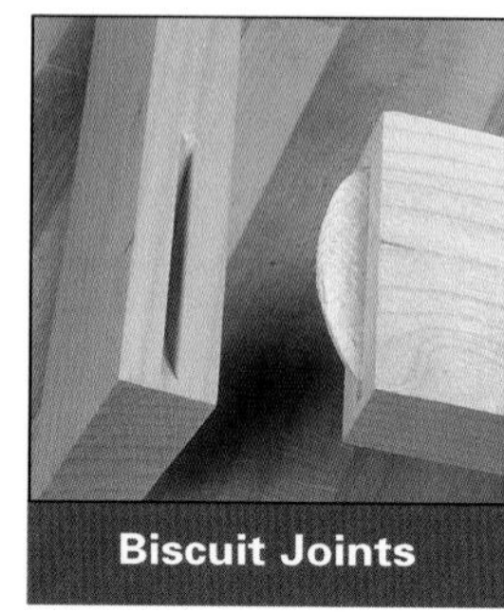

Biscuit Joints

Butt-jointed frames can be used in a variety of situations but are most commonly used for face frame construction in cabinetry. Face frames cover a cabinet's plywood or particleboard edges, giving you a place to mount hinges while providing material for scribing cabinets in place. Face frames are generally glued and nailed or screwed into place, offsetting the limitations of the butt joint. The benefits are twofold: The cabinet face is strengthened and the face frame is more firmly locked in place.

Strengthening Frame Butt Joints

We've all made a frame out of butt joints using hammer and nails; but for the best results, butt-jointed face frames should be strengthened to resist the forces of racking and tension.

Use *screws* through the vertical stiles into the horizontal rail pieces to fasten face frames together. If you use a relatively long thread, the screw will grab enough end grain to hold. Just remember where those screws are located when you apply the face frame to the cabinet. Plug the countersunk holes in areas where they will be visible.

Pocket screws were developed to speed up face frame construction. They pull a butt joint in tightly and actually act as clamps when you glue a frame together. As with all face frame construction, make sure the frame is flat before applying the screws.

Dowels will also hold a face frame together, and you won't have to worry about nailing or screwing into one when you mount the face frame onto the carcase. Drilling for them requires concentration, because it's

Face frames cover plywood edges.

Countersink for a long screw to strengthen a face frame.

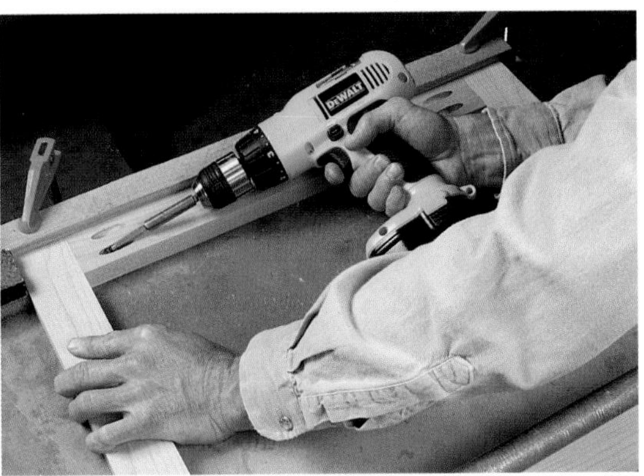

A straightedge helps you line up the face frame when applying pocket screws.

Dowels are an option for face frames, but they're trickier to align than other methods.

Center a biscuit slot in the width of one of your boards.

Check the accuracy of the biscuit joiner fence with a block of wood. This block should fit snug on both ends of the fence. Use a piece of double-sided tape as a shim if the fence is out.

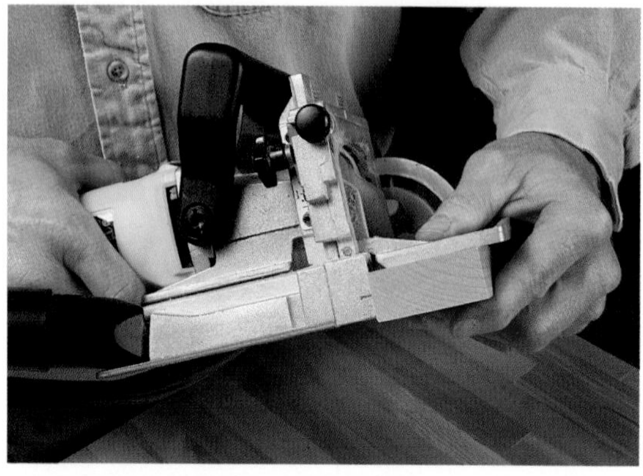
Line up the centerline on the biscuit joiner's edge with the center of the frame stock.

Use a backer board clamped to the bench or pushed against the bench dogs to support the workpiece.

easy to misalign dowel holes. Make sure your frames remain flat, and that the dowels are drilled accurately, whether they are through or blind.

The *biscuit* is probably as simple and strong a method as there is to strengthen butt joints. Because the biscuit is glued into long grain in both parts of the frame, it's very strong. Biscuits can be doubled into extra-thick frames. As with dowels, there's no concern about screwing or nailing through one when applying the face frame. You can even use biscuits in small frames just by offsetting them to an edge where they won't be visible. Biscuit joiners, however, don't automatically guarantee ease and accuracy. There are some things to pay attention to.

ACCURATE BISCUIT CUTS

Here's how to make accurate cuts with the biscuit joiner. Make sure the fence sits parallel to the cutter. Any variation off parallel gets doubled when you make two cuts in pieces to be joined together. Be sure to center the cut accurately in the thickness of the stock to prevent any telegraphing of the biscuit through to the surface of the wood. But even if your mark is not quite on center, if you index from the face side of each board, the members will always go together flush.

Don't hold the workpiece in one hand and try to cut with the biscuit joiner in the other. Use a backer to support the workpiece or clamp the board to the benchtop.

Butt Joint Cuts

Butt joints always get cut in two directions. For most butt joint cuts, which are 90-degree cuts, you cut straight across and straight down a board. When hand sawing, always saw to the waste side of the pencil line and make that pencil line clear and visible. Keep the line clean of debris so you can see it when sawing.

Use a miter saw for frame cuts, but always support long frame members. Use stops to index the cuts. Even if you're cutting only two boards, the time it takes to set a stop is worth the effort, because the boards will come out identical.

Table saws, of course, do an excellent job of crosscutting. If you don't have a sliding table, use a crosscut jig or miter gauge; but check it often to make sure you're cutting square.

➤ **See *"Butt Joints"* on p. 40 for more on crosscutting.**

Cut butt joints so they're flat and square across. If you stack two boards together and cut straight across them but at an angle, the boards won't be the same length.

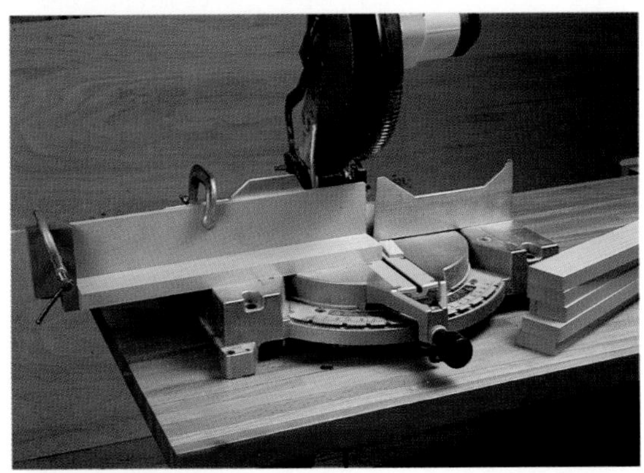

Set up stops to index multiple cuts.

Check how square the table-saw crosscut jig is cutting, especially after many hours of use. Also check the blade to see that it's cutting square to the board's face.

A

C

B

D

E

Butt Joint Reinforced with Screws

Butt joints have the simplest requirements, which are, nevertheless, quite important for good results. Make sure the stock is flat, not twisted or in-winding, and keep all the crosscuts square across the width and face of the boards. Also make sure the edge of the stock is milled square, especially where it will butt into the end of another board (**A**).

Drill through the frame stile with a wide enough diameter bit so the screw head will easily enter the hole. Measure the screw head first to avoid marring the hole. Keep the depth of the holes consistent and deep enough so the screws will have some grab (**B**).

Drill pilot holes for frames when working with thin stock or when using very hard wood. Some screws with an auger-type tip will enter without splitting the wood, but try one out first on a piece of scrap to see how it performs. Be sure to make the pilot hole just smaller than the root of the screw. The root is the part of the screw that is not threaded (**C**).

Put glue on the end grain of the rail for just a little extra holding power. Then drive the screws with the frame flat on the workbench. Push the frame against the bench dogs or a clamped board to prevent it from moving. Lubricate the screws with a bit of wax for easier entry (**D**). Or glue and clamp the frame, let it set up, and then drive the screws (**E**). Fill the countersunk holes with plugs if the frame edges will be visible.

Butt Joint with Pocket-Hole Screws

Pocket holes eliminate any concerns that the screw's countersunk hole will show, because they're applied from the inside face of the frame. They're very quick to apply since the screws are self-tapping. You use only one bit to cut the countersink and the short pilot hole. Pocket screws also eliminate the need for clamping the frame.

Mount the wood into the pocket-hole jig and drill the pocket hole with the supplied bit (**A**). Set the depth-stop collar on the bit before drilling the first hole. Put a shim on the jig and run the bit's tip into it. Then lock down the depth stop. This will prevent you from accidentally drilling into the jig or dulling the bit (**B**).

Drill down to depth and then clear the waste out of the bit and hole (**C**). The drill bit has enough of a pilot bit leading the cut that a small pilot hole will be created for the screw. Set the pocket screw in that hole and drive it home. Remember to glue the end grain of the rail (**D**).

A

B

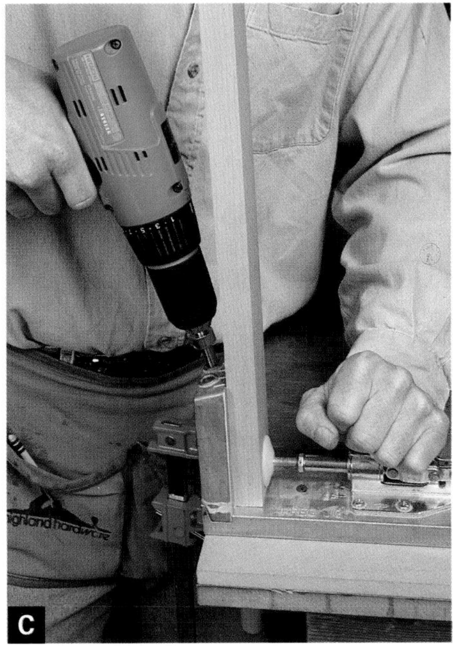
C

D

A

B

C

D

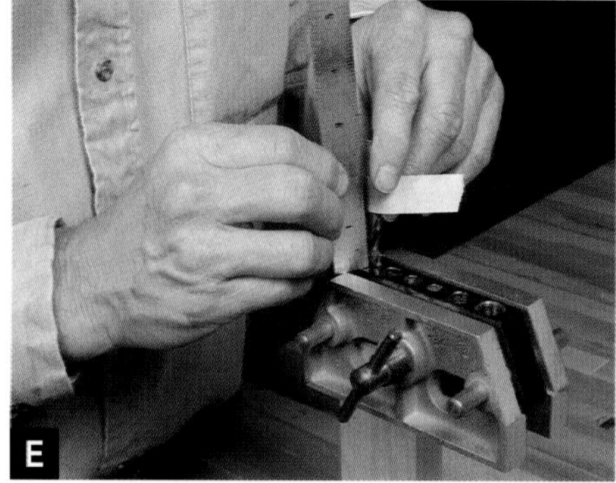
E

Butt Joint with Blind Dowels

Dowel a frame together using a doweling jig to help locate the dowel holes. Be sure to double-check the settings and drill as straight into the wood as you can. Dowels that go in on an angle cause twisted frames. Mark the dowel positions when the face frame is on the bench (**A**).

Place the rail securely in the vise and then set the doweling jig on the end of the rail (**B**).

Align the marks on the jig for the proper-size dowel to the pencil marks on the frame (**C**). Here, I'm using a ¼-in. dowel for a ¾-in.-thick frame. Use a brad-point bit with a centering point to drill the dowel holes. Be sure to take the point into account when setting the bit depth. On larger-diameter bits this amount of protrusion can be significant. No frame will clamp home if the dowels are too long for the dowel holes (**D**). Mark the bit depth with a piece of masking tape (**E**).

Drill each of the rail holes to depth, making sure to line up the pencil mark accurately to the jig mark each time (**F**). Then drill the stiles with the stile mounted in the vise. Use the same depth setting (**G**).

Check the dowel size to the drill bit. If the dowels have shrunk oval, as they're apt to, they may not fit the hole. A quick fix is to cook them a little in a shop oven. They'll shrink enough to make insertion easier. When the glue hits them, the dowels will expand back and lock themselves into place (**H**).

Use dowels with spiral- or straight-cut glue slots. These allow the glue to escape as the dowels are inserted. Put glue at the mouth of a dowel hole. As you put in the dowel, it will push the glue down into the rest of the hole (**I**). Have clamps ready when gluing up a doweled frame. You will have to apply some pressure to get the frames to butt together completely (**J**).

F

G

H

I

J

A

C

B

D

Butt Joint with Through Dowels

The longer the dowel, the greater its strength. Run the dowels through for better holding power and a decorative look. Use this method if you don't have a doweling jig.

Mark out the position of the dowels on the frame (**A**). Use the drill press to drill through the stile. Set up a fence to center the holes in the frame thickness. A couple of pencil marks on the table will index the placement of the board for drilling the holes. Make sure you're using a piece of scrap to protect the drill press table. Drill all the way through each board, clearing the bit often to remove the chips (**B**).

Set up the frame and dry-clamp it together, lining up all the parts correctly. Then drill through the stile into the rail. Mark the bit for the proper depth of cut. Hold the drill level and straight so you don't ream the stile hole larger. Drill each of the holes to depth (**C**).

Cut the dowels a little bit long to allow for any mushrooming that may occur when you pound them in. Put them in the end grain of the rail, check how far they stick out to make sure it's enough, and then get ready to glue the stile. Have a big hammer and some clamps ready. Put glue only on the end of the rail and into the dowel holes. If you put glue on the dowels, it'll get rubbed off as the dowels enter the hole (**D**).

Butt Joint with Wedged Through Dowels

The strongest dowel variation—and the most attractive—is the wedged through dowel. By wedging the dowel, you lock it in place in the board where it has the least favorable gluing surface. Be sure to align the wedge slot so the wedge applies its pressure against the end grain of the dowel hole instead of the long grain. This will prevent any splitting of the long grain when you apply the wedge. At a frame end, leave a horn, or extra wood, on the end of the frame to prevent the short grain from being blown out (**A**).

➤ See *"Butt Joint with Through Dowels"* opposite for drilling methods.

Cut the slots for the wedges with a handsaw after you glue the dowels into the rails. The wedges will be thin when you use a dovetail saw (**B**). Or cut the wedge slot on the bandsaw using a fence to locate the cuts. Make the wedge slot only about one-third of the way down the dowel (**C**).

➤ See *"Making Wedges"* on p. 376.

The wedge fits into a round hole so take a little time before gluing to shape its edges just a bit. A few swipes with a block plane will round the edges enough (**D**). Put glue on the rail end and into the dowel holes. Be ready with the clamps and a clamp block, if necessary, to bring the pieces all the way together. Then remove the clamps and drive the wedge with a metal hammer (**E**). Trim the wedges with a saw close to the edge of the stile, but try not to cut into it (**F**). Then clean up the dowels with a sharp block plane (**G**).

A

B

C

D

E

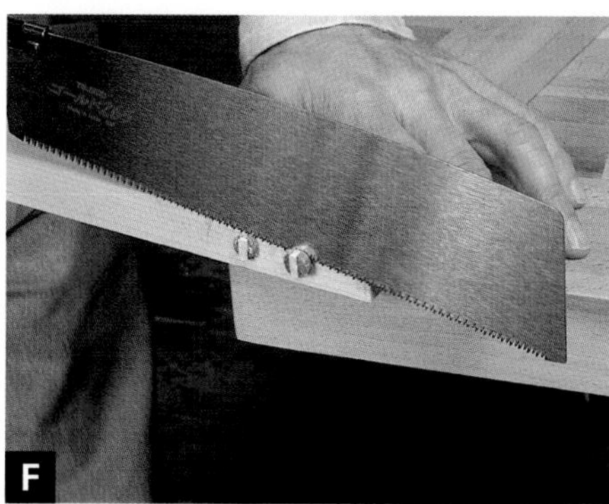
F

G

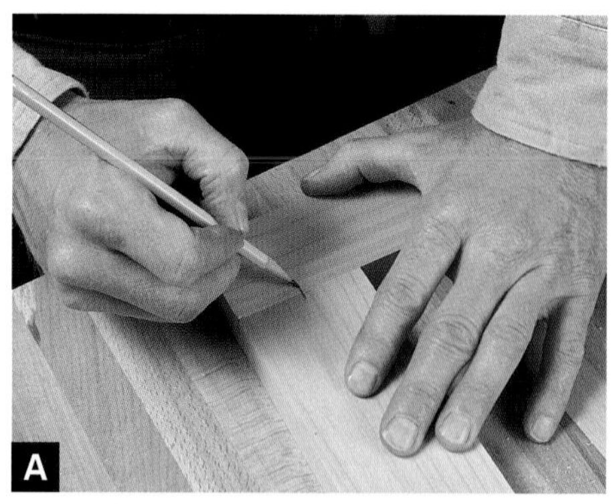
A

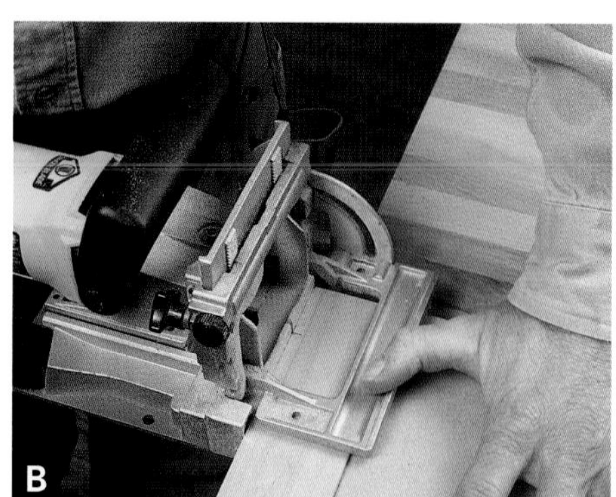
B

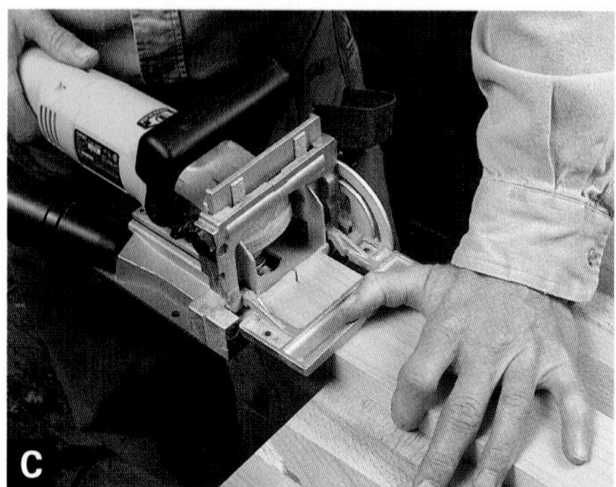
C

D

E

Butt Joint with Biscuits

Use biscuits for a strong and invisible frame joint. Keep the biscuit cut centered in the thickness of the frame. Also index off the face sides of all the frame pieces to ensure a flat frame. Be sure to use a small enough biscuit that the cut doesn't show through at the ends of the board, or offset the cut to one edge if that edge won't be visible. Make a practice cut first to see what diameter cut will be made.

Mark the location of the biscuits onto the frame (**A**). Push the boards into a clamped backer board or bench dogs so they're well supported. Cut the biscuit slots on the stile edge (**B**). Then make the biscuit slots on the rail end. Always keep the biscuit joiner flat on each piece so the slot goes in straight (**C**).

Put glue in the slots using a brush so enough glue gets in (**D**). Have clamps ready to pull the frame together, because the biscuits start to swell as soon as the glue comes into contact with them (**E**).

Butt Joint with Multiple Biscuits

For thicker frames, use multiple biscuits. The biscuit slots are close to the two faces of the boards. Mark the biscuit location across the frame members (**A**). Then mark the depth of the biscuit cuts on the side of the board (**B**).

Set up the biscuit joiner for the first cut and cut all the boards (**C**). Then re-adjust the fence for the second cut (**D**). Make the second set of cuts on all the boards (**E**). Instead of changing the fence adjustment, you can use a flat shim under the fence to raise the biscuit joiner after making the lower cut. The shim has to be flat and of the proper thickness so the upper cut is in the correct position.

TIP If you mill the stock accurately, you can make the first biscuit cut and just flip the board to make the second cut. You'll need two sets of pencil marks, one on each face.

Before gluing the biscuits into the frame members, have clamps ready to pull everything together (**F**).

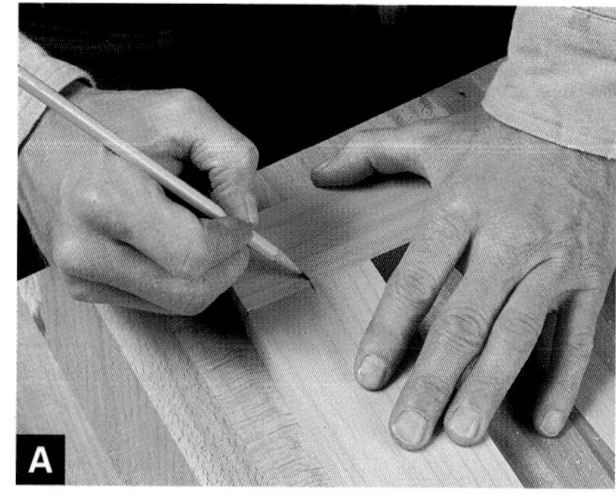
A

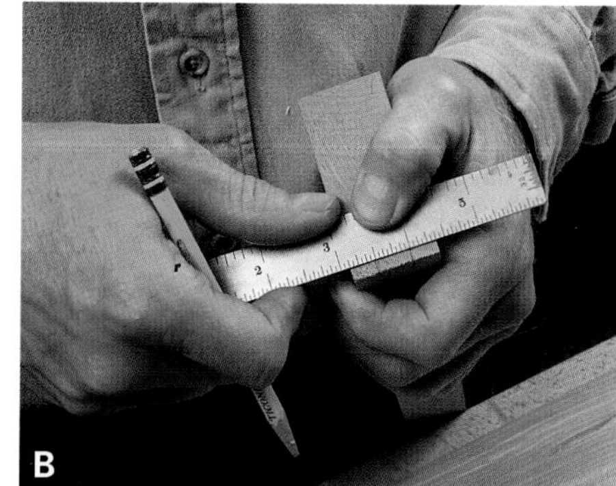
B

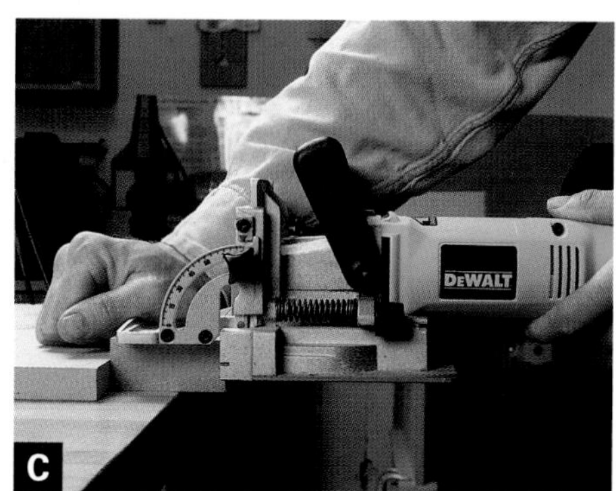

C

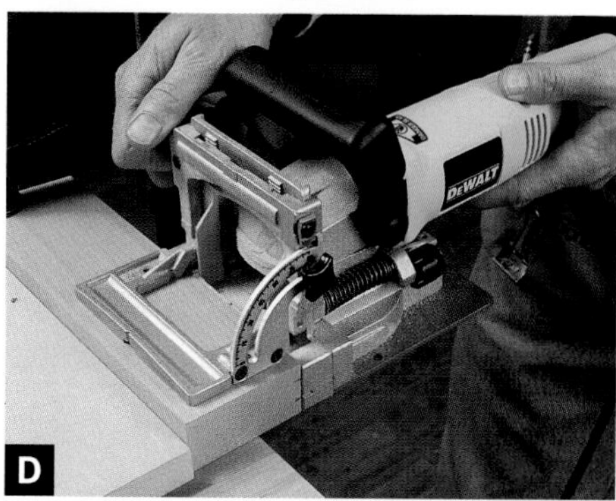

D

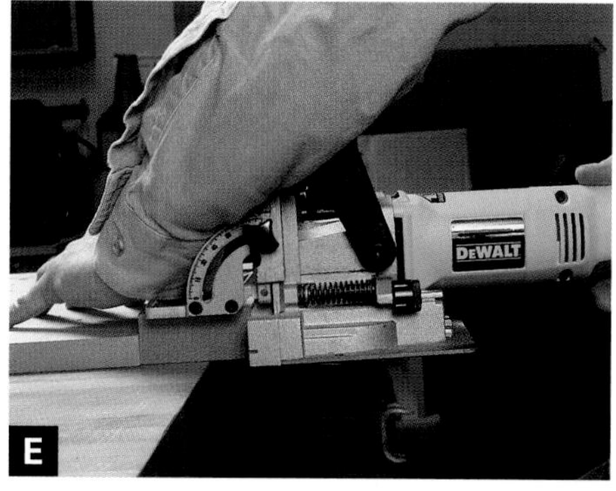

E

F

Miter Joints

Butt Miter Joints

Biscuited Miter Joint

Splined Miter Joints

Mitered Slip Joint

Keyed Miter Joints

FRAME MITER JOINTS are most useful in situations that require a consistent long-grain look around a frame. Because there is no end grain showing in this joint, you can have an undisturbed molding pattern cut right around the inside or outside of the frame. You'll find miters to be the joint of choice for picture and mirror frames. They're also used in face frames and door frames when a molded edge is important or when exposed end grain would be objectionable.

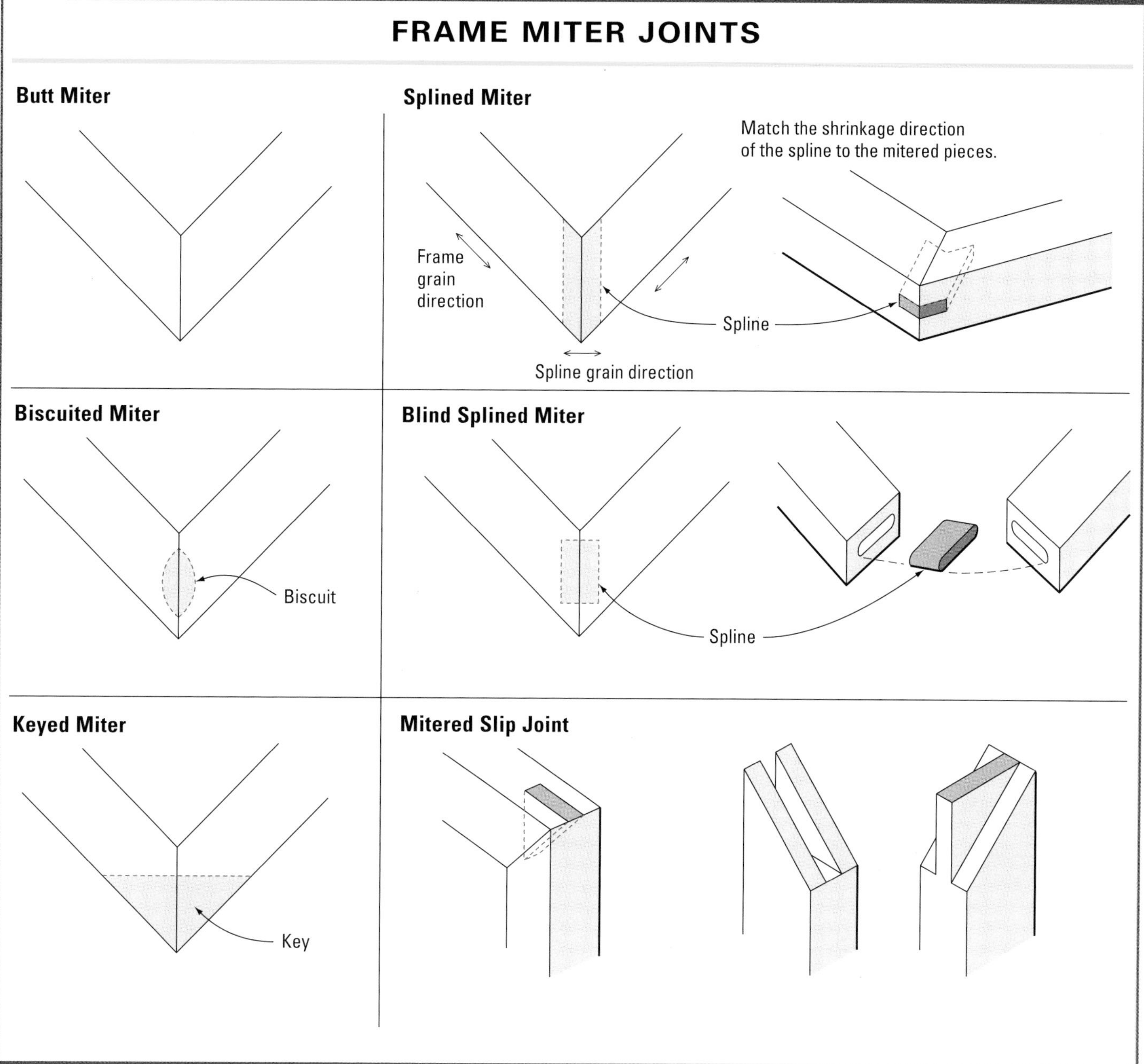

Miter Cuts

Miter cuts require precision. The slightest variation off of true in either direction shows instantly as a gap in the joint. Most miters are bisecting a 90-degree angle, so each miter cut ends up at 45 degrees. Other angles require different bisecting angles; but to keep things simple, always halve the angle of the joint you're making.

It takes practice to make miter cuts perfectly with a handsaw.

BISECTING AN ANGLE

90°
45°
60°
30°
X
C
A
X

Use a compass to bisect an angle. Strike two points (X) along the angle; then strike a line from each point X. Point C is where they intersect. Line AC bisects the angle.

You can cut miter joints by hand and eye with a backsaw or use a carpenter's miter box, but it's difficult to make miters by hand without some final fitting. When cutting moldings in the miter box, always keep the cut running into the molding and not out, to avoid tearout. The cutting direction also depends on what type of saw you're using: European (push stroke) or Japanese (pull stroke).

Miter saws, or compound miter saws, do a better job of reproducing cut after cut at exactly the required angle you're looking for. For longer frame pieces, be sure to support the boards well and to set up a stop to duplicate any cut.

Cut moldings so the cutting action of the saw moves into the molding and not out of it, which causes tearout.

The table saw is the last cutting option for a furniture maker. Miter gauges rarely track accurately in the table's miter slot, usually because of sloppy fitting. You can fit miter gauge bars with inserts to take care of this. Angle the gauge so the saw pushes the frame piece into the gauge; this will give you a safer cut, even if it's slightly less clean. Since you're cutting uphill on the miter, you might see a little more fuzz. Cutting downhill on the miter might be cleaner, but you run the risk of pulling the work into the blade if it slips as you cut.

[TIP] Put a piece of sandpaper on the face of the miter gauge with some double-sided tape to prevent slippage.

Compound miter saws can make accurate miters repeatedly.

A picture framing jig is the best way to cut frame miters on the table saw. The jig uses a very simple geometric concept: the right angle. If you cut a right angle in a piece of plywood and then mount that board on another fitted with runners, but set at a 45-degree angle to the sawblade, you'll always cut matching pieces that make a 90-degree corner. Even if the fence is set slightly off 45 degrees, your cuts will always be complementary. You just need to remember to cut each side of the miter on each side of the jig.

The frame stock can't be too thick or turned on edge, because the blade will reach only so high. But by using this accurate fence and using the two jig runners to track

Angle the gauge so the work gets pushed into it.

This fence piece is cut at exactly 90 degrees, so cuts made to each side of it will be complementary.

in the gauge slots, you can greatly improve your skill in cutting miters. Make the runners out of quartersawn stock to minimize wood movement.

➤ See *"Cutting Miter Joints"* on pp. 106–107 for more cutting techniques.

Use stops on the picture framing jig to index the cuts.

Trimming Miters

Most miter cuts will need some trimming to achieve that really flawless fit. If your block plane is tuned up and sharpened properly, you can make a few judicious passes with it to clean up a miter cut. You can also use a bench plane and miter-shooting board. Always cut downhill on the miter and make sure the plane's iron is adjusted accurately.

A miter trimmer is another option for truing miters. These guillotine-type cutters supply tremendous leverage to slice through the toughest wood. The miter trimmer does require some adjustment and fine-tuning for the best results; but the glass-smooth finish you can achieve makes trimming miters a pleasure.

Trim a frame miter with very light block plane passes.

True your hand-cut miters on a miter shooting board.

The disk sander can also trim miters effectively. Use a one-runner version of the picture framing jig to hold the work up to the disk. Use both sides of the jig to trim matching parts of the joint. Always use the left side of the disk sander so the disk pushes the work down into the table. Make sure the table is at 90 degrees to the disk, too.

Strengthening Miters

The miter joint benefits greatly from some type of strengthening. Miters all by themselves don't offer much in the way of strength, because they're essentially a butt joint with a slight advantage. The grain in a butt miter is halfway between long grain and end grain so it's not an optimal gluing situation. By inserting fasteners, such as nails, brads, or pins, you can tighten up a picture frame joint with ease and add strength.

Hidden fasteners, such as Tite-Joint fasteners, and even bolts can be let in across the back face of a larger miter. But easier and stronger options exist. Biscuit joints between the mitered pieces offer excellent gluing sur-

Set the fence of the miter trimmer at exactly 45 degrees and check that the piece does not slip as it's being cut.

Sand on the left side of the disk so the work gets pushed into the table.

Put a brad across a picture frame joint to hold it fast.

Biscuit joints cut into the miters glue up long grain to long grain.

faces. Dowels can also be used, but they're much trickier to place accurately.

Loose splines placed into the miters offer good gluing surfaces and add a nice decorative touch. They're cut into the miters before gluing. You can call out the fact that the spline is there by using a contrasting-color wood or even by pinning the joint. These loose splines will also help in the glue-up because they prevent parts from slipping around. To make effective and good-looking splines, cut their thickness and length accurately.

Key cuts are made into a miter joint after it's glued. You run the joint across a table-

Loose splines bridge the miter joint, locking long grain to long grain. The grain direction of the spline runs the same way as the frame members for the best strength.

Pinned spline miters have good strength and looks.

KEYED MITER JOINTS

Keyed Miter

Key

Face Keyed Miter

Face keys

Dovetail Keyed Miter

Dovetail key

Butterfly Keyed Miter

Butterfly key

Key cuts across a frame lock the joint and add a design detail.

This face key is quite visible and strong.

saw blade or router bit to make a slot that is filled with another piece of wood. Cutting across the joint reveals long-grain surface, which glues up well with the key. Inlaid keys also work to strengthen a miter joint and give a highly visible appearance to your joinery.

Gluing Miters

One fact about gluing miters is that the miters tend to soak up glue. The end grain pores may be sliced off at an angle but they still suck up glue and can leave a miter joint glue starved. You could just apply extra gobs of glue, but this is messy and unnecessary. Sizing the joint with a coat of glue first to fill the end grain pores helps seal the wood so the adhesive isn't all spirited away.

Figure out your clamping before applying glue. Band clamps provide pretty good pressure for picture frame joints. You can also make up some clamping blocks to help provide pressure right over the joint. Cut small miters in scrap wood and clamp these to the frame pieces. Make sure the clamping handles stay out of each other's way and that the blocks don't slip as you apply pressure to the joint. Good clamping pressure should hold them, but you can also glue sandpaper onto the clamping blocks to prevent slippage.

➤ **See *"Gluing Miter Joints"* on pp. 108–109 for clamping options.**

Sizing a miter joint with glue helps its holding power.

Band clamps provide even pressure for picture frame joints.

Use clamping blocks to put pressure right over the joint.

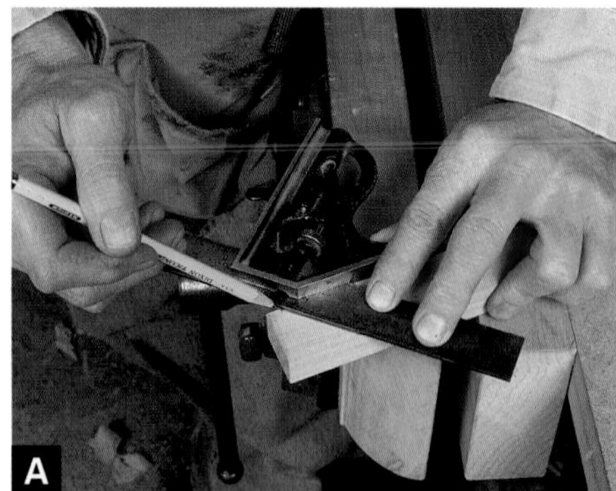
A

B

C

D

Miter Joint

Lay out the 45-degree miter line with a combination square. Hold the square tight to the edge of the board. You can square the miter line down the sides of the board, if you want, for another aid when cutting (**A**).

Cut the miter with a handsaw, but remember that you're always cutting in two directions: across at the angle and straight down the board. Here, practice definitely makes for perfect (**B**). Miter boxes are old stand-bys for roughing out miter cuts. Finish carpenters use them for doing trim work in a house. Line up the saw tight against the 45-degree slot while making the cut (**C**).

Trim the miter by taking very light passes with a block plane. If you're careful and the plane is tuned and sharp, this cleanup pass will improve the miter in a matter of seconds. Be sure to hold the plane square to the face of the board (**D**).

Miter Joint Reinforced with Nails

Simple frames can be strengthened using nails or brads across the joint. Cut the miters using a handsaw or compound miter saw (**A**). Glue up the frame and use a band clamp or miter clamps. After the glue has set overnight you can nail the joints.

Very hard woods should be predrilled to avoid splitting. Keep the frame well supported on the bench over a bench leg so the vibration of the hammering gets taken up by the leg (**B**). Brad nailers also work well for pinning miters. Shoot multiple brads in from the same side so they won't run into each other. Also make very sure to aim truly so the brad stays centered in the frame. Avoid knots and keep your fingers well away from the joint when using a brad nailer (**C**).

Finally, set the nails or brads with a nail set and put putty in the holes before finishing (**D**).

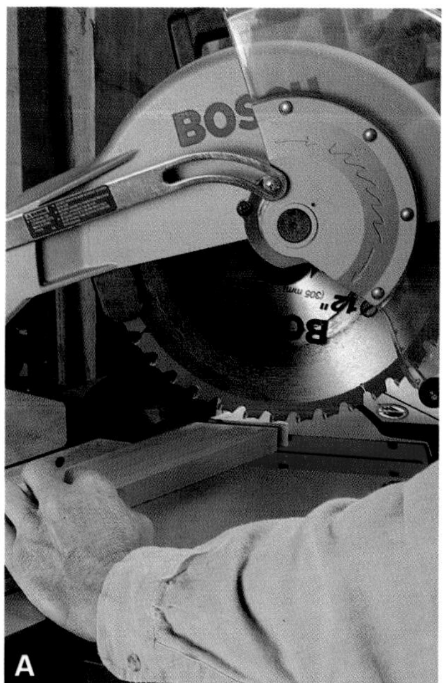
A

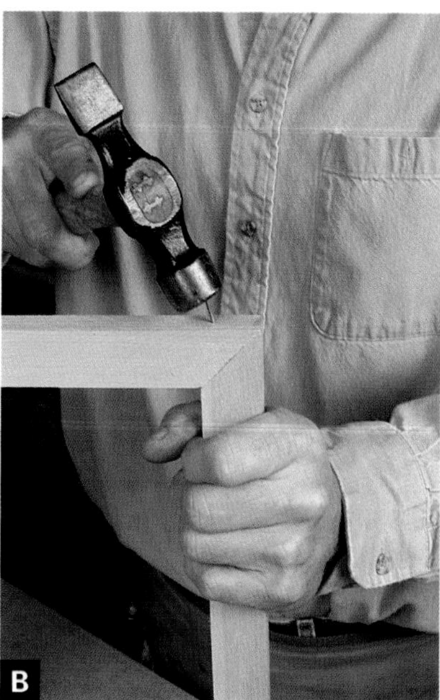
B

C

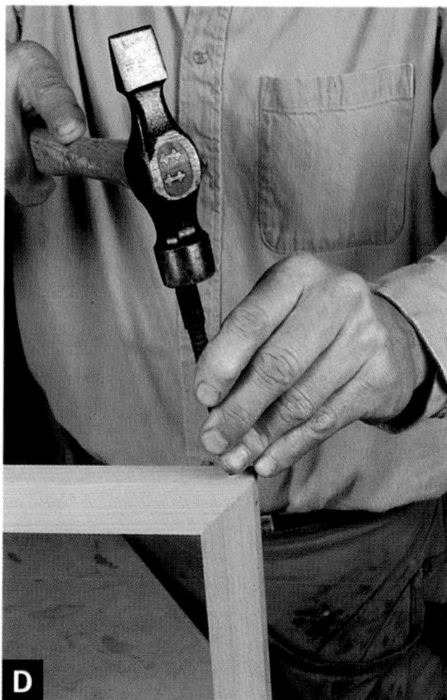
D

A

B

C

D

Biscuited Miter Joint

Use a biscuit across a miter joint to improve its strength. To keep it hidden, the biscuit should be shorter than the length of the miter. The biscuit slot is cut into long grain, so the biscuit will make a good glue joint.

Mark the biscuit location on the face side of the miter joint (**A**). Cut the biscuit slot into each mitered frame member, centering the biscuit slot in the thickness of the frame. If you don't hit dead-on center, remember that as long as you reference off matching faces the slots will line up. Hold the biscuit joiner steady and flat on the face of the frame when cutting (**B**).

Put enough glue in the biscuit slot to allow the biscuit to swell and lock the joint in place. Remember to size the end of the miter joint with glue before gluing in the biscuits (**C**). Have clamps ready to pull the miter together (**D**).

Splined Miter Joint on the Router Table

Make spline cuts along the length of the miters for a loose spline. Match the grain direction of the spline to that of the frame, so they'll shrink in the same direction. The spline can be made of a contrasting wood or the same wood; but remember it will always show, because the exposed grain is part end grain.

You can use the router table for spline cuts that aren't too deep. Mount a straight bit for the size spline required (**A**). Measure for the spline location on a frame member and center this as best you can. Double splines can be used in thicker frames and should be measured for them accordingly (**B**).

You'll cut the spline slot using a spline miter jig (**C**). Set the fence distance off the pencil-marked frame member with the jig in place. Clamp the router table fence down securely (**D**). For deeper slots, don't take one full pass to make the cut. Make several passes to get down to depth. You can clamp the frame member onto the miter jig or hold it securely onto the jig and pass it over the bit for a series of cuts (**E**). Make the second pass using a second fence on the miter jig. Use this fence for boards that have to index off the same face side. This way, even if the slot isn't centered in the frame member, the cuts will match (**F**).

VARIATION Use a slotting cutter in the router table to cut the spline slot. Capture the cutter in a zero-clearance fence, exposing only as much bit as is required. Stack several frame members together for the cut and use a backer for even better support. Remember to index off matching faces.

A

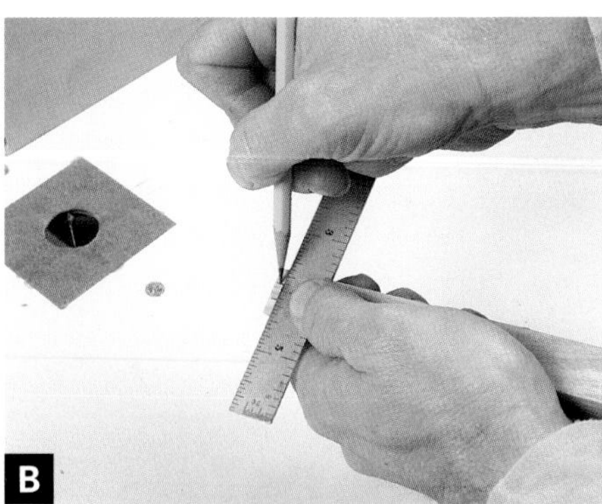
B

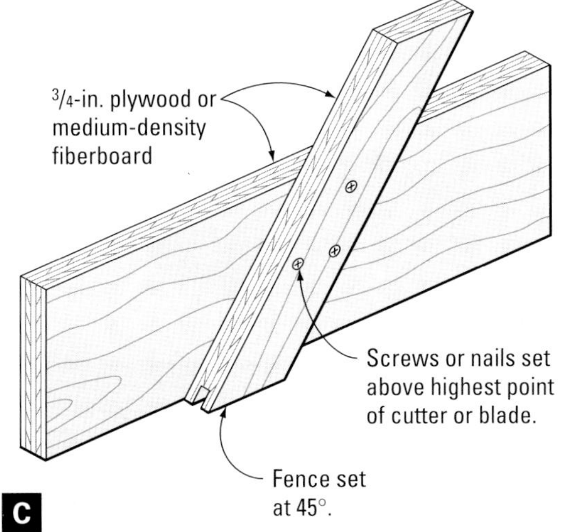

C

D

E

F

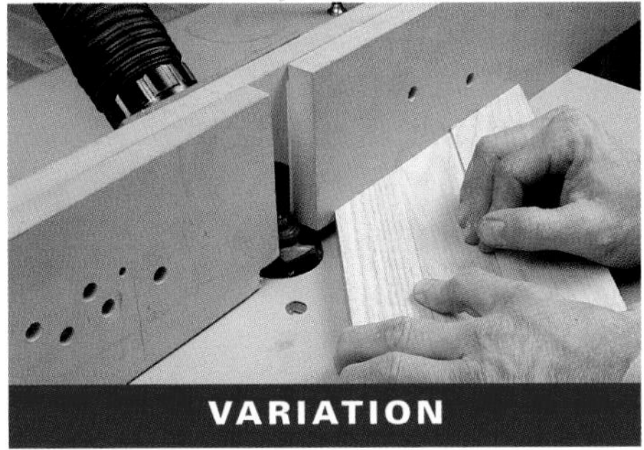
VARIATION

A

B

D

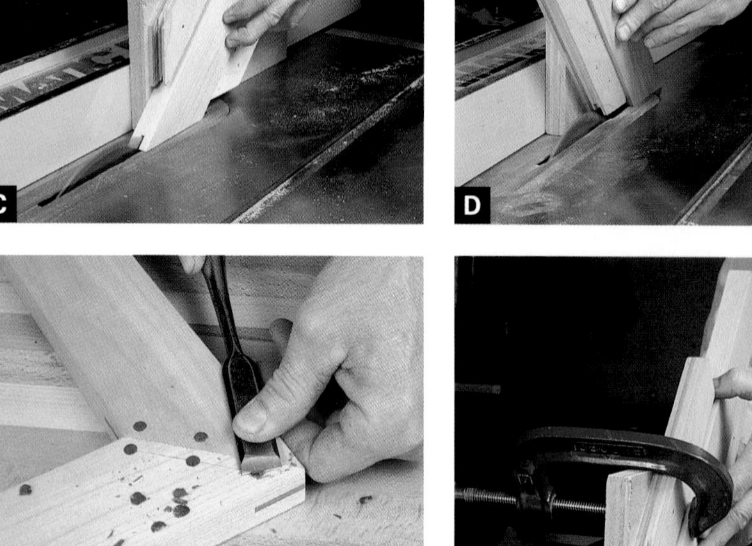
C

E

VARIATION

Splined Miter Joint on the Table Saw

Loose spline miter cuts on the table saw are all made with the blade at full height. Set the fence distance with the board marked out for the cut. Hold the miter jig in place when setting the fence. The cut shown here will yield a simple ⅛-in.-wide slot with a regular sawblade. A thin-kerf blade will cut an even smaller slot (**A**).

Set the blade height for the full height of the slot (**B**). Make the first spline cut by passing the board at a moderate speed over the blade. Too slow a speed and you might end up burning the wood (**C**). Make the matching cut using the miter jig with a second fence on it. Clamp the frame member to the jig or hold it firmly in place as you pass it by the blade (**D**).

VARIATION **Use a dado blade for wider spline cuts. Clamp the frame member to the jig. If you're getting tearout with this cut, use a backer board or put in a gauge line on the back edge of the frame member.**

Pinning the splines with dowel pins gives the joint even more visual interest and strength. After gluing the miter, drill through the spline on the drill press using a brad-point bit. Glue and hammer in the dowels; then clean them flush with a chisel (**E**).

➤ See *"Making Decorative Plugs"* on p. 55.

Blind Splined Miter Joint on the Multirouter

The Multirouter and other horizontally mounted routers do the best job of cutting slots for blind splines for miter joints.

Mount the router with the right size bit for the mortise cut (**A**). Set the table up for a 45-degree cut with a clamped-on fence or use the provided table stops. Clamp the workpiece down securely so it can't move during the cut (**B**). Next, set the bit travel for the width of the cut. Remember to set stops for both sides of the cut (**C**). Then set the depth of cut, zeroing the bit on the workpiece. Make the cut and continue cutting all the pieces. If the cut isn't perfectly centered you'll have to set up a complementary cut for the matching pieces (**D**).

Mill the spline material, rough it out on the bandsaw, and trim it to thickness and width on the table saw. Notice that the spline material is as wide as the mortise cut. It ends up being fairly narrow stock that's best milled in long strips (**E**).

➤ See *"Making Splines"* on p. 222.

Round over the edges of the spline stock to match the round ends of the mortises. Mount a roundover bit in the router table, and set the depth of cut to give a bullnose edge to the spline stock (**F**). If you don't have a roundover bit that matches the mortise, keep the spline stock undersize in width and bevel its edges instead. Glue the spline into one side and then check its length to make sure it's seated properly. Then glue the miter joint together (**G**).

A

B

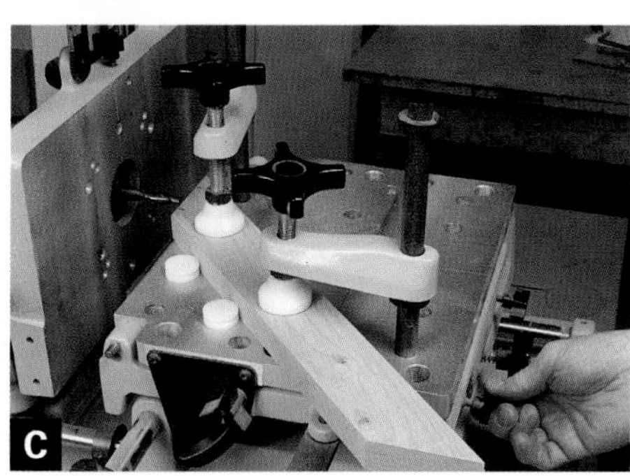
C

D

E

F

G

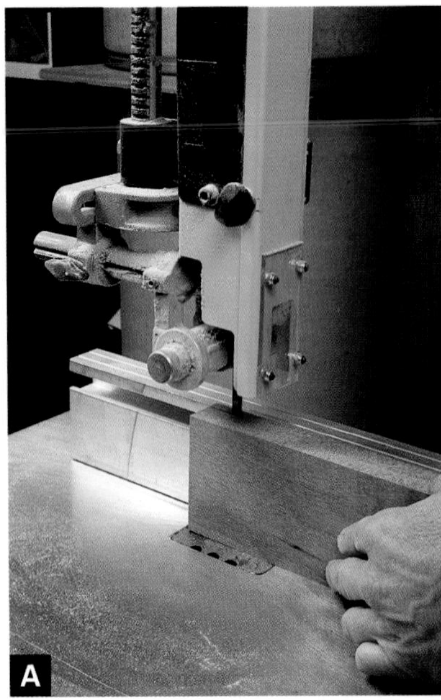
A

B

C

Making Splines

Make spline stock out of the same material as the frame or use a contrasting stock for effect. Remember to run the grain direction of the spline stock in the same direction as the frame. This way all the parts will shrink together in the same direction.

First, rough out stock on the bandsaw using material as wide as the spline (**A**). Then trim to thickness or just oversize on the table saw. Use a push stick to move the wood past the blade. Keep the spline material a bit thicker than its slot so you can plane off those inevitable saw marks (**B**). Cut the splines exactly to length on the table saw or with a handsaw (**C**).

! WARNING When cutting a small piece like this on the crosscut jig, you will trap it between the stop and the blade. So be sure to hang on to it so it doesn't kick back into your face. Use a pencil instead of your fingers to hold the piece.

Mitered Slip Joint

The mitered slip joint is more like a slot mortise-and-tenon joint than a miter joint. But the result shows a mitered joint to the world. Each matching board for the joint is cut differently. Miter cut one board's end and crosscut the other board square. The penciled-out areas on the boards shown in photo **A** indicate what wood has to come out. You'll cut a mortise slot square across the mitered board and make two mitered shoulder cuts on the squared board to establish the tenon.

Use a dado blade and the tenoning jig to make the slot cut straight across the mitered board. Clamp each mitered board vertically in the tenoning jig. Set the blade height so the bottom of the slot is in line with the end of the miter cut. Make all the slot cuts (**B**).

Use the miter jig to cut the mitered shoulder tenon. Set the blade height to start cutting just at the corner of the frame board (**C**). Make the first cheek cut with the miter jig. Make the same cut on all the square-end boards (**D**).

Make the second cut after resetting the saw fence. Since this cut comes all the way out to the face of the board, use a spacer to push each board out just a bit from the jig. Then the blade will make the cut without marring the jig (**E**).

VARIATION **Instead of cutting the tenon in the miter jig, use the miter gauge and a dado blade to cut the tenon boards, holding them flat on the saw table. Make a series of passes to cut each tenon cheek.**

Fit the slip joint carefully so it slides together with just hand pressure. You can clamp across the faces once it's together (**F**).

A

C

B

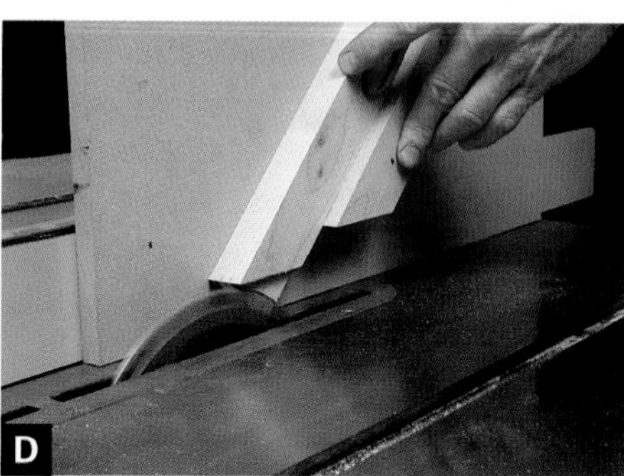
D

E

F

VARIATION

A

B

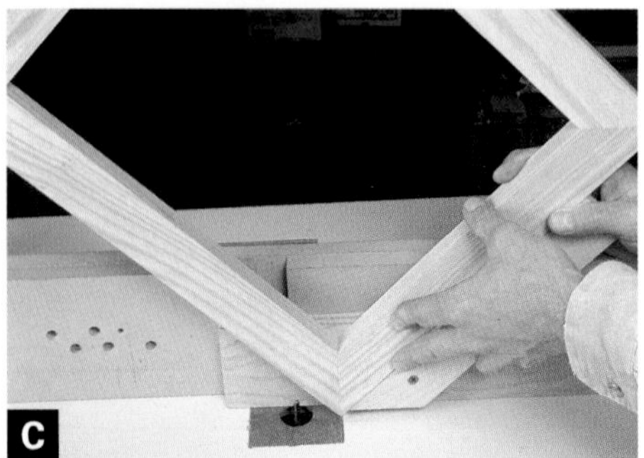
C

VARIATION

D

Keyed Miter Joint

When constructing a keyed miter joint, make the key cuts after the frame has been glued together (**A**). Measure for the key position after cleaning the faces of the frame with a handplane, scraper, or sander. Place the board in a vise to hold it while marking (**B**).

Make the key cut using a straight bit in a table-mounted router. This will create a nice flat-bottomed cut. Use the miter jig to support the frame as you pass it by the bit. Set the bit for the full depth of cut, but don't try to cut at that full depth in one pass. Instead, make a series of passes. Either clamp the frame in the jig or hold it up high in the jig for the first pass and then gradually lower it after each pass for a deeper cut. After each key slot is cut, rotate the frame in the jig to cut the next corner (**C**).

[VARIATION] To make a deeper key cut on wider frames, use the table saw and hold the miter jig up against the fence. It's up to you to hold it tightly to the saw fence.

Mill the key stock on the bandsaw. Rough out the thickness and width on a long stick of wood. Use a contrasting wood to make a nice design element in the frame (**D**).

Cut the key stock to thickness on the table saw. Use a push stick to move the stock past the blade (**E**). You should leave the width oversize and cut the keys oversize in length as well. There's no need fussing with the dimensions, because you'll cut the keys off flush after they are glued in place.

E

F

Plane the keys to fit on a bench hook using a block plane to trim them to size. The block plane will be small enough to work easily on the key stock. Put one key behind another to support the sole of the plane (**F**). When the key fits hand snug in the slot, you can glue it in place. Make sure it fits all the way down into the bottom of the slot, and don't trust a blob of glue as evidence that it's seated. Check to see that the key is flush across the slot (**G**). After the glue has set, trim the overhanging keys on the bandsaw. Then handplane or sand the keys flush to the frame edges (**H**).

G

H

[TIP] Cut down away from the corner in each direction for handplane cleaning. Otherwise you'll be cutting uphill on the key, causing tearout at the corner.

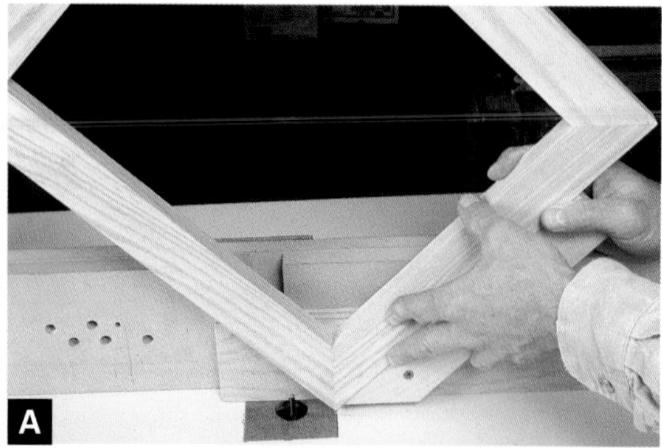
A

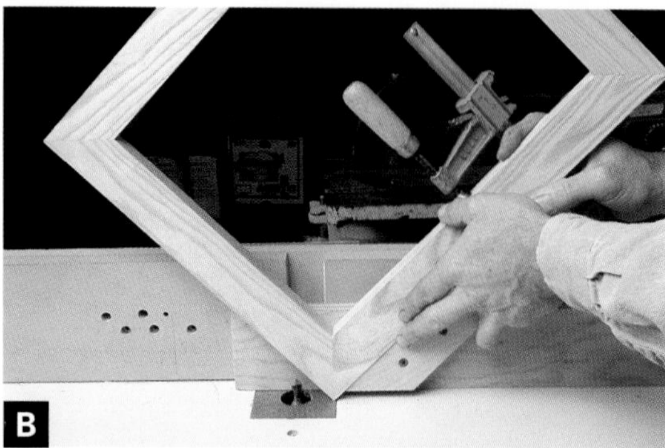
B

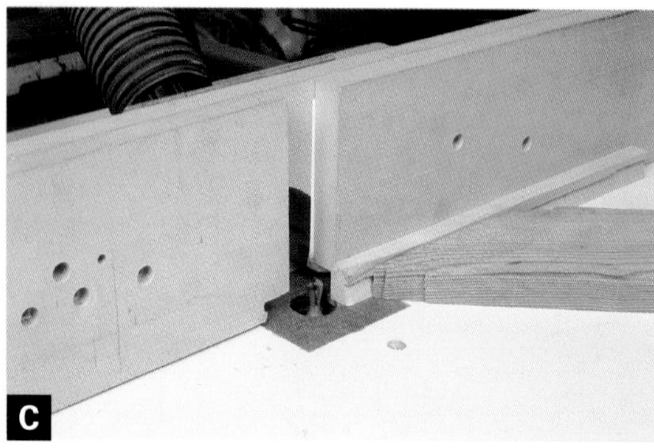
C

Dovetail Keyed Miter Joint

Make the cut for a dovetail keyed miter joint as if you were making a straight key cut. To save wear on the dovetail bit, use the straight bit to remove most of the wood first. You could also use the table saw to cut away some of the waste (**A**). If you center the straight bit on the center of the frame, just replace the straight bit with a dovetail bit without moving the fence. If not, then make your setup with the dovetail bit in place and the miter jig up against the fence. Make the dovetail cut (**B**).

Cut the spline using the same dovetail bit. Mill up some key stock just oversize in width to the full size of the dovetail bit. Make sure it's oversize in height so there will be some wood to run against the fence. Capture the bit in the fence and make the first pass. Then make the second pass, check the fit, and finish up the second pass on the key stock when it fits snug in the dovetail slot (**C**).

Face Keyed Miter Joint

The face keyed miter joint was probably at first a fortuitous mistake. A cut was made when a fence was set incorrectly; but it looked good, so a new method of strengthening a miter was born. The face key cut is like a straight key cut but it's set out at the face of the frame.

Cut both faces of a corner. Set the blade depth for the full depth of cut (**A**). For balance, make a pass along the inside face as well, just flipping the frame over in the miter jig to make those cuts (**B**).

Mill key stock on the bandsaw first and then on the table saw. Make the key stock thicker than the key cut so you can clamp right onto it (**C**).

Glue both keys on at once making sure they seat all the way to the bottom of the key cut. Clamp across them (**D**). Finish the joint by planing the keys flush with the frame's faces and edges (**E**).

A

B

C

D

E

A

C

B

D

Butterfly Keyed Miter Joint

Inlay butterfly keys into a glued-up mitered frame for both looks and strength. Strengthen the miter internally with a blind spline or biscuit. Make key stock out of a contrasting wood. The stock should be wider and thicker than the final size of the keys. Make up a key template out of cardboard or wood and use it to mark out the keys on the wood you'll use for them (**A**).

Rough out the key shapes on the bandsaw, coming just as close as you can to the pencil marks. Cut the keys to length as well. If you can tip your table in both directions, make the cuts at about a 5-degree angle (**B**). Clean the keys to their final shape with a sharp chisel. Keep your fingers behind the blade and push the key into a bench hook or place it in the vise. After shaping the key, slightly angle its sides by about 5 degrees. Do this to the ends as well. This will make the key slightly smaller on one face than the other (**C**).

Measure from the corner to set each key in place. Then scribe around the key with a marking knife, holding the key tightly to the frame with the smaller face held down. Thus when you put in the inlay, the wider part of the key's top face will fill up any little indiscretions in your chisel work. Number each key and set of scribed lines (**D**).

Fill the scribed lines with pencil lead so you can see them more easily; then mount a small-diameter bit in the router. Set the depth of cut for less than the thickness of the key stock. Then rout freehand close to the scribed lines to rout away the ground. Rout in a counterclockwise motion, which yields a climb cut that tends to push the bit away from the cut. This allows you to control the cut more easily. But still remember to take light passes with the bit (**E**).

Clean up the scribed edges with a chisel. Chop straight down into the frame, but be careful at the corners of the inlay ground. As it enters more deeply, the bevel of the chisel will mar an adjacent face. Come at the corners with more of an angle to clean them up (**F**).

Test-fit each key individually until it almost fits to depth. Then put glue in the ground area and side walls and tap the inlay down with a hammer until it fits (**G**). You can use a clamp to make sure it's seated all the way in. Use a plane to cut the inlay flush to the surface of the frame once the glue has set up (**H**).

E

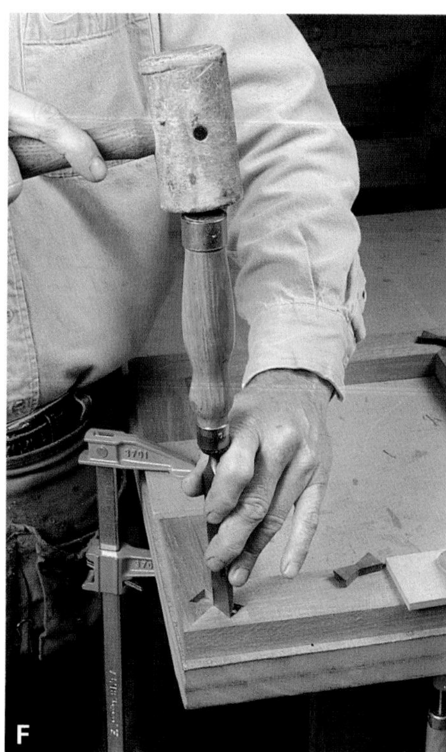
F

G

H

Lap and Bridle Joints

Corner Half-Lap Joints

T or Cross Half Laps

Dovetail Lap Joint

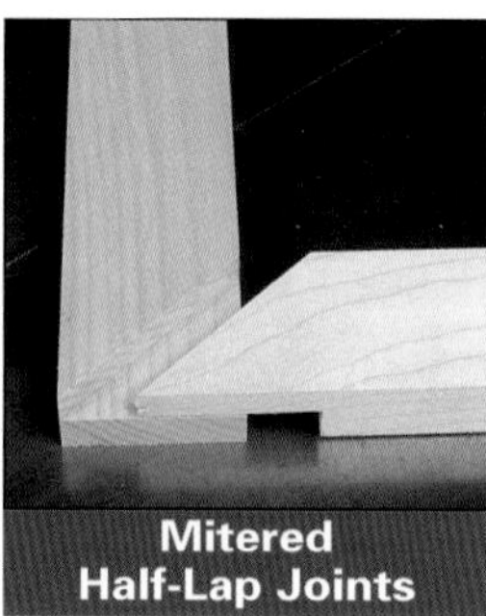
Mitered Half-Lap Joints

Corner Bridle Joints

T Bridle Joint

Halved Joints

One-Third Lap Joint

Bird's-Mouth Joints

Lap joints are used in frame construction when a simple joint of moderate strength is sufficient. Since a lap joint usually consists of only a square shoulder and a flat cheek cut halfway through the thickness of the board, it's easy to cut with a variety of tools. Fitting this joint is also simple, because both parts of the joint are easily accessible. They require no finer tuning than mating two flat faces to one another.

The joint has plenty of long-grain-to-long-grain surface for gluing and the shoulders help resist racking to some extent. But there is little resistance to twisting, so a dowel pin or screw adds strength. Lap joints are used predominantly in narrower members to avoid shrinkage problems. Use them in picture and mirror frames as well as simple frame construction. If used across wider boards, they absolutely require a screw or pin. But their ability to hold tight gets tested as these wider boards expand and contract. In these cases, a glue that stretches a little, such as yellow polyvinyl acetate (PVA), is a good idea.

Because lap joints expose so much end grain and joint line to the elements, they are of limited usefulness in outdoor situations. An epoxy is better for lap joints used outdoors.

One distinct advantage to the lap joint is that it can be shaped in a curved or patterned frame.

Bridle joints straddle a tenoned member on two sides. In this way they are more like mortise-and-tenon construction than lap joinery. Also referred to as slot mortise and tenons when used at a corner, these joints offer a good gluing surface, although their

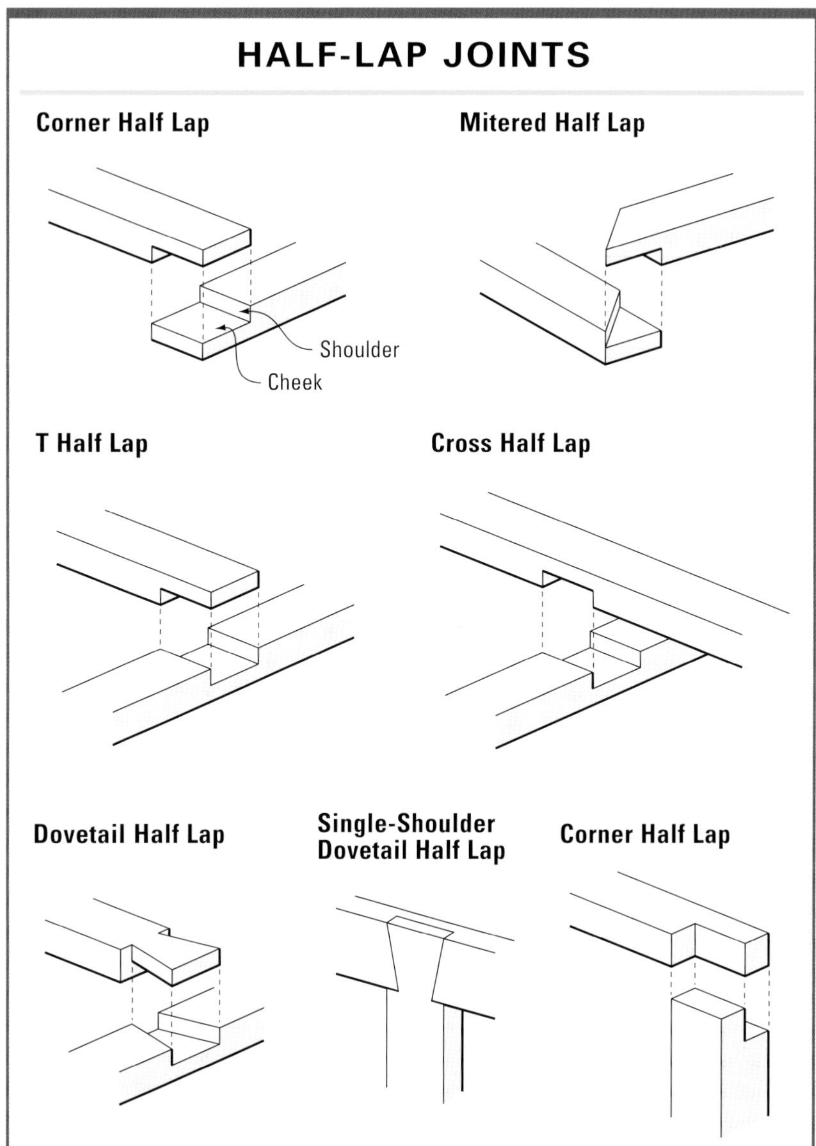

Lap joints are quick to make and provide moderate strength. The joint can easily be shaped, as shown by this mirror frame.

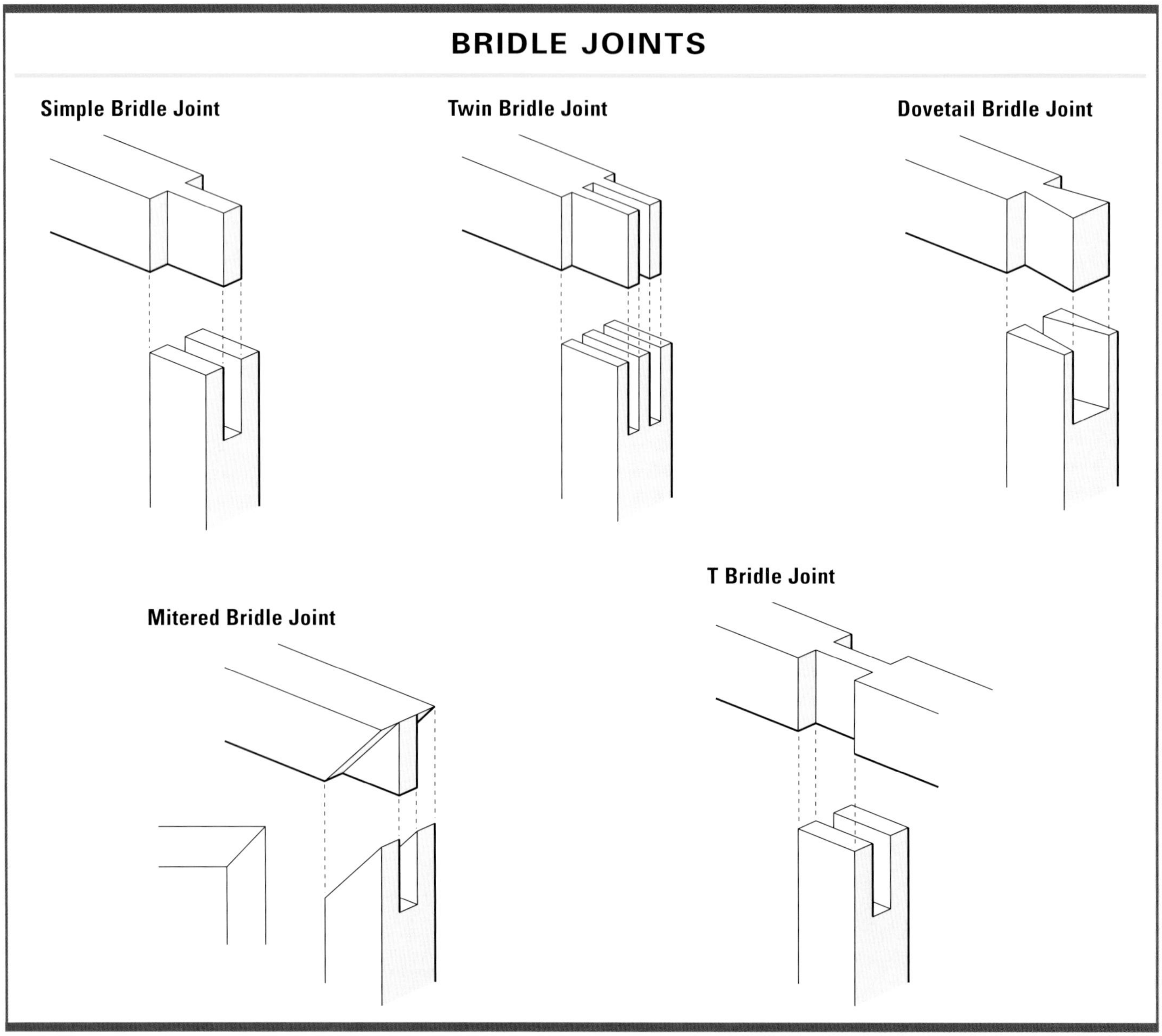

BRIDLE JOINTS

Simple Bridle Joint

Twin Bridle Joint

Dovetail Bridle Joint

Mitered Bridle Joint

T Bridle Joint

The bridle joint shows end grain on both the top and the side.

resistance to racking is compromised by showing through on two sides. With so much end grain exposed, they are also susceptible to moisture gain and loss. But with the addition of a pin, the bridle joint has good strength.

Bridle joints also offer good contrast between the long-grain and end-grain wood

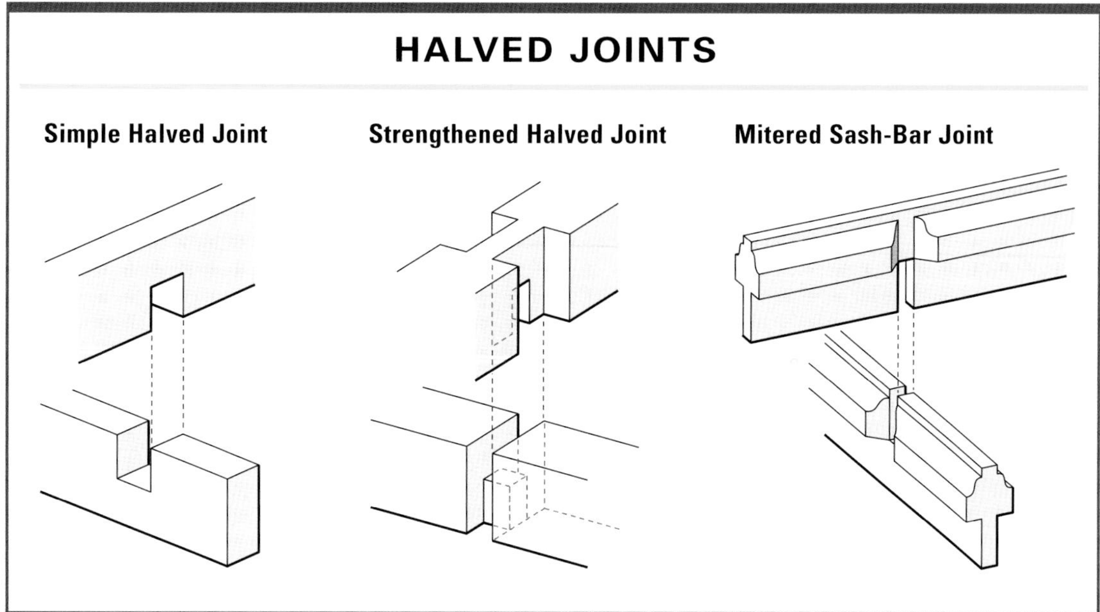

and can be shaped and patterned. They can easily be fitted by trimming with a handplane along the long-grain edges. Use these joints in carcase work when a long rail needs structural support from beneath.

Halved joints are cut in the width of boards. Simple halved joints come in handy for joinery for box dividers or the intersecting members of sash frames. Torsion box construction relies on halved joints to create the interior of the structural carcase. But with no shoulders to protect the halved joint from twisting, it splits out easily along the weakened long grain when cut in wide members. Use strengthened versions of this joint for a longer-lasting fit in situations in which the joint might get bumped or hit.

Cutting Methods

Since most lap and bridle joints have simple squared shoulders, these joints can be cut with a variety of saws and router bits or a combination thereof. Use a method that suits your needs for speed, accuracy, repeatability, and noise level. Any handsaw can make shoulder and cheek cuts, but use a backsaw with crosscut teeth to make the shoulder cut and a ripsaw for the cheek for the best results. The teeth of these saws are designed specifically for these jobs.

The table saw is the obvious choice for making the square cheek and shoulder cuts. But a variety of other power saws can be used for these cuts, including the bandsaw, the sliding compound miter saw, the radial-

Because it doesn't have shoulders to strengthen it, a halved joint is susceptible to breaking.

A cheek cut is best made with a ripsaw, whereas a shoulder cut—made cross-grain—is cut with a backsaw that has crosscut teeth.

Use a sliding compound miter saw for bridle or lap joint cuts. A series of passes will eventually remove the wood for a cheek cut. A stop indexes the shoulder cut.

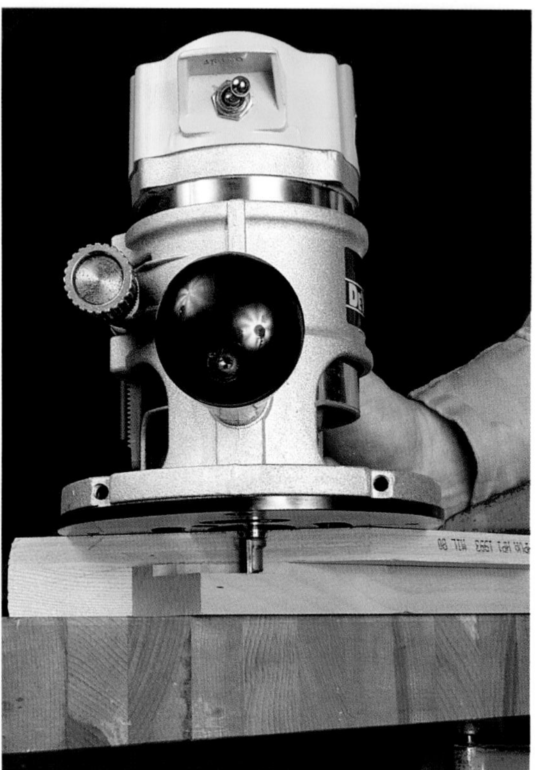
With the aid of a template, this flush-trimming bit cuts out a mitered lap joint.

Rough out the cheeks and shoulder on the bandsaw using a fence.

arm saw, and even a handheld circular saw. Just make sure the saw is cutting accurately to depth by taking practice cuts and checking the results.

In finer work, where the appearance of a joint becomes important, use a router to create perfectly mating cheek cuts.

Using any of the above methods, there is still one step that will improve your speed in cutting and assembly: Whenever you can, rough out the joint first on the bandsaw with two quick cuts. This does several things. By removing the waste, it makes subsequent cuts quicker on the router or saw. It's safer because there's no offcut to kick back on the saw; and, most important, you can use the offcuts to help clamp the joint together. In this way, you won't mar the surface of the boards with clamp heads.

Fitting the Joint

For simplicity's sake, make both cheek cuts for a simple lap joint identical. Take care when laying out the joints, however, to leave the long grain just a bit proud when the joint is finally together. This makes clamping simpler, particularly in bridle joints, since you can put pressure right over the joint without having to use specially cut clamping pads. Cleaning up the long grain is also much simpler than trimming off the hard-to-cut end grain. And the final height of a piece is not compromised as it could be when trimming off the top of a leg compared to trimming the top of a rail.

When just a bit of long grain is left proud of the surface, clamping and cleanup are simple.

Clamping

Because the corner lap joint is so simple to cut, it comes as something of a surprise to see the number of clamps required for glue-up. The clamps are needed since the joint has to be pulled in from three different directions. The same type of clamping is necessary for a bridle joint to ensure a good-looking, good-fitting joint.

All these clamps are required to pull a corner lap joint together.

A

B

C

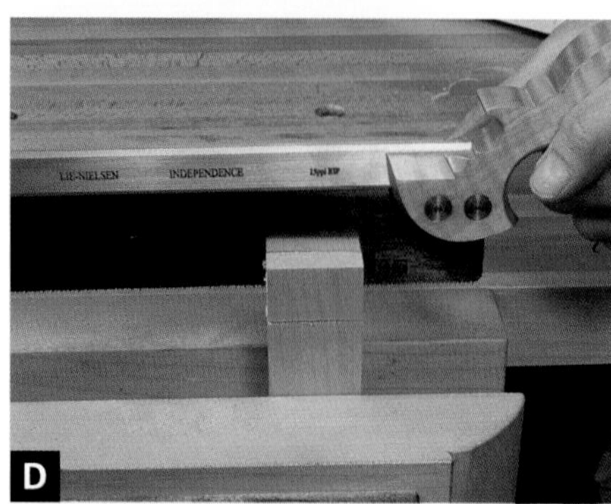
D

E

Hand-Cut Corner Half-Lap Joint

The first step when making a hand-cut corner half-lap joint is to lay out gauge lines on both the edges and the face of the boards. You can fill the lines in with pencil for better visibility. Set the gauge for just under half the thickness of the stock (**A**). Use a square as a depth gauge to set a straight wood fence for a shoulder cut. Set the square for just less than the full width of the stock so clamping is easier. Check both sides of the fence to make sure it's set properly (**B**).

Hold a crosscut saw in tight to the fence and make the shoulder cut down to the gauge lines on both edges. Put a piece of masking tape on the saw and mark the depth of cut on that. Remember to keep the saw straight and held tightly to the fence (**C**). Place the board in the vise and cut the cheek for the lap joint. Use a saw with rip teeth for the best results. You can, of course, use crosscut-style teeth, but it will take longer to make the cut. On wide boards, the backsaw may be too narrow to make the entire cut. Use a regular crosscut saw to finish up the cut (**D**).

Clean up the cheek of the lap joint with a bull-nose plane, shoulder plane, or wide chisel. Make sure the cheek is flat and not twisted (**E**).

Corner Half-Lap Joint on the Router Table

With a wide bit mounted in the router table, you can cut a half-lap joint fairly quickly. Set the bit height to cut just under half the thickness of the stock. First, rough out the joint on the bandsaw so you can set the bit height to its final depth (**A**). Set the fence to make the shoulder cut by using one of the boards as a guide. Clamp the fence in place just under the width of the stock. Have the bit rotated so one of its cutting edges is at a point farthest away from the fence and line up the board just outside that cutting edge (**B**).

Use two or more boards packaged together to make the cuts. You can also use a backer board to help prevent tearout at the rear of the cut. Start at the end of the boards and make full passes across them. Depending on the bit diameter, you may need to make several passes (**C**). Finish up the lap joint cut with the boards running right against the fence (**D**).

A

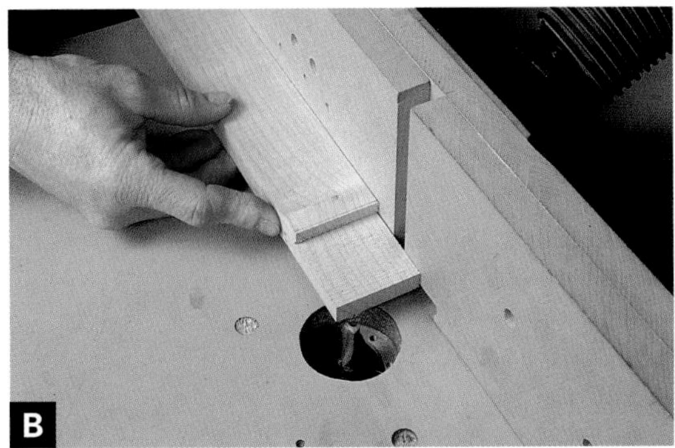
B

C

D

A

B

C

VARIATION

Corner Half-Lap Joint on the Table Saw

To make a corner half-lap joint on the table saw, mark out the shoulder location and depth of cut on the board. These should be set for just under the full width and half the thickness of the stock, which will make clamping and cleanup easier. Set the blade height and clamp a stop on the crosscut jig for the shoulder cuts (**A**).

Make a series of passes to cut the cheek and finally the shoulder (**B**). Most saws with an alternate-top bevel grind leave behind small grooves. Clean those up by moving the board just over top dead center on the blade and moving it back and forth over the blade. Push it forward to cut the next sideways pass and so on until you've trimmed the entire cheek (**C**).

VARIATION **Use the miter gauge with a dado blade to cut lap joints quickly. Move the workpiece past the saw and set the fence up as stop to index the shoulder cut. Keep the feed rate moderate.**

Hand-Cut T or Cross Half-Lap Joint

For a T half-lap joint, cut the first board with a corner half lap.

➤ See *"Hand-Cut Corner Half-Lap Joint"* on p. 236.

Lay the cut board onto the intersecting board with its shoulder tight up against it and mark out the joint using a knife (**A**). Use a pencil to mark the depth of cut for just under half the thickness of the cut.

For a cross half-lap joint, lay the intersecting boards across one another and align them with a square before marking.

Cut a channel with your chisel along the knife mark to help you place the saw (**B**). Make the shoulder cut down to depth. You can put a piece of masking tape along the sawblade and make a pencil mark to indicate the full depth of cut. Saw down to this line. Make sure the shoulders are cut square. You can use a clamped-on fence to help guide the cut if you want (**C**).

Make a series of passes almost to full depth with the saw across the lap joint. Then clean out the waste with a chisel. To avoid tearout, work from both edges in toward the middle (**D**).

Clean out the bottom of the joint with a router plane. Make sure you cut a consistent flat surface across this face (**E**).

Do the final fitting of the joint using a handplane. Trim the edges of the board so it just slides down into the lap cut. This is simpler than trimming the end grain. Check the side-to-side fit by flipping the board upside down and trying it in the joint (**F**).

A

B

C

D

E

F

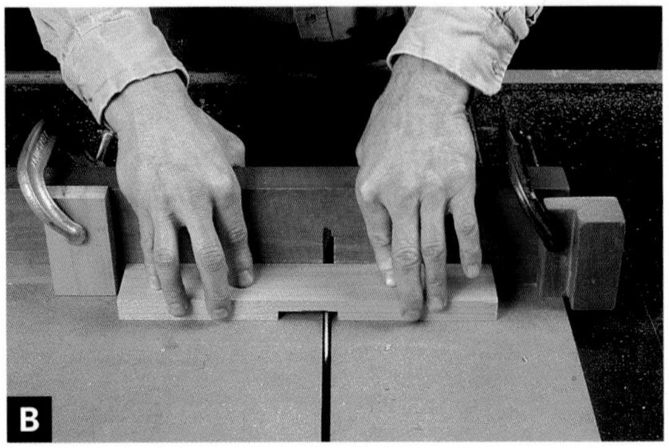

T or Cross Half-Lap Joint on the Table Saw

A

Use this method of cutting a T or cross half-lap joint when joining boards of the same width. Mark out one board for the cross half-lap joint just under the full width of the stock. Also mark out the depth of cut for just under half the thickness of the stock. Set up two stops on the crosscut jig for each shoulder of the joint (**A**).

B

Make a series of passes to cut the joint and then move the workpiece right over the blade. Move it back and forth between the stops at top dead center to clean up the entire face of the joint (**B**).

➤ See *"Corner Half-Lap Joint on the Table Saw"* on p. 238.

VARIATION You can also set up a dado blade to make lap cuts. Use a moderate feed rate to move the boards over the blade.

C

Fit the cross half-lap joint to width by taking handplane passes along the edges of the board. Check the fit by turning the board over and placing it in the joint (**C**).

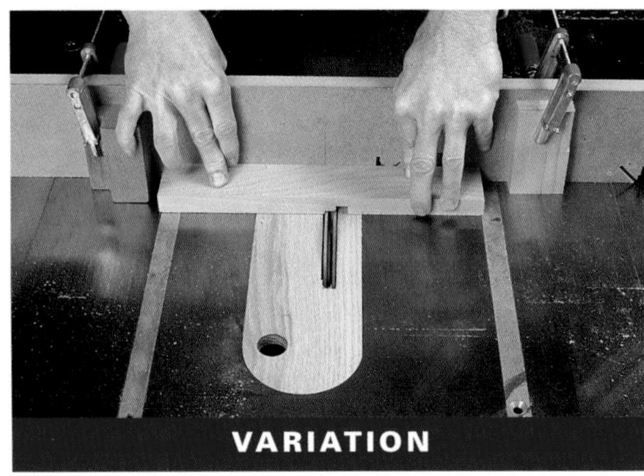

VARIATION

Dovetail Lap Joint

The first step for making a dovetail lap joint is to cut the lap shoulder on the table saw almost to full depth. Then cut the cheek using the bandsaw with a fence (**A**).

[VARIATION 1] Cut the cheek on the router table. Always rough out the cut first on the bandsaw. This way you can set the bit depth to its full height.

Mark out and cut the tail on the bandsaw. Rough cut the shoulder up to the dovetail line and then cut just up to that line. Clean the shoulder cut with a chisel (**B**).

[VARIATION 2] Cut the dovetail cheek and shoulder by hand with a dovetail saw.

Mark out the mating piece by setting the dovetailed board in place on it. Place its shoulder tight up against the edge. Support the back end of the board with a block to level out the dovetailed board (**C**). Rough out the interior of the joint with cuts on the table saw (**D**). Then saw out the shoulders by hand. This will ensure that you'll follow whatever angle you've cut into the tail (**E**). Clean out the remaining wood with a chisel down to depth (**F**).

[VARIATION 3] You can also use a straight bit in the router to cut the lap joint down to depth. Make the cut freehand, being sure to stay away from the shoulders of the joint. If the joint is deep enough, use a top-mounted flush-trimming bit and run the bearing against the shoulders to make the cut.

A

B

C

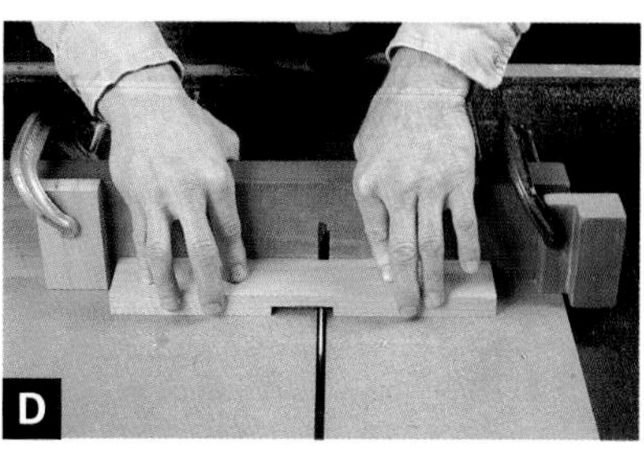
D

E

F

VARIATION 1

VARIATION 2

VARIATION 3

A

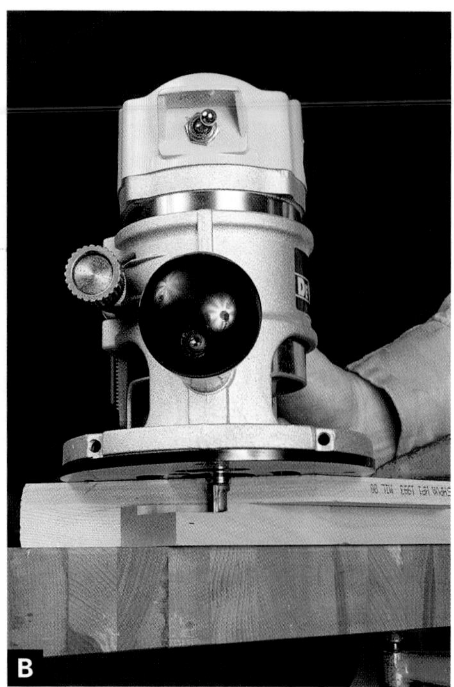
B

C

D

E

Mitered Half-Lap Joint with a Router

To cut half-lap joints with a router, first crosscut one of the boards with a miter cut and the mating board with a square cut. Rout the joint on the square-end board using a miter jig and flush-trimming bit. Clamp the jig in place on the board and set the bit depth for the first pass (**A**). Make sure the top-mounted bearing runs into the fence of the jig (**B**). Drop the bit height to make the second pass. The bearing will run against the first cut you made. Cut to just under half the thickness of the joint (**C**). Cut the mating part of the joint with a right-angle jig clamped onto the piece with the mitered end.

Use the same bit and get down to full depth in a series of passes, as before (**D**).

With this joint, not only do you get the benefit of the lap joint and its gluing surface but you can also carry a molded edge detail right through the face edge of the joint (**E**).

Mitered Half-Lap Joint on the Table Saw

Mitered half lap joints on the table saw are cut in pairs. One side of the joint has a square end with a mitered shoulder on the lap cut. The other side has a mitered end with a square shoulder. Make the miter cuts on the ends of two opposite parts of the frame.

See *"Miter Cuts"* on p. 210.

Cut the mating boards square and to length (**A**). Make the square shoulder cuts using the miter gauge on the table saw. Set the blade for just under half the thickness of the stock and set the shoulder stop for just under the full width of the stock (**B**). Make the mitered shoulder cut on the square-end board. You won't have to change the blade height. Set a stop so the cut starts just at the tip of the board (**C**).

Make the cheek cuts next. Cut the cheek on the square-end board using a tenoning jig with a 45-degree fence on it (**D**). Cut the cheek on the mitered-end board with a regular tenoning jig; hold the piece vertical.

A

B

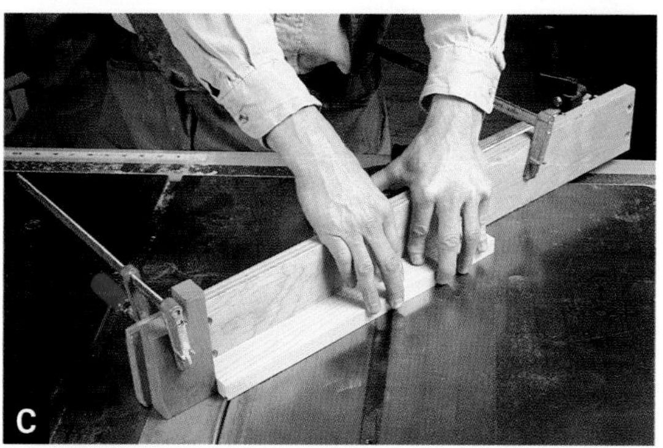

C

D

A

B

C

D

E

F

G

Hand-Cut Corner Bridle Joint

Bridle joints, or slot mortise and tenons, can be laid out with the slot one-third the full thickness of the stock. I prefer to size the tenon a bit smaller, closer to one-quarter of the thickness. But make the slot close in size to one of your chisels for ease in chopping out the waste.

Mark out the depth of the slot on both faces of the boards with a marking gauge. Pencil in the cheek lines across the end of the piece and square those lines down to the gauge line (**A**).

Saw to depth using a backsaw. Keep the sawcut on the waste side of the line (**B**). Chop out the bottom of the slot while holding the chisel vertical. Sight it from the side of the board to make it easier to see how you're holding the chisel. Make your first passes very light and, after each chopping cut, remove the waste. Chop from both faces in toward the middle. You can slightly undercut the slot once you get the cut started (**C**).

Set a combination square off the mating piece for the matching shoulder cut. Lock the square down just under the full width of the stock (**D**). Then use the square to set the fence for the shoulder cuts on the tenoned piece. Make sure the fence is square across the board (**E**).

Cut the first cheek of the tenoned board with a ripsaw down to the shoulder lines (**F**). For a bridle joint with flush faces on the mating boards, check the fit off the first cheek cut. Reverse the cut, placing it against the outside face of the mortised board. If the slot lines up with the outer face of the tenoned piece, the cut is in the proper spot. If it's not deep enough, use a handplane to bring it down to size (**G**).

Corner Bridle Joint on the Table Saw

Lay out the bridle joint so the mortise slot is slightly less than one-third the thickness of the stock. Mark out the depth of cut with a marking gauge to help prevent tearout. Use a tenoning jig to support the board, cutting almost to full depth (**A**).

TIP **An alternate-top bevel blade won't leave a smooth enough surface at the bottom of the cut. Use a flat-grind blade instead.**

Make a series of passes until the slot is cut. For the best-looking joint, clean up the bottom of the slot with a chisel (**B**).

VARIATION 1 **Use a dado blade to cut the slot in one or two passes. Move the stock past the blade at a moderate feed rate and support the piece well. Put a gauge line on the board or use a backer board to prevent tearout.**

Cut the shoulders for the tenon first. Clamp a stop to the crosscut jig fence and set the blade height to cut just under the required height (**C**).

VARIATION 2 **Rough out the cheeks on the bandsaw so you don't have offcuts flying around on the table saw. Use the offcuts for clamping blocks or to glue back onto a tenon that you cut too small. The grain and color will match perfectly.**

Trim the cheeks using the tenoning jig (**D**). Check the fit of the first cheek pass by reversing the tenoned board on the slotted piece. If the slot lines up with the face of the board, the cut is in the right spot (**E**).

A

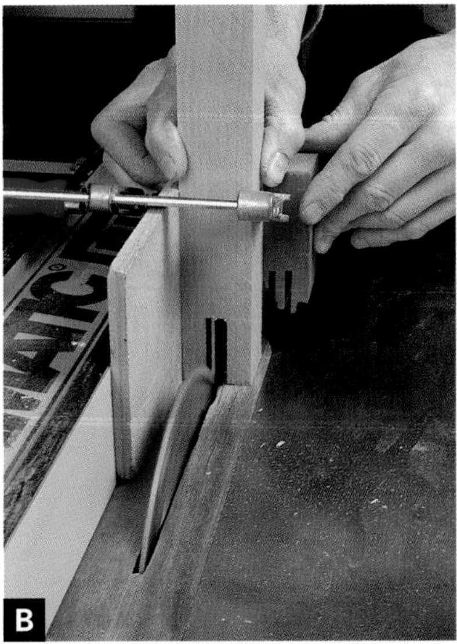
B

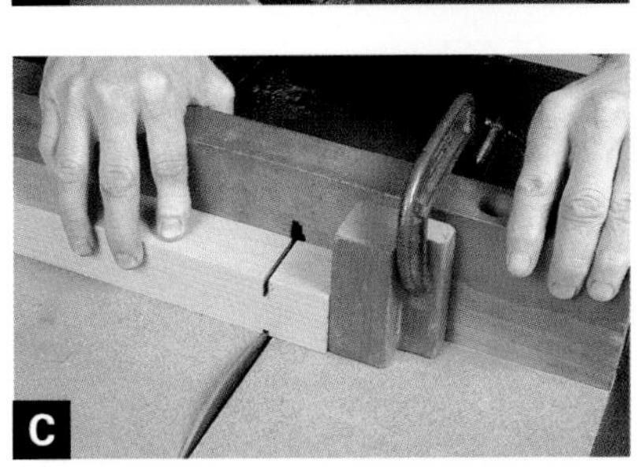
C

D

E

VARIATION 1

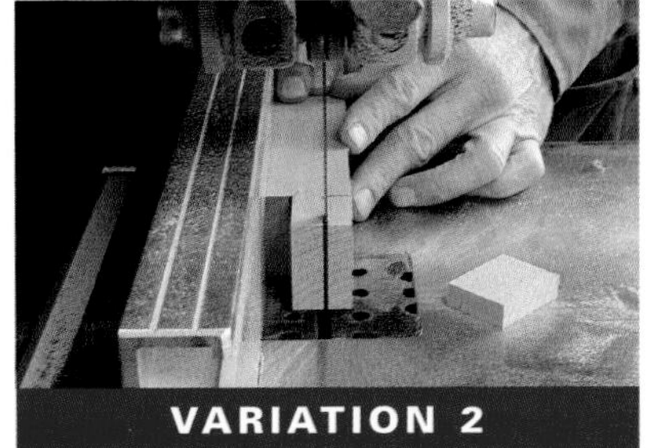
VARIATION 2

A

B

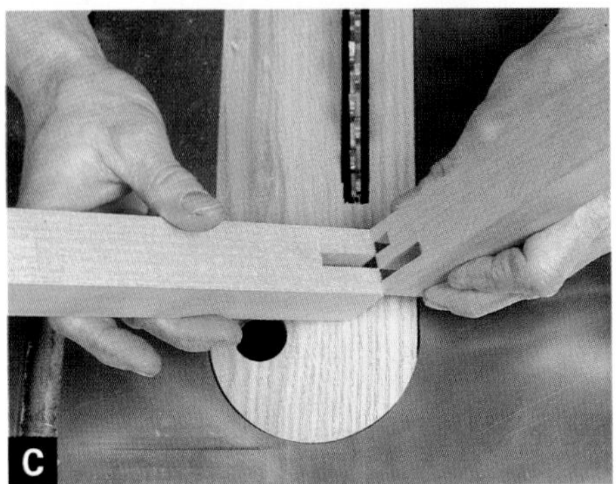
C

D

E

Twin Corner Bridle Joint on the Table Saw

There are almost twice as many cuts for the twin bridle joint as for a simple bridle. Try to work from a center point for these cuts so you can flip the boards to make matching cuts. Start by cutting a slot in the center of one board and work your way out from there.

Use the dado blade and tenoning jig. Adjust the tenoning jig until the blade lines up on the pencil marks for the center slot and set the blade height for the full depth of cut. To center this slot perfectly, make the pass and flip the board for a second cleanup pass. Any off-center discrepancy will be mirrored in the second cut (**A**).

TIP **Put a marking gauge line on the faces of the boards to prevent tearout.**

Next, create the tenon to fit that slot. Mark the tenon on the mating board and move the tenoning jig over to make a first pass (**B**). Cut one slot on this board, flip it in the tenoning jig, and make a second pass. Check to see that the tenon created by these two slots matches the slot in the first board. You can check just the edge of the tenon in the slot (**C**).

When the tenon fits, cut the two tenons on the first board. These will now have to mate up with the two slots just cut. Set the jig to cut a slightly thicker tenon than you need. You can always re-adjust the jig to trim the tenon smaller. Flip the board in the jig after the first cut to cut the second tenon (**D**). Check the fit of each tenon individually by flipping one board around and placing the tenon in its slot (**E**).

➤ See *"Bridle Joints"* drawing on p. 232.

Hand-Cut Dovetail Corner Bridle Joint

To begin a hand-cut dovetail bridle joint, mark the boards with a marking gauge set for just under the width of the boards (**A**). Set the sliding bevel for the tail angle, somewhere between 1:5 and 1:8, and mark the tail down to the shoulder lines (**B**).

First, cut the shoulders with a crosscut saw, holding the workpiece in the vise (**C**). Next, cut the dovetail using a ripsaw, if you have one (**D**). Clean up the corners of the tail piece and pare the cheeks of the tail if needed. You can slightly undercut the shoulders toward the bottom of the tail before marking.

Use a piece of scrap to line up the tail board on its mating piece and knife out the tail (**E**). Cut out the dovetail slot with a dovetail saw down to the gauge lines (**F**). Chop out the waste while holding the chisel right on the gauge line. Remove the waste, cutting from the outside of the joint (**G**).

➤ See *"Bridle Joints"* drawing on p. 232.

A

B

C

D

E

F

G

A

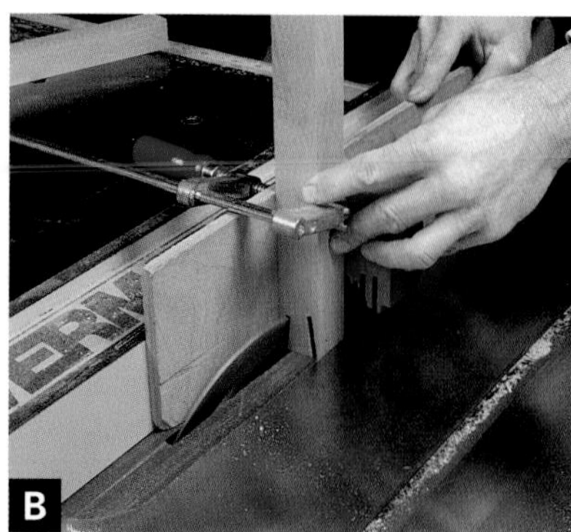
B

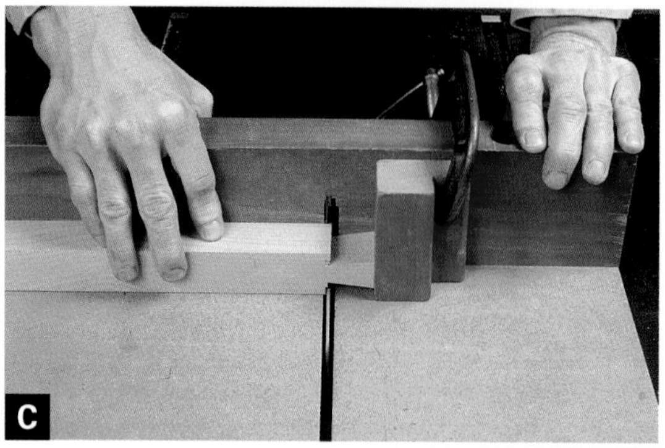

C

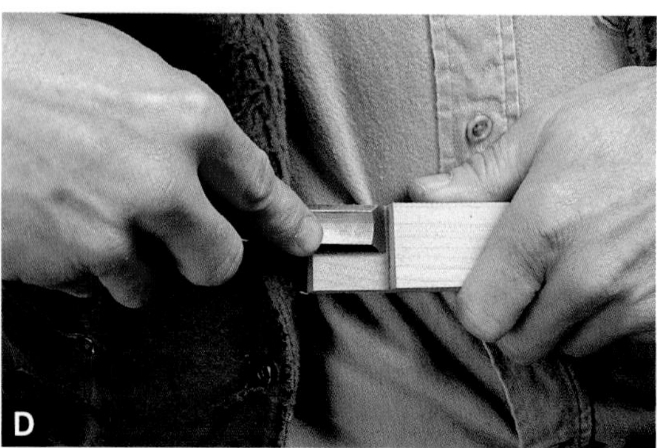
D

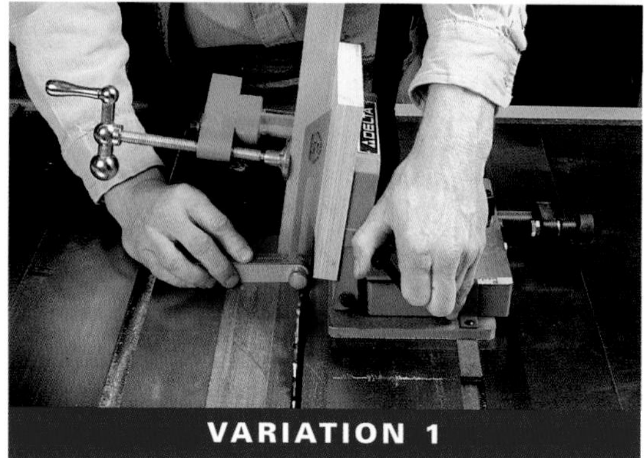
VARIATION 1

Dovetail Corner Bridle Joint on the Table Saw

The dovetail corner bridle joint can be cut on the table saw. Set the sliding bevel for the dovetail angle you want and angle the sawblade to match (**A**). Make two passes to create the tail sides, using a shopmade tenoning jig and flipping the board in the jig for each pass. Be sure the blade height is set so the top of the cut stops just under the marked-out gauge line (**B**).

➤ See *"Jigs"* on pp. 34–37.

VARIATION 1 An alternate method is to angle the steel tenoning jig at the required angle to cut the tail. Keep the sawblade at 90 degrees and use the sliding bevel to set the fence.

Cut the shoulders using the crosscut jig, but first remove the waste on the bandsaw so you don't have offcuts trapped between the blade and the stop. Be sure to save the offcuts. Clamp on a stop for the shoulder cut and set the blade height for just under the angled cheek cut (**C**). Clean up the remaining wood in the corner of the joint with a chisel (**D**).

Mark the tail onto its mating piece (**E**). To cut the slot, you'll have to angle the workpiece in the tenoning jig. Use the saved angled offcuts as shims, taping them onto the tenoning jig. Clamp the workpiece against the shims for the first cut (**F**). Then remove the shims, flip them over, and tape them down. Now you can make the opposite side cut (**G**).

You could also use the bandsaw to make the cuts. Check if your bandsaw tips far enough in both directions to make the cheek cuts.

[VARIATION 2] Angle the bandsaw table first in one direction and then the other to make the slot cut.

➤ See *"Bridle Joints"* drawing on p. 232.

E

F

G

VARIATION 2

A

B

C

D

VARIATION

Mitered Corner Bridle Joint

One board in the mitered corner bridle joint will have a mitered-end cut. The other will be crosscut square at its end. Cut the slot into the mitered-end piece with the dado blade. Clamp the board vertically into the tenoning jig (**A**). The tenoned board will have mitered shoulders. Use the dado blade to cut the cheek and mitered shoulder, holding the workpiece against the miter gauge angled at 45 degrees (**B**).

➤ See *"Mitered Slip Joint"* on p. 223 and *"Bridle Joints"* drawing on p. 232.

After the first cheek is cut, flip the miter gauge to the opposite 45-degree setting and make the second cheek cut. Use stops to index the cut for other boards (**C**). The joint should slide together with light pressure (**D**).

VARIATION **If you don't have a good dado blade, cut the slot with a regular sawblade and chop out the bottom of the slot with a chisel. Cut the mitered shoulders for the mating piece using the miter gauge. Then cut the cheeks using the angled tenoning jig. Rough out the inside cheek cut on the bandsaw to avoid a flying offcut. The outside cheek will simply fall off when you make the cheek pass.**

T Bridle Joint

Cut the slot mortise while holding the work vertically in a tenoning jig.

➤ See *"Corner Bridle Joint on the Table Saw"* on p. 245.

Mark a gauge line on the board to prevent tearout (**A**). Next, cut the bridle joint to fit that slot.

➤ See *"T or Cross Half-Lap Joint on the Table Saw"* on p. 240.

Set up a stop on the crosscut jig to locate one shoulder cut and raise the blade height close to the marked height. Make a series of passes (**B**). Put a spacer between the end of the rail and the stop to cut the second shoulder. Finish up the cut on the first face (**C**).

Flip the board over and make the passes on the second face. Use the spacer again for the second shoulder cut. Check the fit of the tenon to the slot before continuing (**D**). Raise the blade height, if necessary.

VARIATION Clean the waste out exactly to depth with a topside router cut. Clamp another board of the same height close by to support the router base. Use a straight bit and cut freehand or use a top-mounted flush-trimming bit to make the cut if it's deep enough. Clean up any parts you miss with a wide chisel.

Fit each part of the joint separately. Flip the board and check the width of the slot to the board. Use a handplane to trim the board to fit (**E**).

A

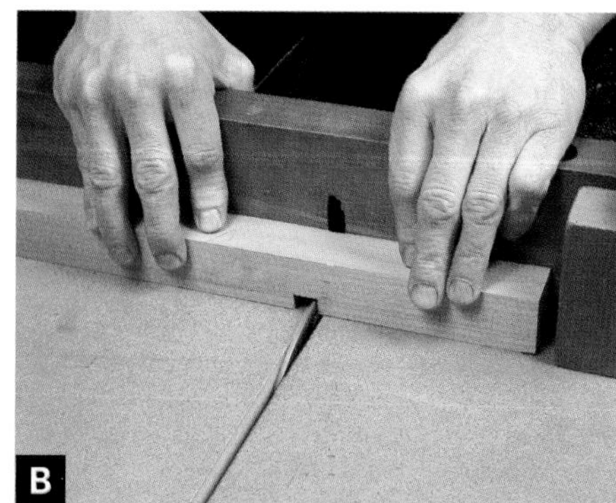
B

C

D

VARIATION

E

VARIATION

A

B

C

D

E

Halved Joint on the Table Saw

The first step to making a halved joint on the table saw is to mark it out for a little less than the width of the stock and a little less than the height of the stock. You will fit this joint by planing the long grain of the boards left proud by these setups.

Put a stop on the crosscut jig off the marked-out joint (**A**). Make a series of passes and check the fit against the mating board; it should be just short of fitting (**B**). Set up a second stop for the other side of the halving cut and locate it precisely; then make the cut (**C**).

Next, make the mating cut on the other board. If you're not sure that the stop is in the proper spot, put a shim at the end of the board. This will push the board away from the stop a few thousandths of an inch. If the cut is still too small, remove the shim for another pass (**D**).

Fit the joint using a handplane to trim wood off the faces of the boards. This will not only remove the milling marks but will more precisely fit the halved joint. Fit each board separately so you'll know where the joint is tight; then put the two together correctly (**E**).

➤ See *"Halved Joints"* drawing on p. 233.

Strengthened Halved Joint

Strengthen a halved joint to prevent cracking at the bottom of the joint. First, lay out the joint on some practice stock to get the depth settings and stops located correctly. One board is marked for a halved joint and two narrow dadoes into both of its faces that are as wide as the halved joint. The other board is marked for the same size halved joint and two wide dadoes, which are at the full width of the stock (**A**).

Set up a dado blade that's as wide as the halved joint. Set the blade height for just under half the height of the stock and cut both parts of the halved joint. Next, cut the narrow dadoes in the faces of one board using the same dado blade and stops. Adjust the blade height so the dadoes leave a section that will just fit into the halved joint cut (**B**).

Then cut the wide dado on both faces of the other board. This dado will be as wide as the stock, so adjust the stops (**C**). Check the depth setting by seeing if the halved joint fits over the dado (**D**).

Finish up the dado cuts on both faces of the second board (**E**). Check the fit of the cuts, but make the adjustments with a handplane if you're close to fitting. Use a bench plane to trim material off the faces of the boards or a shoulder plane to trim the dado depth down a bit (**F**).

See *"Halved Joints"* drawing on p. 233.

A

B

C

D

E

F

A

C

D

B

E

VARIATION

Sash Bar Joint

Sash bar joints use halving cuts. To mate pieces of sash bar stock, however, you must either miter the molding on each piece or scribe and cope one piece to fit around the molding detail of the other. If you don't have the right sweep of gouge, make up a miter block to guide the cutting of the miters. Make the miter block out of two pieces of wood glued to form a corner. Then cut both ends at 45 degrees with a saw.

Make the halving cuts with a crosscut saw (**A**).

VARIATION You can also make the halving cuts through the molding with the dado blade.

Trim the molding to a 45-degree angle using the miter block and a wide chisel. Line up the miter block on the edge of the halving cut or on lines squared out from the halving cut on the bottom edge of the stock (**B**).

On the bottom of the sash bar, make the halving cut. Then carry the cut around to the molding on both edges with the saw. Be careful not to cut past the molding detail when marking with the saw (**C**). Finish crosscutting down to the top molding detail on both faces (**D**); then remove the waste between the saw cuts.

Trim the molding as before using the miter block. Then fit the joint, paring off material as needed for a good fit (**E**).

➤ See *"Halved Joints"* drawing on p. 233.

One-Third Lap Joint

The one-third lap joint is used to create a six-spoked wheel or to make patterns (**A**). All boards are the same width and thickness. Cut them to length after making the joint. Make all the cuts at 60 degrees to the long edges of the boards at a depth of either one-third or two-thirds the thickness of the stock. Each slot that is cut is equal to one full width of a board.

Set up a dado blade with the blade depth at one-third the thickness of the stock. Angle a miter gauge to 60 degrees. Check all the setups on some scrap.

Start with the middle board (board 1). Cut one full-width slot into only one face of this board at one-third depth (**B**).

Mark out the cuts for boards 2 and 3 with a sliding bevel. Mark a 60-degree angle on one face of each board, measure over one full width, and mark another 60-degree angle. Square the farthest ends of the lines over the face of the board, and mark out the second cut at 60 degrees in the other direction across the face (**C**).

Make a slot cut through boards 2 and 3 at two-thirds the full thickness. Make each slot equal to one full board width (**D**). Then reset the miter gauge for 60 degrees on the other side of the blade and cut only board 2 with another pass running in the other direction at two-thirds depth (**E**).

Put boards 1 and 2 together and mark out where the second slot goes onto board 1 (**F**). Reset the blade depth for a one-third cut and make a cut across board 3 (**G**). Finally, cut board 1 at one-third depth on the face opposite its first slot. Be sure to cut this slot in the opposite direction to that of the first slot. Fit and assemble the joint (**H**).

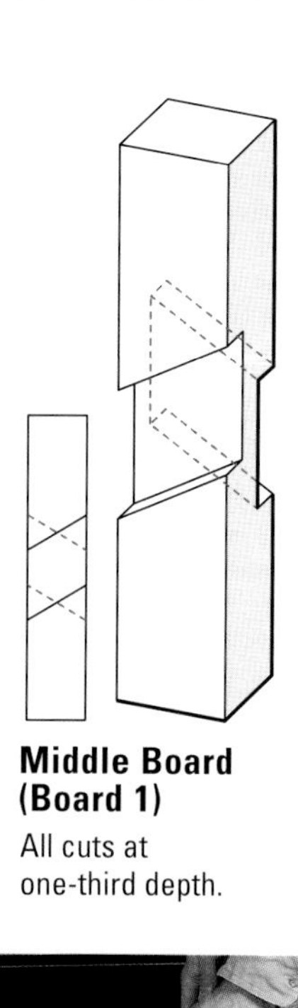
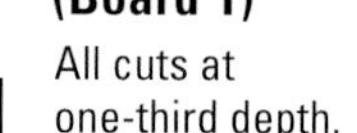

Middle Board (Board 1)
All cuts at one-third depth.

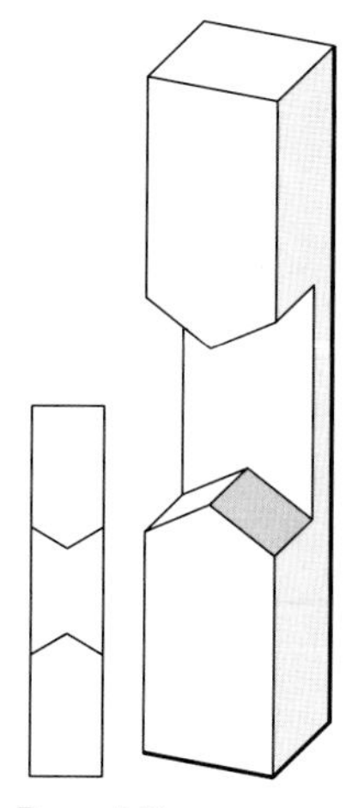

Board 2
All cuts at two-thirds depth.

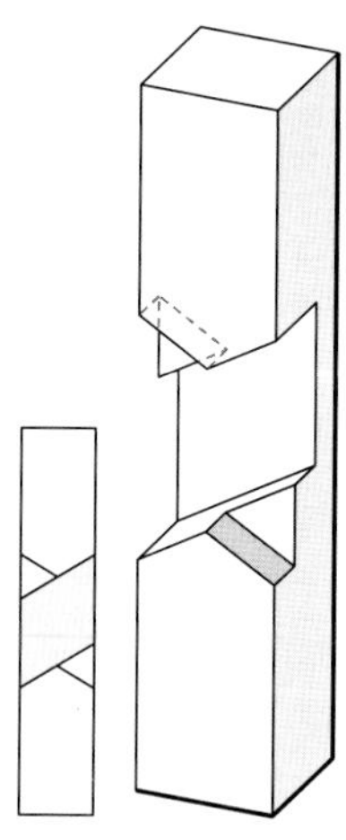
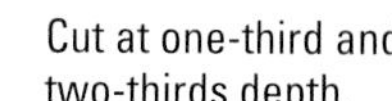

Board 3
Cut at one-third and two-thirds depth.

A

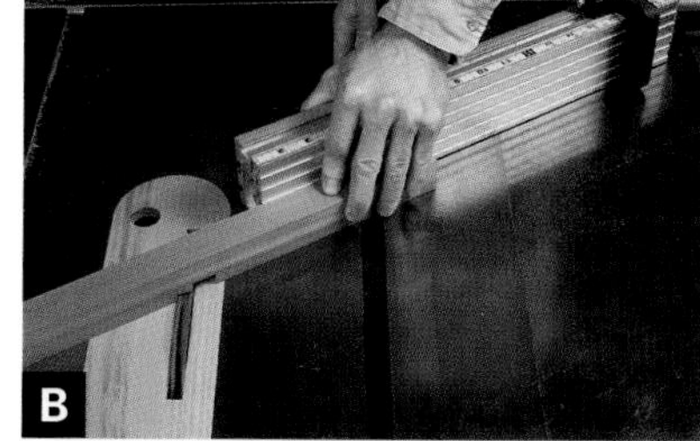

B

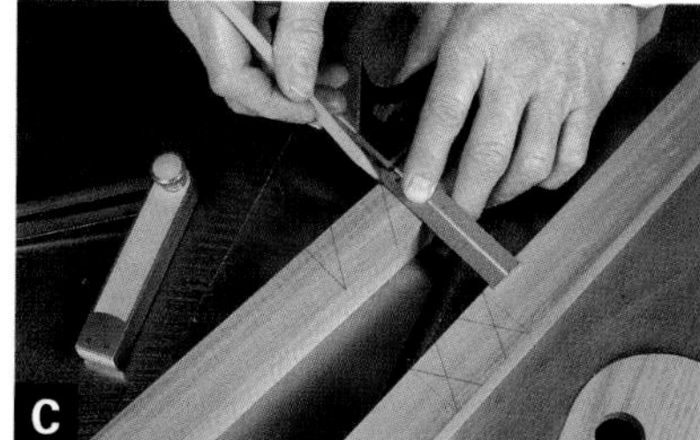

C

D

E

F

G

H

Interior Bird's-Mouth Joint

The bird's-mouth joint is a simple V-shaped notch cut into the edge of a board (**A**). A matching piece fits the notch. You can make the V cut into preshaped molding that will be applied to a piece (**B**).

Set the table-saw blade to 45 degrees and use the miter gauge to hold the molding secure. Cut the notch, making sure the blade height is under the full depth of the notch so it doesn't mar the opposite face of the notch (**C**). Cut both sides of the notch and then clean up the bottom of the notch with a chisel (**D**).

Miter both ends of the mating piece using a picture framing jig. Mark a centerline on the piece and make each cut start right at that line (**E**).

➤ See *"Jigs"* on pp. 34–37.

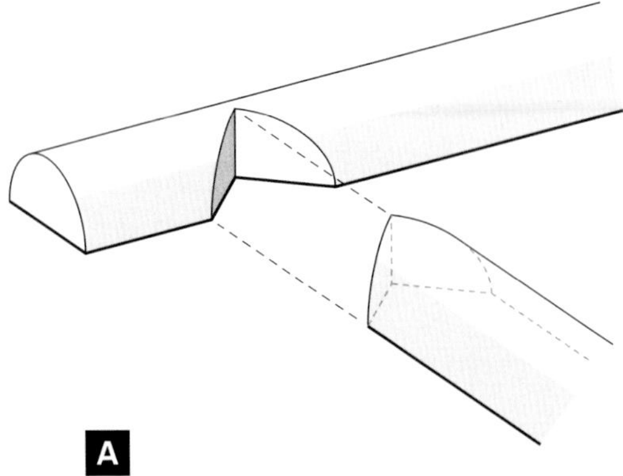

A

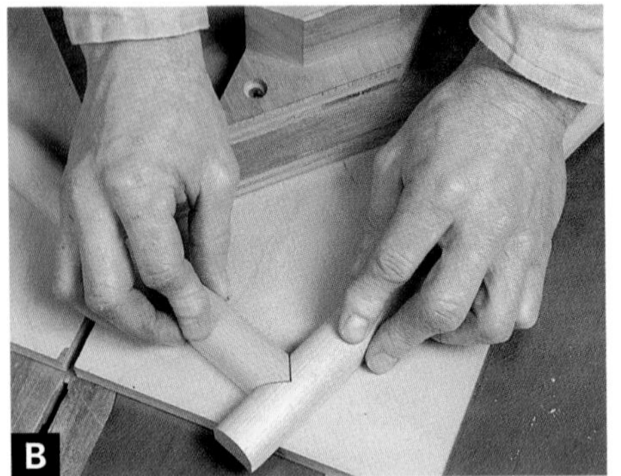

B

C

D

E

Exterior Bird's-Mouth Joint

Use the exterior bird's-mouth joint for structural frame members in carpentry (**A**). Use the sliding bevel to lay out the joint; then cut it by hand (**B**).

You can also set up the table-saw blade at the necessary angle for the crosscut. Cut the bird's-mouth V cut into the end of the board on the bandsaw.

Fit the joint to the edge of a board and strengthen with a fastener (**C**).

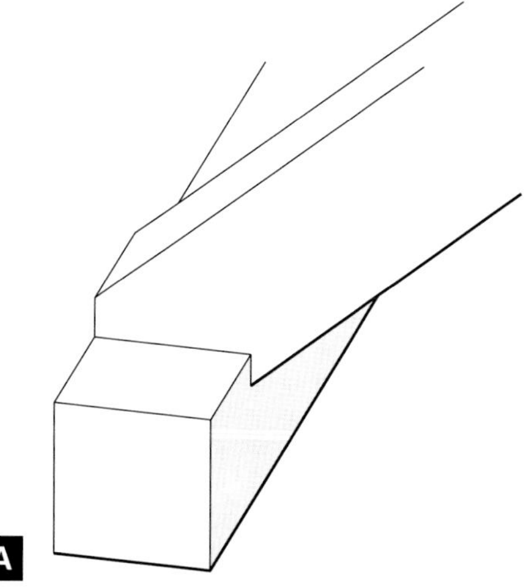

A

B

C

Scarf and Splice Joints

Simple Scarf Joints

Half-Lap Splice Joint

Bevel-Lap Splice Joints

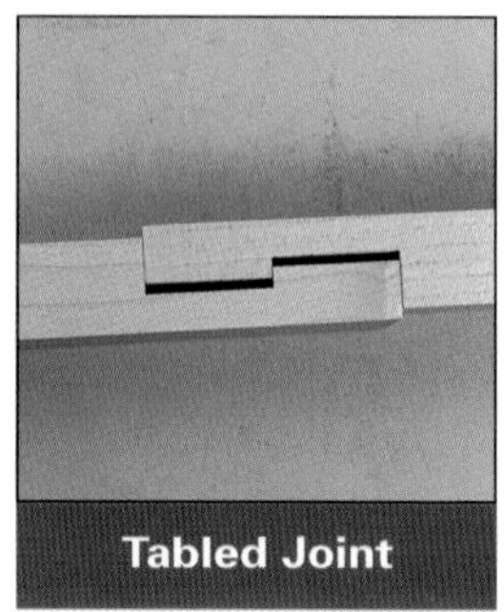

Tabled Joint

Lapped Dovetail Splice

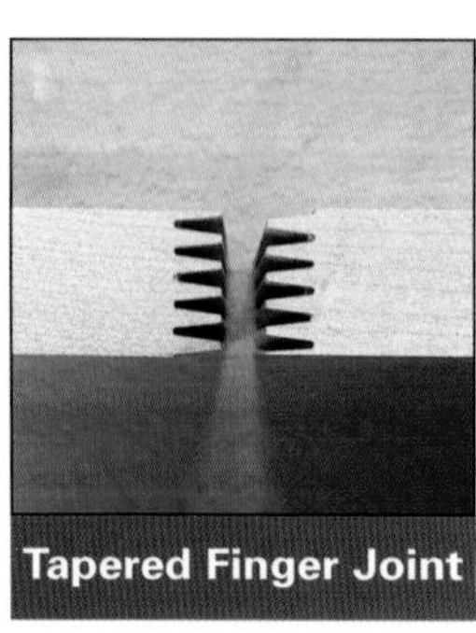

Tapered Finger Joint

Cogged Scarf Joint

Simple scarf or splice joints rely on long low-angle cuts and glue for their holding power. These joints are much like a very low angle miter that is cut to expose as much long grain as possible. Made with slopes of 1:8 to 1:10, the simple scarf joint goes to great lengths to disguise the fact that it's a joint at all; it stretches out the idea of a butt joint until it almost disappears. This is done not only to add strength and maximize the long-grain nature of the glue joint but also to create an almost invisible joint. A scarf joint will blend in far better than a simple butt joint, which always shows a dark glueline, however skillfully cut.

This seamless quality becomes important when a scarf joint is used in an area that's highly visible, such as in long runs of molding or trim work, which generally require some kind of joinery. Scarfing the joints together creates longer lengths while maintaining the long-grain look throughout. Hand rails and boat building are two other areas where scarf joints are used.

There is also a large variety of scarf or splice joints that use joinery designed to resist potential stresses. Some are simple in form, such as the half-lap splice joint. Other splices are used in Japanese temple carpentry. These joints help create long timbers that can withstand the shifting forces of earthquakes. The end-grain splices are very good at resisting tension, compression, and shear forces on the joint.

Cutting Methods

Cutting a simple scarf joint can be accomplished with a good handheld ripsaw. For carpentry work, use a circular saw or chopsaw to make scarf cuts. If you need to cut

The simple scarf joint maximizes the amount of long-grain gluing surface for better strength and a seamless look compared to the simple butt joint.

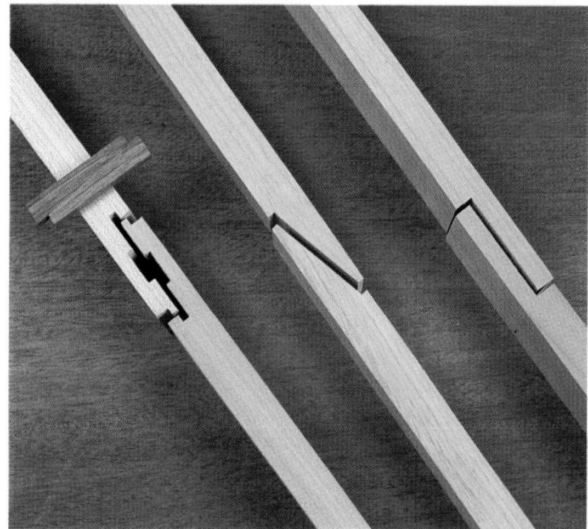

Splice joints can be simple, like the half-lap and hooked splices, or more complex, like the cogged scarf joint.

Scarf cuts on molding are made with a good blade on a chopsaw.

For greater precision and a longer scarf joint with more gluing surface use a scarf jig and a handheld router.

Splice joints can use cheeks and shoulders like a mortise-and-tenon joint to resist the forces of tension and shear.

wide boards or require greater precision, take advantage of router jigs that guide the cutter to make the scarf.

Strengthening the Joint

Simple scarf joints rely on glue for their strength. Splice joints can use cheeks and shoulders, like any mortise-and-tenon joint, to add to the holding power of the glue. Wedges can be used to help hold these joints in fast.

Hand-Cut Scarf Joint

To begin a hand-cut scarf joint, set the sliding bevel to an angle between 1:8 and 1:10, and mark out the boards (**A, B**).

Clamp the boards securely when making the sawcuts (**C**). If you stack the boards together when sawing, they will line up almost automatically (**D**).

To finish, clean up the cuts with a handplane (**E**).

VARIATION You can use a chopsaw to make the scarf cuts.

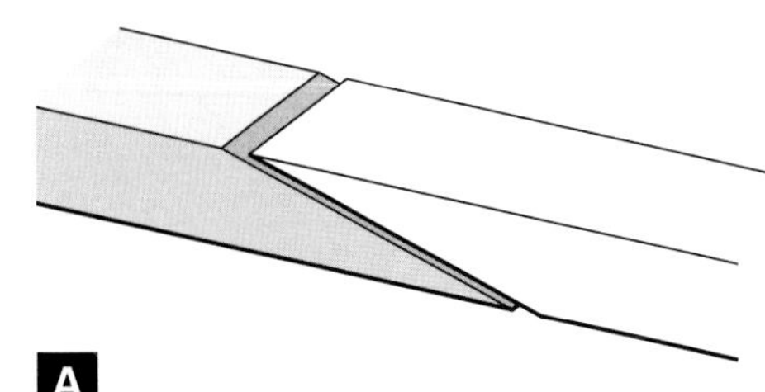
A

B

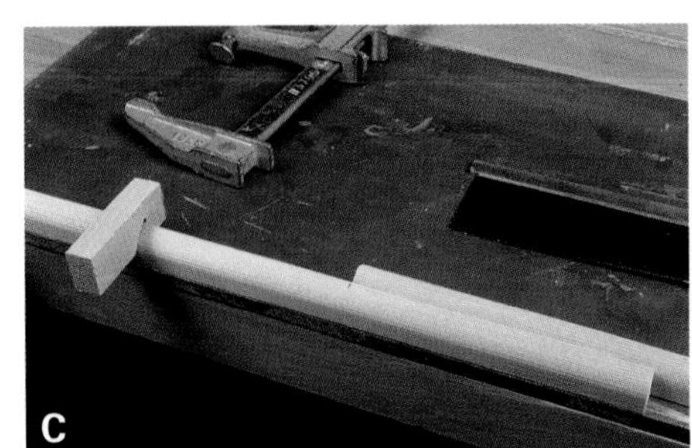
C

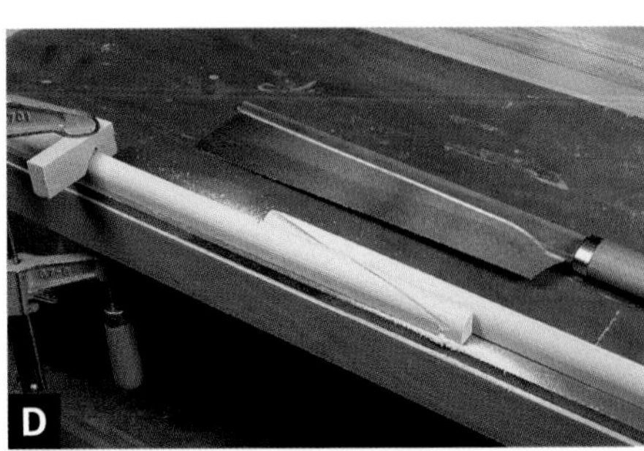
D

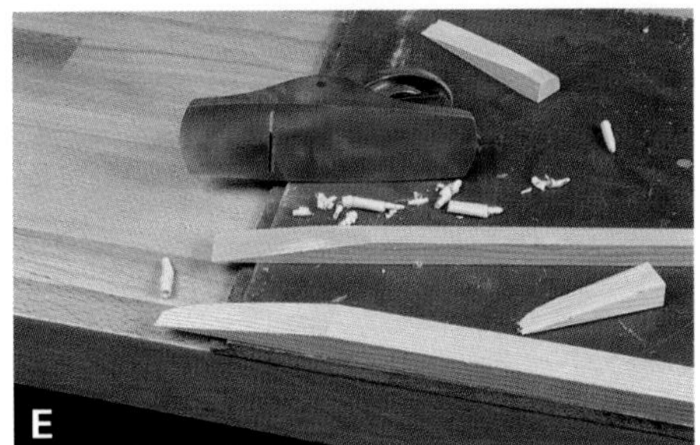
E

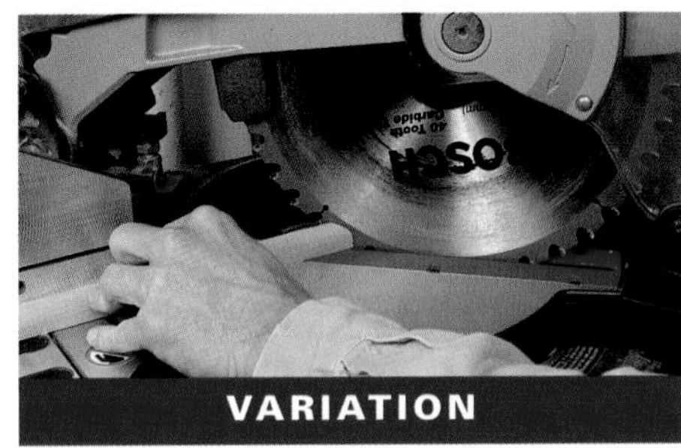
VARIATION

Scarf Joint with a Router

Scarf joints can be cut with a handheld router. Clamp the board to be scarfed in the scarf jig (**A**). The jig's sides are angled at the proper degree for scarf joints. A plunge router rides in a carriage that rests on top of the angled sides.

Rout the scarf, taking several passes to get down to depth. Start up at the beginning of the scarf joint and gradually move down the jig (**B**). With a good, wide straight bit, you should have very little cleanup work to do on the joint (**C**).

A

B

C

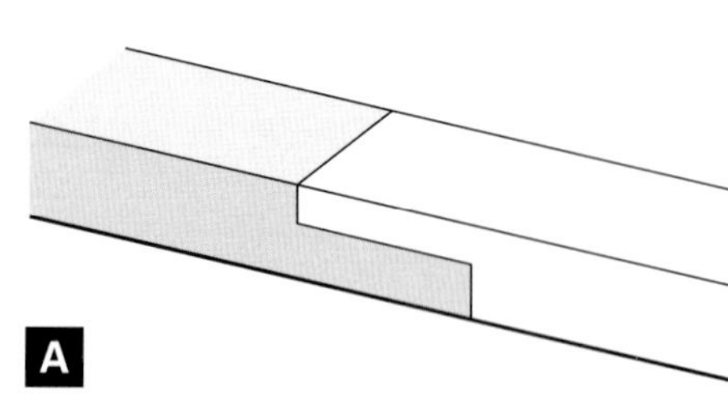
A

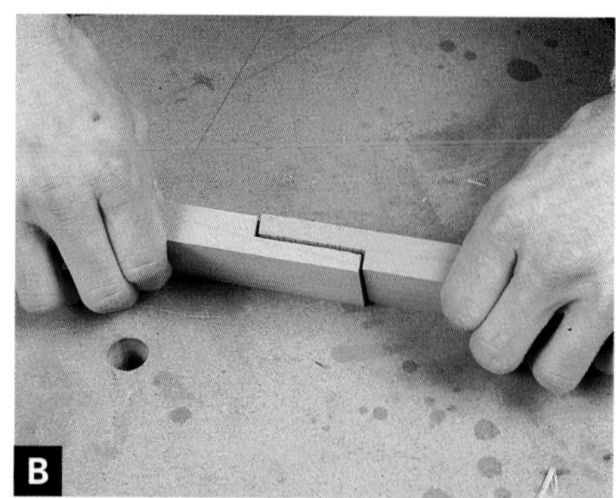
B

C

D

E

F

Half-Lap Splice Joint

The half-lap splice joint is laid out and cut exactly like a corner half-lap joint (**A**). The only difference is that the splice joint is put together end to end instead of at right angles.

➤ See *"Corner Half-Lap Joints"* on pp. 236–238.

The half-lap splice joint is somewhat weak at the corner where the shoulder meets the cheek, especially if any weight bears down on the joint. This joint relies on glue or fasteners to hold it in place (**B**). There are several methods for cutting the joint.

HAND CUT

To cut the joint by hand, first put gauge lines on the face and edges of the boards at just under half the thickness of the stock (**C**). Use a fence to guide the cut. Set up a square as a depth gauge and clamp on a fence. A piece of masking tape on the saw marked out with the full depth of cut can serve as a guide. Saw down to the gauge lines (**D**).

TABLE SAW

The half-lap splice joint can be cut on the table saw. Cut the joint shoulder and cheek but clean up the cut at top dead center of the blade to get a smoother surface (**E**).

DADO BLADE

You can also use a dado blade and the miter gauge to make the cuts for this joint (**F**). Set the saw fence at the proper distance to index the shoulder cuts.

Bevel-Lap Splice Joint

The bevel-lap splice joint differs only slightly from the half-lap splice (**A**). Because of its cheek angle, it does make for a slightly stronger joint in tension. It still needs fasteners and glue to hold it tight.

Set up a marking gauge for a 1:8 angle and lay out the joint (**B**). You'll use the table saw to make the shoulder cuts at 90 degrees to the board. Set up a stop to index these cuts and don't cut past the pencil marks (**C**).

Use the bandsaw to cut the cheek. Follow the line closely but stay on its waste side (**D**). Use a bullnose plane or a wide chisel to trim the joint smooth (**E**).

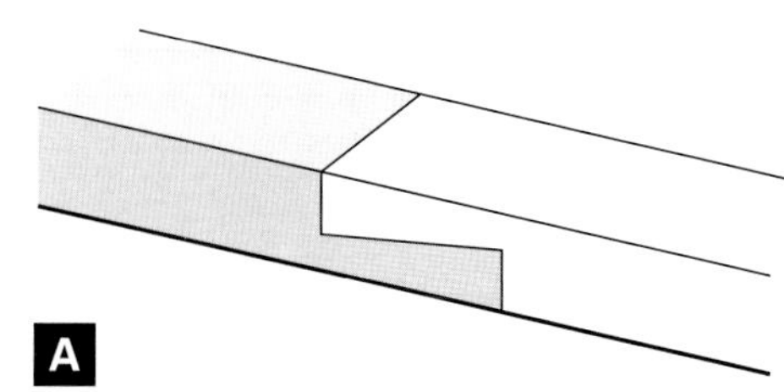
A

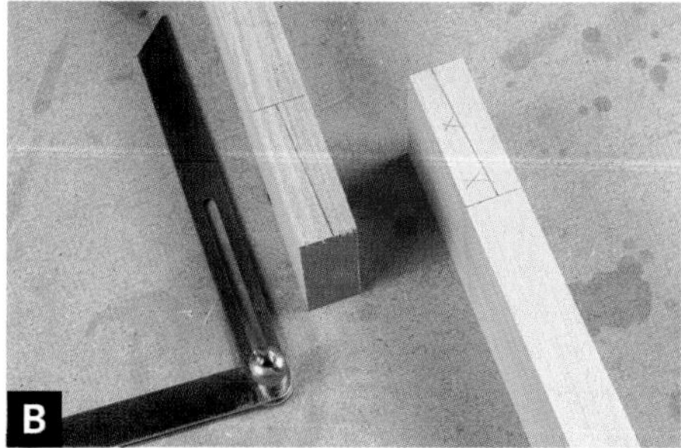
B

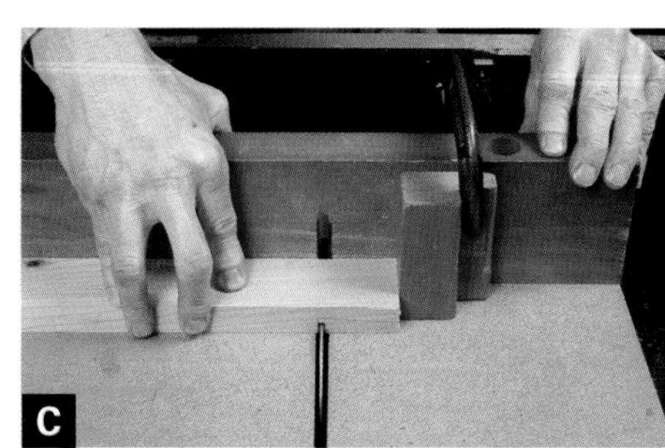
C

D

E

Hooked Splice Joint

The hooked splice joint offers slightly better strength than the simple splice joints, as there is less wood taken out at the shoulder (**A**).

The ends of the boards are cut to a 5-degree to 10-degree angle. Set the table-saw blade to that angle to make the cuts (**B**). First, rough out the cut on the bandsaw. Then, with the table-saw blade tipped, cut the cheek with the workpiece held in the tenoning jig (**C**).

Fit the joint by trimming the ends and shoulders of the boards until they mate (**D**).

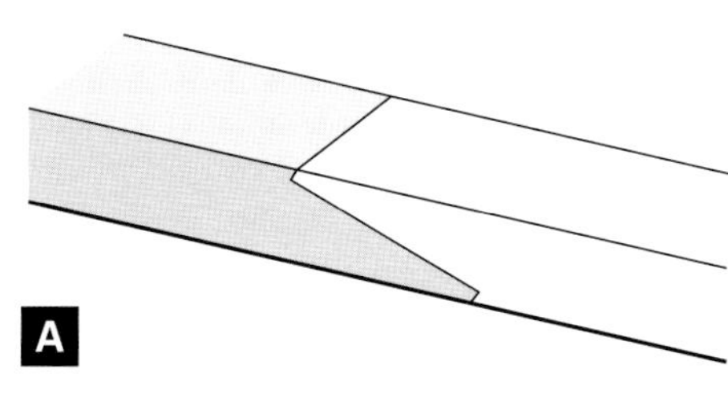
A

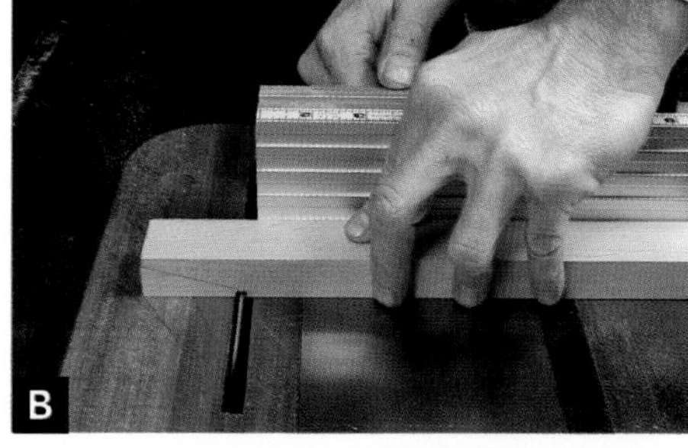
B

C

D

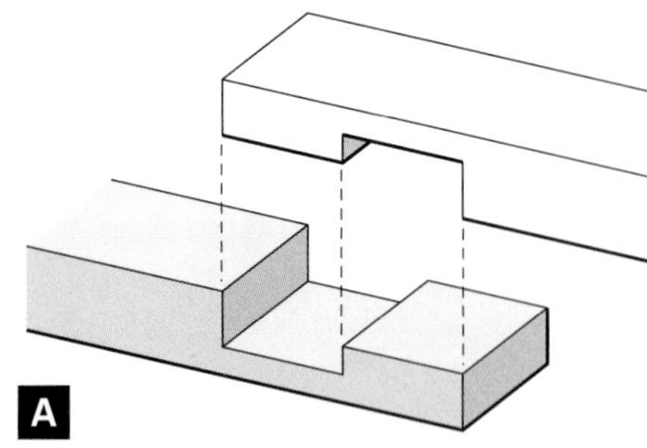
A

B

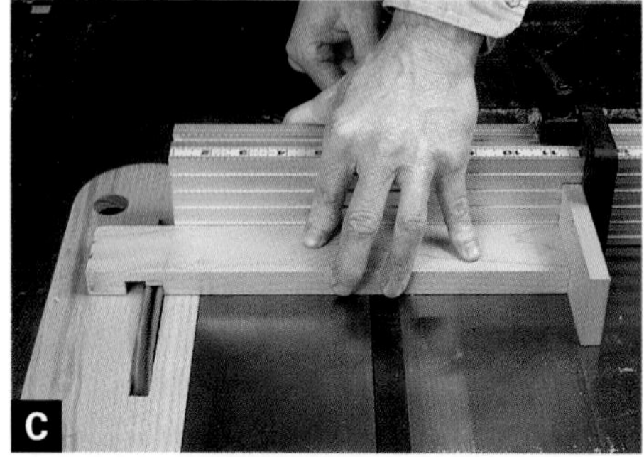
C

D

E

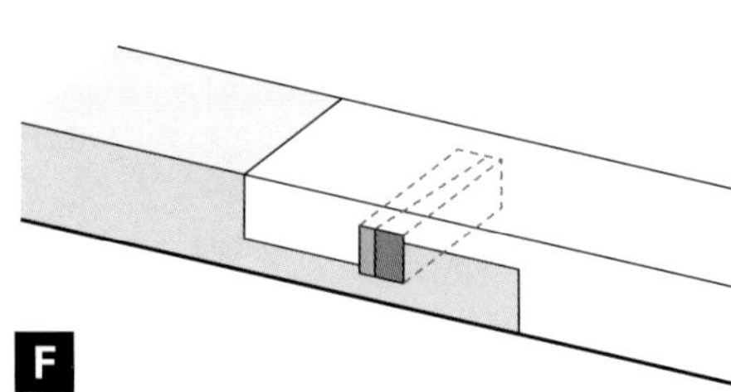
F

G

Tabled Joint

Lay out the tabled joint, splitting the difference between the shoulder and the end of the board for the start of the *large* notch cut (**A**). Set up a dado blade on the table saw and use a stop to index the shoulder cuts (**B**).

Make the dado cut on the first board. The spacer block pushes the board out away from the miter gauge stop for the second pass (**C**). Next, reset the blade height and make the lap cut (**D**).

Fit the joint using a chisel or plane to trim the boards to fit (**E**).

To strengthen a tabled joint, you can cut matching notches in the boards (**F, G**). Folding or double wedges fitted to the notches lock the joint tight.

➤ See *"Making Loose Wedges"* on p. 149.

Lapped Dovetail Splice Joint

Lapped splice joints can be cut using a dovetail (**A**). Mark out the dovetail using a sliding bevel. Don't make the angle too severe, as this will leave weakened short grain out at the end of the tail. Keep the angle between 1:5 and 1:8 (**B**). Mark the shoulder's lines with a marking gauge.

Clamp the piece in the vise and make the shoulder cuts down to the tail lines (**C**). Cut the sides of the dovetail with the piece held vertically in the vise. Clean up the cuts with a chisel (**D**).

You can also use the table saw to create the dovetail. Tilt the blade to the proper angle and use the tenoning jig to hold the workpiece in place. You'll make two passes to create the tail sides (**E**).

Mark out the tail piece for the lap cut and then make the shoulder cut with a crosscut saw. Cut the lap cheek down to the shoulder line (**F**). Clean up the lap cuts with a wide chisel. Make sure the cuts are straight and square to each other (**G**).

Mark out the tail onto the pin piece. Put a scrap block under the end of the tail board to support it during marking out (**H**). Cut the matching shoulder and cheek for the lap part of the joint. Clean up those cuts (**I**).

Saw out the pin at an angle. Saw as deeply as you can go without cutting past the lines. You can chop out a stop at the end of the tail socket and run the saw gently into that (**J**). Finally, chop out the tail socket and fit the joint (**K**).

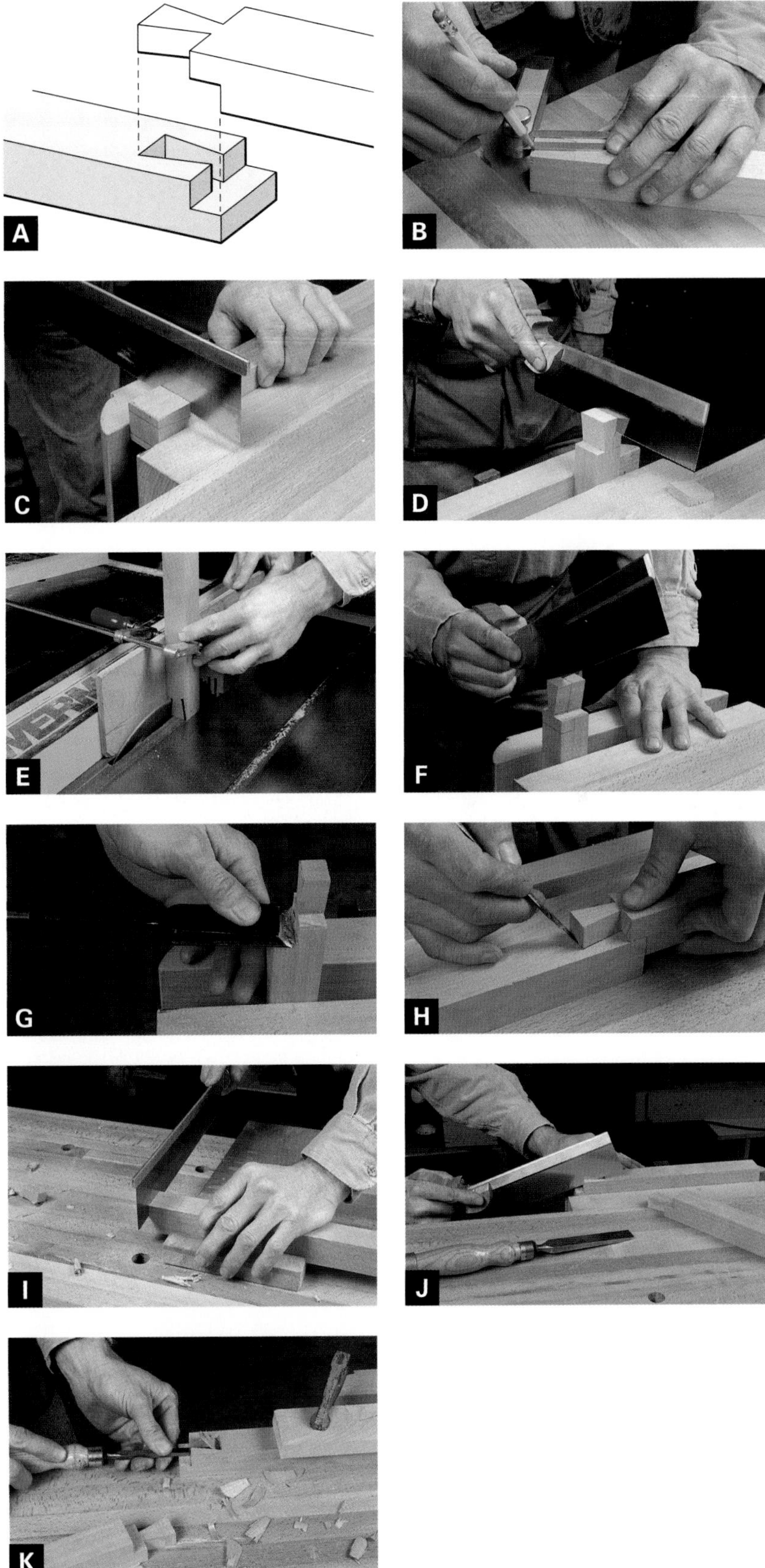

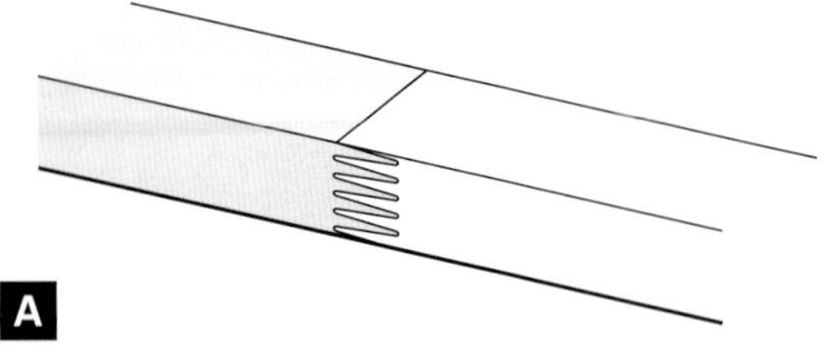

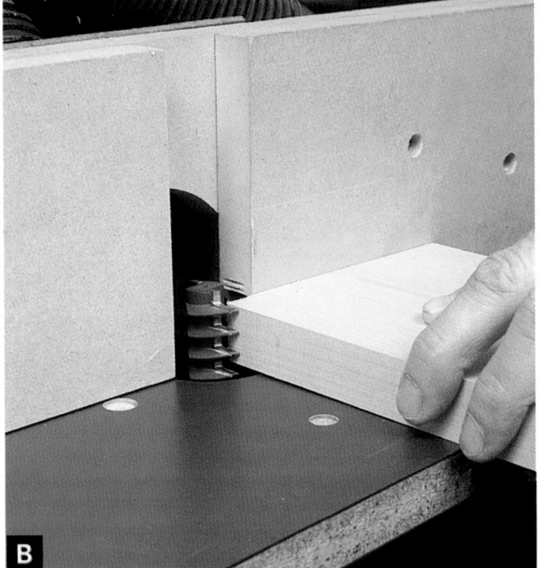

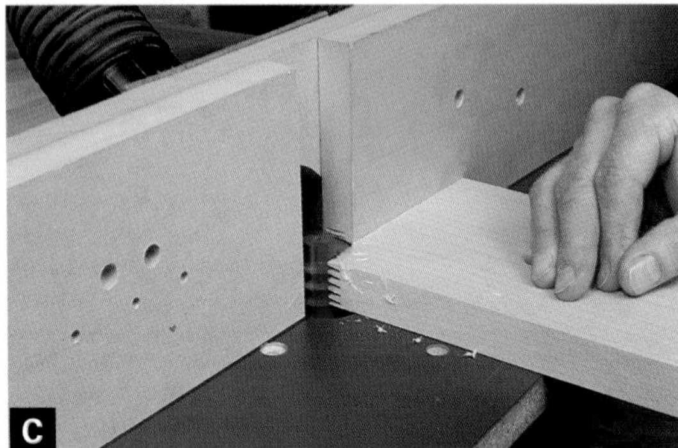

Tapered Finger Splice Joint

Tapered finger joints are showing up in lots of lumberyards these days as we stretch our resources to continue to provide building material (**A**). These joints offer plenty of gluing surface and some mechanical resistance as well.

Set up the finger-joint bit in the speed-controlled table-mounted router. Run the speed down to around 10,000 rpm. Align the cutters to the stock thickness. Both cuts made on the matching boards will be done with one setup (**B**).

Make the pass on the first board with its face side up (**C**). Make the pass on the second board with its face side down. Adjust the bit height and depth of cut until the boards perfectly line up on their faces and the joint closes all the way up (**D**).

Cogged Scarf Joint

To make a cogged scarf joint, lay out the joint on the boards with the scarf running at least as long as the width of the stock (**A, B**). Crosscut the inner shoulders on both boards using the crosscut jig on the table saw. Set a stop to index both cuts (**C**).

Next, rough out the cheek cuts on the bandsaw. Then set the blade height to cut both the notch and the cheek with the board held in the tenoning jig. If you're using an alternate-top bevel blade, clean up the bottom of the notch with a narrow chisel (**D**).

Cut the end rabbet to fit the notch cut. Clean it up flat with a shoulder plane or chisel (**E**).

The cogged cut is made with a simple dado pass. For ease, lay out the notch cuts from the center of each joint so they'll line up (**F**).

Make wedge stock for the folding or double wedges (**G**). Hammer the wedges into place to lock the joint (**H**). Glue them in for a permanent solution.

➤ See *"Making Loose Wedges"* on p. 149.

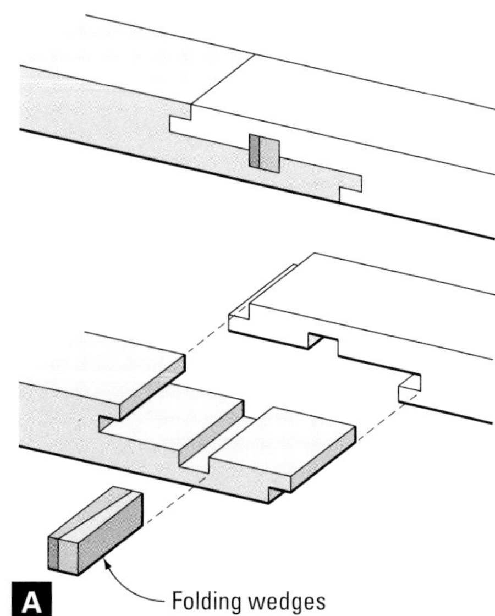

A

B

C

D

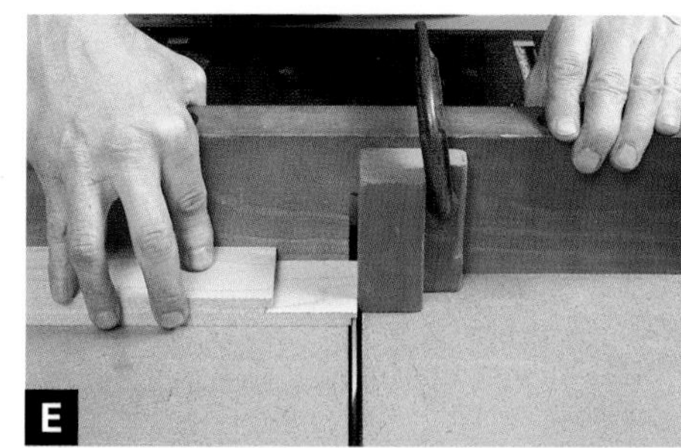
E

F

G

H

Edge Joints

Edge Joints

Edgebanding

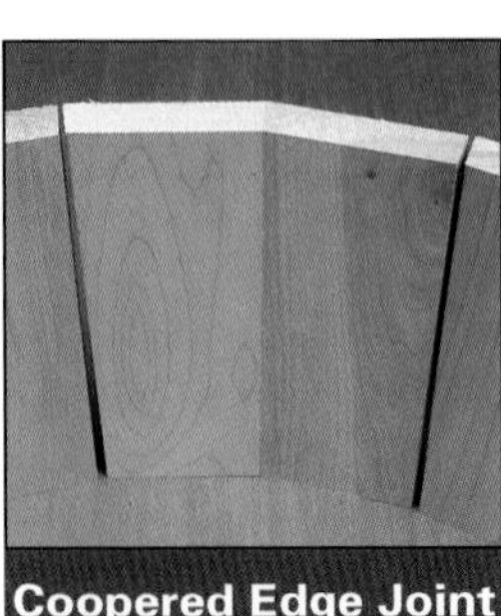

Coopered Edge Joint

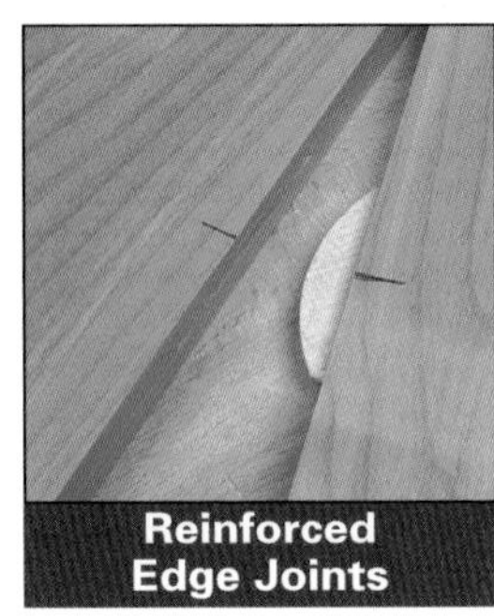

Reinforced Edge Joints

Tongue-and-Groove Edges

If mortises and tenons represent most of the joinery available to a woodworker, edge joints make up the rest. Edge joinery relies mostly on adhesive strength, although there are exceptions. Unglued tongue-and-grooves or shiplapped boards can make up the back of a cabinet, and unglued coopered staves for a barrel can be held in place by an iron hoop. Some edge joints do have reinforcing, like biscuits, dowels, or even a tongue and groove. But these types of reinforcement are used as much for alignment as for strength. What edge joinery depends on is two good mating edges cut straight and true and bonded together with a good adhesive.

Edge laminations put together with a good adhesive are so strong they are often stronger than the surrounding wood. But this strength depends heavily on the mating surfaces being true, clean, and without twist, so as the wood moves it does not put the edge joint under any additional strain. You can pull together any joint with enough clamping pressure, but the joints that will last are the ones requiring only moderate pressure to close.

Edge Joint Uses

You can use edge joints to make simple laminations, construct coopered door shapes, or create wide panels from narrow widths. You can also construct tabletops, carcase sides, and the panels that fit into frames. Edge lamination is used to band the edges of plywood or other sheet-good materials with solid wood.

If you have two good mating edges, you can glue up the boards by just aligning them and rubbing their edges together.

Burned wood will not glue up well. Make sure your surfaces are always clean, straight, and without any twist.

Cover the edges of sheet-good material with a simple edge lamination.

SPRING JOINTS

Note that the gap is exaggerated here for clarity. It should be about $^{1}/_{32}$ in.

Plane in a small gap along the length of the two mating pieces.

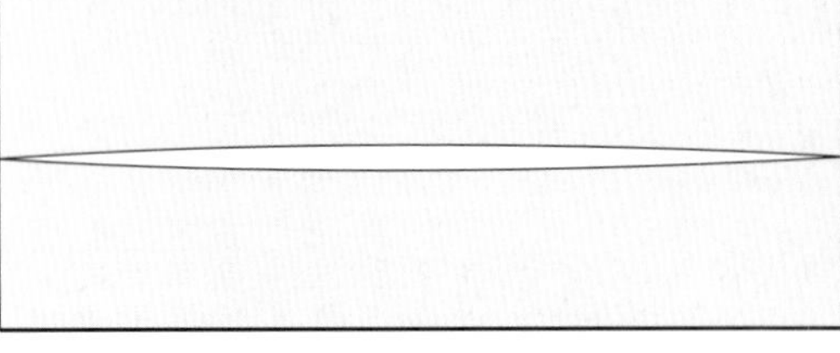

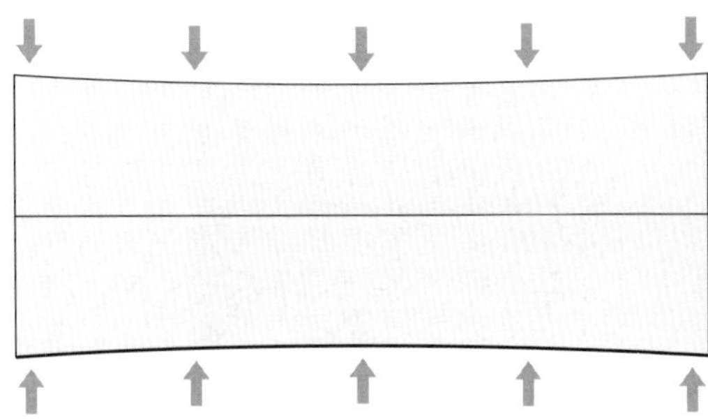

When laminated more pressure is needed in the middle to close up the joint.

The extra pressure created at the ends of the boards allows for a little give where moisture loss first occurs.

To check for a spring joint, look for a little bit of light showing through the middle of the edges. The boards should also have some pressure at their ends when you try to spin one board on the other.

Spring Joints

Edge joinery attempts to do a very basic and yet sometimes difficult task: mating two edges together completely along their entire length. Most boards flex enough even in their width to allow you to clamp out any gaps at the ends of a board. But consider that twice as much moisture loss and gain occurs out at the end of a board through the end grain.

If an edge lamination is going to fail, it will usually fail at the end of a board first. This is where a spring joint really shines. By planing in a small hollow along the length of the boards, you will need to apply pressure to close up the joint. This creates more pressure and a little bit of springback at the ends where the boards start to lose moisture first. Cut this hollow into both mating edges and then check for a sliver of light shining through the joint.

Edge Gluing

Before doing any edge lamination, get in the habit of checking some details for the best results. Arrange the boards for grain direction before joining the edges. Some woodworkers alternate heart sides up or down to minimize cupping. Others run the boards consistently heart side up or down to yield a consistent cup. Still others just choose the best-looking combination of boards.

If you're going to handplane the faces after gluing, line up the grain for a consistent planing direction. Remember that there are eight possible ways to arrange two boards together for a simple edge lamination, so there are plenty of options.

Mark out the face sides and which edges will be glued together. Use flat pipe or bar clamps that you can register the boards on accurately. Have them resting on a good true surface. If the clamps and work surface are flat and you keep the boards flat on the clamps, your laminations have a much better chance of coming out flat as well.

Plane the edges and then dry-clamp the boards together. This will make you get out all the clamps and tools you'll need for the glue-up before the glue starts drying. Check to see that the joint closes up on both faces. Make sure the pressure is consistent across the width and length of the joint. Bang the boards flat onto the clamps at their ends where they tend to lift up.

Use enough glue that you get some squeeze-out when you apply clamping pressure. Use a C-clamp to keep the ends lined up flat or a dead-blow hammer to coax the boards into place. Check both faces for consistent clamping pressure. Add more clamps if needed to get a good consistent pressure. Alternate the clamp heads to even out the pressure.

Reinforcing Edge Joints

An edge joint mates long grain to long grain, which allows ideal gluing surface. For that reason, a glued edge joint has great strength, even without the addition of reinforcements. Tests have shown that an edge joint properly jointed and glued with modern adhesives has greater strength than the original solid wood.

So why reinforce an edge joint? Reinforcements in the form of biscuits, dowels, splines, or tongues and grooves make alignment much easier. Beyond this, reinforcements provide a mechanical connection, which strengthen the joint. Without them, you must depend on the adhesive alone to hold the joint together.

Splines help align edge joints and can be used decoratively. Use plywood splines or use solid-wood splines with their grain running across the groove for the best strength. It's easier to cut a spline to match the grain direction of the mating boards, but it's also easier to break it along the long grain.

Before jointing the edges, mark out the face sides and align the boards for looks or grain or both.

Dry-clamp the boards after planing them to make sure the joint closes up on both faces.

Check both faces for squeeze-out and add a clamp, if needed. Also check to see that the boards are sitting flat on the clamps.

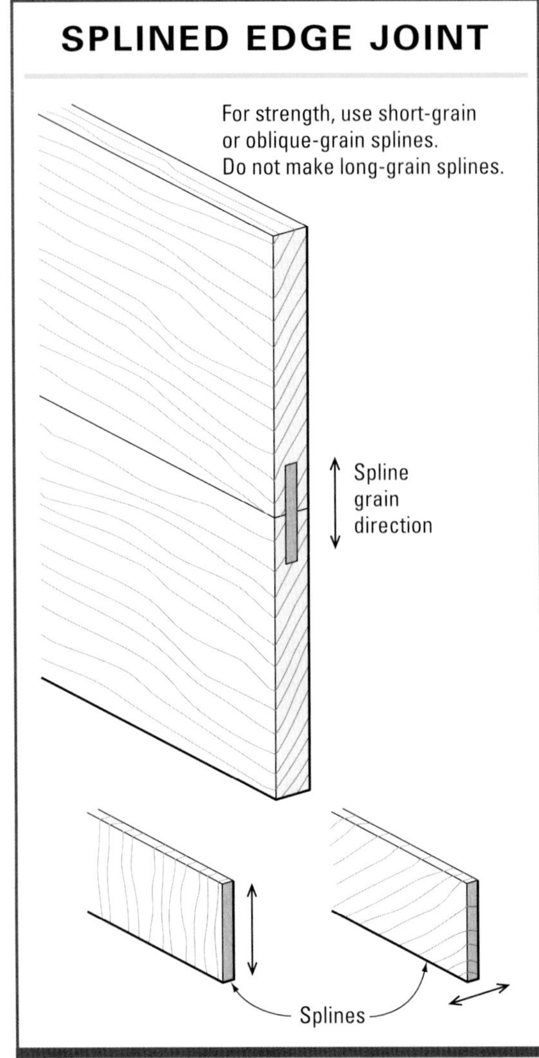

A tongue-and-groove joint is another effective way to join edges. The key to making a strong joint is designing and cutting it to the right proportions.

Edgebanding

Sheet goods are invaluable in cabinet construction, but plywood edges are ugly. Although commercially available edgebanding may be a quick solution, custom edgebanding is more durable and certainly more elegant. Making your own edgebanding allows you to match stock color, especially for unusual species. Custom edgebanding also means more design options, including profiles.

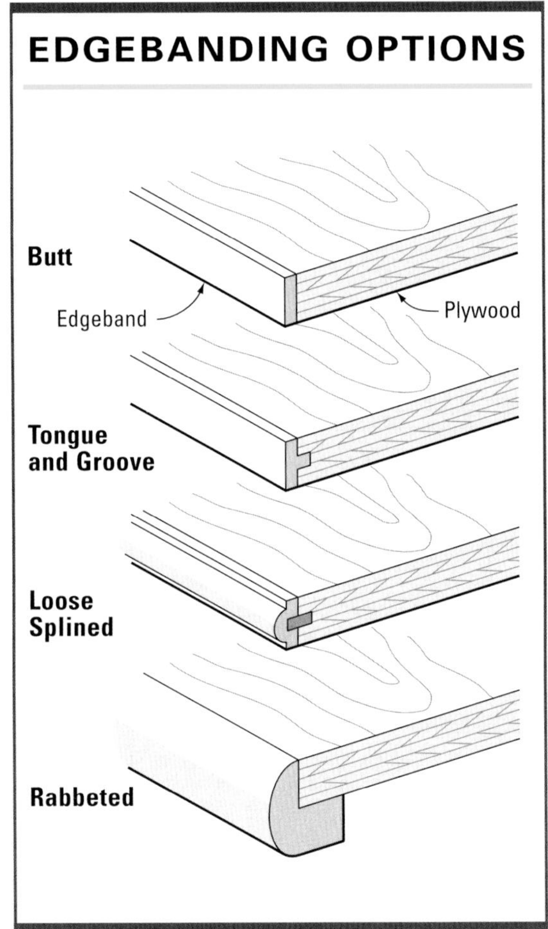

TONGUE-AND-GROOVE JOINT PROBLEMS

Too shallow;
no strength

Too deep;
weak grain

Weak

Too wide;
weak grain

Weak

Too tight

Hand-Cut Edge Joint

If you hand-cut your edge joints, you can plane the mating edges at the same time, which allows you to compensate if the jointed edges aren't dead-on square. When mated, the edges will have complementary angles (**A**).

First, arrange the two boards to be edge jointed on the benchtop for grain direction and looks. Then fold their faces together and line up their mating edges flush on the bench. Put a spring clamp on their ends to hold them in place and clamp them in the vise (**B**). Plane both their edges together using a longer bench plane. A no. 8 jointer plane will work great for this job, because its longer sole doesn't have a tendency to follow any humps or hollows along the edges of the boards. Take long but light and true passes. Try to keep the plane square to the boards' faces. But if you're off square, the plane will cut a complementary pass on these edges so they will always align (**C**).

To check your work, put the two boards together and rub their edges to get a feel for the kind of pressure you can get. If the boards spin freely, then you have a hump in the center that must be removed. What you want is good pressure at the ends of the boards, which indicates you have flat edges. Be sure to examine the entire joint for any gaps, tearout, or twist. Use a shorter plane to put in a hollow for a spring joint (**D**).

Use a shooting board to help you plane more accurately. Place each board in the jig separately and fine-tune your longest handplane so it's cutting square to one side. Run this side along the benchtop and plane the edges at a consistent right angle.

TIP **Put a small wedge under the board so more than just one spot on the plane iron gets used.**

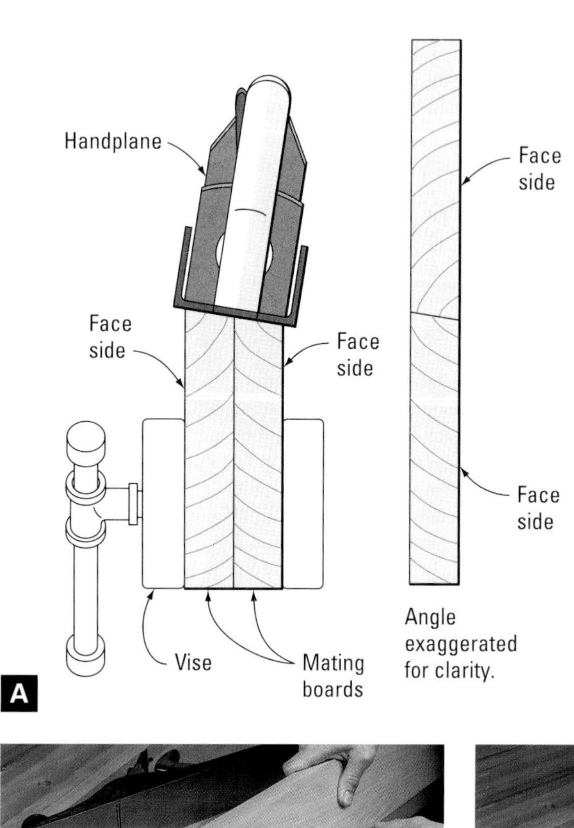

B

C

D

TIP

A

B

C

Edge Joint with a Router

Long or extra-wide panels create edge jointing problems. Most jointers have beds that are too short to handle the panels successfully, plus the weight of a panel can make it difficult to move it past a cutterhead. Make up a router template that you can use to locate the edge cut and to guide the router successfully.

Cut out a piece of some scrap ¼-in. plywood or medium-density fiberboard (MDF) as long as the panel edge and 5 in. to 6 in. wide. Glue a ½-in. by 2-in. piece of MDF onto it to act as the router fence. Make sure the edge of the ½-in. stock is flat and straight, because this edge will be what the router base rides against during cutting. Set up a router with a wide-diameter bit. Make a cut along the ¼-in. MDF to establish the edge of the template (**A**).

Set the edge of the template exactly where you want the edge cut to be and clamp it in place. Rout along the edge, cutting from left to right and with the grain. Keep the base of the router flat against the ½-in. fence. Use a subbase with a flat edge on it if you have one (**B**).

After making the cuts, clean them up using a bench plane. Take an extra pass or two in the middle of the board to make a spring joint (**C**).

➤ See *"Spring Joints"* drawing on p. 270.

Edge Joint on the Router Table

To cut an edge joint on the router table, use a wide straight bit and offset the surfaces on the fence to act as a jointer (**A**). Set up the router table fence with a shim on its outfeed end to mimic the offset of the infeed and outfeed tables of a jointer. Clamp the shim or laminate scrap onto the fence. Then set the fence to capture the bit so that it's protruding from the infeed part of the fence by an amount equal to the thickness of the shim (**B**).

Make the cut moving the wood right to left past the bit at a moderate feed rate. Arrange the grain direction on the board's edge so that you're cutting with the grain. Be sure the wood locates smoothly onto the outfeed table shim (**C**).

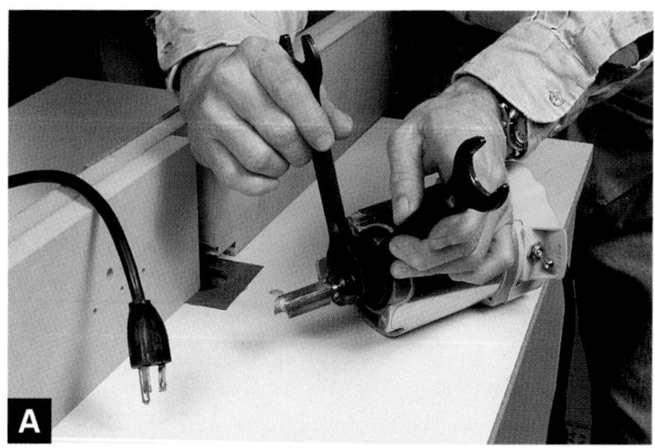
A

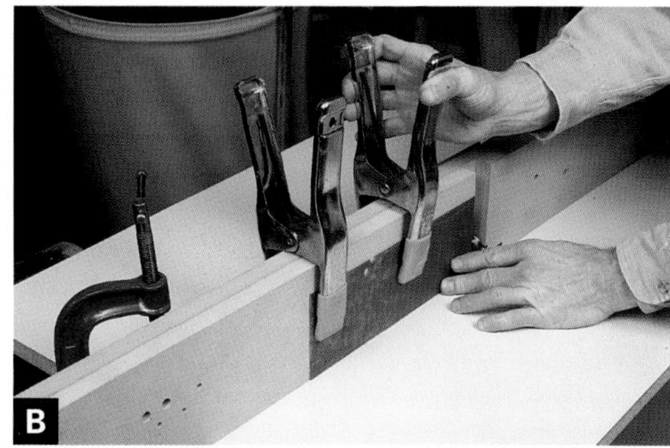
B

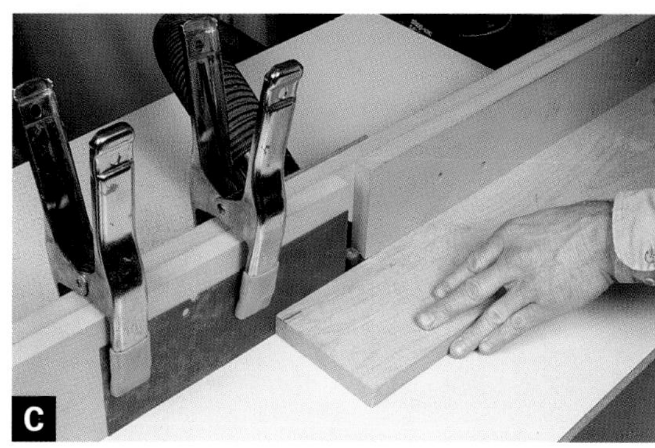
C

A

B

C

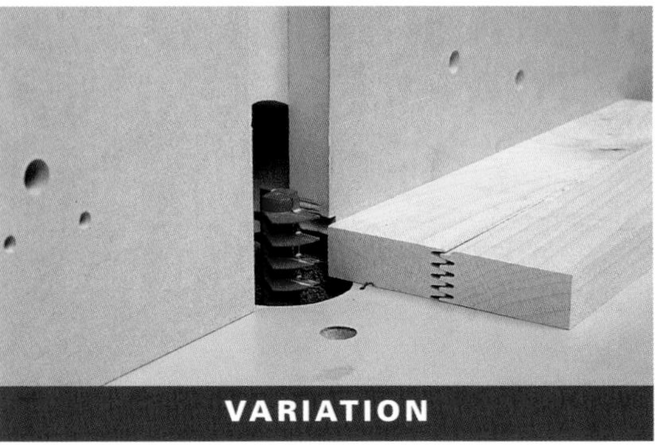
VARIATION

Edge Joint on the Router Table with an Edge-Jointing Bit

To use an edge-jointing bit in the table-mounted router, clamp a piece of ⅛-in. scrap onto the outfeed side of the fence. Line up the cutting edge of the bit to this piece (**A**). Make a practice cut and adjust the fence as needed so only as much bit protrudes as is necessary for the joint (**B**). Adjust the bit height so the boards will match properly (**C**).

[VARIATION] A finger-jointing bit will also make long-grain glue joints. Adjust the bit height and fence location for the best results. Remember to run opposite faces down to the router table.

Edge Joint on the Jointer

When using the jointer to create an edge joint, first arrange the boards for grain direction and face sides. Mark the mating edges. Check the fence on the jointer to see that it's square. Put a light source behind the square to see the setting better. Be aware that every machine has its own quirks when it comes to setting a fence. Take a practice pass after locating the fence (**A**).

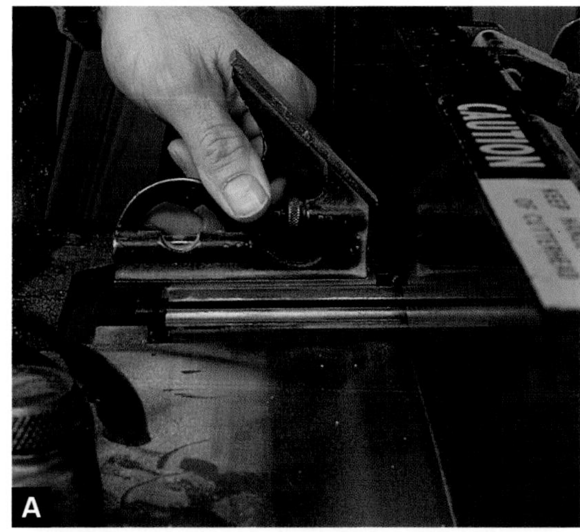

A

Arrange the grain direction on the board's face so it trails down and away from the cut. Make a pass through the jointer while holding the board's edge tight in to the fence at a point just past the jointer knives. Be sure that the board's edge is established on the outfeed table before applying pressure down onto the outfeed table. The speed of the cutterhead should eliminate most tearout if you keep the feed rate slow enough. If you are still running into problems, you can angle some jointer fences to make an angled shearing pass (**B**) or spin the board end for end and take another pass.

B

[TIP] If you run the opposite faces of the boards against the fence, then it won't matter if the fence is out of square a little. Each pass will complement the other.

A

B

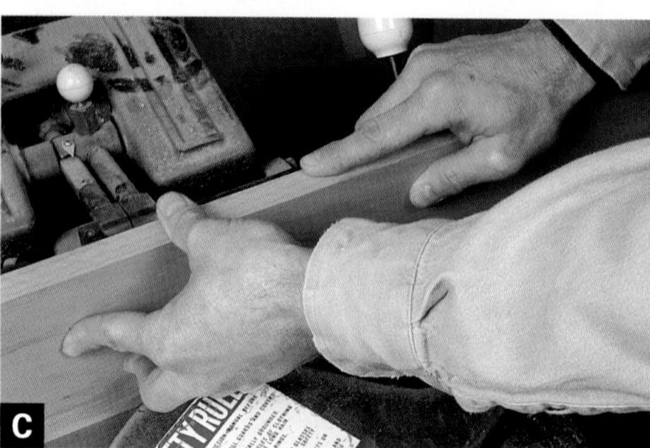
C

D

Spring Joint on the Jointer

To get consistent spring joints on the jointer, you need to remove more wood in the middle of the board, gradually taking less out toward the ends.

Start by flattening the edge of the board with one full pass. Then make another pass, beginning about one-quarter down the length of the board. Lower the board carefully onto the cutterhead (**A**). Continue jointing until you reach the final quarter of the board; then carefully lift the board off the cutterhead (**B**).

Finally, make another full cleanup pass, but this time start to apply pressure downward as you reach the end of the first quarter (**C**). Keep applying pressure and gradually release it at the last quarter, but continue with the pass all the way off the end of the board. Do this to both mating edges.

Then put your boards together and check for a little bit of a hollow along their length. They should also have some resistance at their ends if you try to spin them (**D**).

➤ See *"Spring Joints"* drawing on p. 270.

Edge-Banding Plywood

Edge-banding plywood or particleboard is the kind of cabinet-shop job you become familiar with quickly. Make sure the plywood edge is cut smooth. Some shops joint the edge of their sheet goods on the jointer. This is fine if you have carbide knives in the machine. Otherwise, you will quickly dull the knives. If you don't want to risk your knives, use the table saw to true one edge of the plywood (**A**). Flip the board to make a second cut. If the edge was not at all flat to begin with, flip the plywood one more time to make a third and final truing cut (**B**).

Mill edgebanding material on the planer. Cut it oversize in length and take it down until it's about 1/16 in. wider than the plywood's thickness. If you're getting snipe on the planer, make the stock extra long (**C**). Clean up the edge of the board on the jointer (**D**).

Rip off a strip of banding on the table saw and then rejoin the edge before slicing off another piece. Use a push stick to move the strip past the blade. The thickness of the edge banding is up to you. Some woodworkers like it as thin as 1/8 in. so it almost disappears against the plywood's veneer. I prefer a 1/4-in. edge, which is more likely to hold up over time (**E**).

(Text continues on p. 280.)

A

B

C

D

E

F

G

Use masking tape to help you line up the banding during glue-up (**F**). Put enough glue on both the plywood and the banding that you get a little squeeze-out during clamping. Clean this up before the glue hardens. Also make sure the clamping pressure is even on the top and bottom faces of the plywood. Alternate the clamps on opposite faces or raise the plywood up in the clamps to ensure that the pressure is consistent. A clamping caul helps spread out the pressure (**G**).

H

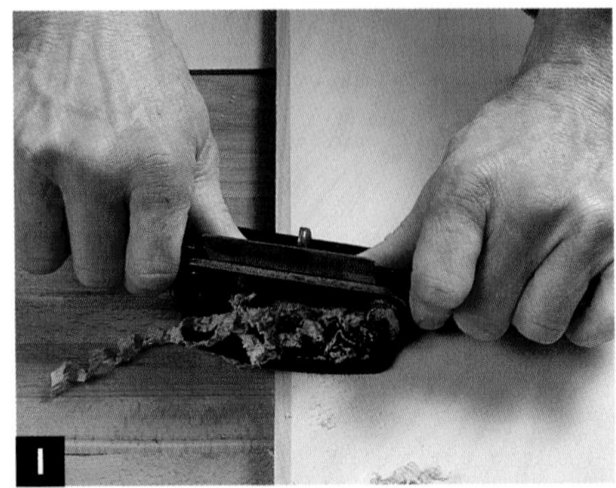
I

Use a flush-trimming bit on the router table to clean up the overhanging edge of the banding. Set the bit height so its bearing rides against the plywood face when you pass it vertically past the bit. Use a fence for extra support (**H**). Scrape the banding flush down to the plywood's veneer. A no. 80 cabinet scraper works well. Just make sure you're cutting mostly on the banding and not into the veneer (**I**).

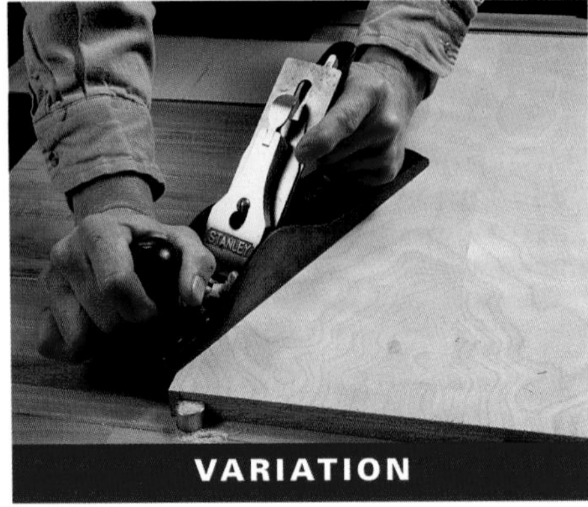

VARIATION

[VARIATION] A handplane will also work well for a final trimming of edgebanding. Keep the pressure over the banding so you don't cut into the veneer and double-check the grain direction of the edgebanding before starting to plane.

Coopered Edge Joint

The first step to making a coopered edge joint is to lay out the curve on a drawing to determine the angle and number of staves required. Use trammel points to draw out the arc of the circle. Measure the total angle of the arc and divide it into as many staves as you want. Then mark out the stave angles from the center. Each board will get cut at half the total angle (**A**).

Mill up the stock to thickness and width, but keep the stock oversize in thickness if the shape of the piece will be rounded. Keep all the boards a little oversize in length.

Set the table saw at the required angle and rip the boards (**B**). Set the jointer fence at that same angle with the sliding bevel (**C**). Joint the boards, holding them tight to the angled fence. Check each joint for a good, flat fit (**D**).

Glue up the coopering in small sections to minimize the problems of applying pressure to angled boards. For a simple two-board glue-up with angle cuts made into both edges, use clamping cauls cut at twice the coopering angle (**E**).

VARIATION You can add tongues to coopered boards. Keep the blade at the coopering angle and hold the board up tight against the fence. This will yield a cut straight into the angled edge. Then joint the edge before gluing and fitting a spline.

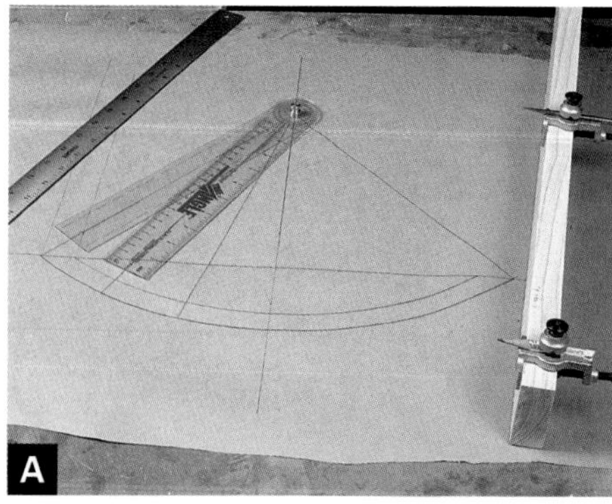
A

B

C

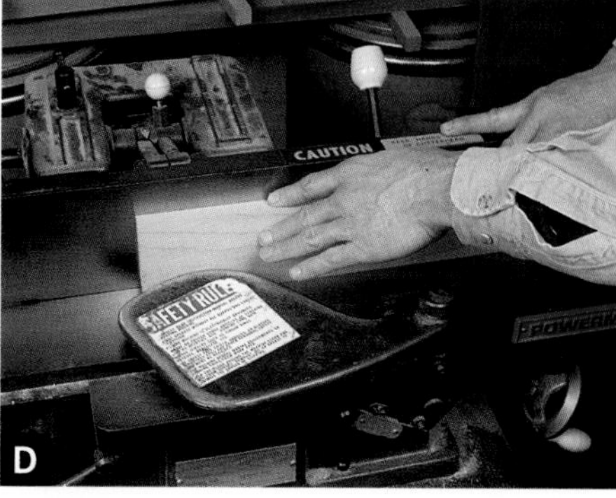

D

E

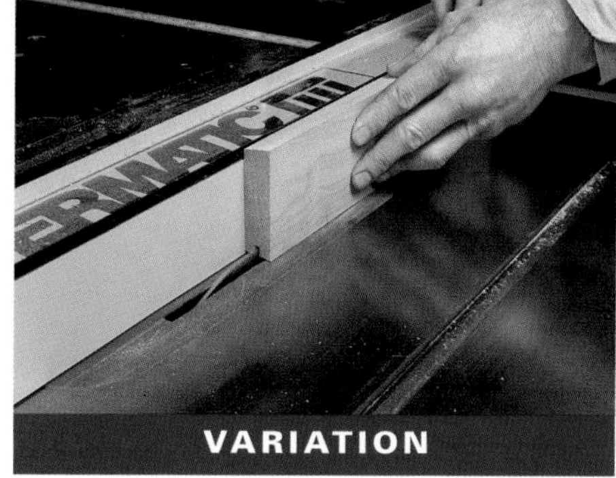
VARIATION

A

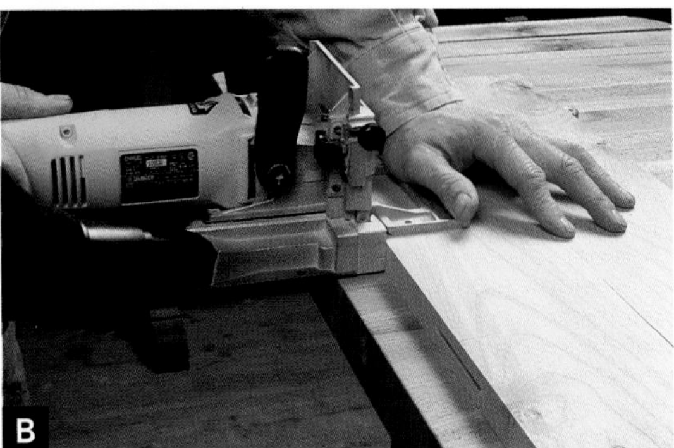
B

C

Biscuited Edge Joint

Biscuits can be used to strengthen an edge lamination; but, more important, they help line up the board's faces during glue-up. This is especially handy when gluing several boards together at once or when gluing long boards, when you might have trouble pulling them down flush to one another.

Plane the edges of the boards flat and smooth. Then mark out the location of the biscuits. Don't put biscuits in any spots where a cut will reveal their location (**A**).

Set up the biscuit joiner so it will center a cut in the thickness of the board. If you index all cuts from matching faces, however, the biscuit slots will line up fine (**B**). Make sure the depth of cut matches the biscuit size. Do a dry-run with the biscuits in place to check that everything will clamp up correctly.

Be sure to apply plenty of glue to the biscuit slots and surrounding wood when joining the boards (**C**).

Doweled Edge Joint

Dowels help strengthen edge laminations but require careful attention so they go in straight and keep the boards flat. Mark out the location of the dowels on the board (**A**).

Place the board in the vise and line up the doweling jig with the pencil mark (**B**). Mark out the drilling depth by placing a piece of tape on the brad-point bit. Then drill to depth, clearing the hole of debris as you enter deeper. Keep the drill held straight and true (**C**).

Use spiral- or straight-fluted dowels so glue and air can escape as you clamp the boards together. Because most dowels dry to an oval shape, cook them in a shopmade oven to shrink them a bit before gluing. This will make their entry much easier; and when the moisture in the glue hits the dowels, they'll expand and fill their holes (**D**).

Be sure to double-check the length of the dowels to their holes before applying glue. Have clamps at the ready to pull the joint home (**E**).

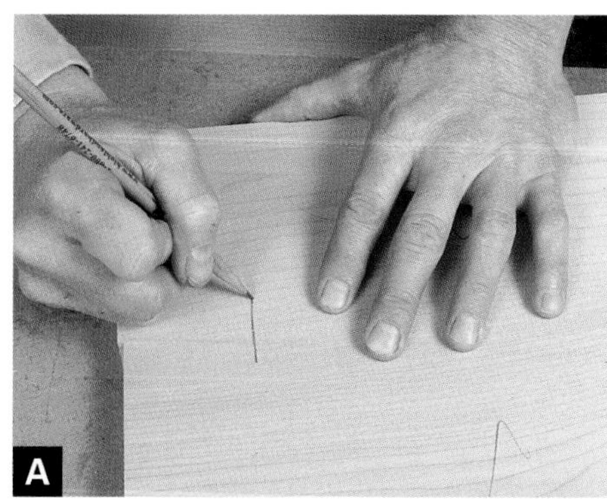
A

B

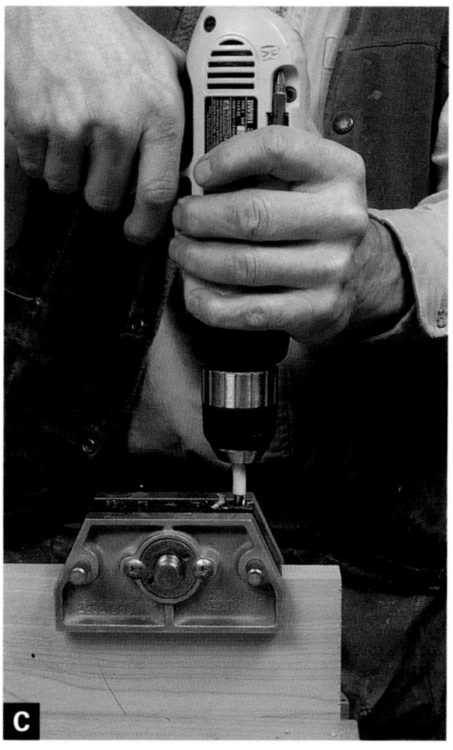
C

D

E

A

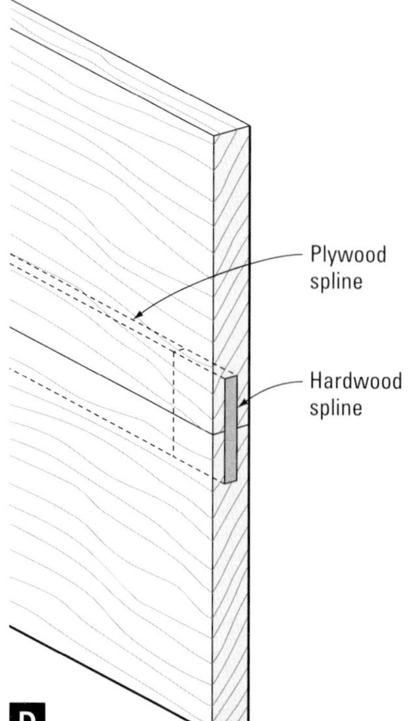

D

B

E

C

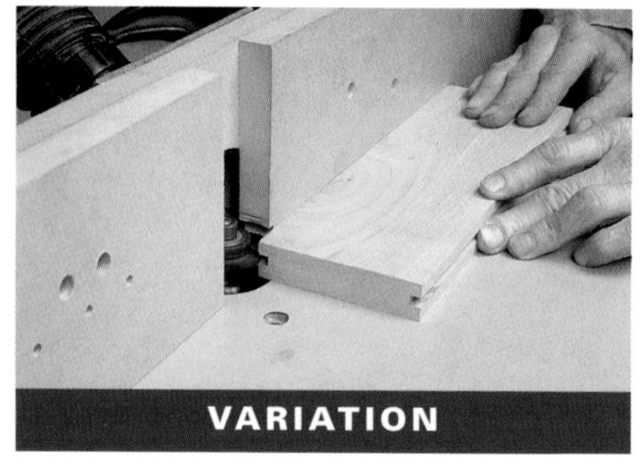
VARIATION

Splined Edge Joint

To make a spline-reinforced edge joint, first make the groove cuts on the table saw, holding the board on edge and up tight to the fence. Then flip the board over to cut with the opposite face against the fence to ensure that the groove is centered. A dado blade will cut a wider groove, if needed, but be sure to keep the feed rate slower (**A**).

➤ See *"Splined Edge Joint"* on p. 272.

[VARIATION] You can use a slotting cutter in the router table to cut the spline groove. Capture the bit in the fence for greater safety and to make a shallower cut; the groove doesn't have to be too deep. Move the work right to left past the bit.

Cut splines out of plywood that matches the groove cut or is a little oversize. Use a push stick to move the plywood past the table-saw blade (**B**). You can trim the plywood's outer faces with a scraper to fit the groove. Keep the spline width just under the combined depth of the grooves so the joint closes up when the spline is in place (**C**).

[TIP] The fit of splines should be just snug but not too loose or too tight or you'll risk a sloppy joint or a cracked one.

Hardwood splines are difficult to fit, because their short grain tends to crack as you put them in and pull them out of a groove. Instead, use plywood splines for most of the groove, but put a hardwood spline just at the end for looks (**D**). Don't worry too much about grain direction; the plywood spline will do the holding job (**E**).

Dovetail Keyed Edge Joint

Add dovetail keys to an edge joint to create a distinctive inlay and to strengthen the joint.

First, mill up the key stock a bit wider and thicker than its final size. Use straight-grained stock and make the keys ⅛ in. to $\frac{3}{16}$ in. thick (**A**). Make up a template of the key shape out of cardboard or ⅛-in. hardboard or MDF. Lay out the keys on the stock and cut the shapes out on the bandsaw. If you can angle the bandsaw in both directions cut each side of the key shape at about a 5-degree angle (**B**). Finish shaping the key with a chisel (**C**).

Use a drum sander on the ends of the keys.

Set the key in position on the glued-up edge joint. Mark out around the key with a marking knife, making sure to put the smaller angled face of the inlay down on the wood. Fill in the knife marks with pencil lead so you can see them clearly (**D**).

➤ See *"Butterfly Keyed Miter Joint"* on pp. 228–229.

(Text continues on p. 286.)

A

B

C

D

E

F

Mount a small straight bit in the router and rout out the ground to depth, coming as close as you can to the knife marks. Use a climb cut so the bit actually gets pushed away from the cut. This will make it easier to cut almost up to the lines, because you can easily control the small-diameter cutter (**E**).

Clean up to the knife marks with a chisel. Make all the paring cuts straight down into the wood. The key shapes shown here have rounded ends, so I cut out the end shapes with a gouge. Use a skew chisel or a no. 1 skew gouge to clean up the corners (**F**).

G

Check the fit before banging the keys home. Press the key in place. Then remove it and look for the shiny spots on the key, which indicate where it's rubbing. You want the key to almost fit all the way down into the joint. The ebony key shown here left behind a little color on the edges of the ground, so I could tell where I needed to remove more wood. Use the skew gouge to pry the inlay up and out of the wood. Place a piece of laminate on the wood to protect it as you pry (**G**).

H

Put glue into the ground area and on all the edges. Put just a dab on the bottom of the inlay as well. Bang the inlay home and clamp it if you can reach it with clamps. Flush the inlay down to the surface of the board with a handplane. Make certain of the grain direction of the inlay before planing to avoid any tearout (**H**).

Hand-Cut Tongue-and-Groove Edge Joint

Tongue-and-groove edge joints can be cut by hand. Use a combination plane to cut a groove in the edge of the board. Make certain the skates on the plane support the iron and aren't set wider than it. Cut with the grain for the easiest results (**A**).

A

Cut the tongue with a rabbeting plane. A no. 78 uses a fence to help you locate the cut. You can also clamp a fence to the board. Use the depth gauge on the plane or mark out the depth of cut on the board. Make sure the iron fits all the way to the edge of the handplane to avoid a stepped cut (**B**).

B

Use a no. 78 rabbeting plane to cut rabbets along the edges of a board. This shiplap joint will allow you to use boards across the back of a cabinet, which will adjust to seasonal wood movement without showing any gaps.

[TIP] Clamp the workpiece in the vise or clamp boards onto the bench to work against.

TIP

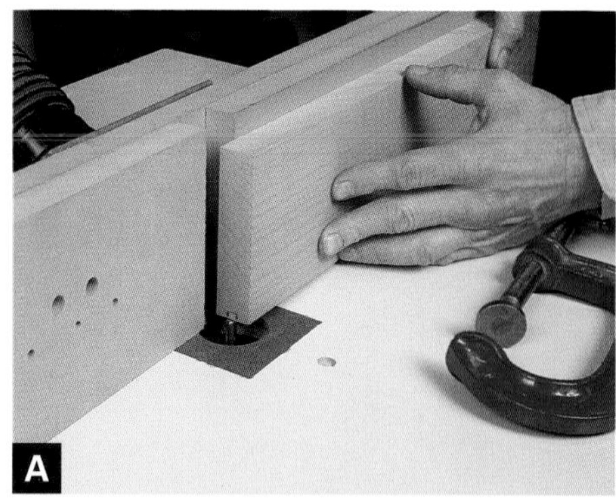
A

B

C

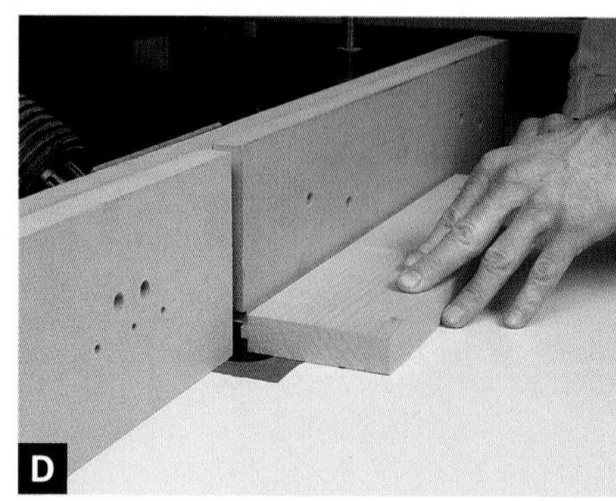
D

E

Tongue-and-Groove Edge Joint on the Router Table with a Straight Bit

You can cut precise tongue and grooves using a straight bit in the router table. Keep the groove size no wider than one-third the thickness of the board. Mount the bit and adjust its height for a ⅛-in.-deep pass. Set up the fence to place the groove cut in the center of the board. Or you can flip the faces against the fence and make the pass twice to ensure a centered groove (**A**).

Make the groove cut while holding the workpiece in tight to the fence. Run the cut twice to clean out any jammed-up chips in the groove or use a single-fluted bit to clear away the chips (**B**).

You can use the same bit to cut the tongue. Run the board flat to the table instead of on edge for easier referencing. Also any tearout that may occur will show up on the edge of the hidden tongue, not on the edge of the board itself. Capture the bit in the fence so only as much bit protrudes as is needed (**C**).

Make the first cut. If you note excessive tearout, make a climb cut first to score the outer edge of the board. Finish up the cut by running the board in the proper feed direction: from right to left. Flip the board over to make the second cut (**D**).

➤ **See *"Climb Cutting"* drawing on p. 21.**

Check that the tongue almost completely fills the groove slot. You can make some minor adjustments with a bench plane, trimming the tongue or groove edge. Or use a shoulder plane to trim the tongue's shoulders (**E**).

Tongue-and-Groove Edge Joint on the Router Table with a Slot Cutter

A slotting cutter in the router table can make the cuts for tongues and grooves. Set the slotting cutter height for the groove cut first. Center it in the work (**A**). Capture the bit in the fence for greater safety and to make a shallower cut. You don't need too much depth for this groove. Flip the board and make the cuts with both faces flat to the table to ensure the groove is centered (**B**).

Adjust the bit height to make the rabbet cuts that will define the tongue. Keep the fence clamped in the same place. Line up the top edge of the bit to the bottom of the groove. Make the first pass, moving right to left past the cutter. If you are experiencing tearout, make a climb cut first (**C**). Flip the board over and make the second cut to create the tongue (**D**).

➤ See *"Climb Cutting"* drawing on p. 21.

A

B

C

D

Mortise and Tenons

Simple Mortises

Simple Tenons

Round Mortises

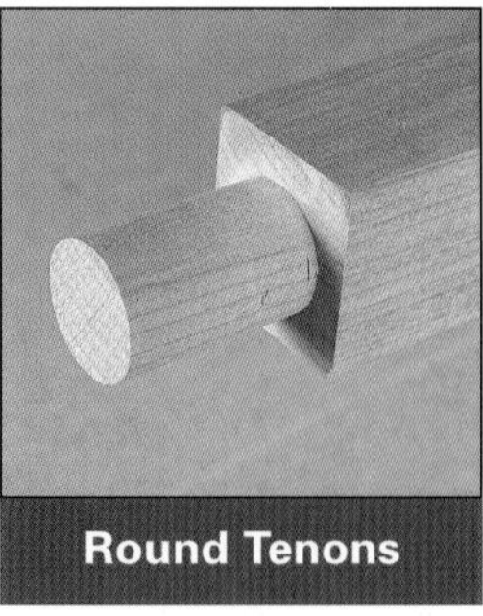

Round Tenons

Loose Tenons

Haunched Joints

Multiple Mortises

Mating Tenons

Strengthened Tenons

Through Mortises

Through Tenons

Angled Tenons

Frames and Panels

Special Joints

If we were to simplify joinery, we would say that all joints are either edge joints or some form of a mortise and tenon. So universal is the use of the mortise-and-tenon joint that it's found in carcase work and frame construction and is included in stools, tables, and chairs. Basically, the joint is used to construct every type of furniture we make.

The basic joint is fairly simple: One part of a board fits into a hole cut into another board. But the shape of the mortise and tenon depends on the purpose of the joint, the methods for cutting it, the speed at which you want to cut, and the joint's impact on the design of a piece.

This 20-year-old walnut stool, made by the author, relies on the strength of mortise-and-tenon joinery.

Advantages of the Mortise-and-Tenon Joint

The mortise-and-tenon joint offers many advantages to the woodworker. It's a load-bearing joint that handles compression forces with ease. When wedged, pinned, or glued, the mortise and tenon also resists tension and racking. The joint gives you all sorts of warning before it fails completely, unlike biscuit joinery. And it will hold together after years of racking, after the tenon shrinks in the mortise, and even after the wood splits in two.

Mortise-and-tenon construction allows builders to lighten their frame members by using smaller, thinner pieces to capture panels in frames. Yet the joint will also hold wide carcase panels together securely. The mortise and tenon, straight or angled, is found in some form or another in almost every table and chair made, allowing relatively small, light rails and legs to support great loads. Tenons can be stopped short of an end or taken through and wedged for better strength and a distinct design detail.

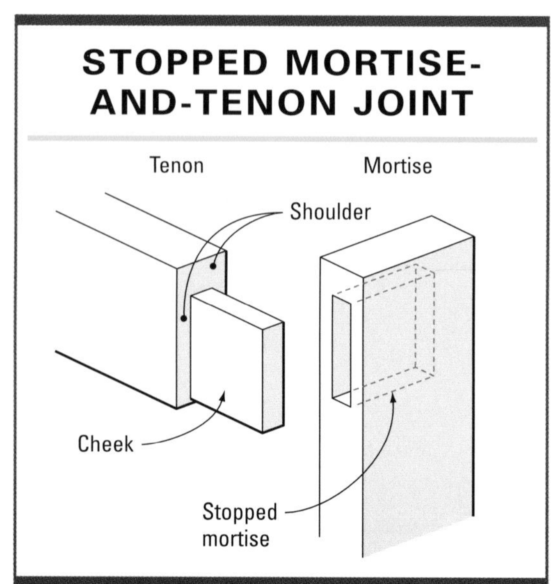

Designing the Mortise-and-Tenon

Let's consider some basic factors in the design of the mortise-and-tenon joint. Size a mortise and tenon to fit your tools. Don't concern yourself with dividing a board into thirds. Match the mortise size to your chisel width, your drill bit diameter, or the size of your router bit.

Try not to remove too much wood when cutting the mortise, because it will leave only thin, weak wood behind. My rule of thumb is to leave at least 1/4 in. of wood on all sides of a mortise. For instance, a 3/4-in.-thick board can handle a 1/4-in.-wide mortise; but if I use 7/8-in.- to 1-in.-thick stock, I prefer to use a 3/8-in.-wide mortise.

Be aware of the stress that will be placed on the joint. If it will undergo twisting forces, keep more wood around the mortise for added resistance. You can increase the strength of a mortise-and-tenon joint by maximizing its gluing surface. A group of short barefaced stub tenons for a window shutter may be perfectly adequate, but a dining room table needs a deeper haunched tenon to provide better strength.

Barefaced tenons are used where tenon members are too thin to allow for twin side

Size the mortise to the tool, not to any formula.

Use deeper mortises to provide more gluing surface and thus more strength.

TENON PROPORTIONS

7/8 in.
3/8 in.
1/4 in.
1/4 in.

Leave a 1/16-in. shoulder to cover the bottom of the mortise.

shoulders. They can be used in situations where many tenons spread out the load or resist force, as in slat construction. Use side shoulders on a tenon to help resist racking and twisting forces. Wider shoulders designed into the rail of a piece help triangulate the holding power of the joint, making the joint more secure.

BAREFACED TENONS

No shoulder

Single shoulder

Double shoulders

Single shoulder

TENON LENGTHS

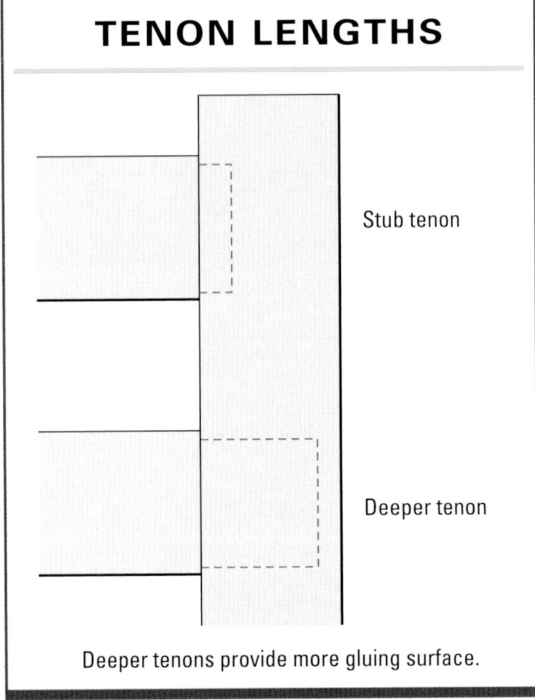

Deeper tenons provide more gluing surface.

The wide rails of this carved walnut arm chair, built by Lonnie Bird, help resist the racking and twisting forces put on a seating piece.

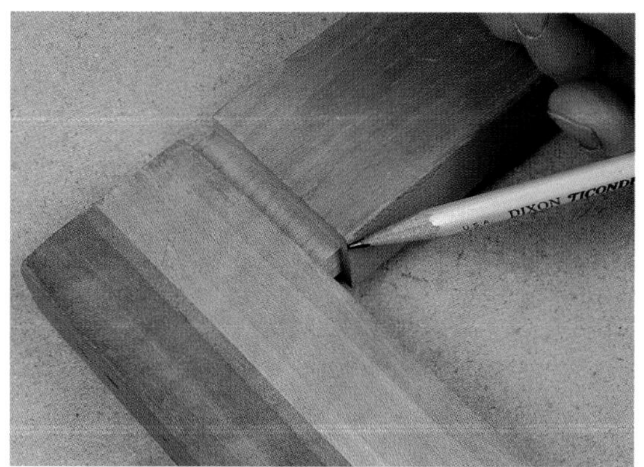

Put a small shoulder at the bottom of a tenon to cover the mortise.

Use shoulders on the top or bottom of a tenon to help hide the mortise and any indiscretions or dings that occur around the mouth of the joint when chopping or fitting it. Even a small 1⁄16-in. shoulder does an admirable job of covering your trail and preventing moisture or dirt from entering a mortise.

In areas where tenons meet up, as in table and chair legs, move them to the outside of the leg to gain greater penetration and strength. The farther you push them to the outside of the leg, the deeper they can go before meeting up. Miter the ends of the tenons where they meet inside the mortise. When the rail can't be moved off-center to a leg, offset the tenon position in the rail itself.

Haunches can be added to help prevent the joint from twisting. They are usually used at the top of a joint where you don't want to expose the tenon, but they can also be used in the center and bottom of wider tenons.

Making the tenons wider works well but only up to the point at which shrinkage in the joint starts to become a problem. Tenons wider than 3 in. should be split into two or

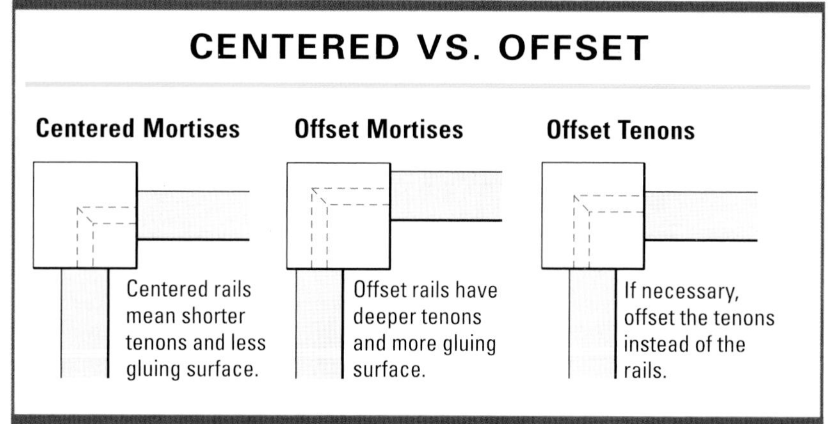

The top of this dining-table leg shows how the tenons can be deeper if moved to the outside of the leg. The pencil marks indicate how far the tenon fits into the mortise.

When a rail can't be offset on a leg, offset the tenon on the rail.

Split a wide tenon into two to minimize the effects of shrinkage. Put a haunch between the tenons and at the top and bottom, if needed.

more tenons to minimize the effects of shrinkage over time. Instead of one large tenon shrinking all at once in the joint, each smaller tenon shrinks individually.

Be sure to consider the orientation of the tenon when you design your joint. The principal goal is maximizing the long-grain-to-long-grain gluing surfaces. Remember that end grain doesn't bond well. If possible, orient the grain of the mortise in the direction of the grain of the tenon. Obviously, this isn't always possible in furniture construc-

HAUNCHED MULTIPLE TENONS

Haunches

One wide tenon in a wide rail will shrink and split. Whenever a tenon will be wider than 3 in., divide it into two or three smaller tenons.

HAUNCHED TENON

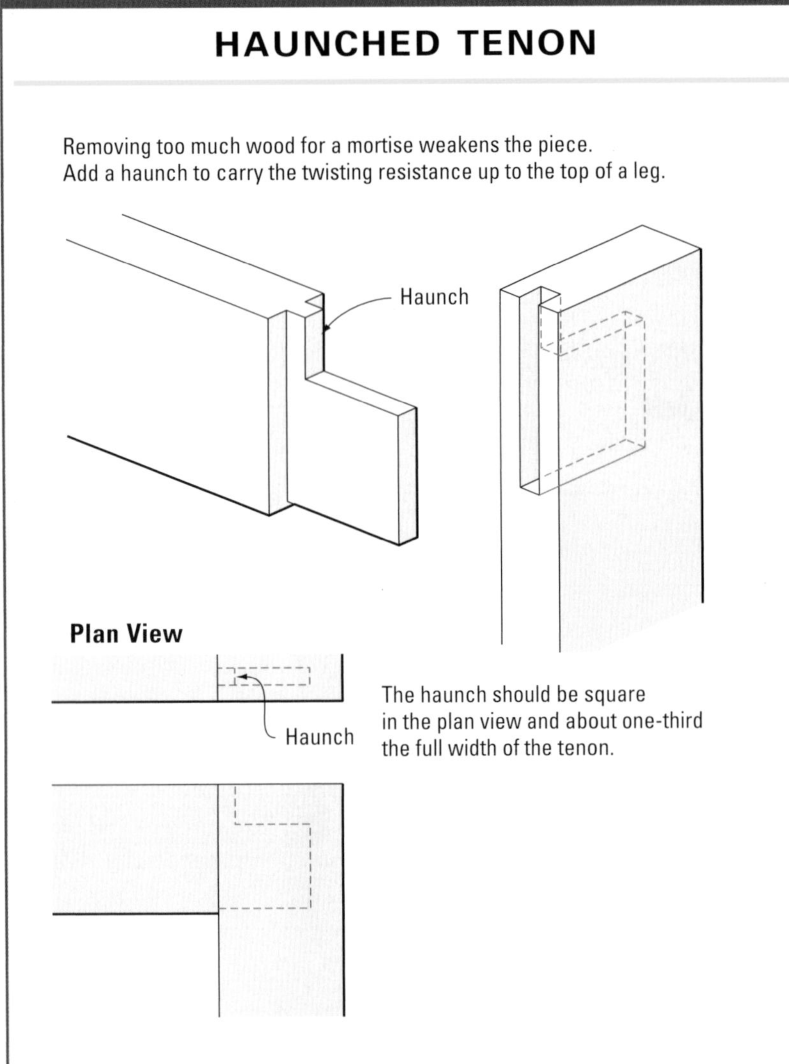

Removing too much wood for a mortise weakens the piece. Add a haunch to carry the twisting resistance up to the top of a leg.

The haunch should be square in the plan view and about one-third the full width of the tenon.

TENON ORIENTATION

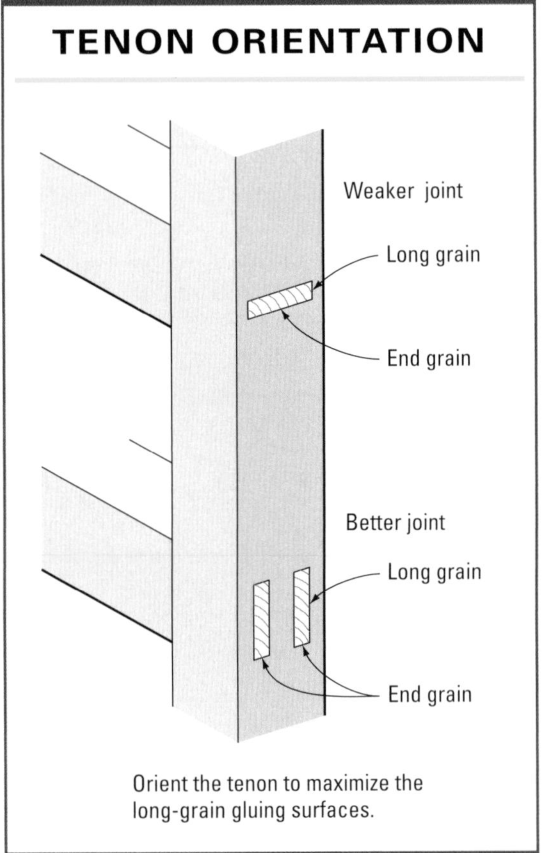

Orient the tenon to maximize the long-grain gluing surfaces.

tion. In that case, consider how the grain orientation will affect shrinkage.

Through Tenons

When you take a mortise through a piece you create new opportunities and new problems. The tenon is longer for greater gluing surface and greater strength. But since the tenon now has end grain exposed, it's more susceptible to the problems of moisture gain and loss. It can shrink and expand in the mortise, causing compression, which can stretch the limits of the glue bond. Wedging the joint minimizes this movement plus adds strength.

Wedges are either pounded into slots cut into the tenon or put through mortises cut through a protruding tenon. The wedges can be left loose or glued into place.

Strengthening the Joint

You have several options for increasing the longevity of a mortise-and-tenon joint. Drill and pin the joint with a dowel, either straight through the joint or by drawboring. Drawboring uses offset holes to pull a tenon in tight to a mortised piece. Foxtail wedging is done from the inside of the mortise. It does the job of strengthening but requires accuracy in the layout. If the wedge is too long, the joint won't close up; but if it's too short, it won't do any real work. The mortise also must be angled out the right amount to accept the width of the wedge.

Wedging the tenon can be done from the outside of the joint as well. Cut a slot in the middle of the tenon so a wedge can be driven into it. Drill in a relief hole at the bottom of the slot to help spread out the pressure. Cut the slot straight in by hand or on the band-

Wedging a through tenon adds a design element while locking the joint in place.

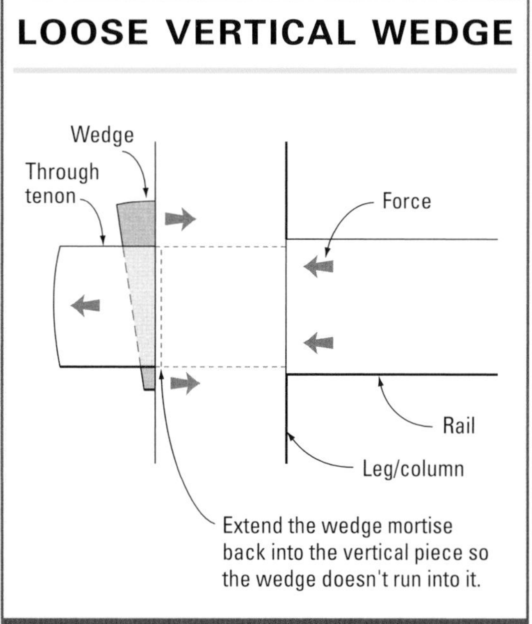

Make sure the wedge is the proper length and width to do the best possible job in foxtail wedging.

The relief hole at the bottom of the wedge slot spreads out the pressure of the wedging action.

ROUND OR SQUARE?

Through joints bring up a broader issue that has to be decided on for almost all mortise-and-tenon joints: Do you round the tenon or square the mortise? Hand-cut mortises will be chopped square so cutting the tenons square is the obvious choice, and lathe-turned tenons are round to fit drilled-out holes. But router-cut mortises end up with round ends. You must either round the tenon with a file and a chisel or square the mortise with a chisel. Through mortises require more care when squaring them because the cuts will be visible.

Squaring the mortise or rounding the tenon is a decision that must be made for every machine-cut mortise-and-tenon joint.

FIXED WEDGES

Single Wedged Tenon

3/16-in.- dia. relief hole drilled at two-thirds tenon length.

Wedge

The wedge is as wide as but shorter than the slot and tapers from 3/16 in. to 3/32 in.

End Wedged Tenon

Double Wedged Tenon

Diagonal Wedge

saw. You can use diagonal wedges and double wedges for design effects.

Be sure to orient the wedge slot correctly to the surrounding wood in the mortise. Avoid wedging that puts pressure on the long grain. Long grain is easy to split, as any wood chopper will tell you. Wedge pressure at the end of a board may also cause splitting out at the short grain.

Mate intersecting tenons together so one helps hold the other in place. Avoid creating short-grain situations that may break out under a strain.

One intersecting tenon locks the other in place.

Cutting the Mortise

There are close to a dozen ways of cutting a mortise. The determining factors are your tool budget, your capacity for noise, your need for speed, and accuracy. If you prefer hand tools, then no router can cut a mortise quietly enough. But if you must make hundreds of mortises for a project, then hand chopping becomes a less romantic choice. Guaranteeing the same size results speeds up a job, making it either more profitable or more palatable. But no matter the tool, always mortise first and then make the tenon to fit.

Use *chisels* that are designed for pounding when mortising by hand. Mortising, registered mortising, and firmer chisels all have enough metal in them to withstand all that hammering. Most have either large handles or handles with hoops to prevent their ends from mushrooming, and they generally have cushioning washers.

WEDGE LOCATION

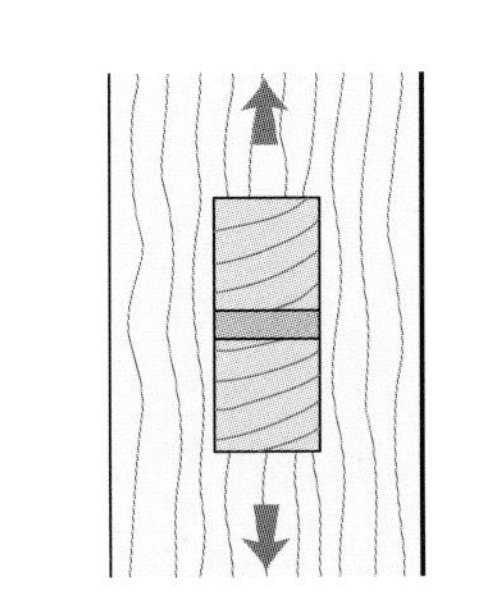

Proper wedge placement puts pressure against end grain.

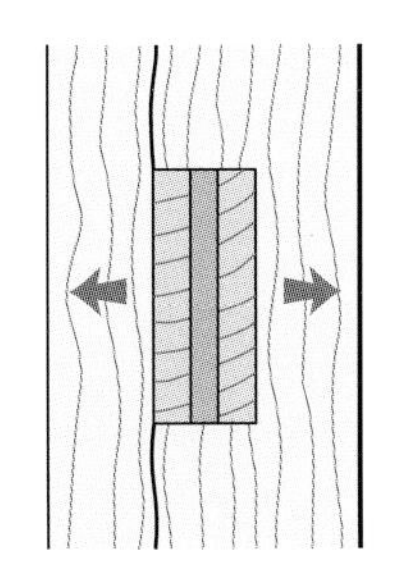

Wedging action against long grain may cause cracking.

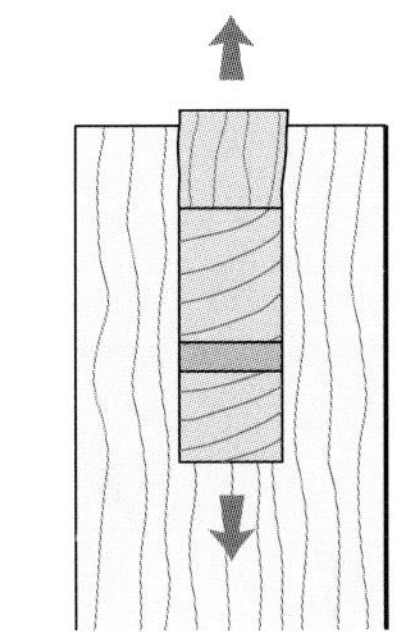

Wedge placed too close to end of board may cause short-grain shearing.

Routers just need to be told where to go for them to mortise accurately. Use spiral-fluted bits for better chip removal or specifically designed mortising bits. Horizontal routing machines do a great job of mortising with their x-y-z movement.

Fitting the Tenon to Mortise

The fit of a tenon to its mortise is more like the fit of a good shoe rather than a sloppy sneaker or a too-tight cowboy boot. The

Use a mortising chisel that's designed for the job.

Use spiral-fluted bits or mortising bits for easier routing.

The Multirouter uses a horizontally mounted router to cut mortises. Clamp the wood to the table, which moves side to side and in and out. The router and bit adjust vertically.

Check for shiny spots on the tenon when fitting it to its mortise. Mark the spots with a pencil and then remove only those areas.

joint slides together with firm pressure and may require a hammer to tap it apart. When trying a joint that just won't fit, check for high spots by holding the tenon up to a light source. The shiny spots indicate where the tenon is rubbing and where you should remove material.

Trim tenons with a wide, sharp chisel or handplane. Handplanes for joinery are specifically designed for trimming tenon shoulders and cheeks. Don't try to trim a tenon with sandpaper or file, as you usually end up rounding the tenon over. Trimming with a table saw is possible if you use paper shims to sneak up on the cut.

When fitting a joint with flush faces, first cut one cheek and check its location to the mortise before going any further. Flip the tenon board around to see that the face of it lines right up with the mortise wall. When the first cheek lines up flush, then move on to cut the second cheek.

Round tenons in green woodworking are always cut in dry wood, but the mating mortise is cut in green or wet wood. The green wood of the mortise then shrinks around

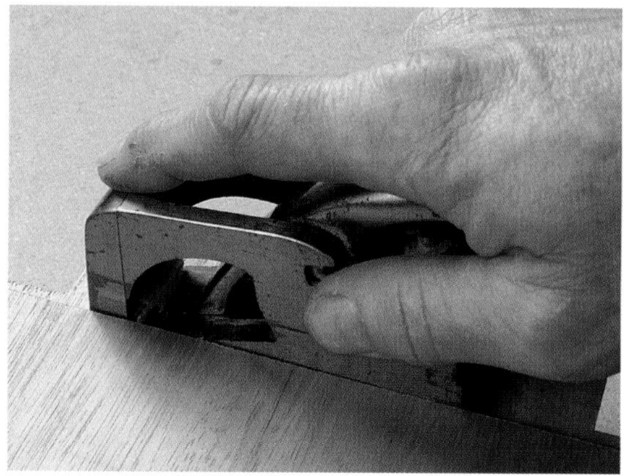
Use a handplane that has an iron as wide as its sole so it can fit right up to a tenon shoulder.

On this tenon-cutting setup, you can use a paper shim to cut just a hair more wood off.

When only one cheek has been cut, you can check the fit of the joint right to the mortise wall to see if more material needs to come off or if too much already has.

the tenon, locking it fast. Fit a too-tight tenon by shrinking it in an oven or pan of heated sand.

There should be room inside the joint for glue both at the cheeks and at the bottom, where excess glue will pool. Always place glue in the mortise to wet its walls, but put more glue at the mouth of the joint where it will be pushed down into the bottom of the mortise. Just a kiss of glue on the tenon's cheeks is enough. Excess glue on the tenon simply gets rubbed off onto the board or will dry hard into a corner.

Put glue in the mortise, wetting the whole joint down; then put a little extra at its mouth. A kiss of glue on the tenon will suffice.

RESCUING UNDERSIZE TENONS

If you cut the tenon too small, take heart. You're not the first to do this. Keep the offcuts around to glue back onto the cheeks of the tenon. The wood and grain direction will match perfectly. Then recut the joint, this time to fit perfectly. Or glue a slice of veneer onto the tenon to fatten it just enough to fit the mortise better. A round tenon can be beefed up by gluing a thick shaving from a plane around it.

Glue on an offcut to a tenon; then recut it to fit.

Hand-Cut Mortise with a Mortising Chisel

To make a hand-cut mortise, first mark out its position on the board by measuring with a ruler or tape measure from the board's end. Square lines across the board to indicate the ends of the mortise (**A**).

Next, set up a mortising gauge or marking gauge to mark out the width of the mortise. Use your mortising chisel as a guide for this. Place the chisel just between the two points on the gauge (**B**). Then set the head of the gauge to place the mortise where you want it in the thickness of the board. Mark out the mortise, holding the gauge tight to the edge of the board throughout. Don't mark past the pencil lines at the bottom of the mortise (**C**).

Make your first chopping cut in the center of the mortise with the chisel set just between the mortise lines. Rely on the width of the chisel to establish the side walls but remember to chop down square to the face of the board (**D**). Continue chopping with cuts at an angle in toward the center of the mortise until you get to the full depth of the mortise. Chop and lever out the waste until you get close to the ends of the mortise. At the ends, chop straight down on the lines. You can undercut the ends of the mortise a bit to help the tenon enter the joint (**E**).

When the mortise is cut, clean the side walls and check all along the width of the mortise, using what I call a drift. This is just a thin piece of wood that you push into the widest part of the mortise (**F**). Where it won't go in is where you need to remove more wood. As you pare, remember to keep the side walls flat and parallel to each other.

Hand-Cut Mortise with a Brace and Bench Chisels

Mark the ends of the mortise with a pencil. Then mark the mortise walls using a mortising gauge set to the width of the chisel (**A**).

Use a brace to drill out most of the waste (**B**). Indicate the depth of cut on the bit with a piece of tape. Be sure to figure in the length of the lead screw of an auger bit, otherwise you might poke through the other side of the board. Hold the brace perpendicular to the board. To see this better, sight from the end of the board.

Drill out the two end holes first. Then finish up the drilling in the middle of the mortise (**C**).

[VARIATION] Instead of a brace, use a power drill. Remember to sight from the end to keep the drill perpendicular to the board.

Clean up the remaining arcs of wood with a sharp, wide chisel. Hold the chisel straight with its back toward the mortise wall. Use the drilled holes as a guide for the cuts and pare straight down (**D**).

Next, chop the ends of the mortise square. Walk a wide chisel over to the end of the mortise, using the existing mortise walls as a guide. Place the chisel between these two marks and chop lightly at first (**E**). Remove the waste and then chop again. Remember to hold the chisel with the bevel side toward the mortise when making these cuts. Clean up each chopping pass with the chisel turned bevel side down to control the cut more easily. As you move down with the chopping, keep cleaning up the side walls.

A

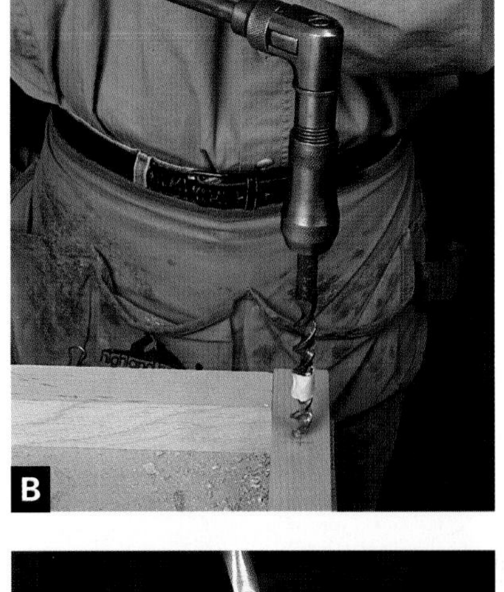
B

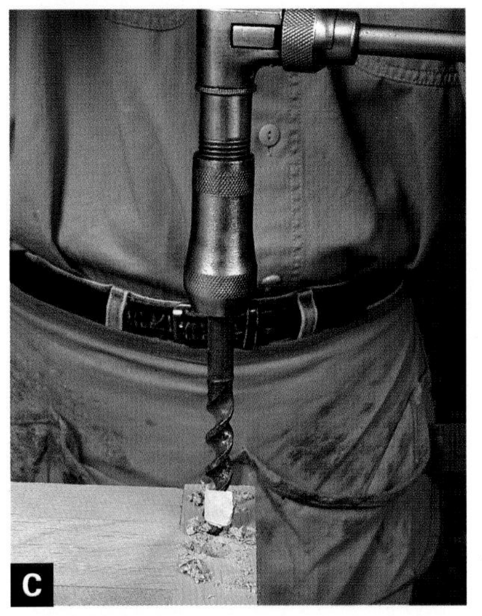
C

D

E

VARIATION

A

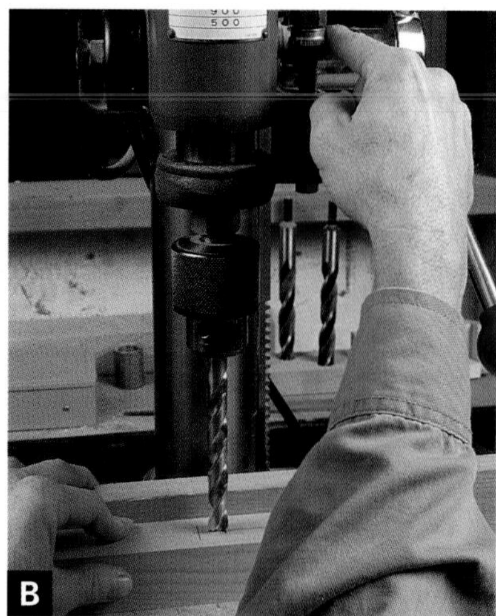
B

C

D

Mortise on the Drill Press

An accurate method of removing the waste in a mortise is to drill it out on the drill press with a fence. Mark the ends and center of the mortise on the board. Set up and clamp the drill press fence using the marked board as a guide. Line up the center of the bit to the center of the mortise (**A**). Set the bit depth by zeroing the bit on the workpiece. The tip of the brad-point bit, which extends beyond its cutting edges, needs to be figured into this measurement (**B**).

First, drill the two outer holes all the way to depth (**C**). Then finish up the middle of the mortise with more boring. Always make sure there's wood for the center of the bit to bite into or the bit will drift off line. If you're careful and slow, you can drill out the very small remaining portion of wood with a good brad-point bit (**D**).

Finish mortising by coming back with the bit and removing all the small arcs left by the first cuts. Make sure the workpiece is held securely when you drill. Clean up the mortise with a sharp, wide chisel.

Mortise on the Drill Press with a Sliding Table

With a sliding table mounted to the drill press, you can cut mortises with metal-working bits called end mills. The sliding table allows for movement back and forth under the bit, which cuts out the mortise (**A**). The best course of action, however, is to drill out the waste first to speed up the mortising and cut down on bit chatter (**B**).

Drill the two outer holes first and then drill the remaining wood in the mortise. The drilling can be done with a bit that's smaller than the final size of the mortise (**C**).

Next, set the sliding table undercarriage in place and put the sliding table on top of it. Clamp the workpiece onto the sliding table fence with the mortise marked out. Chuck up an end mill, line up the bit to the mortise, and clamp or bolt the sliding table undercarriage in place.

Set stops right onto the table to limit its travel and set the length of the mortise (**D**). For multiple cuts, also place a stop on the fence to index the placement of each board. Start to mortise by taking small depths of cut with each pass. Move the sliding table from left to right past the spinning bit when cutting. This will move the workpiece into the rotation of the bit, which will hold the work in tight to the fence and cut down on chatter (**E**).

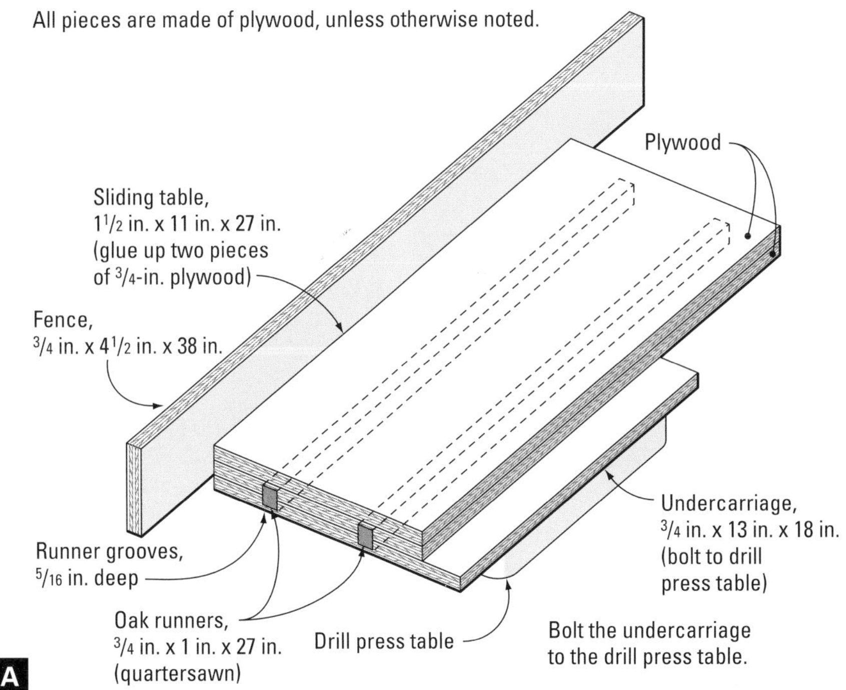

A

B

C

D

E

A

B

C

D

VARIATION

Mortise with a Hollow-Chisel Mortiser

A hollow-chisel mortising machine is designed for one job only: mortising. It uses superior leverage in its control arm to allow you to push through the wood with the chisel while you drill out most of the waste with a drill bit. This bit and chisel arrangement, however, does require perfectly sharpened and tuned bits and chisels for results. After honing the bit and chisel, set the bit through the chisel with a bare 1/32 in. or so between the bottom of the cutting edge of the bit and the chisel points. Otherwise, you will end up burning the steel or not getting through the wood. Also make sure the hollow chisel is properly aligned, parallel to the fence (**A**).

Mark out the mortise on the board and set the fence to place the hollow chisel in the right position over it (**B**). Set the depth of the mortise cut and then clamp the board down in place using spacer blocks if needed under the clamp. First, make the two outer cuts in each mortise and then finish up the middle of the mortise. Be sure to have some wood for the bit and chisel to center on or else the bit will drift off line as you plunge down (**C**). Remember to keep the hollow chisel exit hole pointed to the side to keep the hot chips off your hand or set up a dust collector right near the exit hole (**D**).

[VARIATION] You can place a hollow-chisel mortising attachment on the drill press. You will have to remove the chuck to attach the chisel holder and then reattach it.

Mortise with a Plunge Router and Fence

When mortising narrow stock with a plunge router, clamp several boards together on the bench to provide good support for the router.

First, mark out the mortise (**A**). Use an auxiliary fence mounted to the router fence to give you better support and greater accuracy when cutting (**B**). Zero the bit onto the workpiece (**C**). Then measure up on the depth scale to the depth of the mortise to be cut (**D**). Set and lock down the fence so the mortise is accurately placed in the thickness of the board. Plunge down about ⅛ in. or so with each pass.

To be able to stop the router pass accurately at the ends of the mortise use a simple pencil mark on the wood. Line up the bit at the end of the mortise and then mark the position of the router base on the stock. Come up to this mark each time when you're mortising (**E**).

A more guaranteed method is to clamp a stop to the board that the router base will run into (**F**). Rout between the pencil marks or stops until you're all the way down to full depth (**G**).

A

B

C

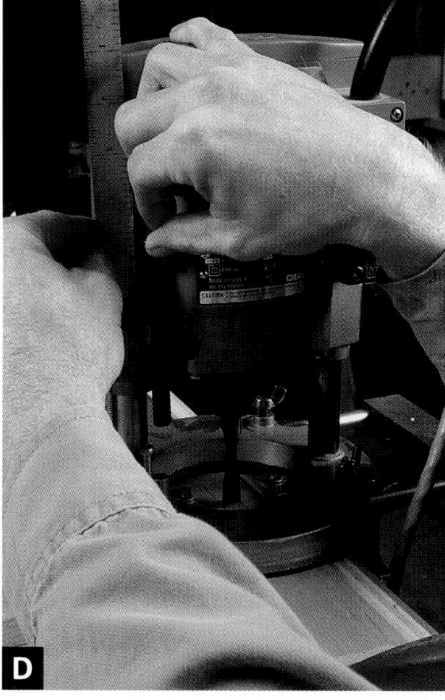
D

E

F

G

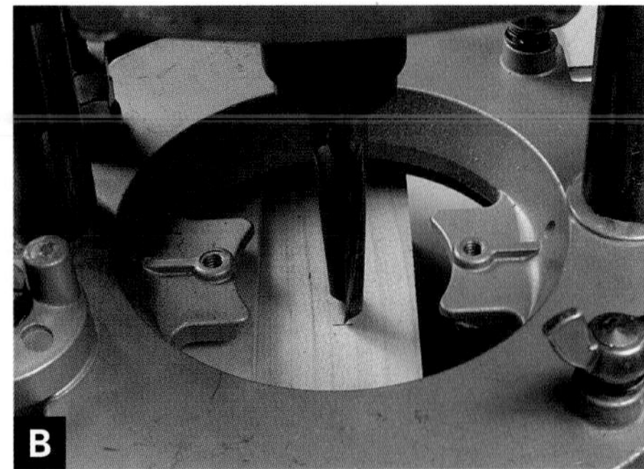

Mortise with a Plunge Router and Universal Jig

Use a universal mortising jig to register the plunge router and fence to make mortising cuts. With a good-size jig, you can cut mortises in material of almost any size or shape. The router fence rides against the outside of the jig while the bit cuts the board, which is clamped to the inside of the jig. Use support blocks under the workpiece, if necessary, to raise it high enough to rout (**A**).

Mount the bit and fence for the plunge router. Set the bit in line with the end of the marked-out mortise. Because my jig has one end stop permanently mounted, I run my fence into this stop and then locate and clamp the mortise under the bit (**B**). The router fence always runs into this stop to establish one end of the mortise.

Next, move the bit to the other end of the mortise and clamp on a stop to the jig to limit the travel of the router. This stop sets the length of the mortise cut (**C**). Zero the bit onto the board; then measure up on the depth scale of the router to set the depth of cut (**D**).

Rout to depth between the stops, being especially careful to keep the router fence tight to the jig (**E**). To index subsequent cuts, clamp on a stop at the end of the board.

Mortise with a Plunge Router and Template

To cut mortises of a consistent size for a project, make up mortising templates to use with the plunge router. With template guides mounted to the router base and a straight bit, you can cut the same mortise slot each time. Location of the mortise in the workpiece depends not only on how you make the mortise slot in the template but also on how you place the template on the board. Mortising templates are also useful for mortising into the ends of long boards, because they provide a wide platform for the router to rest on.

First, nail and glue a ¼-in. piece of Masonite or medium-density fiberboard (MDF) to a 1-in. by 3-in. by 12-in. board. Make sure the edge of the MDF plate is set back from the edge of the board (**A**). Then determine the offset of the mortising bit to the template guide (**B**). Add twice this amount to the length of the mortise to determine the length of the template slot. Mark out the joint dimensions on the inside face of the template (**C**). Use a straight bit as wide as the template guide to cut the template slot. (If you don't have a bit that wide just take several passes to get to full width.)

Set the router table fence so the template slot is centered over the center of the mortise. Remember to figure in the 1-in. fence thickness, which makes placing the fence a little easier. Make some practice cuts at the end of the template to check the setting (**D**).

(Text continues on p. 310.)

A

C

B

D

E

Mark the mortise location on the board. If you want, you can add a stop to the fence to index the cuts, but this will make the template useful for only half the mortises in a frame, and you'll have to make another template for the remaining mortises. With no stop on the template, just figure in the offset amount of the template and place another mark next to the mortise. Clamp on the template, lining up on the offset mark (**E**).

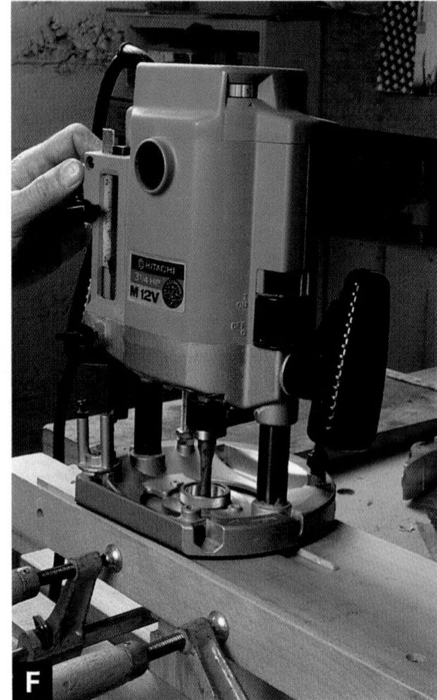

F

G

Set the bit depth by zeroing the bit on the wood with the router in place on the template. Then move the depth stop rod up the proper amount (**F**). Plunge down in the template slot to rout the mortise, making sure the template slots don't fill up with debris during the cut (**G**). Have a vacuum nearby to clear the debris or hook a vacuum hose to the router.

Mortise on the Router Table

Use the router table for shallow mortising. Locate the mortise by measuring the distance from the edge of the bit to the router table fence. Rotate the bit's cutting edge so it's at a point closest to the fence (**A**). Set the bit height for a first pass at ⅛ in. (**B**). This shallow cut lightens the load on the router. Clamp on stops to the fence to limit the travel of the workpiece (**C**). This will set the length of the mortise.

Rout by setting one end of the board against the far stop and slowly dropping down onto the bit. Hold the workpiece tight to the fence as you move down into the bit. As you drop down, move the board back and forth a little until you are finally down to depth. This will minimize any burning caused by a router bit without a center cutting edge (**D**). After the first pass, reset the bit for another ⅛-in.-deep cut (**E**).

VARIATION For most fixed-base table-mounted routers, the depth of cut cannot be adjusted consistently. So you'll often see steps in the cuts, because the bit doesn't stay centered in the base. To increase your accuracy and to speed up the mortising, set the bit at its full depth of cut and use table shims to create each new depth setting. Pull one shim out after each pass. These shims can be made of any flat sheet-good material with a bit slot cut into it.

A

B

C

D

E

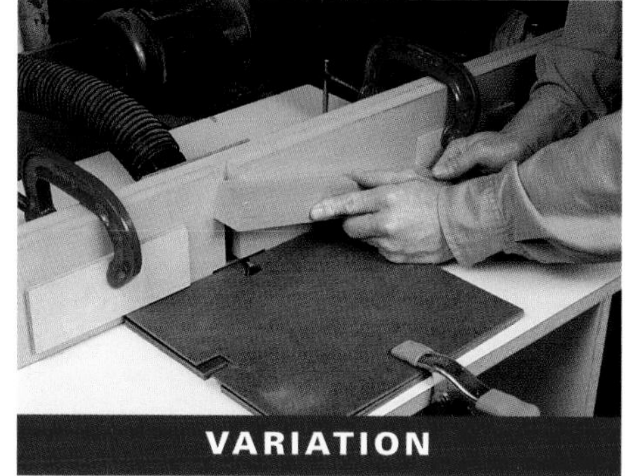
VARIATION

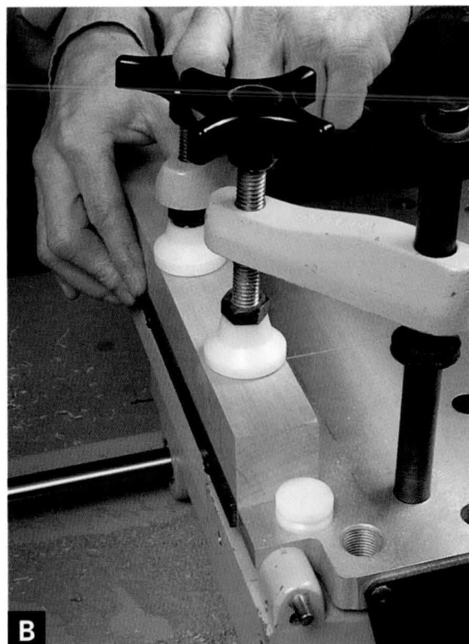

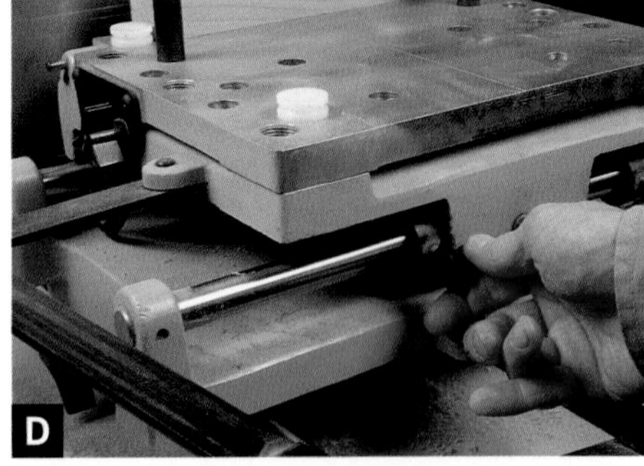

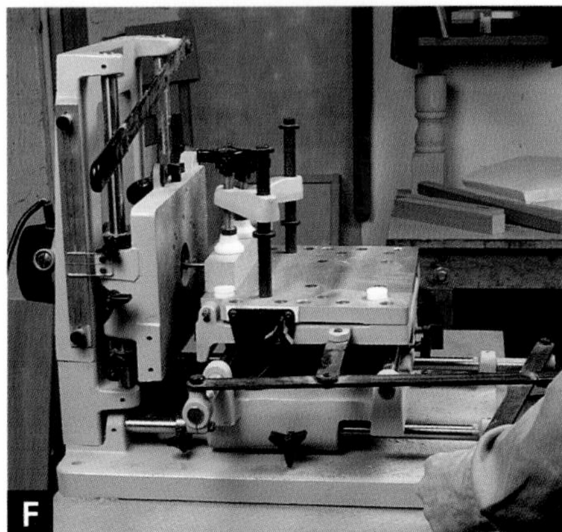

Mortise on the Multirouter

The Multirouter is a horizontally mounted router system. It's one of many designs on the market that use a standard router with a movable table. The Multirouter has movement in three axes: up and down, in and out, and side to side. With a router base mounted to the vertical plate, put the router in place with a mortising bit mounted into it (**A**). The work table has a small fence on it to locate the workpiece. Set the board against it and against one of the nylon table pins that mount into the work table. Clamp the board in place using the table-mounted hand clamps or the optional air-actuated clamps (**B**). Set the bit height off the marked-out mortise.

Adjust the vertical plate with the router and lock it in place (**C**). Set the table travel out at the front of the horizontal table. This will set the mortise length. Place the bit close to the end of a marked mortise and set one of the two table stops. Move the table so the bit is now at the other end of the mortise and set the other stop (**D**). To set the depth of the mortise, zero the bit against the workpiece and measure the depth of cut with a ruler against the bottom stop (**E**). After all these stops are locked down, you can start routing. The setup will take many times longer than it takes to make the average mortise cut. Use the two handles on the table to move the workpiece back and forth and slowly in toward the bit (**F**).

Mortise on the Slot Mortiser

The industry standard for continuous mortising work is the heavy-duty slot mortiser. First, mark the mortise on the workpiece and then clamp the board against the table's short fence. Next, set the bit height with the bit placed up against the workpiece. Adjust the table height until the bit is lined up with the mortise marks (**A**).

Use the stop rods mounted under the table to set the side-to-side travel for the length of the mortise. Use the marked-out mortise as a guide for setting these stops (**B**). The depth of the mortise is set with the stop rods on the side of the cutterhead. Zero the bit on the workpiece and then set the depth (**C**).

To cut the mortise, move the cutterhead into the board for a light depth of cut; then move the table side to side to make the mortise cut. Continue plunging and routing until you're at full depth (**D**).

A

B

C

D

A

B

C

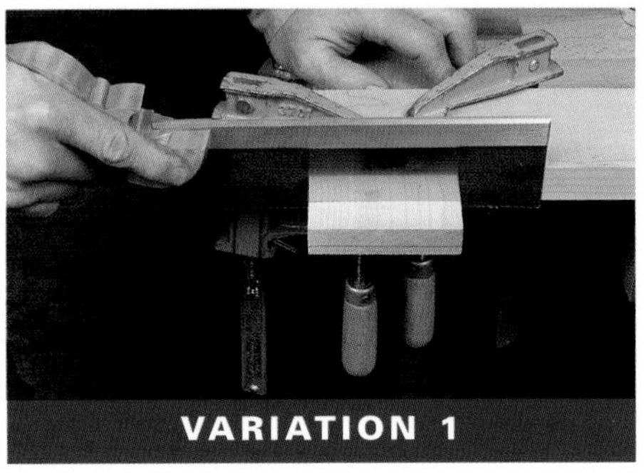
VARIATION 1

Hand-Cut Tenon

Hand-cut tenons demand careful marking out, sharp tools, and patience in the fitting. Always cut tenons after making the mortises. It's much easier to trim a tenon to fit an existing mortise than vice versa.

Mark the length of the tenon or shoulder position with a marking gauge. A wheel-type cutter works best for marking out cross-grain (**A**). Mark out both faces of the board. Lay out the thickness of the tenon or the cheek cuts with a pencil and rule or use the marking gauge again (**B**). Mark both edges as well as the end of the board.

Cut the shoulders first, holding the workpiece tight to a bench hook or with the board clamped to the bench (**C**).

[VARIATION 1] Run the saw against a fence clamped onto the board. If you're careful aligning the fence on both faces and hold the saw tight to the fence, you'll get nice consistent shoulder cuts. Use a combination square as a depth gauge to set the fence.

After making the shoulder cuts, saw the tenon cheeks with a tenon saw or backsaw. On wider boards, cut the cheeks in a series of cuts so you're not faced with one wide cut that might go awry. Start the cheek cut with the board angled in the vise so you can see the lines on both the end and the near edge of the board (**D**). Saw down close to the shoulder cut. Flip the board around in the vise and make a second cheek cut down to the shoulder cut (**E**). Then finish the sawing by placing the board upright in the vise and cutting straight down to the shoulder (**F**).

[VARIATION 2] For narrower boards, saw straight across to make the cheek cuts.

After making the first cheek cut, I find it better to clean it up with a shoulder or bullnose plane before moving on to the next cut. If you've taken off too much wood, you can then adjust the second cut.

After both cheek cuts are made, check the fit of the tenon. Try to leave the tenon a bit fat so you can clean the cheeks with a handplane or chisels for a final, perfect fit (**G**).

D

E

F

G

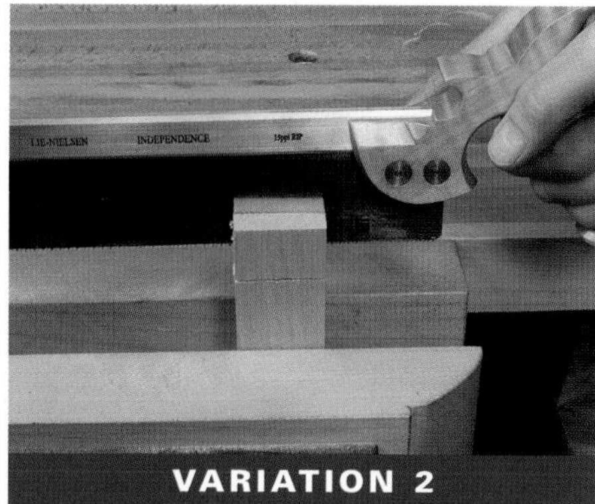
VARIATION 2

A

B

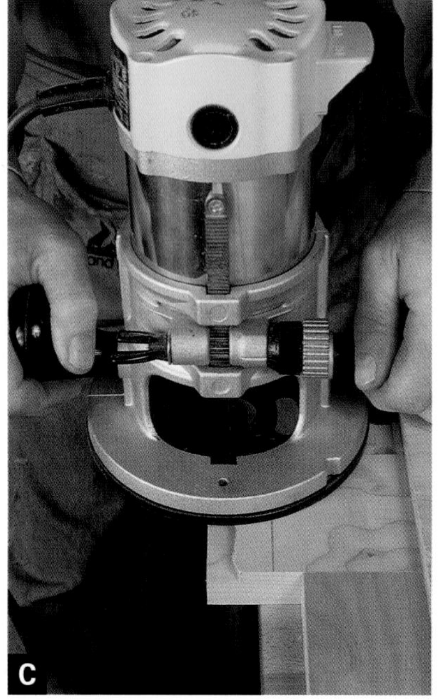

C

Tenon with a Router and Right-Angle Jig

Cut tenons topside with a router running against a clamped-on fence or right-angle jig. First measure the distance from the cutting edge of the bit to the edge of the router base. This is the crucial distance for setting the fence (**A**). Clamp the workpiece down to the bench. Place another board close by it to support the router base and right-angle jig. Use a square as a depth guide to place the jig; clamp it in place (**B**). Set the router bit to cut the tenon in a series of passes, or set it for full depth if you need just a shallow cut.

Start routing first at the end of the board moving left to right across it, gradually working in toward the shoulder. If you cut too slowly, the end grain will burn; so keep the feed rate moderately fast.

For the shoulder cut, hold the router base with one consistent spot on it riding against the jig. Move almost all the way through the shoulder cut. Stop just short of the end; then pull the router away from the jig and off the board. Next, rout back into the shoulder cut for the last 2 in. to prevent tearout at the edge of the board (**C**).

Tenon with a Plunge Router and Fence

Tenons can be cut with a plunge router. Mount an auxiliary fence to the plunge router fence. Mark out the mortise on the workpiece and then clamp the board to the bench with an additional board at the far end of the cut for support. Lock the fence down when the bit lines up on the marked-out tenon. Make sure the cutting edge of the bit is rotated properly (**A**).

Make the pass starting out at the end of the tenon, moving left to right across the board. Keep the router well supported at the ends of the cut (**B**). Finish up the tenon cut at the shoulder, moving quickly across the end grain to prevent burning. Hold the fence in tight to the end of the tenon board and cut almost to the end of the shoulder (**C**).

Move the router off the board and rout back into the shoulder to finish up the cut; this prevents tearout. Keep holding the fence in tight to the board's end (**D**).

A

B

C

D

A

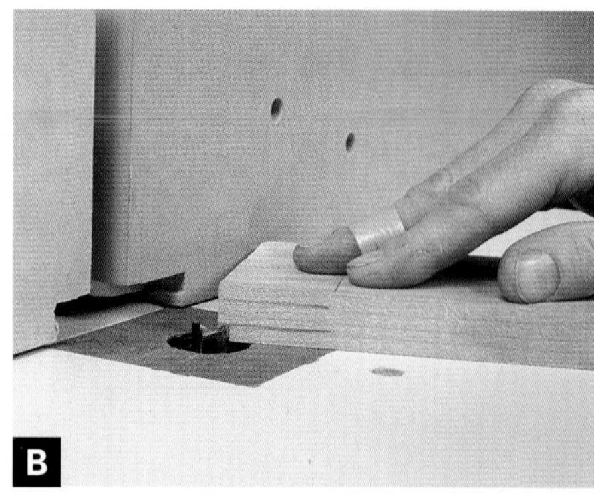
B

C

D

E

Horizontal Tenon on the Router Table

The first step to cutting a horizontal tenon on the router table is to mount a wide bit in the router. Rotate the bit so the cutting edge is at a point farthest from the fence. Measure this distance or set the marked-out tenon up to the bit to locate it and clamp down the fence (**A**). Set the bit height to the full depth of cut, using the marked-out tenon as a guide (**B**).

First, trim the tenons on the bandsaw to eliminate wear and tear on the router bit (**C**). Save the offcuts, just in case you cut a tenon too small. Simply glue the offcut back onto the tenon and recut it.

Use a backer board to support the workpiece when cutting on the router table. Otherwise, this narrow board will rock against the fence. Start cutting at the end of the tenon, moving from right to left across the bit. Gradually work your way in toward the shoulder (**D**). Make the final pass to establish the shoulder by running the board and backer right up against the fence (**E**).

Vertical Tenon on the Router Table

Cut tenons vertically on the router table if the stock is wide enough to move smoothly across the router table and table insert. Narrow boards have a tendency to dip into the bit. Use a push block to help move the workpiece smoothly. Feed the work from right to left across the bit, moving into its rotation.

First, trim the outer face of the board to prevent tearout (**A**). Next, reset the fence to cut a centered tenon and make the full tenon cuts (**B**).

> **WARNING Keep the bit captured in the fence to avoid trapping the workpiece between the bit and fence. Otherwise, when making a trim cut like this, and feeding the piece right to left, the workpiece can be jerked through the cut or pulled from your hands.**

A

B

A

B

C

D

E

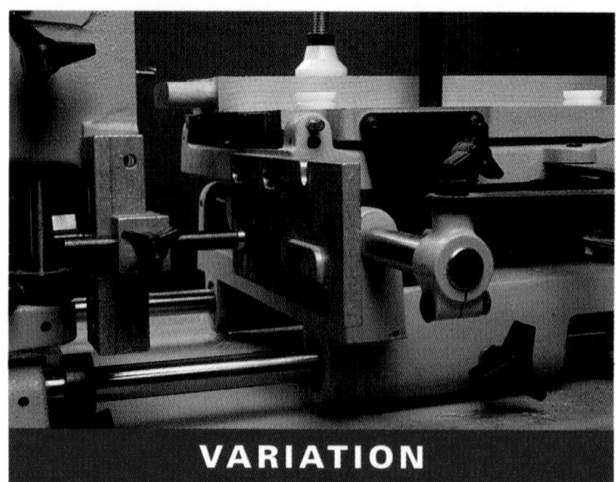
VARIATION

Tenon on the Multirouter

Tenon cuts on horizontally mounted routers like the Multirouter can be indexed to cut in several different ways. I made up a right-angle fence that mounts into the table with the nylon table pins (**A**). I also made up a stop block that fits over the end of the fence. Run the tenon board into such a stop block to index each cut (**B**).

Mount a mortising bit or spiral-fluted router bit in the router. Set the bit depth off a marked-out tenon shoulder and lock down the stop (**C**). Set the bit height off the marked-out cheeks of the tenon. You'll need two stops: one for the top cheek and one for the bottom (**D**).

Cut the tenon a little at a time (**E**).

[VARIATION] The Multirouter can also use tenoning templates that mount to the work table. A stylus follower with a ball bearing rides around the template, allowing you to cut a specific size tenon. Oversize and undersize templates are available to accommodate slight diameter differences among bits.

Tenon on the Sliding Compound Miter Saw

Tenons can be roughed out on a sliding compound miter saw. Set the depth of cut on the saw, holding the board up close to the blade. Mark the mortise clearly. You may need to use an extra-wide fence to get the full travel of the saw at its specified depth of cut. Check this out first before proceeding too far (**A**).

Clamp a stop to the saw fence to index the shoulder cuts. Put the stop at the end of the board closest to the cut (**B**). That way, if any debris gets between the board and the stop, it will push you away from the stop. If you put the stop at the far end of the board, debris could push a cut past the shoulder mark.

Cut the cheeks in a series of passes. After cutting the first cheek, flip the board to cut the other one (**C**).

A

B

C

A

B

C

Tenon on the Bandsaw

Before cutting the tenon on the bandsaw, mark it out on the board. Set the bandsaw fence to cut the tenon shoulders first. Be sure to line up the pencil-marked shoulder with a sawtooth that's pointing away from the fence (**A**).

Saw the shoulders up to the cheek marks, using a backer board for support against the fence (**B**). Narrow boards like the one shown here have a tendency to rock their ends against a fence unless they have support. Or you can feed the work with a miter gauge, if you have one for the saw.

Next, saw the tenon cheeks, slowing the feed rate down as you come up to the shoulder cut. It is common to pop through this last bit of wood and into the shoulder if you're not prepared for it. You could, of course, clamp on a stop to the fence to prevent this. If the tenon is centered, make one cheek cut and flip the board for the second cut. Save the offcuts for your friends who cut their tenons too small: The offcuts can be glued back on and the tenons recut (**C**).

Tenon Crosscut on the Table Saw

Cut tenons flat on the table saw using a crosscut jig. Set the blade height off a marked-out tenon (**A**). Next, clamp a stop onto the jig fence to index the shoulder cuts. I always mark the tenon length on the edge of the board closest to the sawblade so I can line this up easier (**B**).

Make a series of passes with the sawblade until you've cut the entire cheek. Flip the board to cut the remaining cheek (**C**).

These cheek cuts usually end up with numerous ridges, owing to the alternate-top bevel grind of combination sawblades. To clean up these ridges, first wet your fingertips so you can grip the board well. Then move the board right over top dead center on the blade and slide it back and forth over the blade. You will move the board right into the stop, so there's no fear of moving past the shoulder. After one pass, move the jig just a bit farther over the blade and take another pass. Take your time with this, and you'll eventually clean up the entire tenon (**D**).

VARIATION **The dado blade, of course, can quickly remove a great deal of wood. Make sure the dado is cutting a nice flat-bottomed cut. Use the miter gauge. And for this type of cut, you can use the saw fence as a stop for the shoulder cut.**

A

B

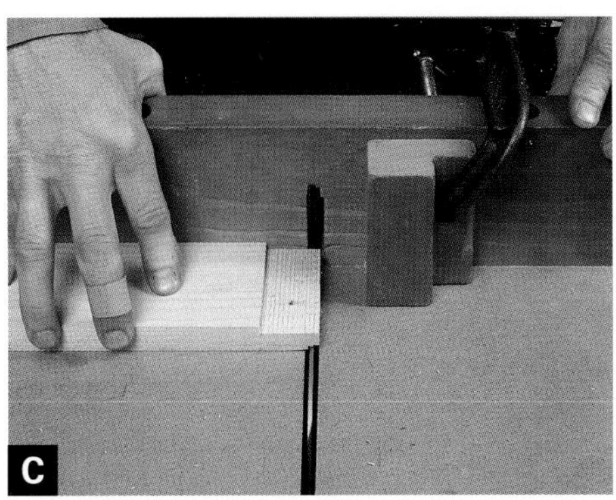
C

D

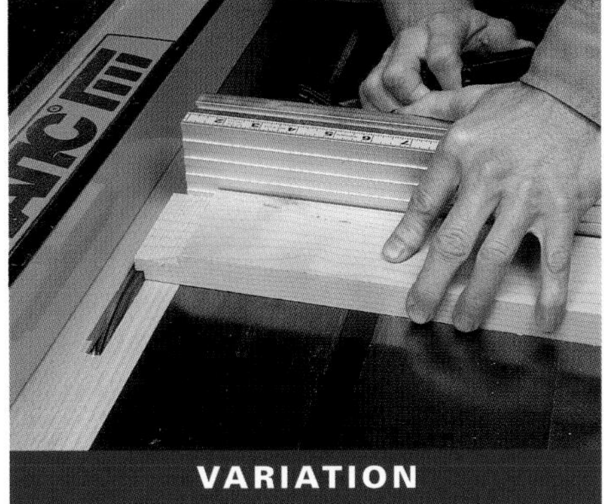
VARIATION

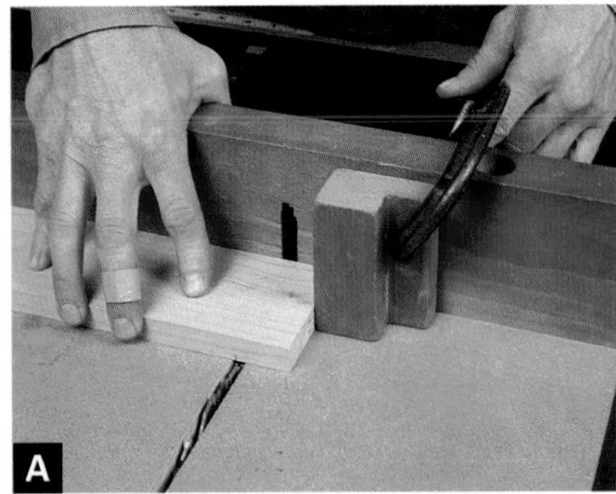

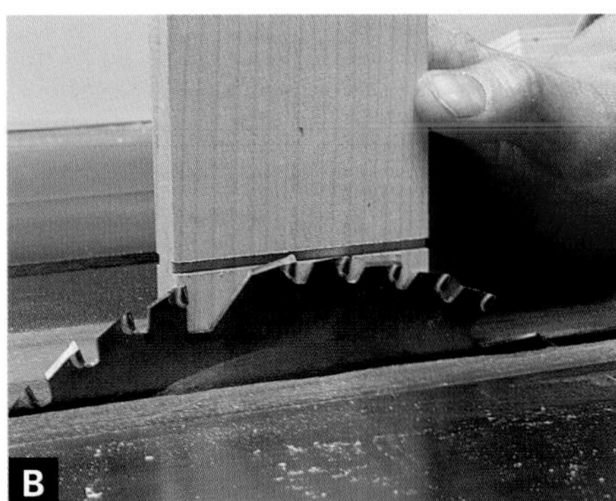

Tenon on the Table Saw with a Shopmade Jig

Before using a shopmade tenoning jig on the table saw, crosscut the tenon shoulders using the crosscut jig with a stop mounted on it. Keep the cut just under the full depth of the cheeks (**A**).

[**TIP**] **Remove most of the cheek waste on the bandsaw. This will prevent any off-cuts from flying around the table saw and will make the tenon cut easier and more accurate.**

Set the blade height for just under the full depth of the shoulders (**B**). You'll use a shopmade tenoning jig to support the tenon board. Place the board and jig next to the blade to set the fence distance (**C**). Clamp the tenon board to the jig and get a firm grip on the jig. Keep it close to the saw fence and perfectly upright when making a pass.

If the tenon is centered, flip the board around to cut the other cheek; then check the fit (**D**). If the tenon is just a hair too large and you don't want to change the fence setting, use a shim for a trimming pass. Place a paper shim between the board and the jig to kick it out toward the blade just a bit (**E**).

Tenon on the Table Saw with a Commercial Jig

To use a commercial tenoning jig, first set the blade height to cut just under the full depth of the shoulder (**A**). Set up the jig with the board clamped in place. Make certain the jig is aligned square and runs accurately in the gauge slot. Fine-tune the position of the jig with the adjusting handle (**B**). Pass the work slowly past the blade using consistent pressure on the jig (**C**).

VARIATION You can use a dado blade to cut the tenon cheeks and shoulders. This can be a heavy cut, so make sure the blade is sharp and that the work is clamped in tightly. Also check to see that the dado blade makes a nice flat shoulder cut with no sawtooth marks to mar the shoulder.

A

B

C

VARIATION

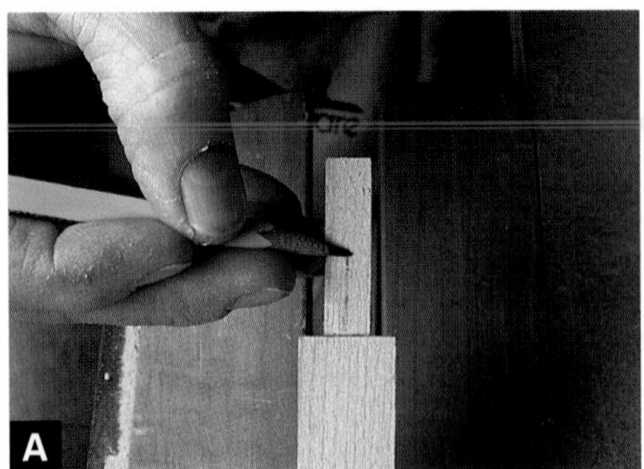
A

B

C

D

Edge Rounding a Tenon by Hand

With every mortise and tenon, you face a choice: Do you square the mortise or round the tenon to fit? Rounding a tenon by hand is best done with the workpiece in the vise.

Use a pencil to mark a centerline down the edge of the tenon (**A**). Use a bastard file to begin rounding the corner. With one of your first strokes, put in a good file cut near to the shoulder (**B**). This will prevent an errant swipe of the file along the edge from running right into the shoulder, Round both corners and then trim to the shoulders with a chisel (**C**).

Make a template from the cutoff of a mortised board to check your work (**D**). After a few dozen roundovers like this, you'll be able to dispense with the template.

Edge Rounding a Tenon on the Router Table

To edge round a tenon on the router table, use a roundover bit that's half the size of the tenon thickness. For example, if the tenon is ½ in. thick, use a ¼-in. roundover bit. Set the bit height to the height of the tenon (**A**).

You can freehand this cut, but you have to be very careful not to run the bit into the tenon shoulder. Watch the bit's rim to get a sense of where to start and stop the cut. A safer method is to set up a fence to capture the bit. Put a straightedge along the fence; when it touches the bit's bearing, lock down the fence (**B**).

Set stops to limit the travel of the workpiece into the bit. Clamp one stop against the fence for two of the edges and make those cuts into the stop (**C**). Reset the stop for the other two edges. These cuts begin just after the shoulder with the workpiece butted up to the stop and then pulled through the bit (**D**).

You'll have a little bit of trimming to do after the routing is done. Use a chisel to round the rest of the edges up to the shoulders of the tenon (**E**).

A

B

C

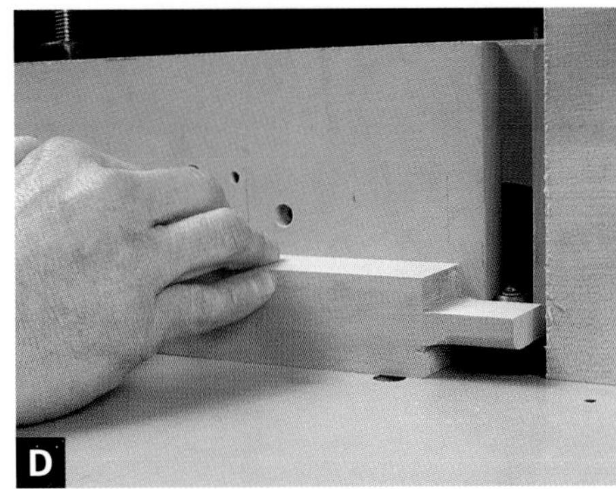
D

E

A

B

VARIATION

Round Mortise with a Brace

The traditional method of cutting round mortises is with a brace. The spoon bit is a chairmaker's bit that allows you to change angles easily as you bore. Make some practice cuts with this bit to get the hang of starting it. It tends to walk a little when you begin to bore because it doesn't have a centering point (**A**).

For the best results, orient the grain direction of the mortise to match that of the tenon. This way each will have its greatest shrinkage—tangential to the growth rings—in the same direction. Drill into a flatsawn face to place the mortise and arrange the grain of your tenon to match. Get started drilling and adjust the bit to cut on the center of the mortise (**B**).

[VARIATION] An auger bit has a lead screw that makes it easier to locate and center for boring. Be careful of splitting out the wood with this bit. When making a stopped mortise, be sure to figure in the length of the screw so it doesn't come through the other face.

Round Mortise with a Drill

Use a power drill with a brad-point bit or twist drill bit for mortising. The brad point locates the drilling center easily. Mark the depth of cut on the drill bit with a piece of masking tape (**A**).

Let the outer edge of the bit score the hole before applying too much downward pressure. This will help prevent tearout around the hole (**B**). Drill to depth, sighting on the bit from the side so you can adjust the drilling angle against a sliding bevel angle (**C**).

A

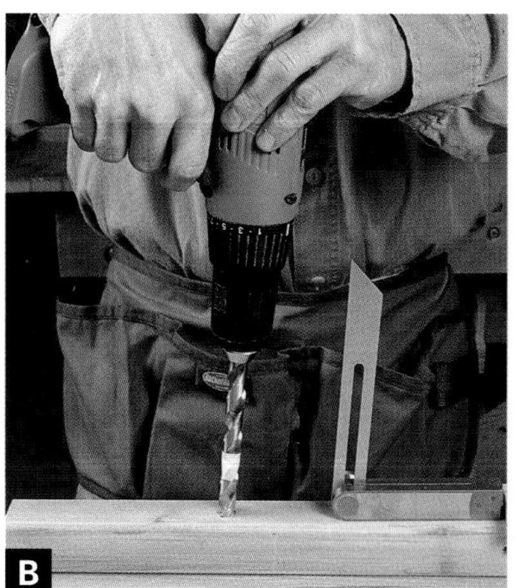
B

C

A

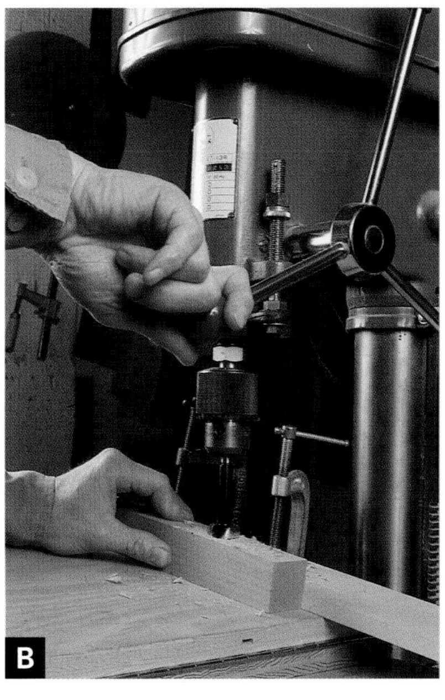
B

Round Mortise on the Drill Press

Mortises drilled straight into a board can be bored with any good drill bit. For angled holes, use a Forstner or brad-point bit. The almost continuous rim of the Forstner bit locates well for this kind of boring. Instead of adjusting a drill press table for a simple drilling angle, use an angle jig. Set a sliding bevel to the proper angle and adjust the jig until the shank of a long-twist drill bit lines up with the bevel. Replace the twist bit with the Forstner bit and lock the jig in place. Clamp a fence to the angle jig to locate the holes (**A**). Find the mortise center and drill to depth (**B**).

A

B

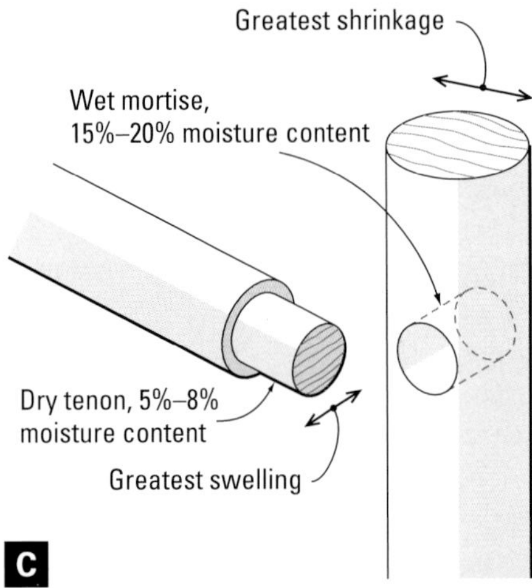

C

Hand-Cut Round Tenon

When cutting a tenon to fit a drilled-out mortise, drill a scrap board using the bit you used for the mortise. Use the board and pencil to mark the diameter of the tenon on the workpiece.

Start shaping the tenon with a spokeshave (**A**). Keep working the tenon down to the pencil mark. Check the fit of the tenon by driving it into a piece of hard scrap with pencil lead on its lip. Remove the wood that has lead smudges on it (**B**).

Green woodworking uses wet and dry wood together to yield joints that shrink to achieve their strength. A dry tenon is fitted to a wet mortise, and their grain directions are oriented so their greatest shrinkage occurs in the same direction (**C**). As the mortise dries out, it shrinks around the tenon, locking it in place. Dry tenons in a makeshift kiln or use heated sand to achieve localized drying (**D**). Localized drying is an especially important technique for making Windsor chairs, for which the rungs have dry tenons at their ends and wet mortises in their middle.

VARIATION Once the round tenon is close to fitting, you can size it by driving it through a dowel pop. Don't force the tenon through the steel plate if it's well oversize; the wood will break or deform.

D

VARIATION

Round Tenon with a Drill and Tenon Cutter

Cut round tenons with a tenon cutter and a power drill for rustic-style woodworking. The example for this technique uses simple branches. For an easy start, use a spokeshave to trim the end of the tenon and then mark out the tenon's length (**A**).

Get the tenon cutter started on the branch. Hold the drill so you drill straight into the branch (**B**). Drill to depth. Clean up any ragged edges on the tenon shoulder with a knife (**C**).

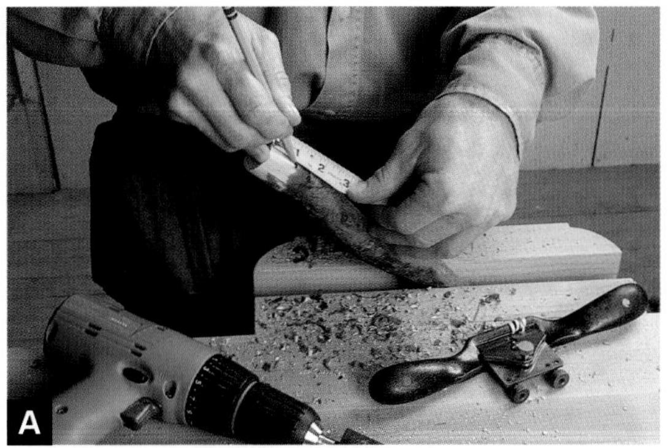

A

B

C

A

B

C

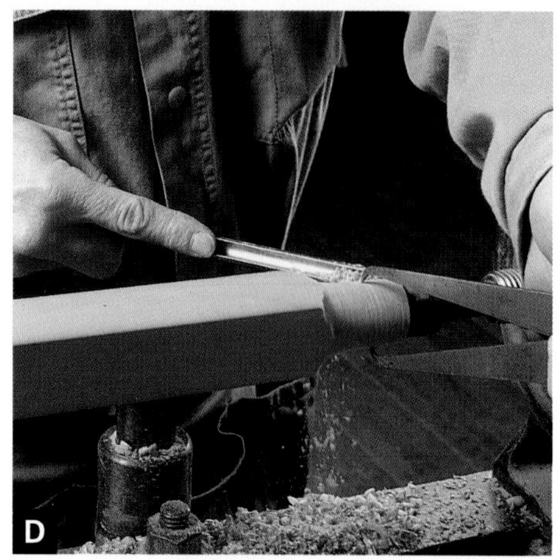
D

E

VARIATION

Round Tenon on the Lathe

Use the lathe to turn round tenons on the end of round or square stock. First find the center of the tenon stock by marking the diagonals across its end. Use the 45-degree angle on a combination square to help locate the center (**A**).

Saw across the marks with a backsaw (**B**). Then hammer in the lathe center. Mount the piece securely in the lathe and make sure it spins freely before turning on the machine.

Begin turning at a slow speed as you start to round the stock with a gouge (**C**). Set some calipers to a little greater than the final thickness of the tenon. Turn the tenon with the gouge until the calipers just slide right over the tenon (**D**).

Clean up the tenon with a skew to size. Reset calipers to the exact size you need and check the tenon often (**E**).

[VARIATION] You can also use a tenon sizing tool when turning tenons. Lock a beading or parting tool in place in the sizing tool at the required diameter. Rough out the round tenon. Then start to cut with the sizing tool. Make sure you apply pressure when holding its end up against the turning tenon; when you get to size, it will slide right over the tenon.

Round Tenon on the Multirouter

You can cut round tenons on the Multirouter by placing the round-tenon template in the template holder. Check the router bit size against the template to make sure you're using the correct bit for the template (**A**). Set the depth of cut by moving the marked-out tenon right under the router bit. Move the stylus pin into the template and lock it down in place (**B**).

Since you're using the full length of the bit to cut the full tenon depth, take your time with this cut (**C**). If desired, rough out the tenon on the bandsaw.

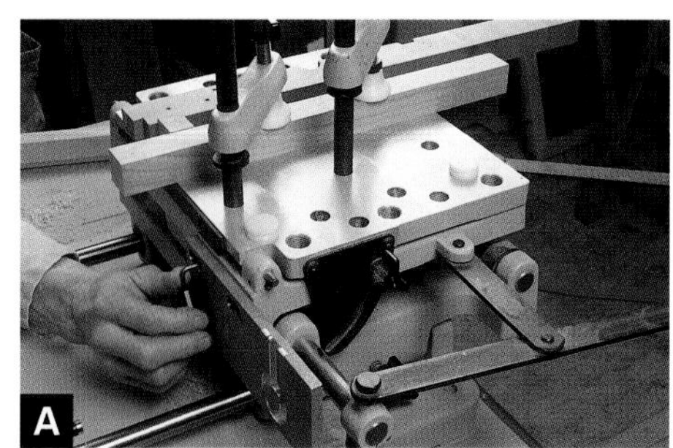
A

C

B

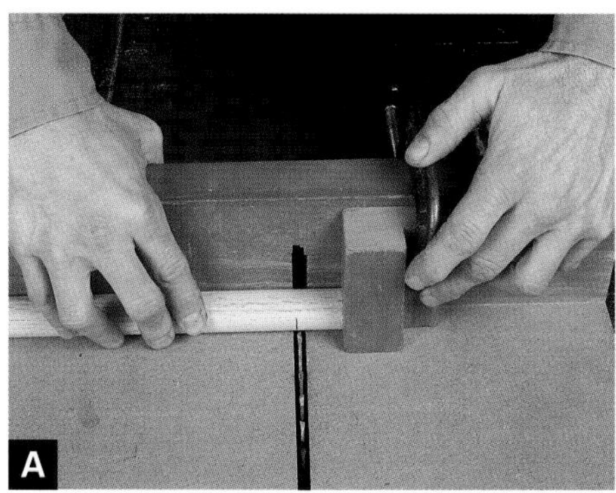
A

B

C

D

Round Tenon on the Table Saw

Round tenons can be cut on the table saw only when you have round stock. Set up a stop on the crosscut jig to limit the length of the tenon (**A**). Set the blade to cut only a small amount of wood (**B**).

Move the dowel rod into the blade and spin it in place over the blade for roughing out. Back the jig up, move the dowel sideways along the fence, and then move back into the blade for another cut (**C**). Reset the blade height for another pass until you're close to the proper diameter. For a final trim pass, bring the dowel directly over the blade at top dead center and move it sideways across the blade into the stop. Rotate it until the tenon is formed (**D**).

Loose Tenon with a Plunge Router and Template

A

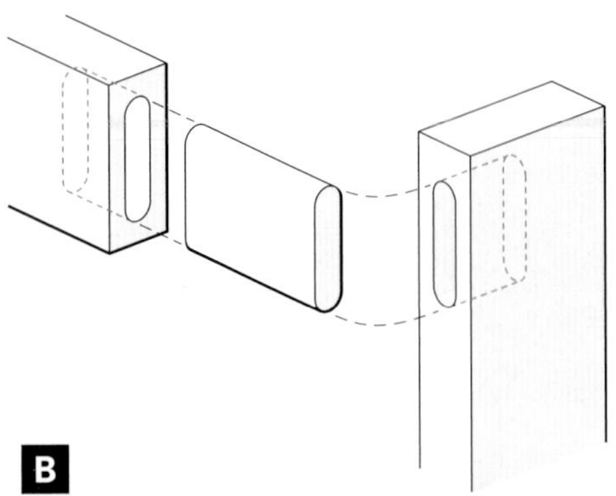
B

Loose-tenon joints are particularly useful for long boards that are too cumbersome to cut tenons on. Use a mortising template to provide a good platform for the plunge router. Measure the offset of the bit to the template guide. Make up the mortising template, figuring in the proper offsets (**A, B**).

C

E

Clamp a long board into the vise at an angle (**C**). Mark out the mortise location on the end of the board, remembering to figure in the offset amount (**D**). Oftentimes, you'll need to place loose tenons in two members of different thickness. Make up the template for the larger member and use a shim to locate the template correctly on the narrower piece (**E**). Place the router on the template and plunge to depth (**F**).

➤ See *"Mortise with a Plunge Router and Template"* on p. 309.

D

F

Making a Loose Tenon

When making up loose tenon stock, keep it in long enough lengths to handle safely. Plane one face and joint an edge of your stock. Then cut the stock to width so it just fits in a mortise (**A**).

Rough out the stock on the bandsaw close to thickness. Replane the face flat if it bows or cups (**B**). Mill to thickness on the planer. For thin stock, use a table insert to prevent the piece from bowing under the pressure of the feed rollers (**C**).

VARIATION You can also cut the loose tenon stock to thickness on the table saw. Be sure to use a push stick.

Cut glue slots in the loose tenon stock on the table saw. These shallow slots will allow glue and air to escape as you drive the tenon home (**D**). Next, round the edges of the loose tenons on the router table. Use a bit half the thickness of the tenon stock. For ½-in. loose tenons, use a ¼-in. roundover bit (**E**).

Rather than gluing the tenon into both mortises at once, I keep it simpler by gluing the loose tenon into one mortise at a time. Check the length of the protruding tenon after you bang it home in its mortise to make sure it seats properly (**F**).

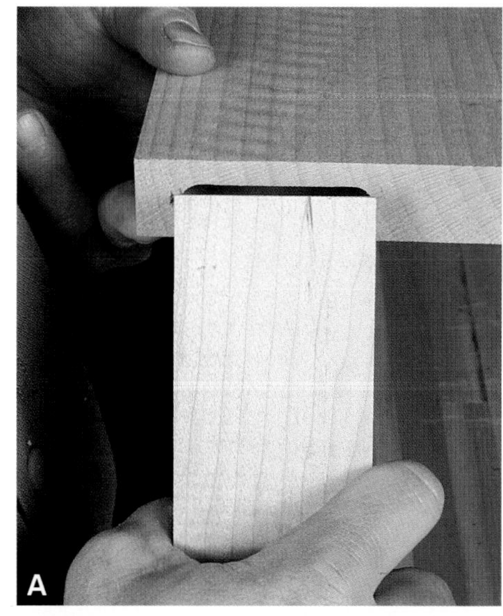

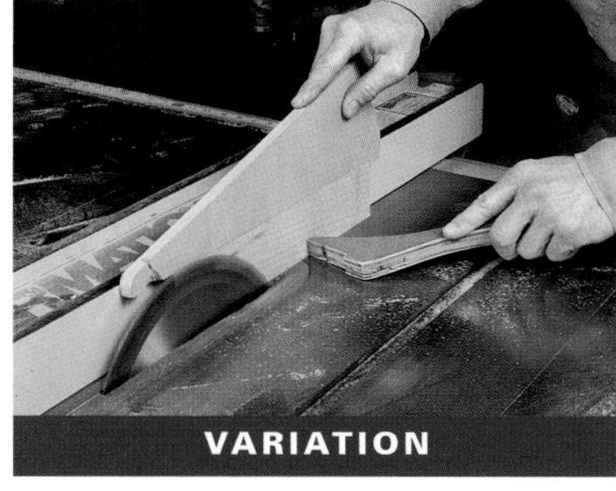
VARIATION

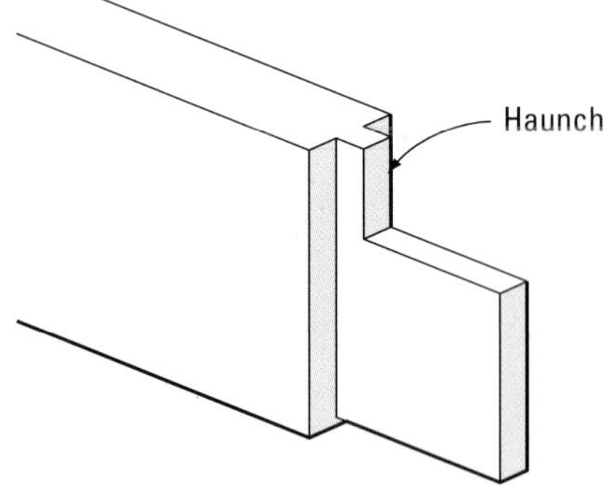

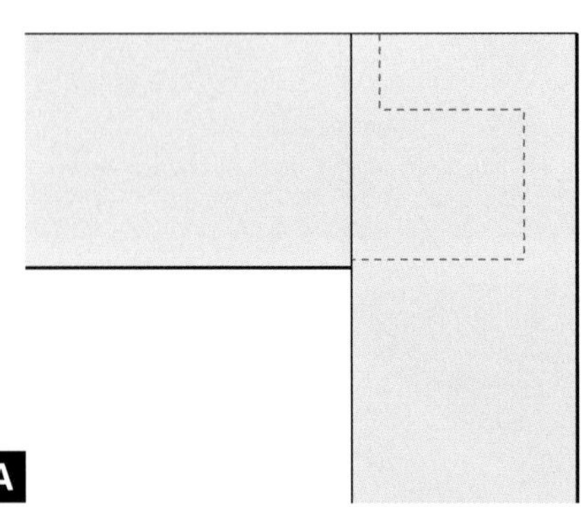
A

B

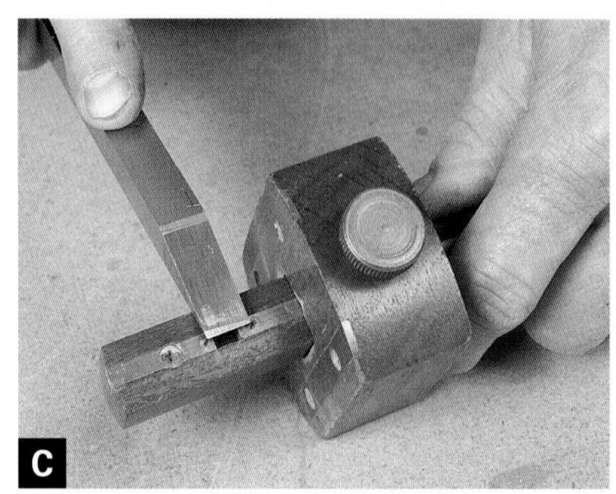
C

D

VARIATION 1

E

Hand-Cut Haunched Mortise and Tenon

You can make haunched mortise-and-tenon joints with hand tools (**A**). Mark out the mortise and haunch position.

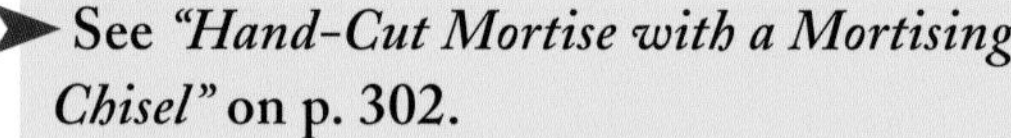
➤ See *"Hand-Cut Mortise with a Mortising Chisel"* on p. 302.

Square lines across the board to mark the ends of the mortise and haunch (**B**). The haunch width should be about one-third the width of the tenon. Set up a mortising gauge or marking gauge to mark the width of the mortise. Use your mortising chisel as a guide by placing it between the two points on the mortising gauge. Then set the head of the gauge to locate the mortise in the thickness of the board (**C**). Mark out the mortise by holding the marking gauge tightly to the edge of the board (**D**).

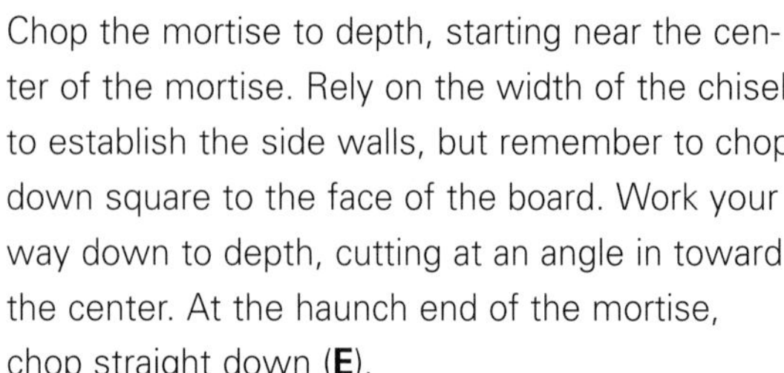
Chop the mortise to depth, starting near the center of the mortise. Rely on the width of the chisel to establish the side walls, but remember to chop down square to the face of the board. Work your way down to depth, cutting at an angle in toward the center. At the haunch end of the mortise, chop straight down (**E**).

When the mortise is cut, clean up the side walls. Check the width of the mortise with a drift—it's a thin piece of wood that you push into the widest part of the mortise. Where it won't fit is where you need to remove more wood. As you pare, keep the mortise walls flat and parallel to one another.

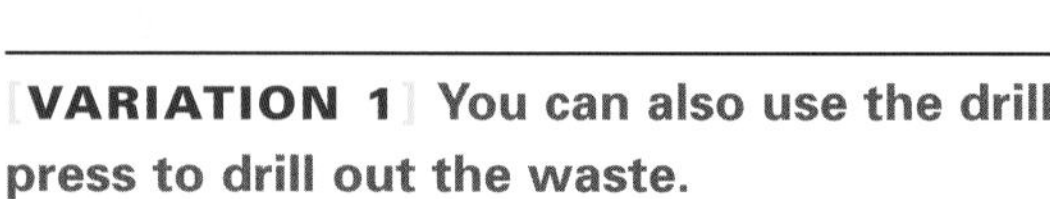
[VARIATION 1] You can also use the drill press to drill out the waste.

Cut the sides of the haunch groove with a handsaw. Mark the depth of cut at the end of the board (**F**). Clean up the bottom of the haunch groove with a chisel or a small router plane (**G**).

VARIATION 2 For a panel groove in the length of a board, use a combination plane, such as this no. 45, to plough the through groove and haunch to depth.

Locate the shoulder position or length of the tenon with a marking gauge on both faces of the board. A wheel-type marking gauge works best for marking out cross-grain (**H**). Lay out the cheek cuts or the thickness of the tenon with a pencil and rule or use a marking gauge. Mark both of the edges as well as the end of the board (**I**).

➤ See *"Hand-Cut Tenon"* on pp. 314–315.

First, cut the shoulders, holding the workpiece tight to a bench hook or with the board clamped to the bench. After making the shoulder cuts almost to full depth, saw the cheeks with a tenon saw or backsaw. After making the first cheek cut, clean it up with a shoulder or bullnose plane before moving on to the next cut. If you've taken off too much wood, you can adjust the second cut.

After both cheek cuts are made, check the fit of the tenon. You can get the corner of the tenon in the joint to see how tight a fit you have. Try to leave the tenon a bit fat so you can clean the cheeks with a handplane for a final perfect fit (**J**).

Next, mark out the haunch size and rip the haunch to width. Crosscut the haunch to length with a backsaw and trim it with a chisel (**K**). To check just the fit of the haunch, flip the board around and place the haunch in its groove.

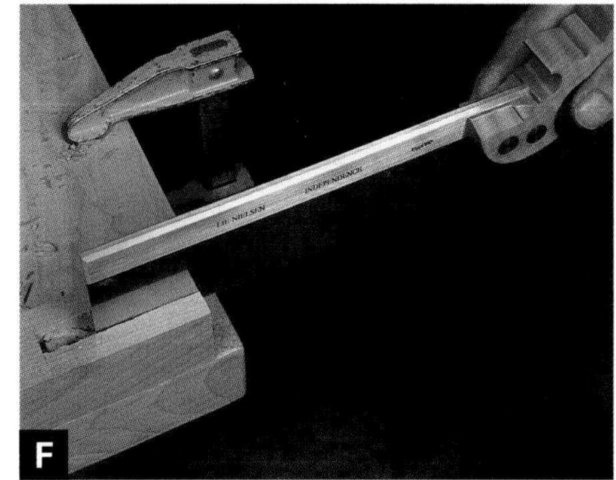
F

G

H

I

J

K

VARIATION 2

A

B

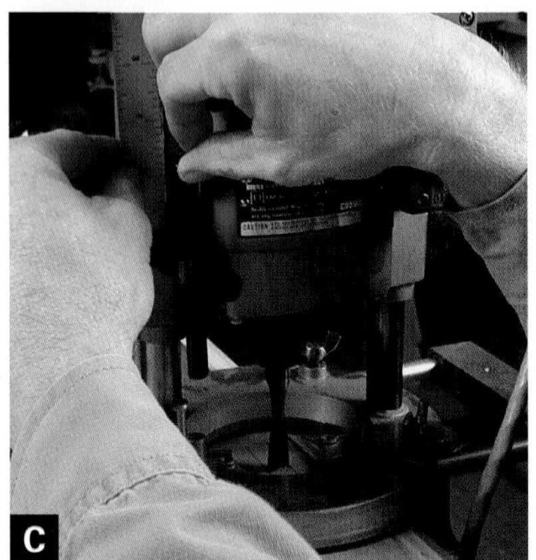
C

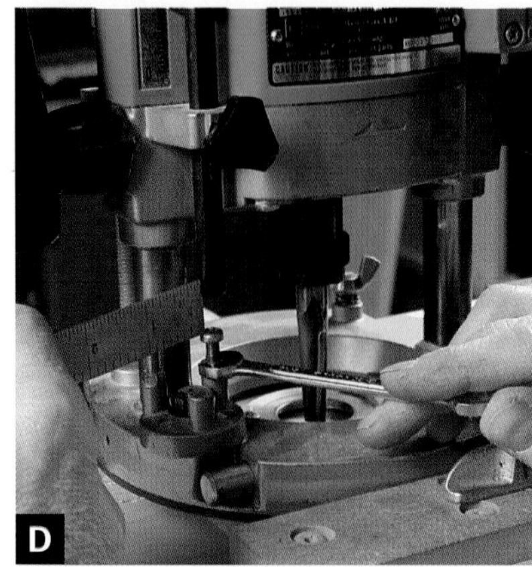
D

E

F

Haunched Mortise and Tenon with a Router

When mortising narrow stock with a router, place several boards together on the bench to provide better support. First, mark out the mortise position (**A**). Then plunge the bit down to the surface of the wood to zero the bit (**B**). Next, measure up on the depth scale for the depth of the mortise cut (**C**). Set a second depth stop for the haunch with another turret stop. You'll have to fine adjust the stop with a screwdriver and/or wrench to lock it down accurately (**D**).

➤ See *"Mortise with a Plunge Router and Fence"* on p. 307.

Place the router over the end of the mortise and clamp a stop to the board (**E**). Cut the haunch groove first. Remember to support the end of the router as you get to the end of the board. A template guide holder left in place in the bottom of the router provides support (**F**).

[VARIATION] You can also cut the haunch groove on the router table with a straight bit and stop. Keep the stop raised up to allow debris to blow under it rather than bunching up against it, affecting the cut.

After the haunch is cut, reset the bit depth on the turret stop for the full depth of the mortise cut (**G**). One stop for the end of the mortise is already clamped in place. Use a pencil to mark the position of the router base for the other end of the mortise and come up slowly to this mark with each pass (**H**).

Make the tenon using your preferred method.

➤ **See pp. 314 to 325 for cutting methods.**

The advantage a haunched tenon gives when fitting the joint is the chunk of wood on its corner that has to be removed. This allows you to take a nibble pass on the saw or with a router so you can check the fit there. If it's too small, no harm is done. Just reset the fence for another pass.

Mark the tenon off the mortise in case any discrepancies in size have crept in (**I**). Put a small shoulder on the bottom of the tenon to cover up the joint. Then cut the tenon to width on the bandsaw (**J**). Make the haunch end-grain cut on the crosscut jig, but set the blade height under the bandsaw cut so you don't have an offcut trapped between the stop and the blade (**K**).

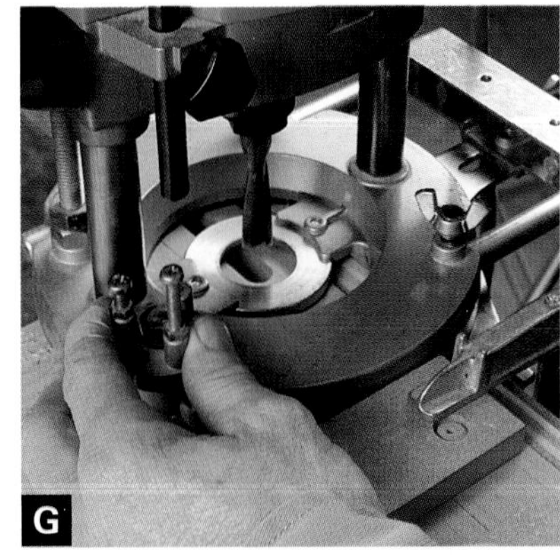
G

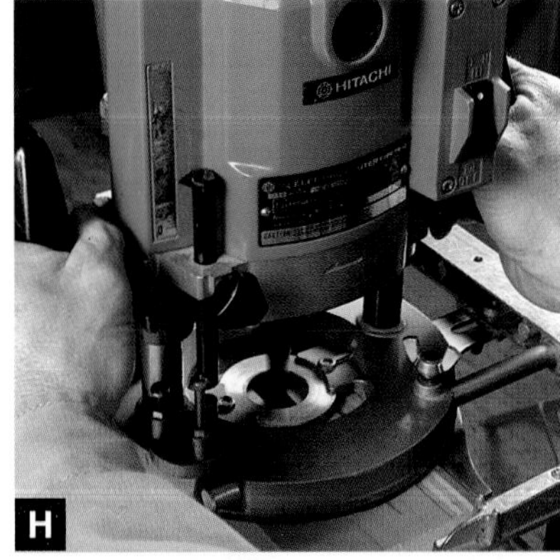

H

I

J

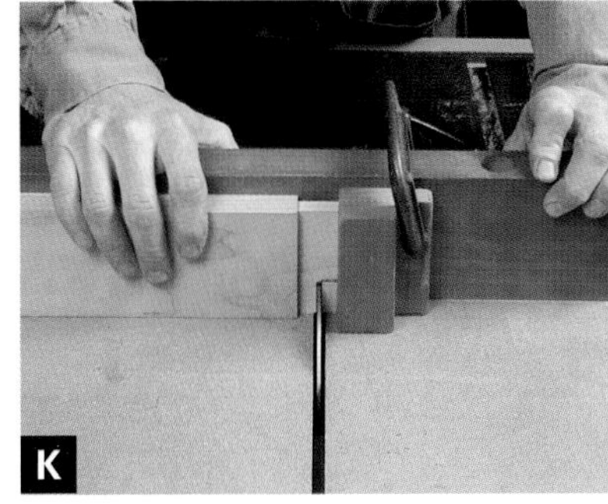
K

VARIATION

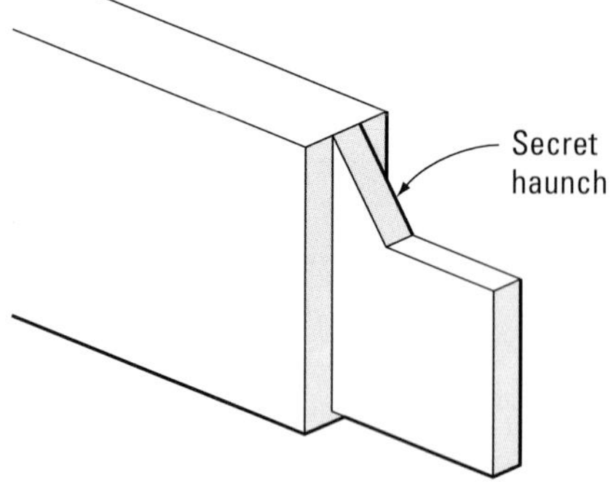

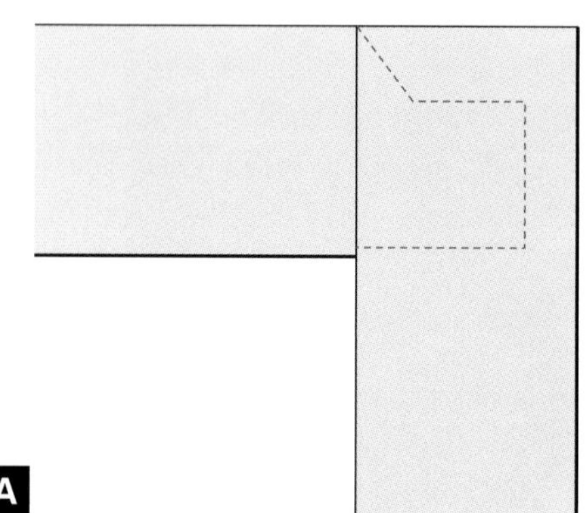

A

B

Secret Haunched Mortise and Tenon

The first step to making a secret haunched mortise-and-tenon joint is to lay out the mortise (**A**).

➤ See *"Hand-Cut Haunched Mortise and Tenon"* on p. 336.

After chopping out the mortise, cut the mortise haunch groove at an angle with a chisel. Keep the groove back from the end of the board (**B**).

Cut the tenon to size with a handsaw down to the haunch line, then rough out the haunch with a sawcut (**C**). Trim the angled haunch to size with a chisel (**D**).

C

D

Double Mortise and Tenon with a Router and Template

A double mortise-and-tenon joint can be cut with a router. Set the double-mortise template in place on the board. You need to pencil in the position of only one mortise and the template offset mark (**A**). Place the router on the template to zero the bit on the wood (**B**).

Rout to depth and use a dust pickup on a router or a vacuum to get rid of the dust. Be careful coming up to the end of the mortises after clearing out debris in the template. You might be surprised by your bit taking a big bite over quite a long length (**C**).

Mark out the double tenons off of the mortises. Set the plunge router fence to cut the tenon shoulders. Leave the tenons a little short so there's room at the bottom of the joint for excess glue. Carefully set the plunge depth to cut the tenons (**D**).

Cut the tenons by working from the end of the board back to the shoulder. Keep the router supported at each end of the cut. Try to move moderately fast across the shoulder cut to prevent burning (**E**).

Cut the double tenons to width on the bandsaw (**F**).

Use the plunge router to cut between the double tenons to establish the rest of the shoulder (**G**). Reset the depth to cut through. Be careful not to run into the tenons with the bit and keep the fence well located on the ends of the tenons. This will establish the space between the tenons in the same plane as the top and bottom shoulders of the joint. Finish up the corners with a chisel.

A

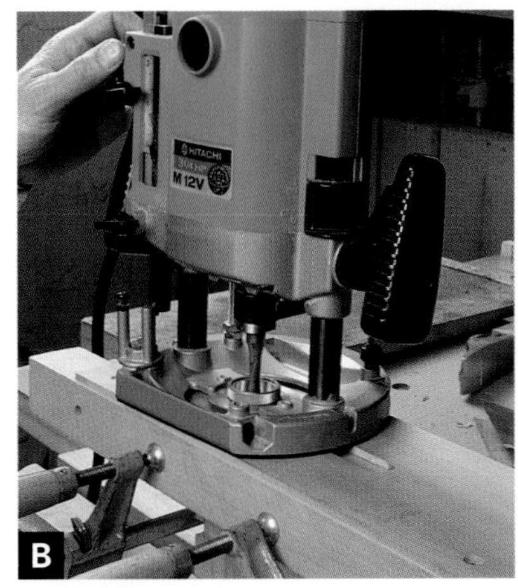
B

C

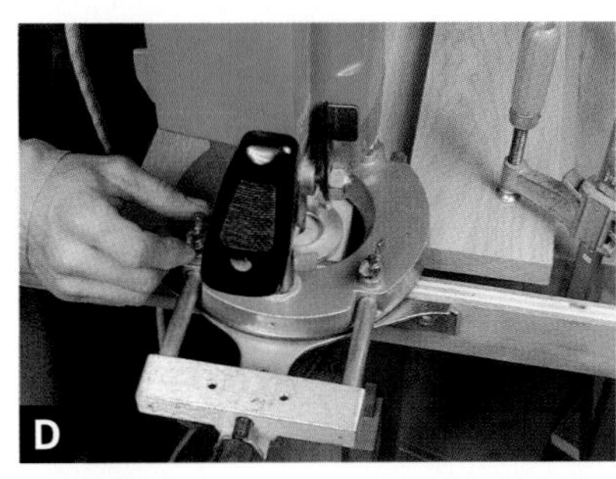
D

E

F

G

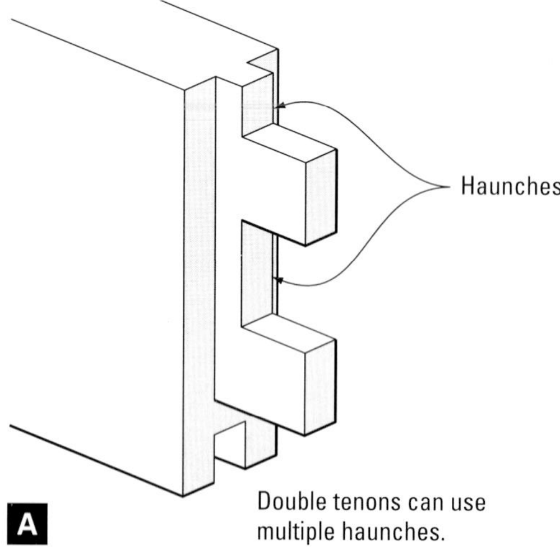

Double tenons can use multiple haunches.

A

B

Hand-Cut Haunched Double Mortise and Tenon

Begin a hand-cut haunched doubled mortise-and-tenon joint by marking out one end of one mortise (**A**). Next, measure and mark out the other end. Then mark out the second mortise. Square lines across the board at these ends (**B**). To mark out the width of the mortise use your chisel to set a mortising gauge. Put the chisel between the two points on the gauge then lock down the head at the distance you want from the edge of the board (**C**). Hold the gauge tight to the board's edge and mark out the mortise. Do not score past the end marks (**D**).

C

D

Start chopping in the middle of the mortises (**E**). Angle the cuts toward each other until you get close to depth; then start to chop straight in. Chop straight down at the ends of the mortises and clean the side walls until they're parallel and the mortises are equal in size.

See *"Hand-Cut Mortise with a Mortising Chisel"* on p. 302 for more information.

E

F

Check the mortises with a drift, which is a thin piece of wood that you push into the widest part of the mortise. Where it won't fit is where you need to remove more wood.

Once the mortises are established, chop in a stop for the saw at the position of the bottom haunch. But don't hit the stop too hard, or it will show past the bottom of the tenon.

Put a depth mark on the end of the board, or use a piece of tape on the saw to mark the depth. Saw out the haunch groove with a backsaw (**F**). Keep the saw in line with the mortise walls and cut down to depth. Chisel out the waste in the haunches.

Because the shoulders on a double tenon are so long, use a fence to help guide the cuts. Set up a combination square as a depth guide to line up the fence. Clamp the fence in place on the wood. Put a piece of masking tape on a crosscut saw and line out the depth of cut on it. Hold the saw right up against the fence and make the shoulder cuts on both faces (**G**).

Chisel away most of the waste with a wide chisel, but pay attention to the grain direction of the board so you don't have a cut split out past the tenon lines (**H**). Use a shoulder plane up tight against the tenon shoulder to cut the tenon to depth. This will only cut out a channel (**I**). Then take a block plane or a bench plane to finish off the remaining wood on the cheek. Get one cheek cut and then move to the next (**J**).

When a corner of the tenon fits in the mortise or you can push the tenon down to the bottom of the haunch groove, mark out the ends of the double tenons and the haunches (**K**).

Saw out between the tenons down to the haunch lines. Remember to keep the saw on the waste side of the cut (**L**). Crosscut the top and bottom haunches out. Then saw out the waste between the double tenons with a coping saw (**M**).

Chop out on the shoulder line between the tenons with a chisel (**N**). Chop from both sides to avoid tearout. Then do the final fitting of the double tenons down to depth.

[TIP] Put a small shoulder on the bottom edge of the double tenon to cover any dents in the mortise.

G

H

I

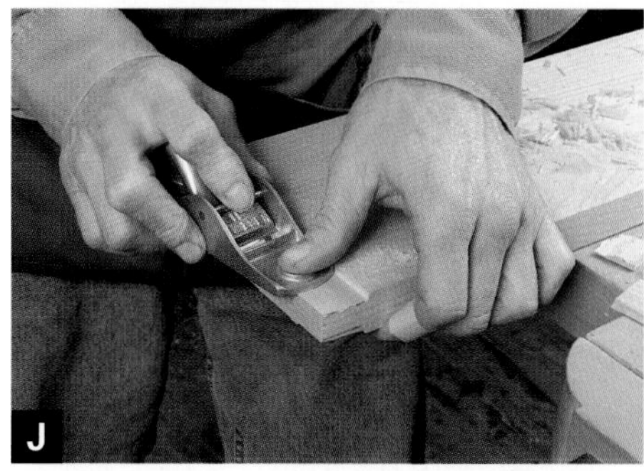
J

K

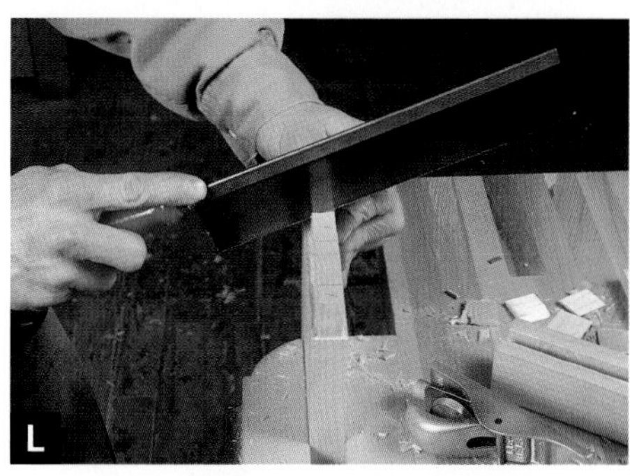
L

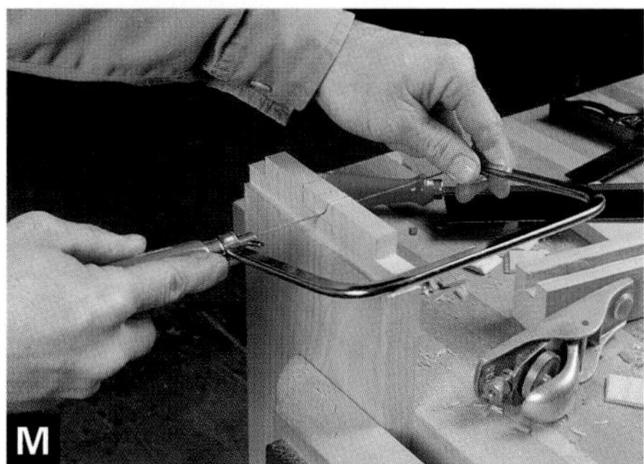
M

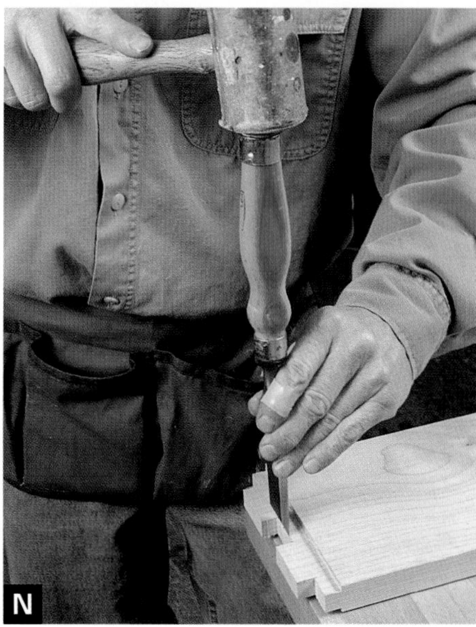
N

A

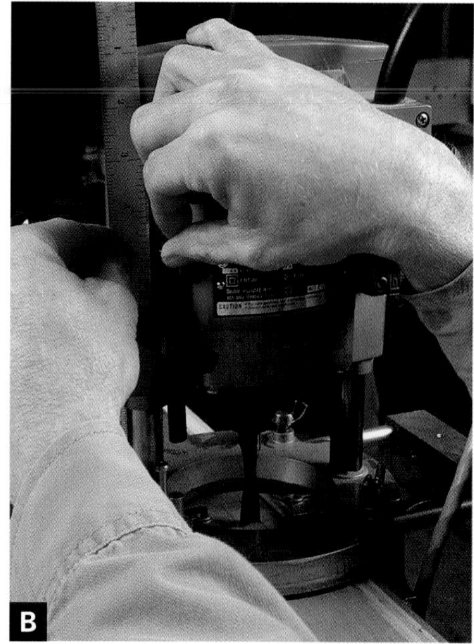
B

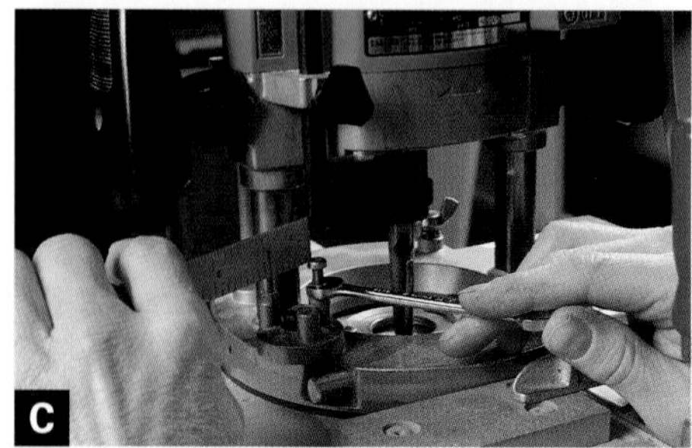
C

D

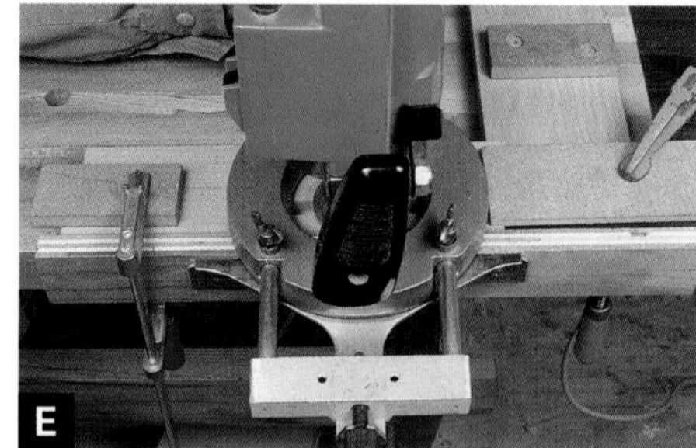
E

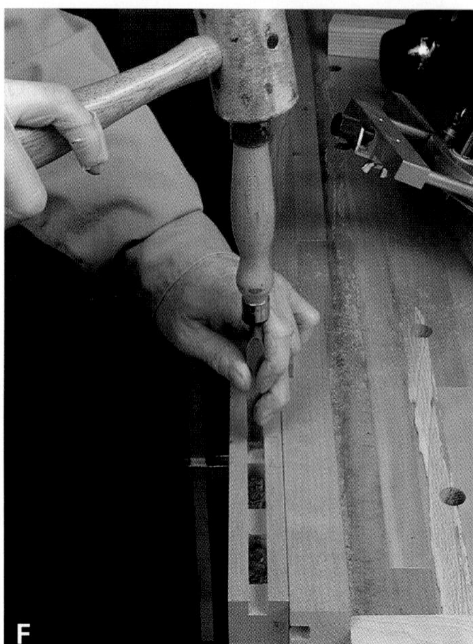
F

G

H

Haunched Double Mortise and Tenon with a Router

Clamp the workpiece down to your bench with two support boards the same height. Put one board next to the piece and the other at its end so the router won't tip during any part of the cut.

Mount a straight bit in the router and zero the bit down on the wood (**A**). Measure along the depth scale for the depth of the mortise (**B**). Rotate the turret stop and set another depth stop for the haunch groove (**C**). Mount a fence on the router to set the mortise in the proper location. Clamp a stop for the haunch groove onto the board that the router base runs into. Rout straight off the other end of the board. Rout out the full haunch groove to depth (**D**).

Next, reset the bit depth on the turret stop to cut the mortises to full depth. Clamp on another stop to limit the router travel for the mortise cuts (**E**).

Chop the mortise and haunch ends square with a chisel. You can slightly undercut these so they won't interfere with fitting the double tenons (**F**). Use the plunge router with a fence on it to cut the double tenons. Work from the end of the board back to the shoulder.

You can use one corner of the tenon board to check the depth of cut, because that corner will be removed to create the haunch (**G**). Cut the tenons to width once they just fit into the mortise slot. Use a jigsaw or the bandsaw to cut them down to the haunch lines. Clamp a block onto the bandsaw fence to stop the sawcuts in the proper location (**H**).

Twin Tenons

Use twin tenons in situations where one full mortise cut would greatly weaken a member. Offset the mortises to provide more wood at the bottom of a rail (**A**).

On the drill press, arrange the mortise cuts so that the setup and stops remain the same for both cuts. You will add a spacer between the fence and the board when you make the second mortise cut.

➤ See *"Mortise on the Drill Press"* on p. 304.

First align the fence for the outer mortise with stops on the fence set at the mortise length (**B**). Drill the two outer holes of the mortise. Then clean up the remaining wood, locating the brad-point bit center on some wood so it doesn't wander (**C**). Put in a spacer for the second mortise and drill that slot (**D**).

Mark out the tenon shoulders with a marking gauge and make the first outside shoulder cut.

➤ See pp. 314 to 325 for cutting methods.

If your goal is to have the faces of the two boards line up flush, make the first cheek cut and check it against the mortise. Flip the mortised piece around and set it against the tenon cheek. If the board's face lines up with the mortise wall, the outside faces will line up as well when you put the joint together (**E**). If it doesn't quite line up, remove as much material as is necessary to bring that first cheek down in size.

Next, work your way through the other tenon cheeks. Cut the interior cheeks on the table saw or bandsaw and chop out the middle shoulder with a chisel.

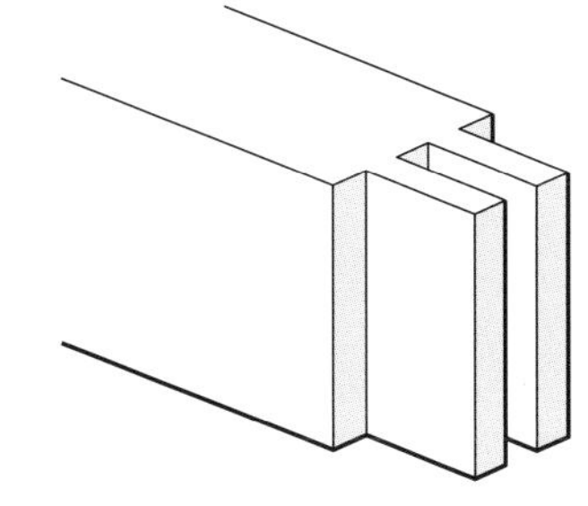

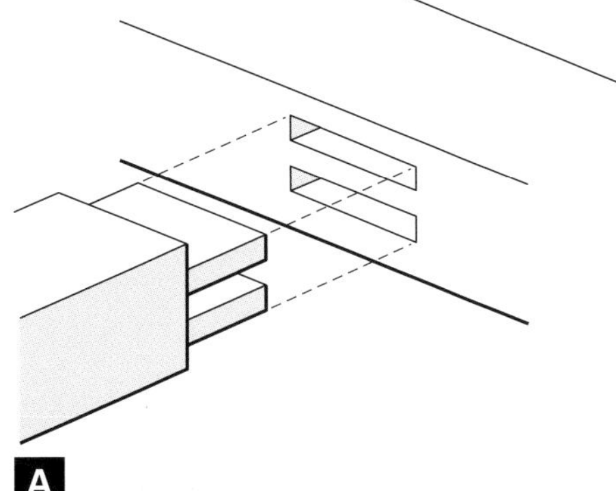

A

B

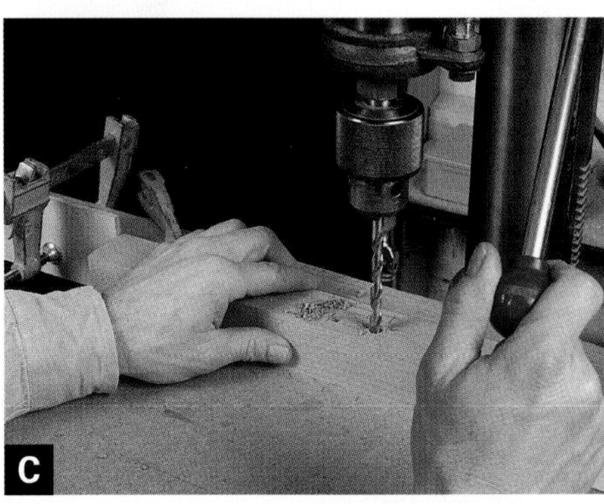

C

D

E

A

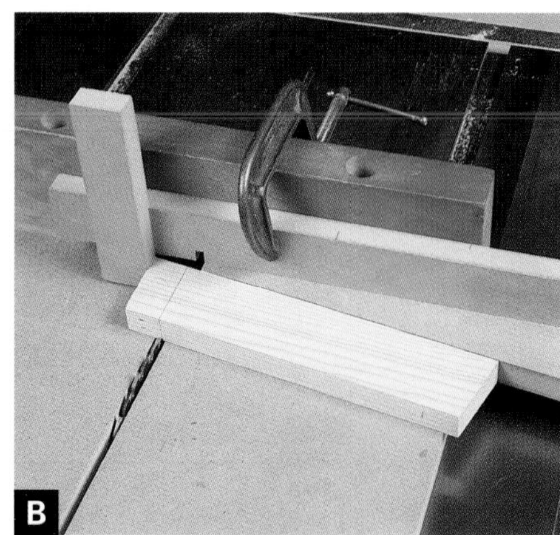
B

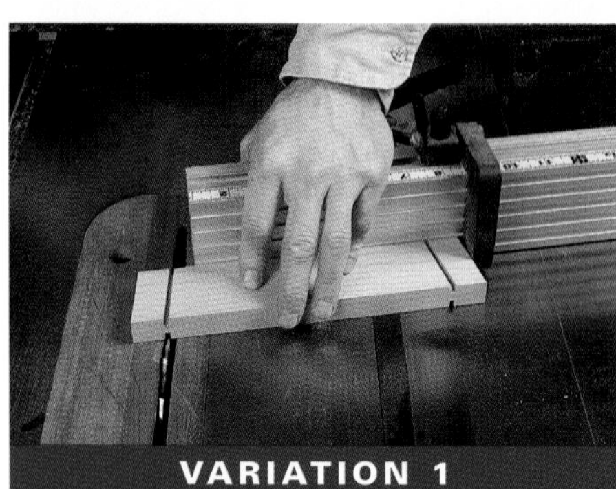
C

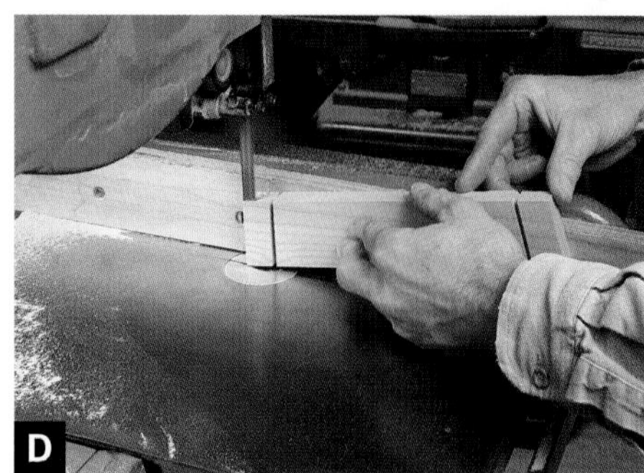
D

Angled Shoulders for Integral Tenon

A simple angle on a tenon shoulder should match the angle of the end of the board for ease in cutting. Mark out the angle and position of the shoulders with a sliding bevel (**A**). Make up an angled fence or cut a piece of scrap to the proper angle to fit against the crosscut jig fence. This angle will complement the angled shoulder. For example, a shoulder of 82 degrees will need an 8-degree angled fence.

Cut one shoulder on opposite faces of the board. You can build in a stop to the angled insert or clamp on a stop to index the cuts (**B**). You'll have to flip the board to cut the matching shoulder. Use a second angled fence or flip the piece of scrap over to line up the second set of shoulder cuts. You must line up the stops very carefully to make sure these angled cuts line up (**C**).

[VARIATION 1] Use the miter gauge angled first in one direction and then the other to make both of the shoulder cuts.

VARIATION 1

Rough out the tenons on the bandsaw carefully, holding the board at an angle. Keep it well supported at the blade for the cut. Then check that both shoulders line up before you tear down the setups (**D**).

[VARIATION 2] Horizontally mounted routers are the simplest way to make angled tenon shoulder cuts. To set the angle, use a standard tenoning fence with an angled shim between it and the board. Then rout both shoulders to create the angled shoulder tenon.

VARIATION 2

Angled Shoulders for Loose Tenon

Angled shoulders on loose tenons eliminate many of the problems with angled shoulder cuts (**A**). This is because you simply make an angled crosscut on the end of the mortised board. Use loose tenons when a mortise cut won't weaken the piece.

Crosscut the boards at the required angle on the table saw (**B**). Mortise for the loose tenon straight into the piece on the horizontally mounted router (**C**).

VARIATION Alternatively, you could first cut the mortise with a template-guided cut and make the angled cut after.

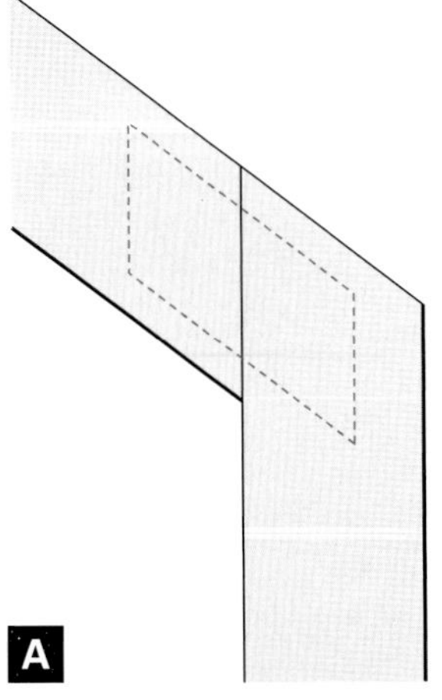

A

B

C

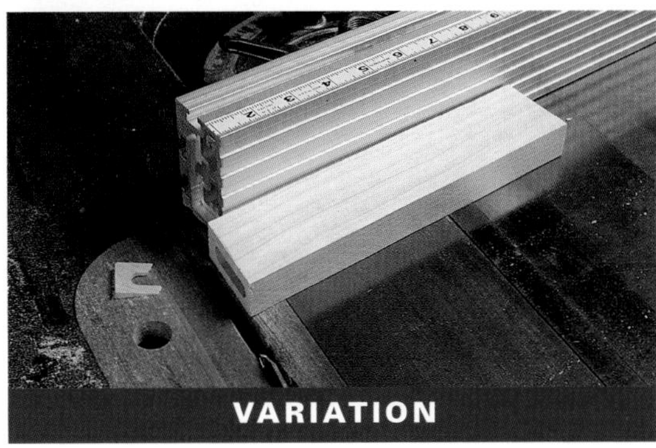

VARIATION

A

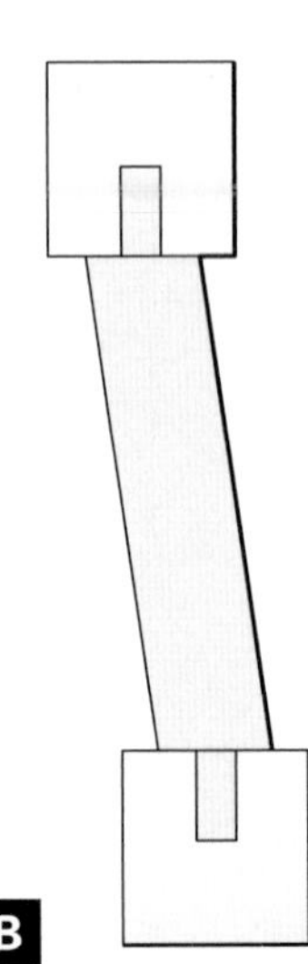
B

C

D

VARIATION 1

VARIATION 2

Angled Tenon

Cut angled tenons vertically with a tenoning jig and dado blade. Angle the tenoning jig to the required angle (**A**). Avoid putting too great an angle on the tenon to prevent short-grain problems at the tenon's end (**B**). Set the blade height and saw the first cheek and shoulder with the jig (**C**). Then cut the second cheek (**D**).

[VARIATION 1] An alternative is to lay the board flat on the table saw and cut the shoulders with the sawblade tipped to the proper angle. Then cut the tenon cheeks with a tenoning jig and the blade still angled.

[VARIATION 2] The Multirouter cuts the angled cheeks and shoulders all at once by raising the table to the appropriate angle.

Mitered Tenon

When tenons meet up inside a table leg, you must allow for the insertion of the mating tenon (**A**). Offset the tenons to the outside of the leg for greater penetration.

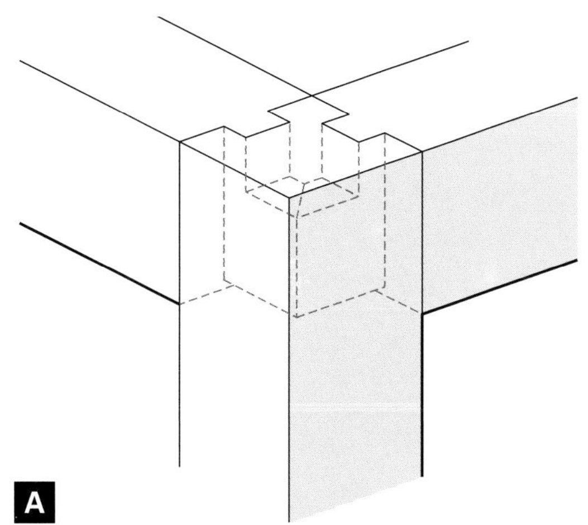

A

➤ See *"Centered vs. Offset"* drawing on p. 295.

Cut the mortises for each leg, but set the depth of cut just less than the full depth required. This means that the bottom of the first mortise won't remove some of the side wall of the other mortise (**B**).

B

➤ See pp. 302 to 313 for cutting methods.

Clean up the remaining ledge of wood with a chisel (**C**).

C

Cut the tenons using your preferred method.

➤ See pp. 314 to 325 for cutting methods.

Miter the ends of the tenons on the miter saw. This is not so much a joint cut here as it is a spacer cut, so don't worry about the miters mating up (**D**).

D

[VARIATION] You can also cut the mitered tenons on the table saw with a miter gauge.

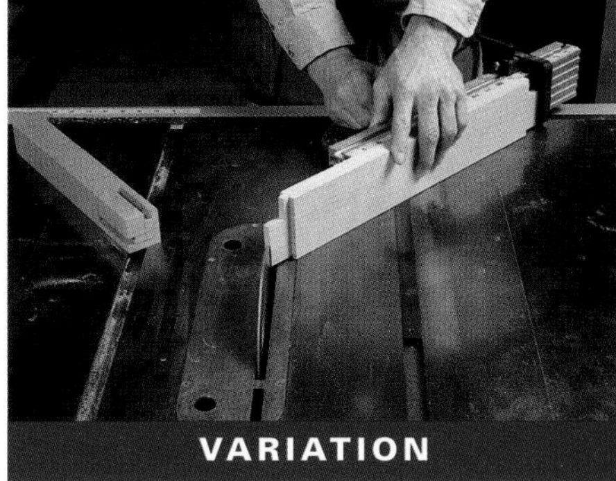

VARIATION

Notched Tenon

Instead of mitering the end of the mating tenons, you can notch the tenons, allowing them to overlap (**A**). Note, however, that this removes gluing surface from the joint.

Mark out the notch position on one tenon. Keep it at half the height of the tenon and just a hair wider. Mark out the notch onto the mating tenon (**B**). Cut the notches by hand with a backsaw (**C**).

VARIATION Cut the shoulder of the notch on the table saw with the crosscut jig and rip it to size on the bandsaw.

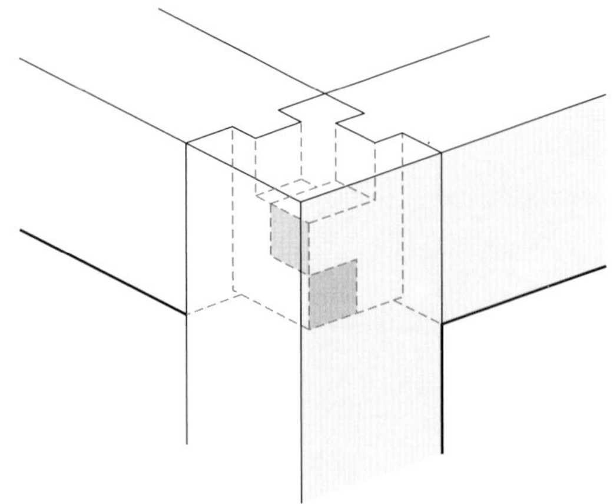

A

B

C

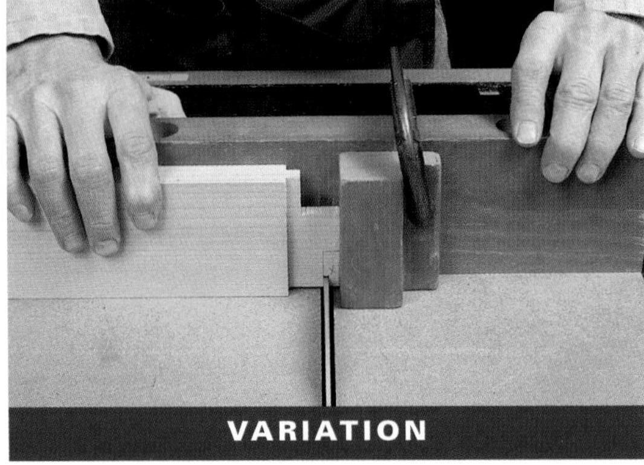

VARIATION

Interlocking Tenons

Interlocking tenons lock one tenon in place with the insertion of the second tenon (**A**). Don't cut too wide a mortise through the first tenon, since it'll end up with easily broken-out short grain. Set up a plunge router and fence to cut the mortises and haunches.

➤ See *"Haunched Mortise and Tenon with a Router"* on pp. 338–339.

Use two depth settings to cut both. Cut the haunch groove first (**B**). Reset the bit depth to cut the double mortises; clamp on stops to limit the router travel (**C**).

Trim the double tenons on the bandsaw to fit the mortises. Mark the haunch line clearly and cut just up to that line or set up a stop on the fence (**D**).

Clamp the double tenon home in its mortise and cut the intersecting mortise through it (**E**). Fit the single tenon to width against the mortise through the double tenon (**F**). Round the tenon shoulders for a round mortise with a file (**G**).

VARIATION **You can use one dowel to interlock with another.**

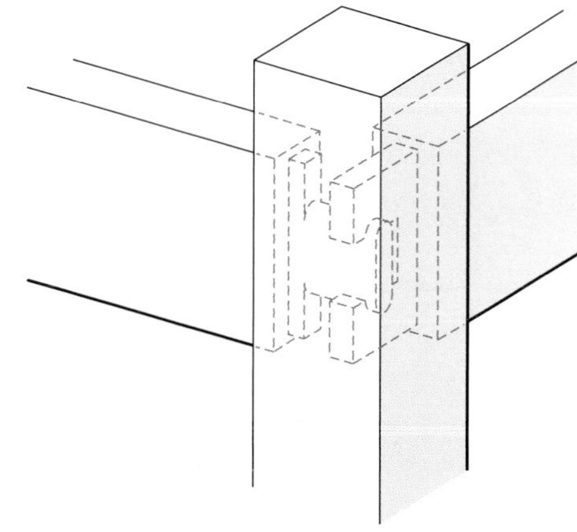

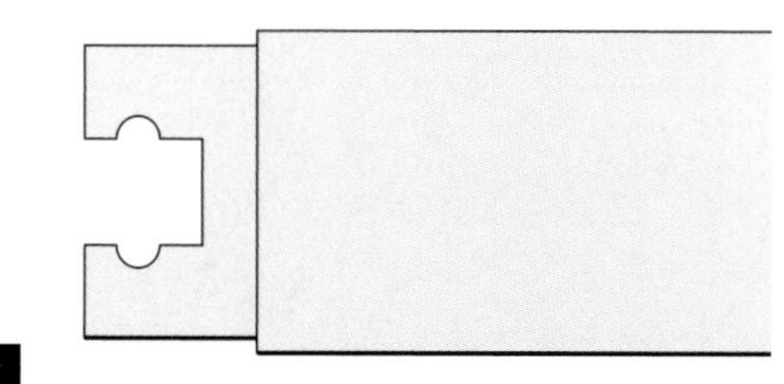

A

Side Elevation

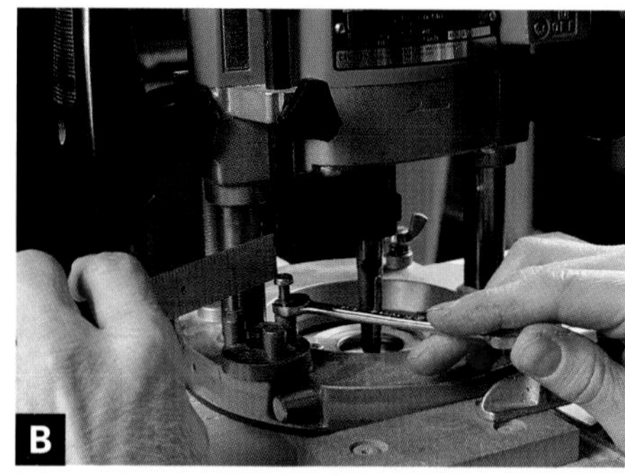

B

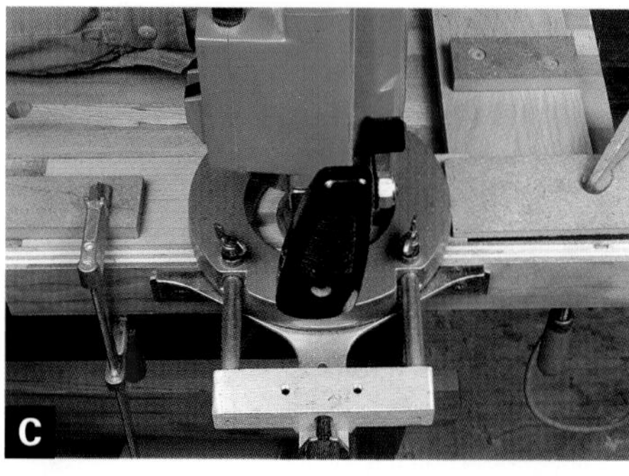

C

D

E

VARIATION

F

G

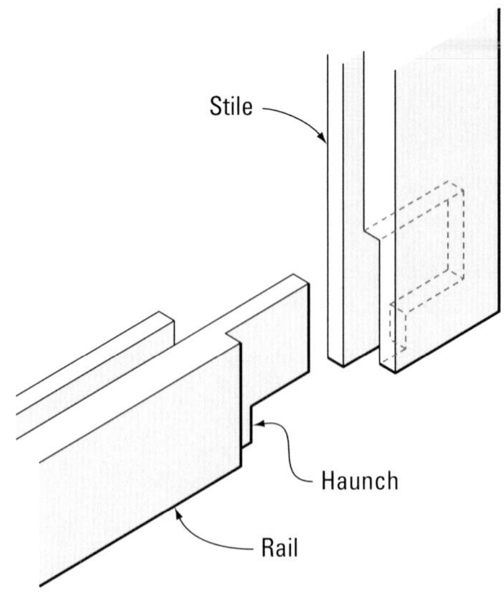

A

B

Tenon with an Offset Shoulder

Hand-cut frame-and-panel joinery sometimes requires offset shoulders on the tenoned pieces (**A**). When a panel is rabbeted in from the back side of a frame, the rabbet is cut straight through the end of the board with a rabbeting plane. This requires a longer shoulder at the back of the tenoned board to fill this rabbet. Router-cut rabbets don't require this offset since you can make all the rabbet cuts stopped when the frame is dry-clamped together.

Pencil in the mortises and rabbets using a square as a depth gauge (**B**). Chop out the mortises to depth (**C**).

C

➤ See *"Hand-Cut Haunched Mortise and Tenon"* on pp. 336–337.

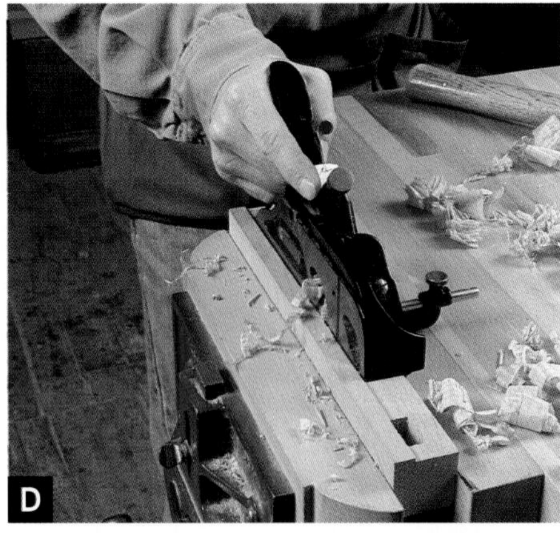
D

Use the rabbeting plane mounted with a fence to cut the rabbet on the back face of the mortised boards. Set the fence so the rabbet lines up on one mortise wall. Cut the rabbets on the tenon boards as well (**D**).

E

Use a wheel-type marking gauge to lay out the shoulders on the tenon piece. First mark out the long shoulder on the back side of the rail and then the short shoulder at the front of the rail (**E**). Next, lay out the tenon thickness using a pencil and ruler or the marking gauge.

Cut the shoulders to depth. Then cut the tenon cheeks with a tenon saw. Clean up the first cheek with a shoulder or bullnose plane before cutting the second. Saw out the haunch with a backsaw.

Mason's Miter

A simple chamfer around the inside edge of a frame or door can be cut after assembly. A bit of final handwork finishes off the detail (**A**).

First cut the mortises using your preferred method.

➤ See pp. 302 to 313 for cutting methods.

Glue up the mortised frame and clean up the faces. Chamfer the inside edge with a 45-degree chamfering bit used topside (**B**).

Finish up the inside corner detail with a chisel. Mark the end of the cut by referencing the chisel off the chamfer. Then carve into that end stop (**C**). Note that the finished joint will always show up a bit darker in the corner because you cut into end grain (**D**).

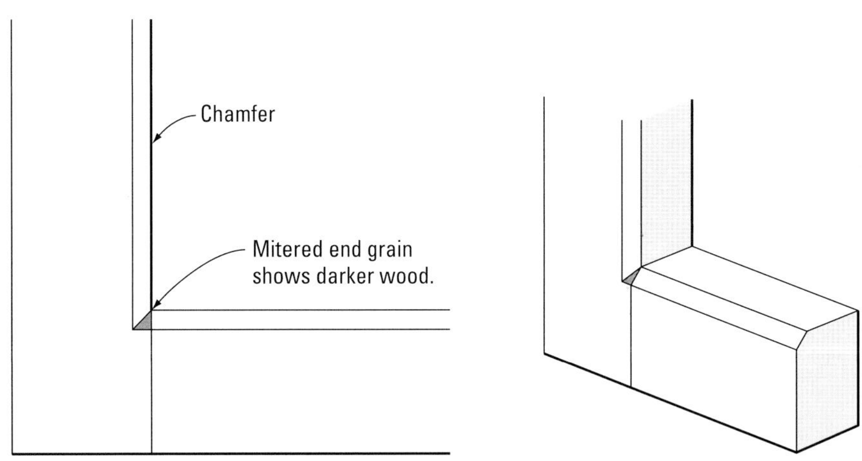

A

B

VARIATION

Mortise and Tenon with Cope and Stick Bits

Cope and stick bits come in a wide variety of patterns and a few configurations. These matched bit sets all cut a stub mortise-and-tenon joint that's in line with a panel groove and a molded edge for frame-and-panel doors. Because of the small amount of gluing surface in these joints, do not expect great strength from them unless you also dowel or screw across the joint.

Cut the stile groove and its molding or sticking with the grooving bit on a speed-controlled table-mounted router. Run the motor speed down around 10,000 rpm. Cut some practice boards to get the bit height just right and remember to use a push stick (**A**).

[TIP] For safety, use a fence lined up with the bearing.

Cut the tongued profile or coped piece on the rail with the tongue bit across the end grain of the rail piece. Use a backer board to prevent tearout and to give you better bearing surface across the fence (**B**).

[VARIATION] Use a reversible bit set to cut both sides of the joint. These bits are less expensive but take some time to reverse the cutter positions.

Mortise and Tenon with Mitered Sticking

Use mortise-and-tenon joints with mitered sticking to create strong door frames (**A**). Purchase material already milled with the sticking or mill up your own. When making up your cutting list, be sure to add in the width of the sticking to each end of the rail.

Cut the mortise-and-tenon joints in the stock (**B**).

➤ See pp. 302 to 325 for cutting methods.

Locate the start of the miter joint by putting the frame together and marking out the width of the rail onto the stile (**C**). Cut the sticking off the stile pieces using the bandsaw and a fence. Come up close to the miter pencil mark or use a stop on the fence to index the cuts (**D**).

Using a paring jig clamped onto the stile, miter the sticking on both stile and rail. Then check your fit (**E**).

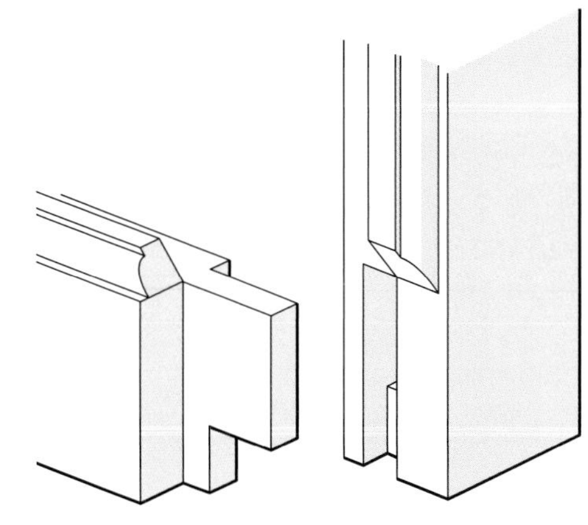

B

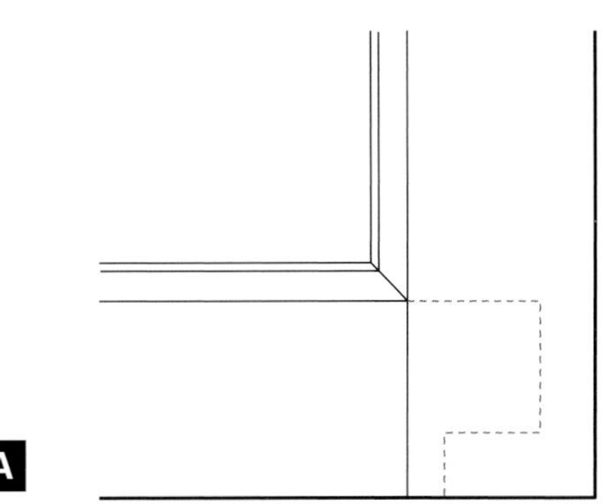

A

C

D

E

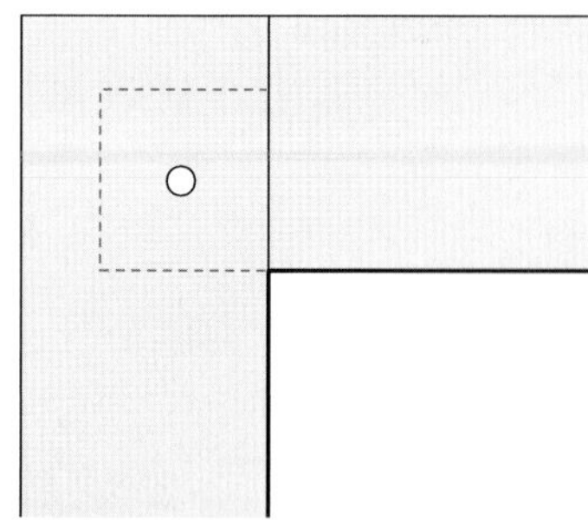

A

B

C

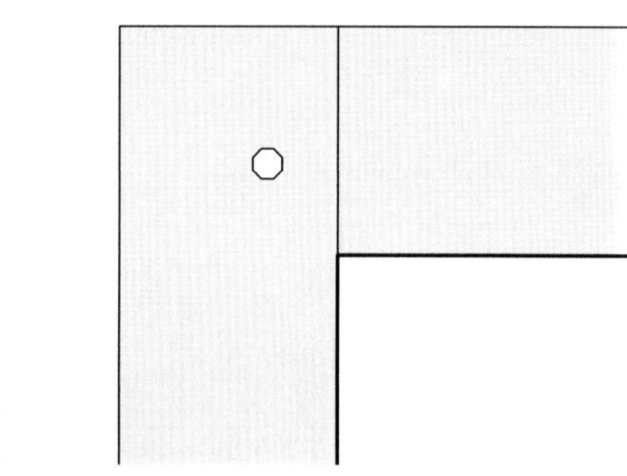

D

VARIATION

Pinned Tenon

To ensure a tenon will hold over time, run a pin through it (**A**). Even if the glue fails, a pinned tenon will remain together.

After gluing up, drill the joint with a brad-point bit. If you want the pin to show through on both sides, use a piece of scrap under the frame to prevent tearout when you drill through. If not, carefully set the depth of cut so the centering point doesn't come through the back (**B**).

Chamfer the end of a dowel pin and add just a bit of glue to the hole before pounding the dowel home (**C**). A more rustic approach is to use octagonal pins in round holes (**D**).

[VARIATION] The pins shown here lock themselves into place because their corners cut into the surrounding wood. Shape the pin stock with a block plane and chamfer the end before inserting it into its hole; avoid making the stock too large.

Drawbore Tenon

Drawboring is more suited to timberframe construction than to fine furniture making, but the joint can be used for furniture if done carefully. The hole drilled into the tenon is offset a bare 1/32 in. toward the shoulder from the hole drilled into the mortise (**A**). When you put in the dowel pin, the tenon shoulder is drawn in tighter to the mortise. For a bridle joint or slot mortise, the tenon hole is closer to the shoulder and higher on the tenon, which pulls the tenon in and down to the mortise. If the offset is too great, the pin won't make it through the holes or will end up stretching out the tenon hole instead of pulling the joint tight.

Cut the mortise and fit the tenon to it.

➤ See pp. 302 to 325 for cutting methods.

Take the joint apart and drill through the mortise with a brad-point bit on the drill press. To prevent tearout inside the joint, drill slowly or place a piece of scrap inside the joint (**B**).

Put the joint back together and mark the hole center on the tenon with the same brad-point bit (**C**). Remove the tenon and remark the hole center just a bit closer to the shoulder (**D**). Drill through the tenon using a piece of scrap under it to prevent tearout and to support the cut (**E**).

Put a heavy chamfer on a dowel pin, which is cut extra long. After you glue in the tenon, bang the dowel through the joint so the chamfer comes all the way through. A chamfered bolt driven through from the other side will help pull things together (**F**).

Drawbored Tenon

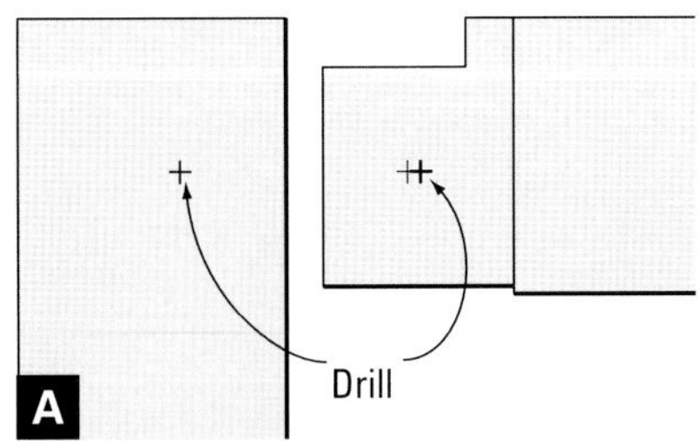

Drawbored Slot Mortise

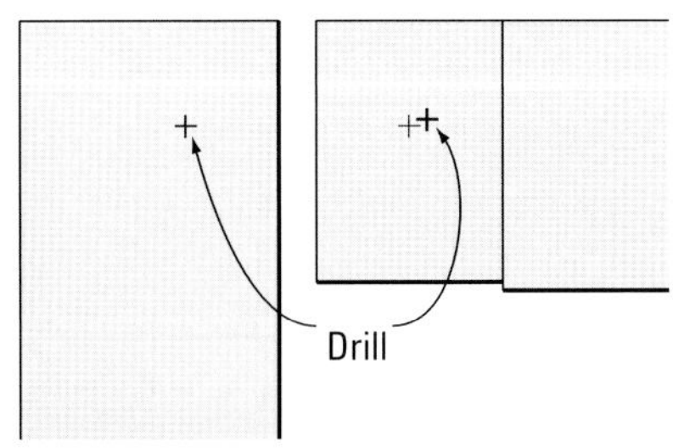

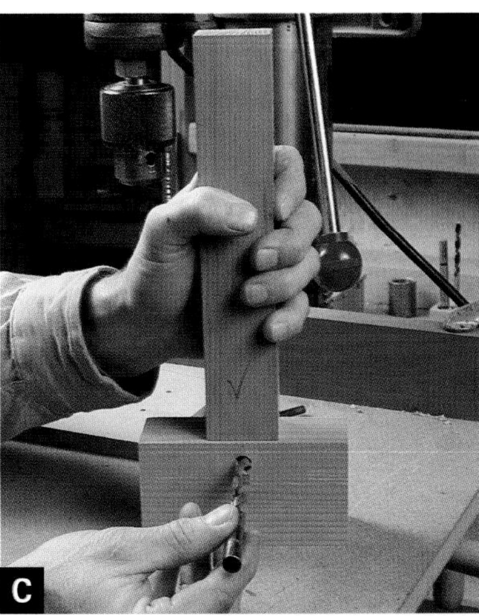

Foxtail-Wedged Tenon

Foxtail, or blind, wedging can be used to strengthen a mortise-and-tenon joint (**A**). But with the number of ways it can go wrong, it's a joint of some questionable merit.

First widen the mortise at its bottom with a chisel. Try not to widen the mortise too much (**B**). Cut the wedge slots with a handsaw or on the bandsaw, putting them close to the edges of the tenon (**C, D**).

Make sure the wedge stock is the proper length and width to do the best possible job for foxtail wedging.

See *"Making Wedges"* on p. 376.

If the wedges are too long, the joint won't go all the way together before it gets wedged. If the wedges are too thin, they won't wedge the joint enough to do any work (**E**). Finally, if the wedge is too wide or its slot is cut too far in from the end of the tenon, the tenon will crack (**F**).

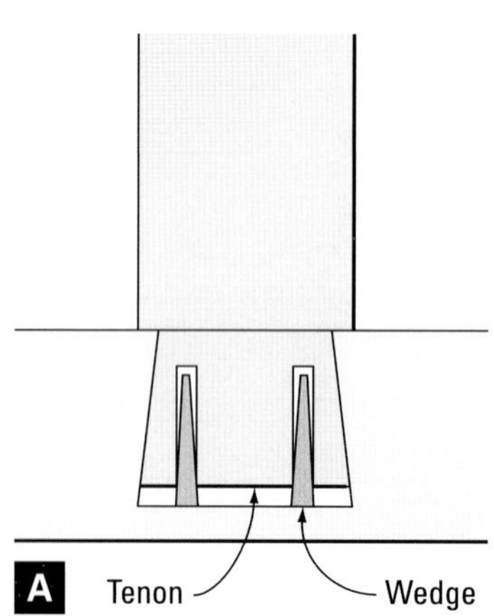

A

B

C

D

E

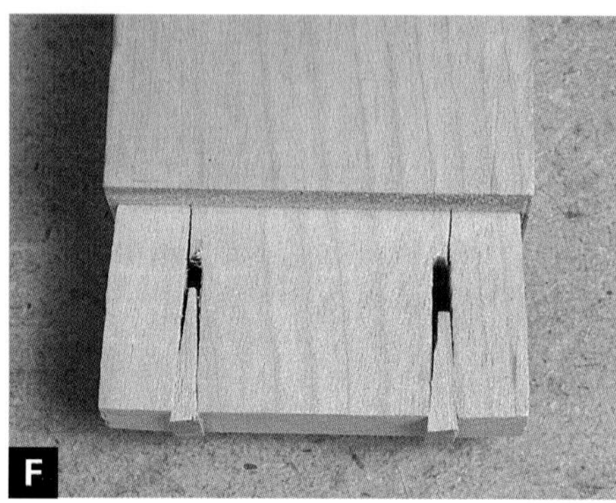
F

Splined Tenon

Add splines to a tenon on a wide board to prevent twisting. An added benefit is that the spline cuts won't remove too much material from the mortised board.

Make the shoulder cuts for the tenon on the table saw with the crosscut jig. Reset the blade height for the cheek cuts or use a dado set to cut the tenon cheeks to size (**A**).

Change back to a regular blade and raise the blade height to cut the slots for the splines. Adjust the tenoning jig to center the spline cut in the tenon shoulder (**B**). Make the first spline cut, rotate the board in the jig, and then make the second spline cut (**C**).

TIP **If you've cut a tenon too small or have a broken tenon in need of fixing, use a splined tenon for the repair. Cut the undersize tenon off, then put a slot in the end of the board and fit the spline to it.**

A

TIP

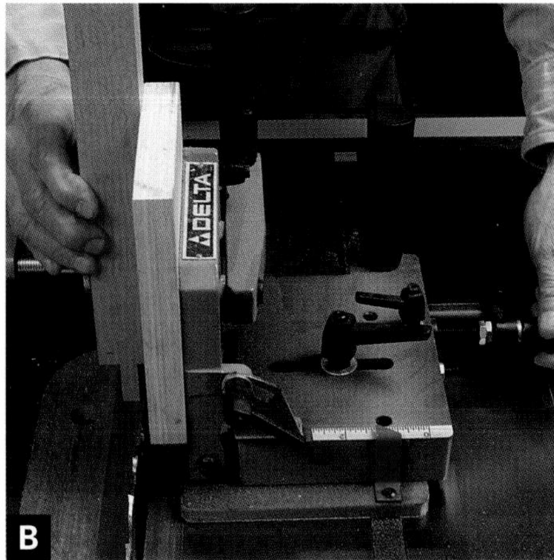

B

C

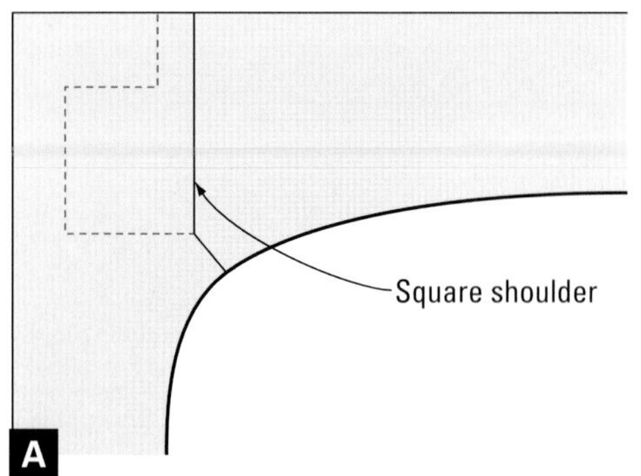

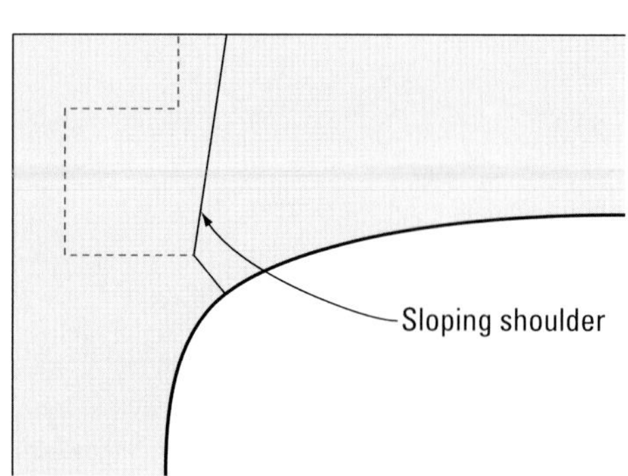

Mitered Shoulder Tenon

Use a mitered shoulder tenon joint where a sharply curved line would cause the tenon shoulder to crumble when shaping. Remove the short-grain problems by creating a mitered end at the shoulder. The rail must be longer at each end by the amount of the shoulder inset (**A**).

Cut and assemble the mortise-and-tenon joint.

➤ **See pp. 302 to 325 for cutting methods.**

Note that the tenon is set up from the bottom of the rail so it's not exposed when mitering. Mark out the position of the bottom of the rail onto the leg or stile. Then pencil in the miter cut on the leg starting from this point. Mark the inset shoulder down to this miter line. A ¼-in. inset is sufficient (**B**). Square a line from the intersection of these two lines back to the leg edge. Then reassemble the rail and leg and mark out the position of this point on the rail, which is where the mitering will start (**C**).

Saw the leg down to the miter line on the bandsaw with a fence (**D**). Clean the face of this cut with a chisel plane or a bullnose plane with its nose removed. Keep good pressure on the back of the plane so it doesn't dive into the cut (**E**). Pare the miter with a chisel and 45-degree block clamped onto the leg (**F**).

Finally, bevel back the shoulder of the rail to match the miter cut (**G**). The finished joint shows how the shaping stays crisp throughout the entire curve (**H**).

Sculpted (Maloof) Joint

The notched chair joint shown here is made with matching router bits (**A**). Lay out the notches on the leg and seat, but remember that the seat notch will be made smaller by the rabbet cut to both faces of the seat blank. Locate the seat notch back from the end of the seat to prevent any weak short-grain problems.

Dado three sides of the leg at a ¼-in. depth. Set a stop for the far side of the dado and use a spacer to index the near side of the cut (**B**). Make a ¼-in.-deep dado notch in the seat that's as wide as the leg after it's been dadoed (**C**).

Use a ¼-in. rabbeting bit with a 1-in. overall diameter to rout rabbets into the top and bottom of the seat notch (**D**). This will leave a ½-in. radius in the corners of the dado. Be careful when entering the cut to rout just in the notch and not around the edge of the seat. It is also important to slow down when exiting the cut to avoid tearout at the edge of the notch. This will cause some burning of the end grain. Or you can score the edge with a knife or make a climb cut back into the notch.

Mount a ½-in. roundover bit in the router table and round over the inside corners of the leg to match the round corner of the seat notch (**E**). Check the fit of the joint and adjust where necessary. If the leg is too wide, take a few handplane passes and round over the edges again. If the leg notch is too large, take a shoulder plane to the dadoes (**F**).

Drill the leg for one or two screws. First, countersink with a brad-point bit; then drill through the leg for a pilot hole (**G**).

Fit the joint together, glue it, and drive the screw. Then start shaping the joint (**H**).

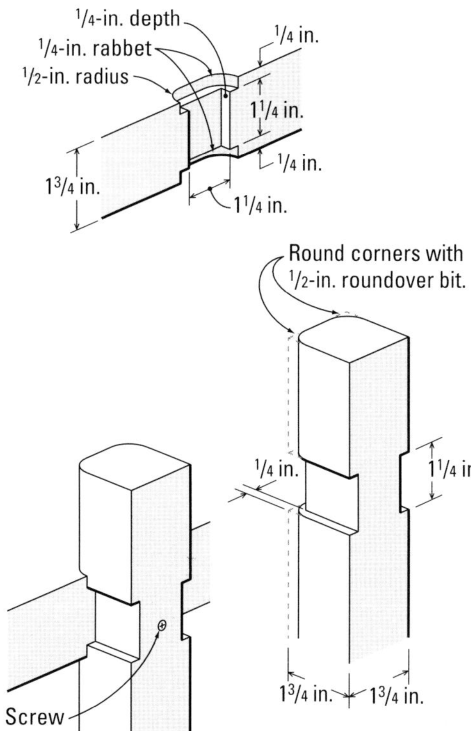

A

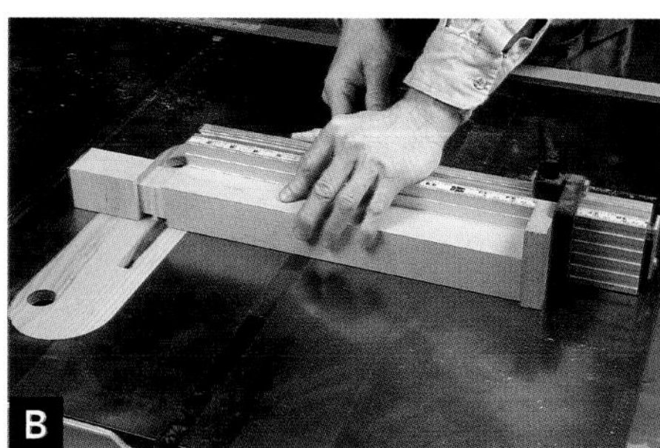

B

C

D

E

F

G

H

Step 1
Lay out and cut the mortise; make the first miter.

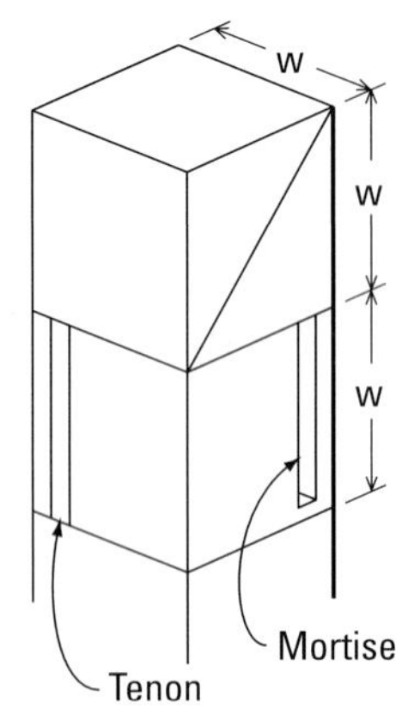

Step 2
Cut the tenon.

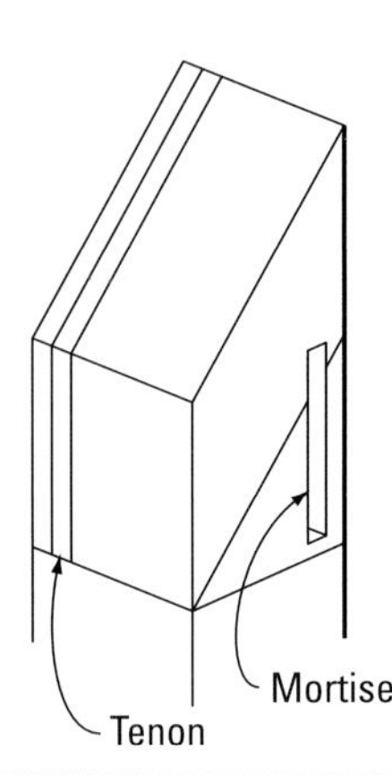

Step 3
Cut the second miter.

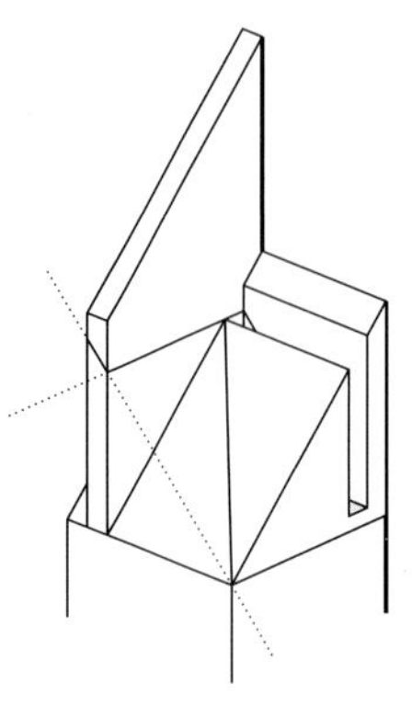

Step 4
Trim the tenon.

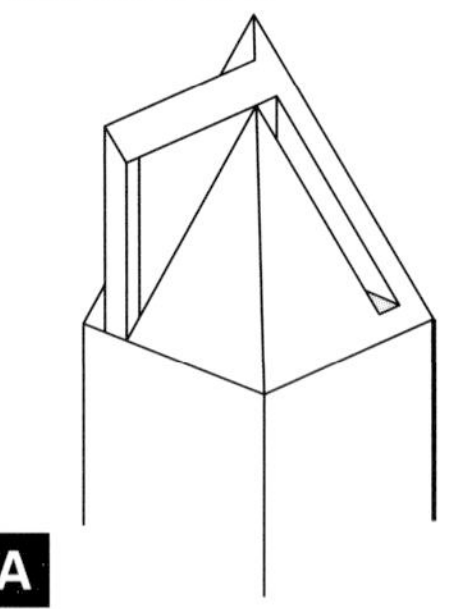

Step 5
Clean with a chisel.

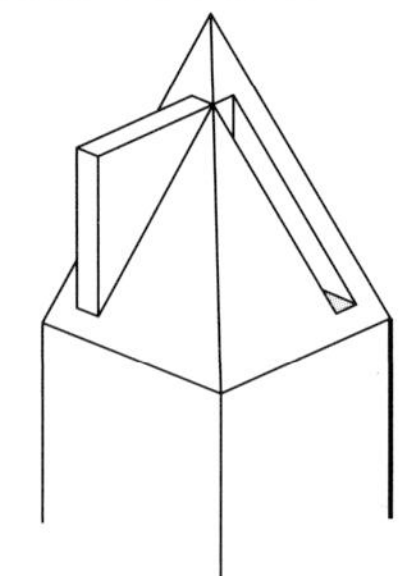

Finished Joint

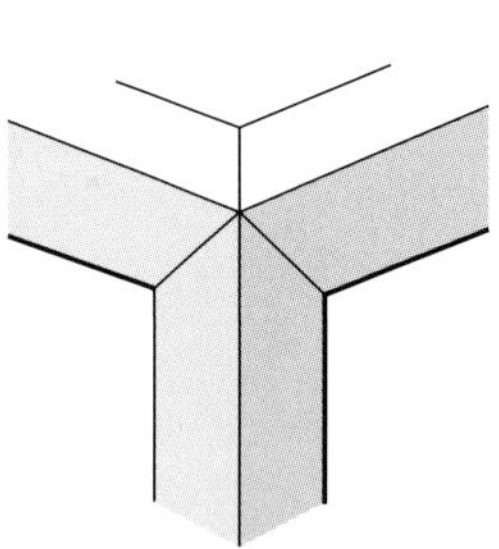

A

B

C

Triple Miter Joint

To make the elegant triple miter joint, you must have great precision and greater patience (**A**). For ease, make all the pieces square and the same size. Then tune the saw and miter gauge so that they're cutting accurately at 45 degrees. Each piece will be cut exactly the same with two miters, a mortise, and a tenon. Cut the pieces longer at the end by the width of each mating piece. So for a table, the rail will be cut long by the width of two legs, and each leg will be cut long by the width of the rail. This extra wood will help in the cutting of the joint.

First, lay out and mark the pieces for their miters, mortise, and tenon. Draw a 45-degree miter line that extends down from the corner. Then square this line across the two inside faces. The distance from the end should be equal to one side of a board. Draw another miter line or measure down from the first line the same distance, again equal to one side of a board. Mark this line around both faces. Position your mortise and tenon on these faces between those two lines, but move the mortise up off the bottom line by 1⁄16 in. The penciled-out spots indicate where wood will be removed (**B**).

Next, make the mortise cuts.

➤ See pp. 302 to 313 for cutting methods.

The width and depth of the mortise depend on the stock. For this example, I used 3⁄8-in.-wide by 7⁄8-in.-deep mortises set in 3⁄8 in. from the edge of each board.

Next, make the end miter cut across all of the boards.

➤ See *"Miter Cuts"* on p. 210.

Then reset the table-saw blade height to cut the first angled tenon shoulder at 45 degrees. Index the shoulder position by running the mitered end of the board against the saw fence (**C**). Re-adjust the miter gauge to run at 45 degrees in the opposite direction and reset the blade height. Cut the second angled tenon shoulder (**D**).

Cut the tenon cheeks using a tenoning jig made up at a 45-degree angle; but for the inside cheek cut, remove the waste first on the bandsaw or with a handsaw. This will prevent that offcut from being trapped between the sawblade and the jig. The waste piece on the outer cheek will just fall off (**E**).

Now, cut the second miter from the tip of the board back, making sure again that the angle of the miter gauge is right on (**F**).

You'll next have to trim the tenon so it fits the mortise height. Crosscut the tenon to height on the saw but don't hit the miter (**G**)!

Finish trimming with a chisel, working cross-grain. Make a bandsaw cut to trim down the width of the tenon. Then put in a small shoulder at the bottom of the tenon to match the mortise and cover up the joint (**H**).

D

E

F

G

H

A

B

C

D

Hand-Cut Through Mortise

Chop hand-cut through mortises with a chisel to yield square corners.

➤ See *"Hand-Cut Mortise with a Mortising Chisel"* on p. 302.

Measure out the mortise on the board and square lines across it to mark the mortise's ends. Square these lines around the board and mark out the mortise on the opposite face as well. Double-check the layout lines by measuring again from the end of the board. The distances should be the same (**A**).

Use a chisel to set the width of the mortise. Place it between the two points on a mortising gauge; then set the head on the gauge to place the mortise where you want it on the board. Mark both faces for the mortise (**B**).

To speed up the mortising, drill out the waste on the drill press. Chuck in an undersize bit and use a fence to locate the cut accurately. Drill the two outside holes first and then finish up the middle. Use a piece of scrap on the drill press table to protect it (**C**).

Finish up the through mortise by chopping from both ends in toward the middle and cleaning both faces so they end up parallel and straight (**D**).

Through Mortise on the Drill Press

The drill press accurately cuts through mortises with the aid of a fence.

➤ See *"Mortise on the Drill Press"* on p. 304.

Drill from one side all the way through the board. Put an auxiliary table on the drill press table and a piece of scrap on top of that so you can drill into it. Clamp these both in place so they don't move around on you as you drill (**A**). Set the bit depth of cut so it drills all the way through the board and a little way into the scrap (**B**).

Drill the two outside holes first; then drill the remaining wood in the center of the mortise (**C**). Always have some wood for the centering point of the bit to grab into so the bit doesn't wander. Leave the mortise ends round and round the tenon or chop the mortise ends square with a chisel.

A

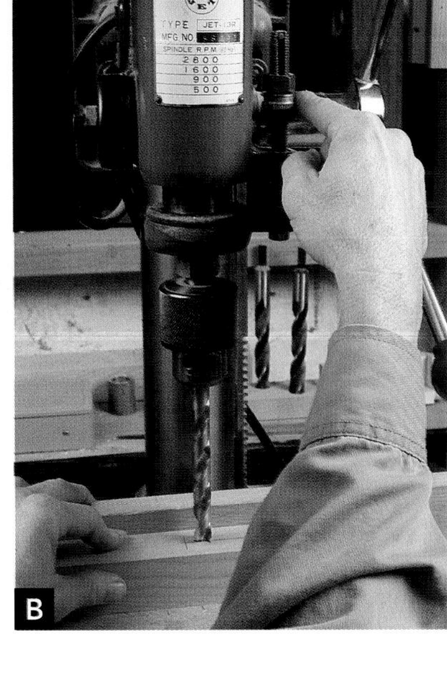

B

C

Through Mortise with a Plunge Router and Fence

Use a plunge router to cut through mortises with round ends.

➤ See *"Mortise with a Plunge Router and Fence"* on p. 307.

You'll have to round the tenon to fit the mortise. Use a bit that's long enough to cut through the wood without marring the topside of the mortise with the shank of the bit or the collet nut. You can rout through into a piece of scrap or stop the cut just short. I prefer the latter method, as it prevents errant cuts into the benchtop. Support the plunge router with boards the same height, putting one at the side and another at the end of the cut.

Mark out the mortise on one face. Set the router fence off these marks (**A**). Using a cardboard shim on the bench as a guide, set the bit depth to come almost through the board. Push the plunge router down to the shim and lock the depth stop rod (**B**). Rout through the mortise. The little bit of wood that's remaining is easily pushed through with a pencil (**C**).

Clean up the remaining bit of wood with a chisel and round file.

Through Mortise with a Plunge Router and Template

Through mortises can be cut with a handheld router and a template.

➤ See *"Mortise with a Plunge Router and Template"* on p. 309.

A

B

You'll have to round the tenon to fit the round end of the mortise. Make sure the bit is long enough to cut through the board and that the collet nut doesn't run into the template guide. Use a piece of scrap under the workpiece to prevent tearout when routing through or stop the mortise just short of coming through. Set the template in place, and put the plunge router on top of it to set the bit depth. Place a piece of cardboard or paper on the benchtop, push the bit down until it hits the cardboard or paper, and lock down the depth stop rod (**A**).

Rout to depth just short of the other face, remove the template, and punch through the remaining wood (**B**). Clean up the exit side of the through mortise with a chisel and round file.

A

B

C

Wedged Through Tenon

A tenon wedge should be aligned so it applies pressure against the end grain of its mortise rather than the long grain. This will avoid any tendency for the long grain to split out. First, cut the mortise and fit the tenon cheeks.

➤ **See pp. 302 to 325 for cutting methods.**

Next, cut the tenon to height so it just fits inside the length of the mortise. Use the bandsaw to trim it down to size. Check the fit from end to end of the mortise (**A**). Then round the tenon ends if the mortise has round ends.

➤ **See *"Edge Rounding a Tenon"* on p. 326 and p. 327.**

Because of the pressure that a wedge exerts on a tenon, especially in dry wood, don't widen the mortise. This increases the risk of splitting out the tenon when you apply the wedge. Keep the mortise at one length throughout and concentrate on a smaller wedge doing its job of creating pressure.

To avoid the risk of splitting out the bottom of the tenon with the wedging pressure, drill a 3⁄16-in. relief hole about two-thirds of the way back from the end of the tenon on the drill press (**B**). This hole will spread out the wedging pressure around a circumference instead of concentrating the pressure at the bottom of the wedge slot, where cracks will occur. Cut the wedge slot down to this hole on the bandsaw, using a fence to guide the cut (**C**). Make the kerf about 3⁄32 in. wide.

➤ See *"Fixed Wedges"* drawing on p. 298.

[VARIATION] For a design detail, use diagonal or double wedges in the through tenon. Cut a diagonal kerf in the tenon with a handsaw.

Make the wedge from a harder wood than your tenon. Cut the wedge to about twice the thickness of its slot and make some extra wedges that are a bit thicker. If you find that your wedges are going in too easily, use the thicker wedges for the remaining tenons. Cut the wedges to length at about three-quarters of the full length of the wedge slot. You'll find that the wedging force will tend to fill up most gaps that show at the edge of a through joint.

Put glue in the wedge slot and use a hammer to drive the wedge. When the sound changes from a thud to a ping you've gone as far as you can with the wedge (**D**).

➤ See *"Making Wedges"* on p. 376.

D

VARIATION

A

B

End-Wedged Through Tenon

Use end wedges on through tenons that have square ends. These wedges won't cause any tenon splitting because they're applied to the outside of the tenon, not the inside.

➤ See *"Fixed Wedges"* drawing on p. 298.

Cut the mortise and tenons using your preferred method.

➤ See pp. 302 to 325 for cutting methods.

Widen the mortise with a chisel to allow room for the wedges to enter. Check the angle of the chisel work against the shape of the wedges (**A**).

➤ See *"Making Wedges"* on p. 376.

Make sure the tenon is completely home in its mortise before driving the wedges in. Support the tenoned piece or have a clamp on it to prevent any movement as you drive in the wedges. Use a spot of glue in the wedge slots (**B**).

Wedged Through Dovetail Tenon

The wedged through dovetail tenon combines the mechanical advantage of the dovetail with the holding power of the wedge (**A**). You can run the wedge from the inside or outside face of the joint. As the wedge pressure is applied, the angled tenon locks into the mortise.

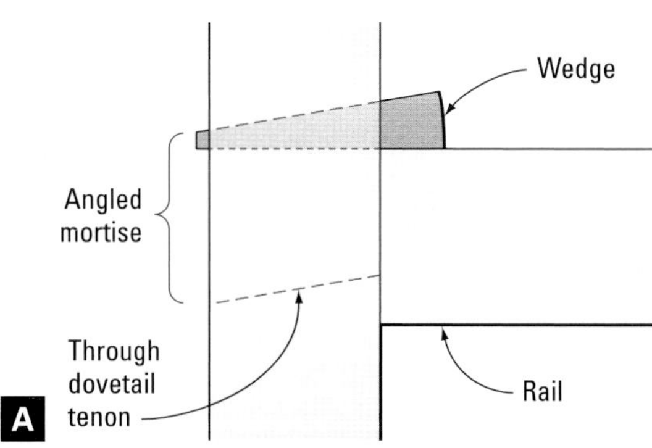

A

Cut the through mortise.

➤ See pp. 302 to 313 for cutting methods.

Next, angle both ends of the mortise along two parallel lines laid out on the board. These lines are set at the angle of the wedges, which is 7 degrees to 8 degrees. Make sure the mortise ends are chopped flat and work them from both edges in toward the middle to avoid tearout (**B**).

B

The angle on the tenon can be cut on the bandsaw or with a handsaw. This angle must match the mortise angle. Don't put a shoulder at the top of the tenon because the wedge has to slide along the top edge.

➤ See pp. 314 to 325 for cutting methods.

Assemble the joint and drive the wedge from the inside to lock the joint in place (**C**). Fit the joint by trimming the wedge or tenon angle.

C

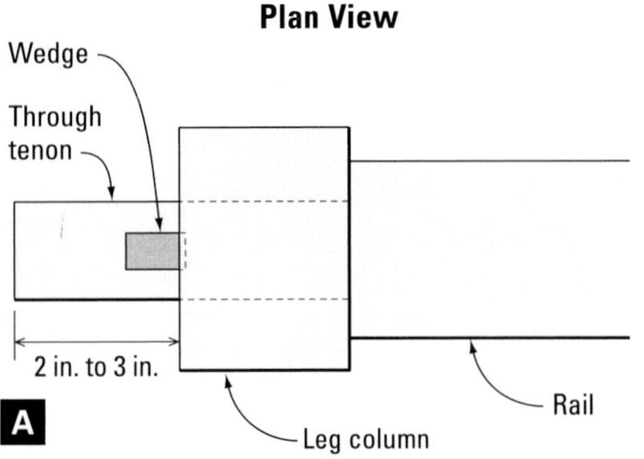

Vertically Wedged Through Tenon

Through wedges fit through a protruding tenon to lock it in place. Wedges can be left loose or glued in place. The tenon itself can fit quite loosely through the mortise for knockdown construction, because the wedge and tenon shoulders do all the work in this joint. You can also fit the tenon snug enough to be glued.

Make sure there's enough wood at the end of the tenon to prevent blowing out the grain when you bang the wedge home. Extend the tenon out 2 in. to 3 in. to accommodate this (**A**). Put two wide shoulders on the tenon; these will pull tight against the mortised piece when the wedge is applied. Small shoulders at the top and bottom of the tenon also help cover any dents in the mortise. The wedge size depends on the thickness of the tenon. The wedge mortise itself should be narrow enough to fit through the tenon without weakening the tenon side walls but thick enough to provide some strength.

Run the tenon home through its mortise and mark out the face of the mortised piece onto the top of the tenon (**B**). Pull the joint apart and mark out the full size of the wedge mortise on the tenon (**C**). The wedge mortise extends back beyond the face of the frame member so that the wedge doesn't bottom out against its own mortise wall. The wedge mortise is angled on both sides, although only its outer edge needs to be angled to match the angle of the wedge. Angle the drill press table to match the wedge angle and lock the table in place (**D**). Keep the angle at 7 degrees to 8 degrees.

Mortise through the tenon by drilling with a brad-point or Forstner bit. Bore the two outer holes first and then finish up in the middle. Put a piece of scrap under the tenon to support the drilling and to prevent tearout (**E**).

Chop the end of the wedge mortise square on its outer end only (**F**). Line up the chisel to match the angle lines drawn on the tenon. If you placed the other end of the wedge mortise far enough back, you can leave that end round. Lightly back bevel the bottom of the wedge mortise to prevent tearout when driving a tight wedge through it (**G**).

➤ See *"Loose Wedged Through Mortise and Tenon"* on pp. 147–148.

D

E

F

G

Horizontally Wedged Through Tenon

The advantage of a horizontally wedged through tenon is that it's easier to mortise through the tenon's thickness than through its height (**A**).

Angle the drill press table and drill out for the mortise.

➤ **See pp. 372 to 373 for cutting methods.**

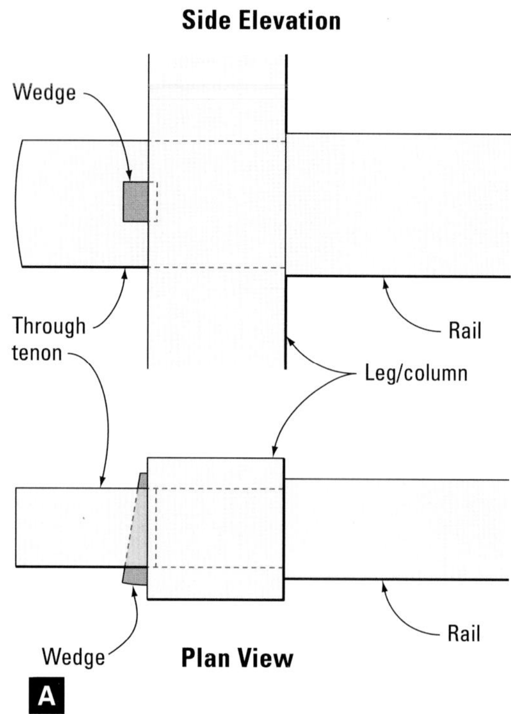

Chop the mortise end square and at the required wedge angle of 7 degrees to 8 degrees (**B**). Support the tenon from underneath with some scrap when chopping. Remember to extend the wedge mortise back beyond the face of the mortised piece so the wedge doesn't bottom out on its own mortise.

B

Bang the wedge home with a metal hammer; when the hammering sound changes from a thud to a ping you know you've gone far enough (**C**). Leave the wedge unglued for easy knockdown or glue it in place.

C

Through Tenon with Folding Wedges

Folding or double wedges can be used horizontally or vertically (**A**). They push against each other in a straight-walled mortise that goes through a protruding tenon. This makes the mortising for through wedging simple.

Mark out the face edge of the mortised piece onto the side of the tenon (**B**). Pull the joint apart and mark out the full size of the wedge mortise. Make sure its rear wall extends back so the wedges don't bottom out on their own mortise. Cut the through mortise on the drill press straight through the tenon. Place a piece of scrap under the tenon to support the drilling and to prevent tearout (**C**). Then chop the wedge mortise out square on its outside end only (**D**).

Make up the folding wedges so they fit easily through the wedge mortise.

➤ See *"Large Through Wedges"* on p. 377.

Cut the wedges' angle at 7 degrees to 8 degrees. Adjust how far the wedges enter by trimming their straight back edges (**E**).

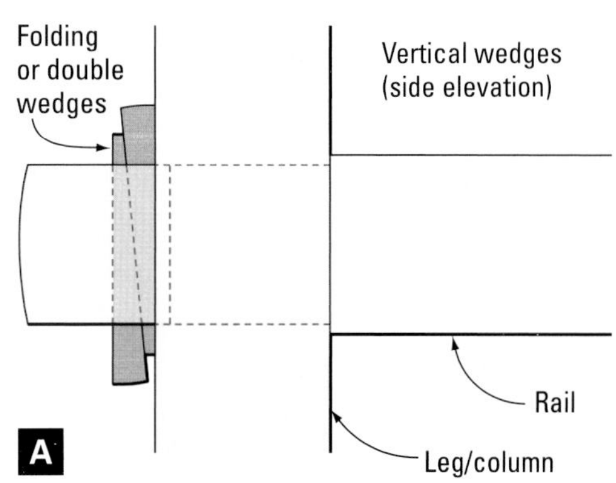

Making Wedges

Wedges that fit inside or through a tenon can be of different sizes, each of which requires a different cutting method.

SMALL INTERIOR WEDGES

Rough out the wedge stock for the smaller interior wedges on the bandsaw, bringing the stock close to width and thickness. Then use the table saw to trim the stock to width and a little oversize in thickness. Use a tall push stick that fits easily between the blade and fence to pass the wedge stock through (**A**).

Fit the wedges accurately to the width of their through joints (**B**). Handplane them so they fit easily through their mortises.

Then cut them at about an 8-degree angle with a jig that holds them upright as you pass them by the sawblade. Set the saw fence so the final thickness of the wedge is about twice the width of the wedge slot (**C**).

Cut the wedges to length with a handsaw. Their length should be about three-quarters the full length of the wedge slot (**D**).

WARNING Be sure the table insert fits tightly around the blade so the wedge stock doesn't slip down into the saw as you pass it by. Or use a piece of scrap plywood to cover the blade area, or clamp the wedge stock to the jig.

LARGE THROUGH WEDGES

Rough out larger through wedges on the bandsaw. Then plane them to thickness on the planer or pass them by the sawblade to cut them close to thickness. Handplane the milling marks off to get the wedges to final thickness. Check their thickness against their mortise.

Make a simple taper jig out of plywood or medium-density fiberboard (MDF) for cutting the wedge angles on the bandsaw. Mark out the desired angle of the wedges on the jig and cut this out cleanly. Keep the angle at 7 degrees to 8 degrees. Crosscut the wedge stock to length and then fix it to the jig. Adjust the bandsaw fence to cut wedges to the proper width (**E**).

There are numerous options for wedge shapes so let your design skills take flight. Clean up the saw marks and trim the wedge to its final size with a bench plane held in the vise as a jointer. Use a small push block to hold the wedges and to protect your fingertips (**F**).

➤ See *"Making Loose Wedges"* on p. 149.

E

F

List of Contributors

TO THOSE MANUFACTURERS WHOSE HELP WAS SO INSTRUMENTAL:

Lie-Nielsen Toolworks and Tom Lie-Nielsen

The J.D.S. Company and John McConegly

Laguna Tools and Catherine and Torben Helschoj

Garrett Wade Company and Gary Chinn

Toolguide and Festo and Michael McGibbon

Freud, U.S.A., and Karen Powers

Hitachi Power Tools and Kristin Boesch

Keller Jigs and David Keller

Black and Decker and Joan Mellott

Leigh Industries and Ken and Matt Grisley

To everyone at Woodcrafters and especially Dan Baker

Further Reading

CABINET MAKING

Ellis, George. *Modern Practical Joinery.* Linden Publishing.

Joyce, Ernest. *Encyclopedia of Furniture Making.* Sterling Publishing.

Tolpin, Jim. *Building Traditional Kitchen Cabinets.* The Taunton Press.

CRAFTSMANSHIP

Krenov, James. *The Fine Art of Cabinetmaking.* Sterling Publishing.

Nakashima, George. *The Soul of a Tree: A Woodworker's Reflections.* Kodansha International.

Pye, David. *The Nature and Art of Workmanship.* Cambium Press.

WOOD TECHNOLOGY

Forest Products Laboratory. *Wood Handbook: Wood as an Engineering Material.* Forest Products Laboratory.

Hoadley, R. Bruce. *Identifying Wood.* The Taunton Press.

———*Understanding Wood.* The Taunton Press.

DESIGN

Aronson, Joseph. *The Encyclopedia of Furniture.* Crown Publishing.

Editors of *Fine Woodworking. Practical Design.* The Taunton Press.

Graves, Garth. *The Woodworker's Guide to Furniture Design.* Popular Woodworking Books.

Morley, John. *The History of Furniture: Twenty-Five Centuries of Style and Design in the Western Tradition.* Bulfinch Press.

Pye, David. *The Nature and Aesthetics of Design.* Cambium Press.

TOOLS AND MACHINERY

Bird, Lonnie. *The Bandsaw Book.* The Taunton Press.

———*The Shaper Book.* The Taunton Press.

Hack, Garrett. *Classic Hand Tools.* The Taunton Press.

———*The Handplane Book.* The Taunton Press.

Lee, Leonard. *The Complete Guide to Sharpening.* The Taunton Press.

Mehler, Kelly. *The Table Saw Book.* The Taunton Press.

Nagyszalanczy, Sandor. *The Art of Fine Tools.* The Taunton Press.

———*Woodshop Jigs and Fixtures.* The Taunton Press.

Rogowski, Gary. *Router Joinery.* The Taunton Press.

WOODSHOPS

Landis, Scott. *The Workbench Book.* The Taunton Press.

———*The Workshop Book.* The Taunton Press.

Nagyszalanczy, Sandor. *Setting Up Shop.* The Taunton Press.

———*Woodshop Dust Control.* The Taunton Press.

Tolpin, Jim. *The Toolbox Book.* The Taunton Press.

WOOD FINISHING

Charron, Andy. *Water-Based Finishes.* The Taunton Press.

Dresdner, Michael. *The New Wood Finishing Book.* The Taunton Press.

Jewitt, Jeff. *Great Wood Finishes.* The Taunton Press.

———*Hand-Applied Finishes.* The Taunton Press.

Index

N

O

P

R

S

U

V

W